Acknowledgements

Thanks to the following people for their ideas and help as we wrote this book:

Katherine Ragsdale, Cynthia Johanson, the Bushman, Pat Renner, Dave Platt and Dan Jenkins at GTE Spacenet, Clark Miller, and Emil Paska who's still out there in the PC trenches.

This book owes much to the generosity of Swan Technologies, who loaned us a 486/33 EISA computer for disassembly and photographs. Many thanks to Adaptec, Addstor, Advanced Micro Devices, American Megatrends, Inc., ATI Technologies, Central Point Software, Creative Labs, Dariana Technology Group, DiagSoft, DTK Computer, Inc., Gibson Research, Iomega Corporation, JDR Microdevices, Logitech, Ontrack, PC Power and Cooling, Stac, Storage Dimensions, Symantec, and TouchStone Software Corporation, who sent us products, photographs, or both.

Special thanks for the enthusiasm and creativity of Steve Berkowitz, Kathleen Joyce, and Laura Specht of MIS: Press. Our flow chart designer, Lora McLaughlin, tweaked the photos and converted them into electronic format. And Nick Ferrone, the line art artist.

Finally, we thank our friends and family who encourage and support us.

Fix Your Own PC
2nd Edition

**by Susan Sasser, Mary Ralston, and
Robert McLaughlin**

**Photographs by P. Hampton-Renner
Flow Chart Layout by Lora McLaughlin**

MIS: PRESS

A Subsidiary of
Henry Holt and Co., Inc.

First Printing

ISBN 1-55828-232-7

Printed in the United States of America

10 9 8 7 6 5 4 3 2 1

MIS:Press books are available at special discounts for bulk purchases for sales promotions, premiums, fund-raising, or educational use. Special editions or book excerpts can also be created to specification.

For details contact: Special Sales Director
                         MIS:Press
                         a subsidiary of Henry Holt and Company, Inc.
                         115 West 18th Street
                         New York, New York 10011

Trademarks

Throughout this book, trademarked names are used. Rather than put a trademark symbol after every occurence of a trademarked name, we used the names in an editorial fashion only.Where such designations appear in this book, they have been printed with initial caps.

Table of Contents

Introduction

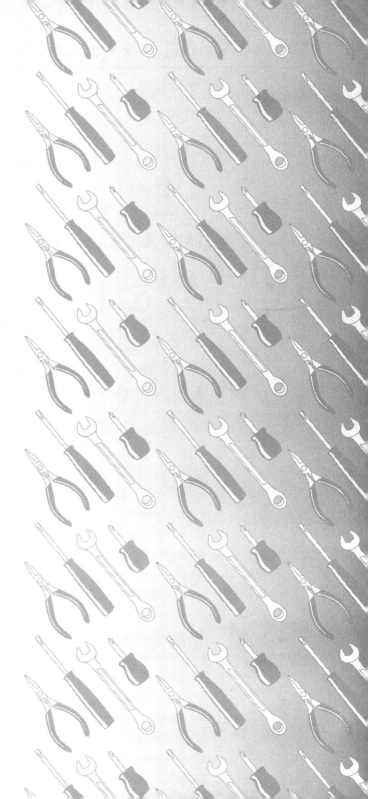

If you have the original *Fix Your Own PC*, welcome back. You'll find information on fixing and upgrading the new machines and components, updated repair flow charts, and new photographs and illustrations to help you find your way.

If you're a new reader, this book will give you the skills to diagnose and repair your PC clone and to make intelligent repair and upgrade decisions about your computer. You may only want to undertake minor repairs and upgrades yourself, but you'll have a pretty good idea of what's wrong with your machine when it has problems, what upgrade components you can add yourself, and how to communicate with your computer repair shop.

What's New in This Book

✔ *Information on diagnosing and repairing 386 and 486 computers, with photos to help you identify the parts*

✔ *Video upgrade choices*

✔ *Hard drive types—IDE, ESDI, SCSI*

✔ *Single inline memory module (SIMM) memory*

✔ *Sound boards*

✔ *Windows 3.1 requirements*

✔ *Upgrade options*

We've added reference tabs in the margins and color to help you find the section you want, and a lay-flat binding to make it easier to use beside the computer.

What's Still Here

✔ *Diagnosis and repair for XTs and 286s.* Many of these computers are still chugging away in your homes and offices. As they age and need expensive repairs, you'll replace them, so the next edition of *Fix Your Own PC* might not deal with XTs at all.

✔ *Diagnosis of monochrome, Color Graphics Adapter (CGA), and Enhanced Graphics Adapter (EGA) video cards and monitors.* If they're still working, we tell you how to keep them going. When they need an expensive repair, we'll tell you to upgrade.

What Hasn't Changed in Computers

✔ *Serial and parallel connections.* Connection and cable standards don't change, one PC generation to the next.

✔ *Floppy drives.* These haven't changed much since the 3.5-inch drive became popular.

✔ *Power supplies, keyboards, and other such necessities of computer life.*

✔ *Basic hard drive information.* They're bigger and use different types of controllers and methods of laying the information down, but they're basically the same, from the quaint 10 Mb to the featherweight 2.5 inch drive in your notebook portable.

What Computers We Deal With

The only computers we deal with in this book are the familiar IBM-PC clones—everything from widely advertised brands to Joe's Garage XL-Turbo Blaster. At heart, they're all the same machine, based on the familiar IBM PC/AT/386/486 design. All are based on the Intel family of 80x86 CPU chips. Millions of these machines are in use, and many millions more will be assembled and sold before they reach techno-oblivion. The supposed end of the dynasty is the Intel 80586, now code-named the P5. This chip is really a Reduced Instruction Set (RISC) chip, with a disk operating system (DOS) facade that lets you use your old software.

Someday, PCs won't be "downwardly compatible" anymore. You won't be able to run Lotus 1-2-3 V.2.2 or WordPerfect 5.1. Some of you will keep on using DOS applications and others will want to move on to whatever is the fastest machine available. Even if you basically just want an automatic typewriter, you'll want to run friendlier, fancier software, and you'll upgrade and replace your PC, no matter how hot it seems now. The upgrade cycle seems to take about 18 months, we've observed. At that point, things start to break, or you want to upgrade a specific part of your PC.

This book will tell you when and how to repair, what to upgrade, when to replace, and how to avoid the bad repair shops and communicate with the good ones.

Why to Beware Computer Repair Shops

Your PC is more complicated than the typewriter it replaced. The computer is both an electrical device and an electronic device: it contains plenty of gears and bearings and springs, as well as chips and microprocessors. Because it's both electrical and electronic, repairing it is both easier and harder than repairing your toaster or food processor. Oddly enough, you can repair your computer much more easily and safely than you can repair your toaster. (Wonder why? See Chapter 12 in Section 2. A sealed power supply is a safe power supply.) Interchangeable parts and components pop in and out with finger-pressure or a couple of screws.

Because the PC is an electronic device, it's the ultimate Black Box to the unschooled owner. If you don't know what's going on in those chips and controllers and cables, a computer repair shop can tell you just about anything, and you have no choice but to believe it. They're usually telling you the truth, but sometimes not. Some dealers' repair shops are run on a profit-sharing basis: the manager of the repair side is paid according to the profits he makes on repairs.

One candid small dealer told us that he found, to his dismay, that he was forced to charge for unneeded repairs because his margin was so thin on hardware sales. He got out of the retail business, as a result, but he was an exception. It may be your day to walk in with a minor repair when the dealer has a cash-flow problem.

What this Book Can Do to Help

If you've already ruled out the possibility that your hard drive needs replacing, know for sure it's something else, and can describe the diagnostic steps you took to make sure, your chances of getting an honest repair for an honest price have just zoomed. And you'll know what was going on inside that Black Box.

We believe that anyone who wants to can master the insides of their PC clone. No exotic skills are required, other than the ability to think clearly and use a screwdriver. If you're a novice user, you may have to look up terms in the glossary or consult the component descriptions a few times, but you'll be amply rewarded for the effort involved the first time you fix your own machine. If you're an experienced user, computer professional, or even repair technician, we hope that this book will be informative as well as useful.

Computer Repair Economics

When an electronic part in a computer goes bad, you might think it is a simple matter to identify the offending chip, replace it, and go on about your business. The problem is that this method takes time. A lot of time. The cost for the repairperson's time often exceeds the cost for a whole new part.

Here's why. The average technician in the Washington, D.C. area is paid about $15 an hour. A good business rule of thumb is that labor must bring in three times what it is paid. So to just break even, the computer store must charge you $50 an hour for the technician's time. To make a profit, the store should charge you $75 an hour, assuming that the technician is hard at work during every hour of the technician's 40-hour work week. In the Washington area, the average charge is $75–$110 an hour for "bench work" (diagnosis rather than simple part replacement) and $175 an hour for the same type of diagnosis at the customer's location.

The average component repair, as opposed to replacement, takes about three hours. This time includes determining which part is bad, removing it, repairing it, replacing it, and testing it to make sure the repair was made correctly. The average three-hour repair costs $225 and carries a 90-day warranty.

For a comparison, here is the cost of the parts required to assemble a typical 25 MHz AT/386 clone as of July 1992—the price for a particular component remains substantially the same, even though quality and capacity improve over time:

- ✔ 200 watt power supply—$55
- ✔ 386 mainboard—$200, without memory
- ✔ Case—$50
- ✔ 80 Mb hard drive—$300
- ✔ Hard/floppy controller—$40–$175, depending on type
- ✔ Super Video Graphics Array (SVGA) card—$200 and up
- ✔ SVGA monitor—$300
- ✔ 1.2 Mb floppy drive—$40
- ✔ 1.4 Mb floppy drive—$40
- ✔ 2.44 Mb floppy drive—$70

All parts carry one-year warranties; hard drives once carried only a six-month warranty. They're better built now, though we don't think they last much longer than two years. We just don't see as many crashing in three months, as we used to.

As we look at the list, only the SVGA monitor, the hard drive, and possibly the video card cost much more, brand new, than the average $225 repair. And a new replacement part has a warranty nine months longer than a 90-day warranty on a repaired component. Note that a malfunctioning monitor can be repaired by any competent television repair technician.

It's clear from these figures that replacing an offending board is not only quicker and simpler, but far more cost-effective.

The Repair Process

For any repair, determining which part is causing the problem consumes the greatest amount of time. Although a variety of test equipment is available to us in the shop, the most important tool we, and you, have is being able to think logically and to follow a step-by-step process to isolate the faulty part. Very little of our time is spent actually replacing the part. We can replace a floppy drive in 5 minutes, a mainboard in 20 minutes, and a hard disk in 40 minutes. Figuring out which part to replace can take at least an hour—sometimes much longer. For example, the symptom is the screen message, "Abort, Retry, Ignore, Reading Drive (C:)." This can be caused by any of the following:

- ✔ A bad track, which the manufacturer located and printed on the drive label, was not entered as bad when the drive was formatted. Now data has been placed on this bad track.
- ✔ The heads of the hard drive have drifted out of alignment with the tracks, causing some spots to be unreadable.
- ✔ The hard drive cable has lost connection or has been damaged.
- ✔ The hard drive is failing and must be replaced.
- ✔ The hard drive controller is bad and must be replaced.
- ✔ The 12-volt line on the power supply is too high, too low, or unstable, and the power supply must be replaced.
- ✔ A memory chip or SIMM is bad and should be replaced.
- ✔ The direct memory access (DMA) controller on the mainboard is bad. The mainboard must be replaced.

This book tells you what to do if you have the screen message "Abort, Retry, Ignore, Reading Drive C:" It helps you determine which problem is the one you are facing and how best to solve it. The appropriate repair for this problem can be as simple as running a software program or as expensive as replacing the hard disk and controller. The troubleshooting charts in Section 3 provide you with a step-by-step process to determine what the source of your problem might be and what to do to correct it. The appendices list all the error messages we have been able to gather up, to help you decipher weird screen messages.

Tales from the Back Rooms

The three of us met at a Washington, D.C. area computer clone chain, where we were the hardware guru, service manager, and lead-store manager. The chain is no longer in business, and we are now involved in other aspects of the computer industry. During our days at the clone chain, we saw more than our share of horror stories, some of our own creation. Under the pressure of building IBM clone XTs, ATs, and 386s (some 100 machines a week for a five-store chain) we committed our share of computer atrocities, but we saw even worse examples from factory-authorized service centers. The most memorable examples include memory problems, hard drive problems, and power supply problems.

Memory Problems

One gentleman walked in asking if we could fix his Kaypro XL (XT clone), which he had purchased from another dealer. He was getting assorted nonmaskable interrupt (NMI) errors, and memory allocation error messages. One computer repair place said the problem was bad software and reloaded his hard disk. A second shop (certified by Kaypro, Compaq, and IBM) said the problem was bad memory and replaced nine chips, charging $275. We examined the machine and discovered that the problem was the power supply. It was clear that neither repair shop had tested the computer after the repair or had any intentions of standing by the warranty.

Another computer came in for repair from a customer complaining of NMI errors. A standard diagnostic program said there was no problem with the memory. But an examination of the memory chips themselves showed that one of the chips that was supposed to be a 41256 was really a 4164.

Hard Drive Problems

At our service center, we saw many instances of data lost on hard drives because a non-run length limited (non-RLL)-certified hard disk was RLLed. The trouble didn't show up until six months of data were suddenly missing. Now, we suspect some known-bad drives are being sold in clones as good drives, under the pressure to stay in business. It's a good plan to open up a new computer and look around inside, or have the technician do it when you take delivery. Anything that looks funny should be questioned. Odd-looking stickers on the hard drive, for example. Bad sectors are always identifed at the factory and noted on a sticker, but any others need an explanation.

Because shops don't keep a repair history, it is common to have the same repair done and redone. Here's an example: the customer's computer displayed "non-system disk error" on boot. The standard repair is to just reformat the disk—not replace any parts. The hard disk was formatted three times before the customer screamed. When the hard disk was replaced, the problem remained. The hard disk and controller were replaced—same problem. It turned out that the stock hard disk controller did not support the wedge stepper motor in the stock hard drive. We finally fixed the problem by throwing away the hard disk controller and replacing it with another type. Note that the problems never showed up with any diagnostic program.

Some hard disk problems aren't caused by the hard drive or controller. A customer brought in a Kaypro XL, purchased from a national chain. The hard disk failed intermittently. Over a period of nine months, the computer was brought back and forth to the vendor at least ten times. On the last visit, the vendor insisted the problem was "due to microwaves emanating from the Russian Embassy" (the machine was located in a building across the street from the Soviet Mission to the United States). Upon examination, the problem was found to be cracks in the mainboard in the slot area. We replaced the mainboard, and fortunately the manufacturer extended the warranty to cover the period of "microwave interference."

Power Supply Problems

We know of a machine that kept bouncing back and forth from the service department to the customer, with the technician reformatting the hard disk instead of replacing it, until the technician finally replaced the hard disk, then the mainboard, despite the fact that the same problem kept recurring. Eventually someone thought to check the power supply. Putting a voltmeter on the power supply revealed that the 5-volt line was putting out closer to 7 volts, and was causing parts to run too hot and refuse to communicate with each other. If the 5-volt line had gone to 10 volts, the customer might well have had bits of fried plastic inside his machine, or an exploded capacitor. Yet the power supply is one of the last parts the average shop thinks to check. Another machine had constant problems copying from one floppy drive to the other. The cause, again, turned out to be the power supply, not the floppy drives themselves.

Brand-Name, No-Name, or Mail Order?

Though our clone chain committed its share of mismatches and other build-up problems, we are constantly reminded of the poor quality of famous brand-name factory-authorized repair. Some Compaq owners came to our shop for diagnosis and then went back to the Compaq dealer and said, "Replace that part, and don't argue." Compaq's dealer-only service policies, as well as forgetting it was basically a clone maker, may have had something to do with the company's slide.

We are also amused at the hype about famous brands' engineering and manufacturing, compared with our no-name clones. Although our chain can, and does, use parts that we've scraped the barnacles off of ourselves, we didn't see much better quality from big name brands. Computer parts are manufactured all over the world, are interchangeable, and suffer the same ups and downs in quality.

Many of our customers could afford any machine on the market, but preferred our no-names for their overall quality and performance. These customers weren't one-man offices, but some of the best-known corporate headquarters in the Washington, D.C. area. When most customers realized that the same parts were going into all the computers, whether a true no-name or one of the myriad "what's-that" brands, the prestigious brand name machines lost more and more market share to the clones.

Currently, we recommend buying mail-order machines or brand-name clones, rather than the true Joe's Garage clones. If you know a good local dealer, stay with her, but be aware that the sharp drop in prices has forced many clone shops to put out shoddy machines and then go out of business.

We, like you, want reliable computers and need prompt warranty repairs.

We bought four new computers in the last two years. The clone from a small local chain became an orphan when the shop closed three months later. Although it was sold as a 25 MHz 386, when we opened it up for a repair job we saw that the original chip had been pried out and a 16 Mhz chip substituted. The screwdriver marks were obvious on the sides of the socket. The BIOS chip set failed in 15 months. Since the motherboard was an orphan, we had to replace it. Should we have opened up the case on delivery to see if it was as advertised? You bet. The owner was too busy meeting deadlines to run the new machine through the paranoia inspection. Meantime, three mail order clones work just fine. Only one has required service—a hard drive failed warranty. The manufacturer took care of it.

When Is It You, and When Is It Them?

It's easy to be humbled by a techno-whiz. If a new set of SIMM strips doesn't work, don't assume you put them in wrong. You may have been sold the wrong part. That happened to us, twice in a row, when upgrading a new Macintosh Quadra. If software doesn't work right, it probably is a bug, not your hardware, causing the problem. Some software vendors, like WordPerfect, have excellent records in owning up to their bugs and issuing updates. Others, like Microsoft, are much less market-driven. As an example, Windows printer drivers are provided by the printer manufacturer, not Microsoft, who merely distributes them but takes no responsibility. If you have a printer that isn't one of the major brand names, you may have a difficult time getting a fix. Excel, for example, occasionally gives the Canon BubbleJet a fit. Hardware manufacturers are much less able to answer customer questions and provide new drivers than software vendors. You may have to locate and query several divisions of a manufacturer before you find the guy who writes the drivers.

While vendors are still spotty in their support of users, repair departments are up to their usual tricks, too. You have to wonder if the bad guys in the business are out there running Seminars for Scumbags, teaching the art of fake repairs and techno-babble. It may pay to mark parts in your computer with your initials, as California investigators did when they checked out car repair shops. Some of the worst computer repair technicians would probably claim they always mark parts that way and it's their initials, not yours.

Some dealers are condescending and irresponsible when you return faulty merchandise. They insist that the machine is perfectly all right when the printer goes through a $25 inkjet cartridge every twenty pages or so, for example. When this happened to a relative of ours, a complaint letter to the company president produced an apology and a replacement.

So trust your instincts when something seems wacko. You're probably right. If you find an honest repair shop, tell the world. It's tough to make a living in computers these days.

How to Use this Book

This book is divided into three sections—chapters, data pages, and flow charts. The chapters contain tips for solving a variety of common problems, background reading, and our opinions and prejudices. The data pages contain specific instructions for identifying, diagnosing, and replacing the individual computer components. The flow charts show you how to trace the cause of computer symptoms to find the probable cause. If you have a problem right now with your computer, turn to the data pages if you're sure you know the cause. Confirm your diagnosis with the flow charts. Come back to the chapters to see what we think about replacement parts and upgrades.

Keeping your generic or name-brand PC clone repaired and running well can be much easier than repairing standard household appliances, if you have a little knowledge and some curiosity. We hope at the very least you avoid paying too much for the wrong repair.

Section 1
The Chapters

Chapter 1
The Parts of a Computer

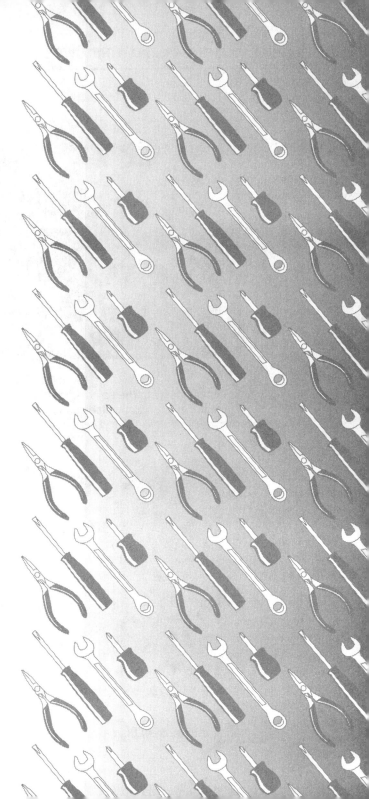

This chapter introduces you to your computer's anatomy and to the individual components, which we discuss in detail later in the book.

You should turn off the computer and unplug it before you remove its cover and go through this chapter. There is no electricity in the computer when it's off and unplugged. In fact, there is very little shock hazard when the computer is on, as long as you never disassemble the sealed power supply or the monitor.

If you have disconnected the power cord, it's time to take the cover off your computer and look inside. Figures 1.1 to 1.3 on the next two pages show you how. You will remove the screws that hold the cover on, then gently pull the cover forward, up, and off. If you have a desktop computer with the Baby AT case, or a tower model that stands upright on the floor next to your desk, look at Figures 1.8 to 1.11 on pages 21-23—the cover screws may be hidden on the back or the sides, and the plastic front piece probably snaps off and on. It makes sense, of course, to look for mounting screws before yanking on anything plastic.

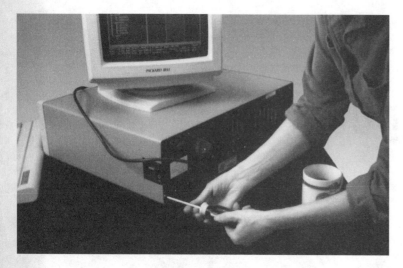

Figure 1.1
*Start by removing the screws holding the top cover onto the case.
Typical full-size clone cases use five Phillips screws, one at each
corner and one in the top center, but designs vary.*

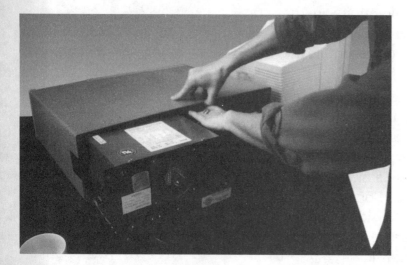

Figure 1.2
Slide the cover off the case, taking care not to dislodge cables.

Now look around inside the computer. You will see circuit boards, gray ribbon cables, a shiny metal power supply box, and a couple o f hard drives and/or floppy drives. Figures 1.5, 1.6, and 1.7 on pages 18-20 show three typical PCs (fully disassembled) to help you identify the parts in your computer, but don't get down to specifics yet. Glance at your computer, then at Figures 1.5 and 1.6. Remarkably similar, aren't they? The parts in your computer look a lot like the parts in the photos. And it would take an expert to differentiate between the XT clone parts in Figure 1.5 and the AT clone parts in Figure 1.6. Even the 486 EISA computer in Figure 1.7 (the newest, fastest, and most expensive computer in this book) looks a heck of a lot like the humble XT clone in Figure 1.5. Whether clone or true- blue IBM, desktop or tower model, XT or 286/386/486, these personal computers share the same design.

Modular Design

Throughout this book we'll load you down with specific detail about this mainboard design or that hard disk design. Those details are important. You can't ignore them. But first let's look at the big picture.

The biggest circuit board in your computer is the *mainboard* (also called the *motherboard*). *Expansion cards* (smaller, special-purpose circuit boards) plug into sockets on the mainboard. These sockets are called *bus slots* or *expansion slots*, and the particular kind of bus slot on your mainboard tells us a lot about the mainboard and your computer's capabilities.

Your computer has a *power supply* (a transformer which converts 110 volt AC current into low-voltage DC current to run the computer).

The power supply is easy to identify, since the computer's AC power cord plugs into the back of it. It's a shiny metal box, often 5-7 inches on a side sprouting many wires and connectors to power the guts of your computer.

Both floppy drives and hard drives are separate electro-mechanical boxes connected to the rest of the computer with gray ribbon cables and 4-wire power connectors from the power supply box. You should be able to recognize your floppy drives even though the computer cover is off—the diskette-insertion slot is a familiar landmark.

All PCs use this modular design: mainboard, expansion cards, power supply, drives connected with cables. The details vary from computer to computer, but the underlying design is a good one and remains popular despite technical advances.

Take a little time to familiarize yourself with your computer and its innards. See how the power connectors hook up to the mainboard. You'll also notice some skinny wires that lead to the drive indicator light, the speaker, and the power-on indicator.

If your PC is older, the memory chips are arranged in rows of nine and are in a segregated section of the mainboard off to themselves. All the chips have identifying numbers stamped on them. If your computer is newer, it may use SIMM strips instead of individual memory chips. SIMMs are slanted, upright 3-inch strips with 8 or 9 chips in a row on the strip. A typical SIMM holds 1 or 4 Mb of RAM. It's okay to press down on the chips and strips to make sure they're seated firmly, but don't poke around inside the computer with a screwdriver. You'll also notice that the mainboard is attached to the case with a few screws, or a couple of screws and some plastic standoffs that poke through holes in the board. None of these parts are hard to install.

Figure 1.3
The AT clone cover has just been removed. You don't need a special tool bench to work on your PC. The dining room table works fine.

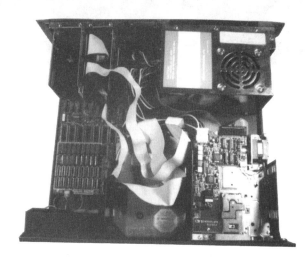

Figure 1.4
The XT clone cover has been removed. This XT has both floppy and hard drives, and three expansion cards (from left, MGP video card, hard drive controller with two ribbon cables, and floppy drive controller with a single ribbon cable).

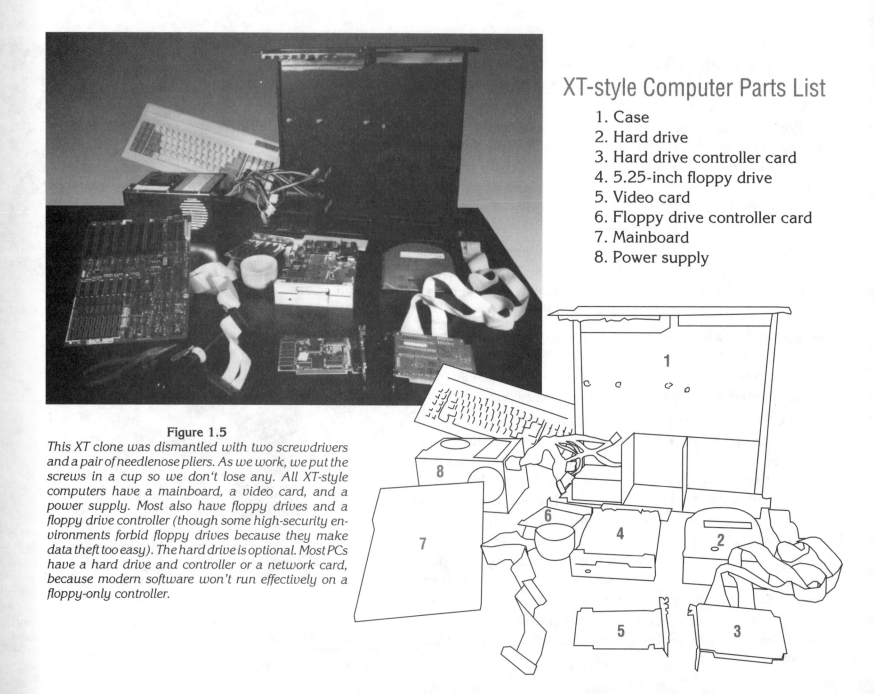

XT-style Computer Parts List

1. Case
2. Hard drive
3. Hard drive controller card
4. 5.25-inch floppy drive
5. Video card
6. Floppy drive controller card
7. Mainboard
8. Power supply

Figure 1.5
This XT clone was dismantled with two screwdrivers and a pair of needlenose pliers. As we work, we put the screws in a cup so we don't lose any. All XT-style computers have a mainboard, a video card, and a power supply. Most also have floppy drives and a floppy drive controller (though some high-security environments forbid floppy drives because they make data theft too easy). The hard drive is optional. Most PCs have a hard drive and controller or a network card, because modern software won't run effectively on a floppy-only controller.

AT-style Computer Parts List

1. Computer cover
2. Case
3. Hard and floppy drive controller card
4. Hard drive
5. Mainboard
6. Power supply
7. Battery pack
8. Video card
9. 5.25-inch floppy drive

Figure 1.6

This AT/286 computer was easily dismantled. All the screws you need to remove, plus a handful of white plastic standoffs to mount the mainboard, are shown in the center with the two screwdrivers you'll use. AT-style computers, like XTs, always have a mainboard and a power supply. Though some of these computers have the video circuitry right on the mainboard, most use a separate video card. Look for a single drive controller and floppy drives, hard drives, or both. Though some AT-style computers have a serial port and a printer port on the mainboard, most still use one or more I/O cards for the serial and parallel ports.

486 EISA Computer Parts List

1. Power supply
2. Case
3. Front cover
4. Floppy and hard drive controller
5. Video card
6. 3.5-inch floppy drive
7. SCSI hard drive
8. Mainboard
9. I/O card
10. 5.25-inch floppy drive

Figure 1.7

The 486 EISA computer is far more sophisticated than the XT and AT-style computers shown in Figures 1.5 and 1.6, but it's no harder to disassemble. In fact, new computers use more snap-out and squeeze-and-slide parts and fewer screws than the old ones did. Look for a power supply and a mainboard. Because 386 and 486 computers often integrate a number of "extras" right on the mainboard, your 386 or 486 may well not have a separate serial or parallel I/O card. If the ribbon cables from the floppy and/or hard disks plug directly to the mainboard, the drive controller circuitry is on the mainboard as well.

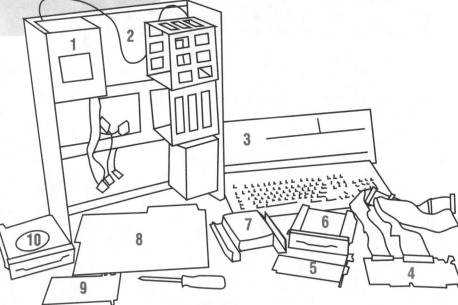

Cards are replaced by removing one screw, pulling up the old card, then aligning the new card with the slot and pushing down. The greatest difficulty, and it's minor, is ensuring that the card is firmly in place.

Figure 1.5 shows an XT clone, fully disassembled and labeled. Figure 1.6 shows an AT clone, again disassembled and labeled. Figure 1 .7 shows a 486 EISA computer. 386 computers will look a lot like the AT clone and/or the 486 computer, depending on the particular brand of 386 and the motherboard design. Read on if you need help with this "386," "486 EISA," and "AT clone" jargon.

Figure 1.8
The screws holding the cover to the case on the "Baby AT" case are on the sides. If you remove the case often, consider replacing the original Phillips screws with plastic thumb screws, to keep from having to deal with stripped threads.

How to Tell Whether You Have an XT, AT, or 286/386/486 Computer

You may not know which type of PC you have. You may have bought an unlabeled clone at a garage sale or have no documentation. The easiest way to find out what you have is to open the case and look at the brand name and number silk-screened onto the CPU chip. Though some computers tuck the CPU chip and part of the motherboard under the drives to save space, the CPU itself is easy to find. It is usually the largest chip on the mainboard and is set in a network of copper circuit traces. The CPU might be labeled 8088, 80286, 80386, etc. But some CPU chips aren't marked that straightforwardly. If you have an XT-style clone you might find a V20 or V30 CPU chip (V20 and V30 are NEC's clones of the 8088 and 8086 chip, respectively) or you might have an 8186 (a souped-up version of the 8086). 386 and 486 computers might have 386/SX, 386SLX, 386/DX, etc. printed on them instead of a simple 80386 or 80486. Use your ingenuity, you'll find the right chip.

CPU chips with higher numbers are larger and more powerful. An 8088 chip isn't much bigger than other chips on the mainboard; it's about two inches long and half an inch wide. 80286 chips are roughly an inch square, and 80386 and 80486 are big square chips that you can't miss. Figures 12.1 to 12.4 on pages 115-118 show typical 8088 (XT-style), 80286 (AT-style), 80386, and 80486 mainboards.

Figure 1.9

The 80386/25 case has just been removed, showing the compact "Baby AT" case with five expansion slots instead of the eight slots on standard size AT mainboards. Note that the basic components look much like the XT components. This mainboard has some longer 16-bit slots, a faster CPU chip than the XT, and more than four times as much RAM as the XT.

An 8088 CPU chip means you have an XT clone. IBM's XT, the first computer in the IBM PC family with a hard disk, was widely cloned. Some XT clones used the Intel 8086 CPU chip (a slightly faster half-sister of the Intel 8088 microprocessor), but most clone makers used the same 8088 CPU that IBM had used in their PC and XT computers. Because of the memory addressing limits of the 8088, the XT clone can only utilize 1024K (1 Mb) of memory. The upper limit of random access memory (RAM) is 640K—the computer needs the top 384K of memory addresses for the video card, the hard disk, and the read-only memory basic input/output system (ROM BIOS). Most XT clones run at a faster clock speed than the IBM XT, but they're still glacially slow compared to the newer 286, 386, and 486 computers.

An AT/286 computer is a clone of IBM's AT, which is based on the Intel 80286 microprocessor chip. This microprocessor can address 16 Mb of memory, but it almost always operates with the Microsoft disk operating system (MS-DOS, the operating system designed for the 8088 microprocessor). DOS is limited to the capabilities of the least common denominator—the 8088 microprocessor. Consequently, programs operating under MS-DOS cannot use memory over 1 Mb without a special program to open that RAM up. To get around the memory limit of DOS, many programs are able to use what is called *expanded memory*. Expanded memory cards can be added to both XTs and ATs. Most expanded memory cards are installed in ATs, though, because XTs aren't fast enough to justify buying an expanded memory card to do complex work.

An AT/386 computer is built around an 80386 microprocessor. The 386 microprocessor can theoretically address 2 gigabytes (2 billion bytes) of physical memory, but no one makes a computer with that many memory chips (too pricey). The normal AT/386 hardware design limits physical memory to 16 Mb. The last 15 Mb of this memory is extended memory, which can be used either as extended or as expanded memory in 386 or 486 computers if you run a memory manager such as 386MAX or the EMM386 program in DOS 5.0. The 386 chip also provides 64 terabytes (64 trillion bytes) of *virtual memory*. The 64 terabytes is called virtual memory, because computer programs think this memory exists but it isn't really there. For the ordinary DOS user, the most important difference between 386 and earlier chips is the virtual 8088 mode, which makes the 386 computer look like several 8088 computers running simultaneously on the same machine. Three programs which use this virtual mode are VM/386 from IGC Corporation, Microsoft's Windows 386, and Digital Research's concurrent DOS.

The AT/486 or 486/EISA computer is built around the 80486 microprocessor. The DX version of the 486 chip includes special math functions which were not integrated into previous microprocessors. 8088, 80286, and 80386 microprocessors will work with a special math coprocessor chip if you install one, but you have to buy the 80x87 coprocessor chip separately. The SX version of the 486 lacks the math functions and appears to the software to be a very fast 386. The 486 is different from the 286/386 line in some important ways. It is only pretending to be an 80x86 chip. Inside, it's talking RISC. Reduced instruction set chips do only a few things, very fast. Workstations like the SUN, Hewlett-Packard, and others are RISC machines.

Figure 1.10
The 486 EISA computer has a tower case. The screws holding the cover to the case are at the back.

Bus Designs—ISA Versus EISA and MCA Mainboards

When you compare the four mainboards in Chapter 12, or the disassembled computers in Figures 1.5, 1.6, and 1.7, it's easy to see that the major difference between an AT-type computer and an XT-type computer is the expansion slot size. 286/AT and 386/AT computers (and 486/AT computers too) have

Figure 1.11
The plastic front cover pops off Swan's 486 tower machine.

Explore Computer

longer 16-bit expansion slots, sometimes mixed with shorter 8-bit slots, while an XT has only the short 8-bit slots. The AT is a 16-bit machine, with many internal data transfers being made 16 bits at a time. This 16-bit AT bus is called the ISA (Industry Standard Architecture) bus. 16-bit transfer via the ISA bus provides some of the speed advantage 286 and 386 AT computers demonstrate when compared to computers using the 8-bit XT bus.

The EISA bus provides a quantum leap in bus throughput (that's capacity, measured as data bits transferred per second). EISA, which stands for Extended Industry Standard Architecture, accepts both standard ISA and EISA cards. It provides 8- or 16-bit transfers through the standard ISA cards and 32-bit transfers through the EISA cards. Only a few EISA cards are on the market, primarily high-end hard drive controllers and local area network (LAN) cards. Super-fancy EISA video cards priced at $3,000 apiece probably won't interest you, unless you work at Industrial Light and Magic and need to bring work home.

The EISA bus provides "bus mastering," which allows components like hard disk controllers and LAN cards to talk to each other directly, rather than going through the computer's CPU chip to communicate. An EISA LAN card has four or five times the throughput of a 16-bit ISA LAN card because it doesn't have to ask the CPU for permission to talk to the hard drive. This is a good moment to thank Swan Technologies for loaning us a 486/33 EISA computer to disassemble, test, and photograph. Their order number is 800-468-9044.

Micro Channel architecture (MCA) is IBM's proprietary 32-bit bus with bus mastering. Unlike EISA, MCA is not compatible with ISA—MCA bus connectors accept only MCA cards. Like EISA, MCA is a very fast bus.

Standard Hardware

Other than mainboard and power supply, the major components of a computer are:

- ✔ Floppy drives and controller cards
- ✔ Hard disks and controller cards
- ✔ Video cards
- ✔ Parallel printer ports
- ✔ Serial ports

✔ Game cards

✔ Modems

As manufacturers learn to pack more features into each chip it becomes simpler to manufacture one multi-purpose circuit board rather than many individual expansion cards. In the early 1980's each parallel port or serial port required an individual expansion card plugged into a bus expansion slot. In the 1990's, powerful new computer mainboards routinely include the electronics to control multiple parallel and serial ports. Many mainboards also feature hard and/or floppy disk controller logic right on the mainboard rather than on a separate expansion card. Other computer manu-facturers continue to use plain-vanilla mainboards, but stuff parallel ports, serial ports, a game port, and a floppy or hard drive controller onto a single expansion card. This design is cheaper to manufacture than multiple single-purpose cards. So new computers need fewer expansion cards to cover the basics. But exotic new add-ins have proliferated, so power users are still complaining that they don't have enough expansion slots.

Installing and maintaining the standard devices listed above should present no problems. The installation problems arise when exotic bits of hardware—things no one dreamed would be stuck in a PC when it was designed—are inserted into the computer.

Exotic Hardware

Almost anything can be and has been tucked into the obliging PC/XT/286/386/486 machine. Exotic hardware components are those not supported by the design of the BIOS or the PC architecture. Here are some examples:

✔ 3270 cards

✔ Network cards

✔ Bus mice

✔ Fax boards

✔ SoundBlaster boards

✔ Scanners

✔ A/D (analog to digital) and D/A (digital to analog) boards to monitor scientific experiments or control machinery

Figure 1.12
*When sliding the cover back onto the case, be careful not to tear
any cables or wires loose.*

✔ IEEE (Institute of Electrical and Electronics Engineers) standard bus interfaces to monitor lab equipment

✔ EPROM burners to create new BIOS ROMs from Electronically Programmable ROM (EPROM) chips

✔ IC (integrated circuit) testers

These are only a few of the items that can be inserted into a computer. The trick with these devices is to install them so that they are not in conflict with other devices already in the computer. The possible conflicts are:

✔ Two or more devices with the same or overlapping I/O addresses.

✔ Two or more devices with the same or overlapping ROM addresses.

✔ Two or more devices trying to use the same IRQ (interrupt) or the same interrupt vector simultaneously.

These conflicts can be avoided, to some extent, by reading the technical specifications in the documentation that comes with the hardware. In most cases, this hardware consists of a card that fits into a mainboard slot. Make sure that each new piece of hardware can coexist with existing cards. Use a utility or diagnostic program to find out which interrupts are in use, and which are available to your new device. We like QAPlus best, but PC Tools, Norton Utilities, and many other programs report on interrupts and addresses. For more details see Chapter 16, which covers peripherals, including installation and troubleshooting tips.

Reinstall the Cover

Now that you've looked around inside the machine, put the cover back on the computer, tucking in the cables as shown in Figure 1.12. The computer should boot up when you turn it on, but if it doesn't, don't panic. The problem is most likely that you loosened a cable in the process of pulling off the cover. Turn off the computer, take the cover off again, and push all the cables back in place.

Chapter 2
Diagnostic Programs

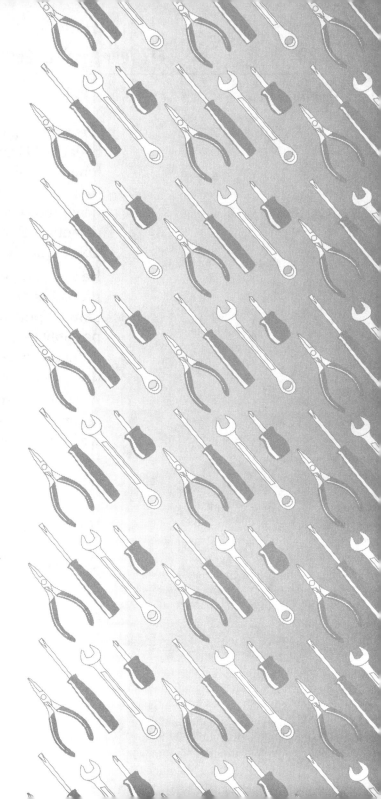

This chapter describes some of the diagnostic programs that are currently available, including the configuration utilities used to prevent hardware conflicts when installing new boards. We also discuss the advantages and limitations of these programs and explain how the diagnostics do what they do.

If you need to know precisely how healthy your computer is, can a diagnostic disk tell you? Is a repair recommendation based on diagnostic tests always accurate? Unfortunately no—on both counts.

Repair specialists, computer columnists, and diagnostic disk manufacturers promote these disks as infallible and all-encompassing, claiming that these programs have the ability to coax secrets from deep inside your computer.

You don't try to drive nails with a pair of pliers (maybe you do, but try to think for a moment like someone who doesn't). Diagnostic disks, like pliers, are handy for a variety of chores. But they won't do everything.

We remember an inexperienced technician in our shop replacing four or five hard drives in a row because his diagnostic disk kept reporting sector read/write errors on the drive. A new drive would function well when first installed, then report increasing errors during all-night read/write testing to confirm that the repair was done correctly. Each morning he examined the error log, saw the new read/write errors, and assumed that the hard disk he had replaced the previous day was defective. Because diagnostic disks have no way to test the power supply, the true cause (a bad power supply) wasn't discovered for a few days.

Here's another example of confusion in using diagnostic programs. A customer with printer problems tested her machine with a general-purpose diagnostic disk. The disk reported that the parallel port was working, so the customer (quite reasonably) assumed the problems couldn't possibly be due to a bad printer port. She returned the printer, complaining that it was defective. In fact, the parallel port wasn't working correctly, though it passed all the tests this particular diagnostic program could administer. The solution was to replace the port, not the printer.

A printer began malfunctioning intermittently on a network workstation. It was a fairly new computer, so we didn't believe the printer port had failed. We assumed the new network software we were installing was either bad or misconfigured. We ran QA Plus diagnostics, though, which found the bad port and saved us reworking all the steps in Novell 3.1 Print Server. In this case the diagnostics served us well.

Whole-Machine Versus Disk/Data Diagnostics and System Snoopers

Let's divide the world of diagnostic disks into three categories: those that attempt to test the entire machine, those that concentrate on the disk drives, and those that report on the hardware and software installed in the computer, but don't attempt to test it.

QA Plus and CheckIt, for example, are multi-purpose diagnostic programs designed to test the entire computer. They test memory, the microprocessor, the DMA chip(s), the numeric coprocessor, the floppy and hard drives, the serial and parallel ports, the video, the mouse, and the keyboard. They also provide full system configuration information (including the interrupt and memory addresses used by each piece of hardware).

Disk/data diagnostic programs, by comparison, concentrate only on the disk drives. They test and analyze the hard disk and/or the floppy disk, painstakingly reading each sector in search of corrupted data. These programs usually include some very sophisticated data recovery utilities. A typical disk/data diagnostic disk provides intensive testing routines, bad sector lock-out, file-moving utilities, and a sector-by-sector hard disk editor. The big three in this category are PC Tools, Norton Utilities, and SpinRite.

System snooper utilities report the hardware and software installed in the computer, plus the interrupts and addresses used by that hardware. They often call themselves configuration utilities or system information utilities. You are probably familiar with Norton's System Information (SI), PC Tools System Information, ASQ from the makers of 386MAX, or WinSleuth from Dariana. QA Plus and CheckIt also report the system configuration.

All are good programs. Some are practical for the new user; others are invaluable for veteran computer jocks. Some are more suited to one diagnostic/repair situation than the others. We'll discuss individual programs in the last half of this chapter, but first it makes sense to consider the general limitations and potential of any diagnostic program.

How Diagnostic Programs Work

Imagine that your computer is a patient in the hospital. Diagnostic disks require a conscious patient. They are excellent at testing one limb at a time (the serial port, extended memory, or keyboard, for example). The patient must be conscious, though, or they are useless. We'll use the serial port test to explain why.

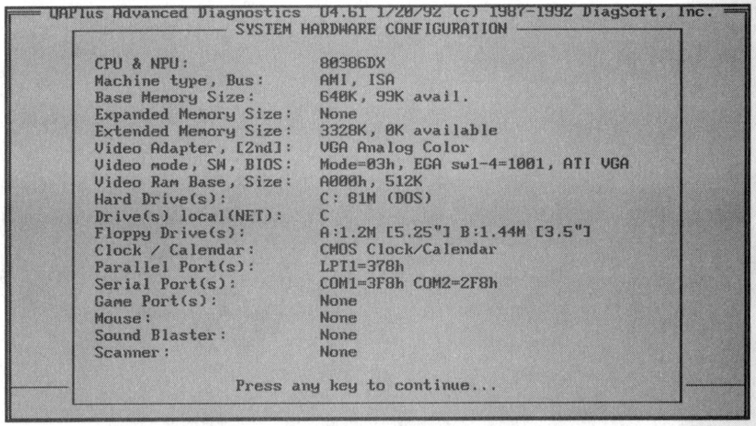

Figure 2.1
Diagnostic packages can report system configuration in considerable detail as well as diagnose problems. This system information screen is from QA Plus.

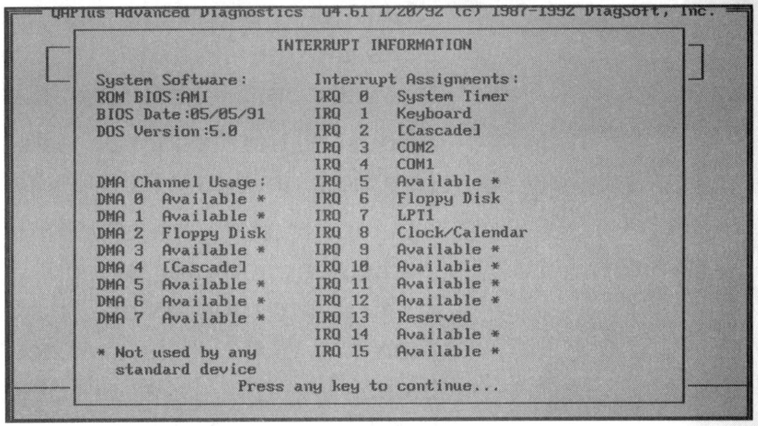

Figure 2.2
Dianostic programs are invaluable in reporting which interrupts are in use and which are available. When you add a new card or suspect a conflict, here's the place to turn.

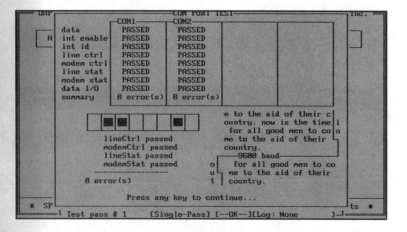

Figure 2.3

This is a sample diagnostics report, in this case of a serial port.

Let's use CheckIt as an example. The program runs the serial port through some pretty fancy hoops, sending data out on the TX (transmit data) line, checking for correct reception on the RX (receive data) line, and testing for correct signals on the RTS, CD, and DTR lines. Never mind if this TX, RX, and RTS stuff is all gibberish. If you really want to know all the details, buy *The RS-232 Solution* by Joseph Campbell (Sybex Computer Books, 1984). Probably you don't want to know, that's why you're considering buying a diagnostic disk. CheckIt will be able to tell fairly quickly if some aspect of your serial port is malfunctioning.

The problem is that CheckIt does not operate the serial port on its own—CheckIt asks the CPU to operate the serial port. It's like asking the patient to perform the test and then report the results when the test is done, without interpreting the results. For this serial test to run reliably, the power supply, mainboard, CPU, BIOS ROM, minimal RAM memory, video, and keyboard must all be functioning moderately well. Some parts, like the CPU, the memory, and the power supply, must be just about perfect or the serial port test will bomb—whether or not the serial port is bad.

Almost all the diagnostic tests are like this serial port test. They require a living, breathing patient (a functioning computer) both to run the test and to communicate with the diagnostic software.

Diagnostic software is ideal for torture-testing a running computer. If you must certify that a particular computer is good, you can 't beat diagnostics. Diagnostics will test all day or all night, without any supervision. They will test the machine longer, in greater depth, and more creatively than any of us users ever could—except by using the machine, and that's the problem. Many technicians run 72 hours of sophisticated diagnostics on a particular machine, then hand the machine to the user, swearing that everything is perfect. Within five minutes of normal use, the machine breaks and the technician looks like a fool. There was nothing wrong with the diagnostic disk, nothing wrong with the technician, and nothing wrong with the user. It's just that computers create endless new ways to fail.

Limitations Inherent in the Testing Process

Suppose your diagnostic disk tells you that something in a particular system (such as the floppy drive system) is malfunctioning. Is this true? Probably, but not necessarily. Certainly something is malfunctioning and the diagnostic disk noticed the malfunction while testing the floppy drive system. Nevertheless, that doesn't absolutely prove that the problem is in the floppy drive system. For example, a bad power supply could provide bad voltage to a working floppy disk, causing that disk to choke when reading from a floppy.

On the other hand, the conclusive test for a bad power supply is to replace it and see if the symptom goes away. The problem is much more likely to be a bad drive (out of alignment, for instance) than a bad power supply. The technicians and programmers who collaborate on these diagnostic disks give you their best guesses. These are excellent guesses, but they are not necessarily correct.

Using a diagnostic program to pinpoint a problem is therefore more of an art than a science. It's an art because diagnostics don't tell us which part is bad, only that *a* part is bad. Because any one of several components may cause a given symptom, it's impossible to know exactly which component is to blame—you can only guess which component is most likely causing the problem.

If you have tried the repair recommended by a diagnostic disk and get the same symptom again, don't just replace that part two, three, or four times. It was a good guess, but not the right one. Now you've got to start looking at other possibilities.

The Untestables

Here are some parts of the computer that no diagnostic program can ever test. Think of them when you get stumped, when the likely suspect is clearly not the right one.

Low Memory

No memory test program can write patterns to low memory and read the patterns back. If it did that, the computer would stop working. Low memory contains the interrupt vector table, the stack, and various system files (these terms are defined in the glossary). In other words, this is the autonomic nervous system of the computer. If you damage the low memory, the patient is dead— you can hardly test its reflexes. Most memory test programs say they are testing the first 64K of

RAM, but they're really not. The newest versions of QA Plus are an exception. QA Plus moves what it can out of low memory before testing, then turns off the interrupts and tests the bottom 16K of RAM.

Floppy Drives

No diagnostic program can test drive alignment without a special factory-formatted floppy test disk. Most diagnostic programs do not contain such a disk. QA Plus, our favorite diagnostic program, now sells a floppy drive diagnostic package that includes a factory-formatted disk. We don't see many floppy drive alignment problems anymore, so we haven't tested it. Floppy drives are more apt to have problems with mechanical parts like latches and springs. If the floppy drive does have an alignment problem, it will still require special shop equipment to fix it.

Power Supply

No diagnostic disk can test the power supply. Slight long-term voltage deviations can cause two kinds of problems: overvoltage and undervoltage. Long-term overvoltage conditions stress every motor and every chip in the computer. If you are constantly replacing parts, try checking your power supply output voltages with a meter. Even one excess volt will burn out a delicate hard disk or expansion card in a matter of weeks.

Chronic undervoltage produces its own set of symptoms. A hard disk that is getting less than 12 volts, for example, may not come up to speed the first three times you turn on the computer in the morning. The fourth time, though, it may work fine and seem okay all day. Low voltage can also cause mysterious intermittent computer lockups.

Power Line Interference

When an air conditioner turns on, it may well produce a momentary dip in the line voltage, followed by a spike. Thunderstorms are also notorious for the voltage spikes they cause. Some of these line (115 volt, wall current) spikes come through the power supply and travel through the 12- and 5-volt DC lines to the chips.

A momentary dip in current will cause the voltage to drop so low that the memory chips start to forget things. When this happens, the computer locks up. Perhaps you didn't see the lights brown out for an instant during the voltage drop. It doesn't matter. A voltage drop lasting only 1/1000 second can lock up the computer.

If your area has problems with "dirty power" that include unannounced brown-outs and power drops, you might want to invest in a line conditioner, an $80 device that boosts the power during momentary drops and acts as a surge protector as well. These dips in power can do bizarre things to computers.

Similarly, a momentary voltage spike to the hard disk head may well write gibberish in the middle of the hard disk—or worse, to the boot sector or the FAT (File Allocation Table). You will not notice this problem until you go back and try to read the file or boot from the hard disk. This is where routine use of disk maintenance programs can pay off. Run PC Tools DISKFIX or Norton Disk Doctor on a regular basis so they can catch and repair these problems. If the boot sector is trashed, try SpinRite, Disk Doctor, or DiskFix. It might be able to repair the boot sector, and if not, may be able to trick DOS into working properly anyway. The manual has the details.

Hard Disk Versus Hard Disk Controller

A diagnostic program can test for accurate data storage and recovery, and many programs have very sophisticated in-depth hard disk testing routines. What happens when a hard disk system flunks these tests? Unfortunately, there is no way to eavesdrop on the hard disk controller and the hard disk as they attempt to read or write data. If a bad controller is sending incorrect control signals to the hard disk, you'll have a data storage failure. If the controller is good, but the hard disk doesn't correctly follow the controller's directions, you'll also get data storage failure. Even a bad cable can cause intermittent failures. Refer to Chapters 5 and 15 if you think your hard disk is failing.

Diagnostic program error messages, your computer's BIOS ROM error messages, and DOS error messages are all based on educated guesses. Use the information these error messages give you, but know they are not infallible. We list common error messages in the appendices and suggest approaches to try if one of these messages appears on your screen.

Specific Diagnostic Programs

This section describes several of the diagnostic programs that are currently on the market.

Diagnostics

QA Plus and CheckIt—Whole Machine Diagnostics

QA Plus and CheckIt are whole-machine diagnostics—they investigate the complete PC. Both do the job competently, but any diagnostic can be fooled. Each tests the hardware in slightly different ways. Both are good programs, useful for the amateur and for an experienced technician. QA Plus is the stronger and more complete of the two; CheckIt seems to be a subset of QA Plus. There is now a Windows version of QA Plus called QA/WIN that gives you a graphic display of basic and Windows configuration, including interrupts, memory mapping, network information, and so forth. As this book goes to press, QA/WIN has several shortfalls. We still prefer the non-Windows version of QA Plus. For home use, CheckIt is perfectly okay, but for networks or big installations, we'd use QA Plus.

These whole-machine programs are great for finding two or an even number of bad memory chips. This kind of error can be frustrating because it doesn't cause a memory parity error, so you get no error message on the screen. Both QA Plus and CheckIt will locate the particular bad memory chip for you if you tell the program precisely how the memory chips are arranged on the mainboard. But if you know that much, you probably can figure it out yourself.

Neither CheckIt nor QA Plus comes with a manufacturer-formatted floppy disk to test alignment. (QA Plus sells it separately.) Alignment isn't repairable in the field anyway. Remember that misaligned drives have trouble reading disks recorded on a different computer, and another computer (or even another drive in your computer) will have trouble reading data recorded by the misaligned drive. A misaligned drive has no trouble reading disks that it recently recorded. Very old disks may have been recorded in better days when the drive was still in alignment.

Both CheckIt and QA Plus use serial and parallel *loopback* tests (loopback means the test sends data out some pins and reads it back to others). Buy a wrap plug, or read the directions in Chapter 16 if you want to solder one up at home. But just because the diagnostic says the parallel or serial port is good doesn't necessarily mean that the port is good. Here are the limitations.

One parallel port test program only tests one of the eight data lines. What if one of the other seven lines is failing? The program tests all 8 bits inside the latch chip on the parallel card, then assumes that if one of the data lines works, all eight do. This is a good guess, but sometimes it won't be true. By comparison, a diagnostic program written by a computer manufacturer and disseminated to their dealers for warranty repairs, loops back six of the eight parallel port data lines. Again, if the problem is in the seventh or eighth bit (the seventh or eighth data line) the test just won't find it. That's why the final test for a parallel port is to run it with a printer and see if it performs properly.

The serial port test, with wrap plug installed, loops back from transmit to receive and tests the control lines by wiring them together in two bunches. This covers every single important line in the serial port. So a clean bill of health from a serial port wrap plug test is more likely to accurately reflect a truly functional serial port. Nevertheless, the final proof is always whether the serial port works properly with a serial printer, external modem, or other serial device.

Diagnostic and Data Recovery Utilities

Now let's consider the major hard disk diagnostic/data recovery utilities. Hard disk diagnosis and data recovery are closely allied, so much so that many programs perform both jobs. All of these utilities will examine a disk for bad sectors, move important files, and perform other repairs. Refer to Chapter 10 for information about data protection and recovery. What kind of testing do they do on the hardware itself?

PC Tools

PC Tools DISKFIX will repair the most common hard disk problems that cause read/write errors or no-boot problems. It also contains a handy list of DOS and CHKDSK error messages and related troubleshooting advice.

PC Tools COMPRESS will unfragment the files on your hard disk so DOS can read those files faster. This is important because a fragmented file is hard to recover unless you have been running a disk monitoring program which tracks your file deletions or one that saves the "deleted" files in a temporary directory until you purge them for good. And DISKFIX now allows you to non-destructively low-level format your hard disk and set the interleave for maximum speed. If format and interleave are new concepts, see the glossary and Chapters 5 and 15.

But DISKFIX is not designed to detect hardware failure and identify the bad part, it's designed to repair mangled data on a functioning hard disk attached to a functioning controller with cables that are installed right side up. If the hard disk is not plugged into a four-wire power cable or the data cable is disconnected, DISKFIX chokes completely.

Norton Utilities Advanced Edition

The Norton Disk Doctor (NDD), like PC Tools, repairs common hard disk problems. Use Speed Disk to defragment your files. This speeds up file reads slightly, and improves your chances of recovering accidentally deleted files. Norton's Calibrate will set your hard disk to the optimum interleave. But the Disk Doctor, like PC Tools DISKFIX, is primarily a software-repair product (it repairs data storage glitches, moves data off bad sectors of the hard disk, and recovers lost files and directories). Like PC Tools, it gives no useful advice if the hard disk cables are unplugged or misinstalled.

SpinRite

The original version of SpinRite worked only on MFM hard drives. This limitation has been corrected in SpinRite II, in that it now works on SCSI, IDE, ESDI, RLL, and MFM drives. SpinRite will not low-level format ESDI, IDE, or SCSI drives, but the rest of SpinRite's repertoire works on all drives.

SpinRite is famous for maximizing hard disk throughput by setting the interleave to the perfect value for your hard disk and your particular computer system. It is also capable of rewriting the boot sector, a nice feature if your boot sector has been trashed by a voltage spike in a thunderstorm. But SpinRite is no help if you have incorrectly installed the cables.

Disk Manager

Well-known as a hard disk installation utility, Disk Manager also provides hardware troubleshooting diagnostics for hard disk controllers and drives. Unlike the other disk/data diagnostics we have reviewed in this section, Disk Manager does not attempt data recovery. But Ontrack (the publisher) will salvage corrupted data for a fee. Also unlike the other programs in this list, Disk Manager sometimes realizes that the cable or hard disk might be misinstalled. But other times it interprets a physical installation problem (e.g., no data cable) as a case of ultra-weird hard disk hardware.

Configuration (System Information) Utilities

System snooper diagnostics report which hardware is installed on the computer. You must know which interrupts and memory are in use when installing new cards, especially network, MIDI, fax, and other exotic hardware items. Each expansion card needs its own interrupt and a memory address area all to itself. All the diagnostics and system utilities that we've discussed here (except SpinRite and Disk Manager) provide lists of interrupts and addresses, showing which are free and which are already in use in your computer. Try CheckIt, PC Tools, the Norton Utilities, 386MAX, WinSleuth, or whatever you've got laying around.

Summary of Diagnostic Programs

Diagnostic disks can't tell you everything, but they are very useful. You should consider buying one of the whole-machine diagnostics if you need to test or repair your computer. You'll also need a configuration utility to figure out how to set the switches and jumpers on new expansion cards. All the utility programs we mention here, except SpinRite and Disk Manager, include a system information configuration program.

Because each of these diagnostic programs uncovers slightly different types of problems, you'll probably be best off investing in one of the disk/data diagnostic programs as well as a whole-machine diagnostic. These diagnostic programs are good. But always remember that your brain, especially if you are an experienced technician, is better. And nothing beats the old eyeball when troubleshooting misinstallation problems like cables, switches, and jumpers. Use the diagnostics and consider their repair recommendations—but don't follow them blindly.

Chapter 3
Common Problems and Solutions

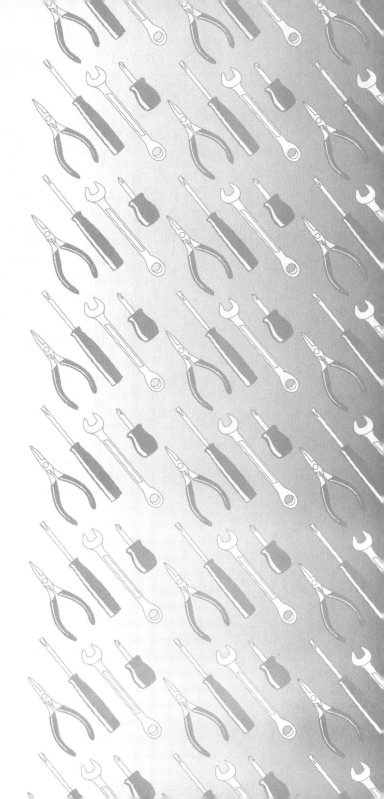

Your computer was working fine yesterday. Today it's sitting there, apparently dead, exhibiting big, expensive symptoms. It flashes a sullen error number on the screen and refuses to boot. It won't recognize setup. The printer won't work. The monitor is blank. What do you do?

Back when computer stores were staffed by salespeople who knew computers and could diagnose and remedy simple problems, you'd call Jenny, Sid, or Rashid. They'd ask you a few questions, have you try a few things, and, if their first suggestions didn't work, suggest you bring the computer down so that they could look at it with you.

But the economics of computer retailing have driven Jenny, Sid, and Rashid out of sales. Some computer stores forbid the salespeople to ever open a box, and wisely so. The computer supermarkets are staffed with clerks in matching tee shirts, not computer-literate salespeople. As a result, you'll end up with the machine in the repair shop, at the by-now familiar charge: $50 minimum, $75 an hour bench time.

Often these charges are unnecessary—this chapter tells you how to diagnose some common problems yourself.

Check the Cables First

Always check the cable connections first if your computer appears to be dead. With the jumble of cables worming out of the back of the computer, it's easy for one of them to get unplugged. Test all the connections and press them together. This may sound elementary, but you'd be surprised at the number of dead computers and printers that work fine when they're brought into the repair shop—their owners simply forgot to check that they were plugged in and turned on.

If the cable connections are okay, follow the suggestions in the rest of this chapter. If the quick fixes in this chapter don't get you up and running, consult the troubleshooting charts in Section 3. Follow the chart's questions and answers to point you to another troubleshooting chart that will suggest a solution. As we point out in the previous chapter, any single problem may have many causes.

Coaxing a Printer to Speak to You

The causes of a printer malfunction can range from a broken or disconnected cable (the most likely) to a bad printer port (the least likely, since parallel ports don't break down overnight). The switch boxes or the printer itself are also potential culprits.

Test the possible causes in this order:

- ✔ Cable
- ✔ Switch box (if there is one)
- ✔ Printer
- ✔ Parallel port

Test the cable by trying a known-good one. Test the switch box by removing it from the circuit and attaching the cable directly to the computer and printer. Test the printer by hooking it up to another computer. If you don't have access to spare parts, take the printer to your dealer's showroom to test out various hookup possibilities. You'll have to carry the printer and computer around to hook up your equipment, but it's cheaper than paying for a technician to diagnose the problem—and if anything needs to be dropped off for repair, you're already there. This is one of the reasons we prefer no-name clones assembled at Joe's Garage and Computer Store—the big-name chains discourage bringing in your machine to set up on the fancy cabinets to test out cables and switches on your own. If your computer was mail-ordered or bought from a techno-supermarket, take the printer into your office to hook up. Most offices have as much equipment floating around as our old clone chain.

Soothing Slow and Noisy Disk Drives

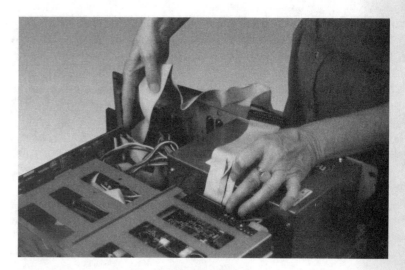

Figure 3.1
Press the floppy drive cable in place, both at the disk controller (right hand) and at the floppy drive (left hand).

Disk drives often break down gradually and can no longer read or write files as effectively as they once did. The usual cause is dirt adhering to drive heads. The drive is open to the elements: it inhales dust, smoke, grease, and other household pollutants. To prevent or treat dirty drive heads, buy a disk cleaner kit. Apply the cleaning solution to the special absorbent disk provided in the kit, then insert the disk into the drive. Issue the DOS DIR command to direct the drive to read the disk. You'll get an "Abort, Retry, Fail" message, but meanwhile the head accesses the disk and the cleaning solution. Press **R** (Retry) a few times to make sure the head is clean; a couple of revolutions removes the dirt. This is the generic method for using the cleaning disks; check the directions on your kit for specific procedures.

Occasionally, a floppy drive malfunctions because its cable is loose and must be pressed back in place. To correct this problem, turn off and unplug the computer, then open the computer case and trace the cable to its attachment and press it firmly, as shown in Figure 3.1. There's no danger to you or the cable, but remember to turn off and unplug the computer before you open the case.

If these fixes don't solve your problem, see Chapters 4 and 5 for further help. A noisy floppy drive, for example, may have been born that way, or it may be due for replacement. Instructions for replacing a floppy drive are provided in Section 2.

Reviving Failed Hard Disks

Hard disks almost always fail either at bootup or when the machine has been on long enough to get hot. The solutions we give here apply only to hard disks that fail at bootup.

The primary cause of hard disk failure at bootup is a loose cable or a popped card. Turn off and unplug the computer, open the computer case, and press the card back in place, as shown in Figure 3.2. Then press the cable into place.

Flakey Power Supply

Figure 3.2
After turning off the computer, push the hard disk controller down firmly to reseat it.

Another cause of hard disk failure is a malfunctioning power supply. A symptom of this problem is a disk that boots properly then dies as the machine gets hot. The message that appears on your screen is something like "Seek error, Abort, Retry, Fail." Don't keep replacing the hard disk and controller if you're continuing to have this problem. What's happening is that, instead of providing the proper 5 volts to the motor, the power supply is putting out 8 or 10 volts. The motor is running too fast and getting too hot, so it is registering its problem by not being able to read or write properly. Not all drives choke on a malfunctioning power supply, but the less expensive drives often do.

Did Your Computer Lose Its Setup on the Bedpost Overnight?

On 286, 386, and 486 machines, a common bootup error message is "Invalid Configuration Information" followed by "Hard Disk Failure." Your problem may be as simple as some dead batteries. All you need do is open up the case, replace the batteries with fresh ones and run the setup program. If you have a 286 machine, it's important to keep a boot disk with the setup program on it so you can handle these situations. Make sure that you get such a disk with your computer when you take delivery from the computer store. The setup program is usually stored on the hard disk, but you need another copy for those times when you need to boot from drive A. 386 and 486 machines have setup in ROM now, so you don't have to keep track of the disk.

The experience of solving a hard disk problem by replacing some batteries brings up one of our favorite engineering horror stories. It concerns two different early name-brand 286 machines that had the batteries soldered to the mainboard. The batteries were supposed to last five years, but they expired prematurely. The unfortunate owners were informed that they had to buy new mainboards—an expensive proposition. More than one of these owners bought clones as replacements for their name-brand computers. Why? Because clones had plain old AA batteries that are easy to replace. Newer mainboards for 386 machines have lithium batteries that are supposed to last the same five years, and also succumb much sooner. A battery pack costs about $5 but can be hard to find. Be sure you don't buy the more expensive AT replacement battery pack by mistake. The four-pin plug doesn't fit the two-plug outlet on the common clone mainboard.

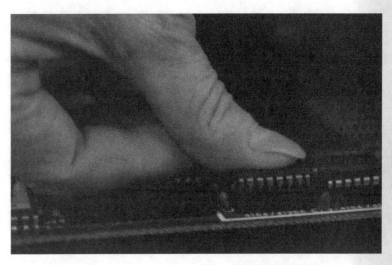

Figure 3.3
Press memory chips down firmly with your thumb. This will reseat a poorly seated chip.

This tale illustrates why we prefer clones assembled with modular components to national brands. When you replace parts in a name-brand computer, you often have to buy expensive name-brand parts. If you're considering buying a name-brand computer, be sure to ask about the compatibility and price of replacement parts.

Recovering Memory Failures

Memory problems often reveal themselves with a nonmaskable interrupt (NMI) error message on your monitor. If you have an XT or 286, the most common cause of memory failures is a popped memory chip. You can easily fix this by turning off and unplugging the computer, opening the case and pressing down on the chips with your thumb, as shown in Figure 3.3. Press down all the chips, one by one, to make sure they're seated. If you have a 386 or 486 machine with SIMM strips, shown in Figure 3.4 on the next page, make sure the strips are tilted and snapped into place properly. More subtle memory problems can show up as intermittent malfunctions in almost any component, such as the hard disk.

Figure 3.4
Make sure SIMM strips are securely clipped and tilted into place. This mainboard has been removed from the machine to show detail better.

It's best to discharge static electricity by touching some other metal surface before you begin working inside your computer. You should also wear a grounded wrist strap and avoid scuffing your feet back and forth on wool rugs while working on the machine. Standing on a special pad isn't really necessary. Grounded wrist straps are available inexpensively at electronic parts stores.

Missing Device Drivers

The symptoms of a missing device driver are usually something like this: your computer boots, but drive D has disappeared, the scanner has stopped scanning, or you can't get back on the network.

First, check your CONFIG.SYS file. It must include all the "device=" statements required to load all your device drivers. Most present-day computers (any that are more complicated than an 8088 with two floppy drives) boot with AUTOEXEC.BAT and CONFIG.SYS files.

Add-on peripherals and boards are often shipped with installation disks that contain alterations to the AUTOEXEC.BAT and CONFIG.SYS files. Before you install an add-on, copy your files to AUTOEXEC.OLD and CONFIG.OLD, then rewrite the originals to add the necessary "device=" statements. The lines required by the device driver will now be in your CONFIG.SYS file, and you'll have the backup files in case something goes radically wrong and you want to look at the old instructions.

A corresponding problem crops up with Windows. The WIN.INI file contains specific instructions to the computer about Windows setup. New software writes additional lines into WIN.INI; the well-mannered software makes a copy of the old file and keeps it for you, in case you de-install or need to make other changes. If you get strange symptoms, ill-behaved software or the stray neutron may have zapped your WIN.INI file.

Nonworking Color Monitor

For the most part, perform no repairs, other than adjustment, on a color monitor. You can, however, try removing the fuse at the back of the monitor and putting it back in. The fuse may be perfectly good, but due to heat or being moved around, it may not be seated quite right.

Liquid on Keyboard

This fix for spilling cola on your keyboard sounds crazy, but a reliable source assures us that it works on Zenith, Wang, and most clone keyboards. Disconnect the keyboard cable, remove any batteries inside the keyboard, then hold it under the hot water faucet until it's thoroughly rinsed. Let it drain and dry out for a couple of days, then plug it in. Don't try this one on a laptop. We owe this quick fix to Clark Miller, former Data Manager at George Washington University's Law School and a true computer guru.

Chapter 4
Maintaining Floppy Drives

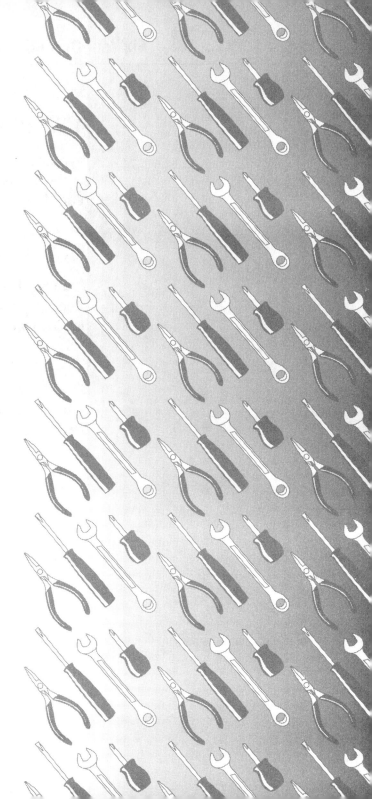

In the last chapter we took a look at the most frequent computer system problems in general. In this chapter, we'll look at problems that are specific to floppy drives.

Your computer frequently communicates with other computers via floppy disks. Even if your office computer is hooked to a LAN, you probably use Sneaker Net a lot. You install new programs and share data with floppies, so the quality and status of the lowly floppy drive should interest you as much as the health of your car's windshield wipers. Floppy drives aren't very glamorous, but if they don't work when you need them, you're in trouble. Figures 4.1 and 4.2, on pages 51 and 52, show typical AT-style 16-bit controller cards with floppy drives attached.

Floppy Drives

How to Determine Whether a Drive Is Aligned

If you have cleaned the floppy drive heads, but the drive still doesn't read/write correctly (for example, it won't read disks recorded on the floppy drive from a different machine, or it will no longer read disks it recorded a month or a year ago), see if the drive is in alignment. Alignment means:

✔ the heads of the drive are physically aligned with the tracks on the floppy disk, and

✔ the heads write at the proper level (an electronics term similar to "volume" on your stereo).

You may not realize your brand new disk drive is out of alignment until you try trading disks with other computer owners. We had a shipment of 1.2 Mb drives in our shop, for instance, that tested fine in new machines, but couldn't read disks recorded on other machines. So be sure to swap disks with friends before your machine goes out of warranty.

Drive alignment is checked and adjusted on a special disk alignment machine. Any competent dealer has one of these machines. If you don't want to take your computer to the repair shop to determine if the drive is in alignment, you can run one of the programs that includes a special diagnostic disk to tell you if your drive is in alignment.

However, only a trained technician with an alignment machine can realign your drive. Don't be surprised if the bill for this service is close to the price of a new drive. This is a 90-minute repair job, because the drive must be removed from the machine, tested, adjusted, and reinstalled. Remember the economics of computer repair: the typical repair is 2 hours at $75 an hour. For $50 you can buy a new floppy drive and install it yourself in about 30 minutes, start to finish, using only a Phillips #2 screwdriver.

In our shop, we only realign drives for computers if no replacements are available, as is the case for CP/M (pre-IBM-PC) machines. Again, the economics of repair dictate replacement, not repair, of most bad floppy drives. Replacement is your only option when 3.5-inch drives go bad—many brands are built in such a way that realignment is impossible. You need to be sure, however, that it's the drive, and not another component of the drive subsystem, that needs to be replaced.

How to Judge Which Component Needs to be Replaced

There are four basic components to the floppy drive subsystem:

- ✔ Disk
- ✔ Disk drive
- ✔ Cable
- ✔ Disk drive controller

Each component can be tested in turn to determine if it is the cause of the drive failure.

Try formatting a disk, then copying a file to it. If you get the DOS message "General failure reading," "Data error," or "Track 0 failure," try another disk—disks die over time. If two or more disks don't work, then there is a problem. Make sure, by the way, that you're using the proper type of disk. If you try formatting a high-density disk in a low-density drive, you'll sometimes get a "Track 0 bad" message, even though the disk is okay. It's just the wrong type for the drive heads to cope with.

If you try to format and the drive grinds away with the indicator light on without completing the format, try a fresh copy of your DOS disk. The FORMAT.COM file may be damaged. We know, because in our early learn-troubleshooting-at-home days, one of us replaced both her floppy drives because neither one would format a disk. Two new drives and $180 later, she still had the same problem. It turns out her old working copy of DOS was too addled to send the proper directions to the floppies—so no format. With a fresh copy of FORMAT.COM, everything worked perfectly.

If the machine has recently been worked on, check to make sure the floppy drive cable is properly installed. If it is installed correctly, check to make sure that the A drive, and only the A drive, has a terminator. If both the cable and the terminator are okay, then break out your diagnostic disk, such as QAPlus, and see if the drive works.

If QAPlus's floppy drive test says the drive is bad, replace the cable before junking the drive. Run the floppy drive test again. If it still says the drive is bad, replace the drive. A bad controller is rare, but if the new drive flunks the test, it may be the controller. Replace the controller and test again. If it's still bad, try the power supply. If it's still bad, replace the mainboard.

Unfortunately, it is usually impossible to independently verify that either the power supply or the mainboard is bad. Often the only symptom is poor floppy drive performance, the exact symptom that brought you here in the first place. So, if you know the disks, the drive, the cable, and the controller are all good, yet you still have floppy drive problems, try a new power supply next. Don't be frightened by this. Only once in about ten thousand repairs will you go beyond replacing the controller.

If you replace a floppy drive, try to get a decent replacement brand. Quality fluctuates with all brands, so ask around about recent recommendations.

Possible Floppy Disk Problems

Sometimes data disappear from a disk. You can't find a file you're positive is on the disk or you see gibberish when your word processing program retrieves it. The disappearance has four possible causes:

- ✔ The floppy has been mistreated.
- ✔ The floppy just died from natural causes.
- ✔ The floppy has been damaged from a failure of the drive.
- ✔ You made a mistake by accidentally deleting the file or by reformatting the disk.

Loss of data because of mistreated floppies is common. Store and handle your floppies gently. Don't let anything, including your fingers, touch the media surface through the rectangular opening. Don't expose the floppy to magnetic fields, such as magnetized screwdrivers. Don't use a floppy as a coaster, staple it, or post it on the refrigerator with a magnet, as one customer did. Data can generally be recovered if the disk is not physically damaged. Use the same recovery utilities you'd use on a hard disk. Refer to Chapter 10 for data recovery information.

Loss of data due to disk old age is prevented the most easily. If your data is your life, buy "lifetime warranty" disks that guarantee complete data recovery. If the disks start to lose files, you'll need to mail them back to the manufacturer, who rebuilds the data and returns the disk to you. If you don't buy warranteed disks, make a habit of dating your disks and occasionally making extra copies. A new working copy every six months is about right, if your disks are well-cared for. You may have tax and accounting data that are valuable enough to protect even further, by keeping backup copies of the data disks in another location. Fires and theft do happen.

However often you back up, think of disks as disposable items. Store only a few files on a floppy, not your entire work. Floppies don't cost much. We've heard of graduate students who own three floppies and keep reusing them until they die, thus losing their research.

The third probable cause of data loss is failure of the floppy drive subsystem. As long as the drive has not physically damaged the media surface of the disk, it is possible to recover data. Please note: If the surface of the disk is damaged by the drive, the floppy drive is broken and must be replaced. If the media surface is intact, the recovery methods outlined in Chapter 10 may help.

The fourth cause, user mistake, is the most common cause of data loss from both floppy and hard disks. The user types "del" or "format" and, despite being warned and required to confirm the command, zaps her data. Thousands of hours of work are lost this way. The long-term solution for this problem is better training and procedures, even though data can often be recovered.

Figure 4.1
Typical AT-style floppy drive system with disk, disk drive, cable, and an AT-style controller capable of regulating both hard drives and floppy drives on a single card. Photo by Mel Chamowitz.

Disk/Disk Drive Compatibility

Some of you are still using your XTs with 360K drives, so we remind you of disk compatibility problems.

Some quick math shows that a 1.2 Mb disk contains four times the information that a 360K disk does. What isn't so obvious is that the head on a 1.2 Mb disk drive is only one-fourth the size of the head on a 360K drive. When a 1.2 Mb floppy writes in 360K mode it leaves big gaps (big strips of background medium surrounding the skinny little track written by the skinny little 1.2 Mb head). When a big, wide 360K drive head tries to read the skinny little tracks, the head gets as much background as actual recorded information. This produces read errors. For this reason, only a 360K drive should be used to format or write a 360K floppy. However, a 1.2 Mb disk drive should have no difficulty reading a 360K disk. Microfloppies are a bit more compatible. The heads are the same size, so a 1.44 Mb disk drive doesn't leave gaps when writing or formatting 720K disks.

Figure 4.2
Most new PCs are configured with both a 3.5-inch and 5.25-inch drive.

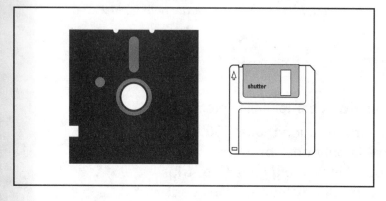

Figure 4.3
A 5.25-inch floppy disk (left) and a 3.5-inch disk (right).

If 1.44 Mb and 720K disks have the same size heads, how does the 1.44 Mb disk hold so much more data than the 720K version? The difference is that the 1.44 Mb disk is a high-density disk and the 720K disk is a low-density disk. The terms low-density and high-density describe the number of sectors per track on the floppy. A high-density floppy has 15 or 18 sectors per track; a low-density floppy has 8 or 9 sectors per track. In addition, the various sizes of disks differ in the number of tracks per side. And not every version of DOS is capable of supporting the newer high-capacity disks.

3.5-Inch Drives: Smaller Is Better

As far as your computer is concerned, there is little difference between 3.5-inch drives and 5.25-inch drives. If you have an XT, you can even replace one of your older drives with a 3.5-inch drive, to gain some compatibility with newer machines. You'll need to upgrade your DOS version to 3.2 or above in order for the machine to recognize the drive, however, and you'll also need to add a special command to your CONFIG.SYS file in order for the computer to format disks in 720K format (otherwise, it will format the 3.5 inch disks in 360K format). DOS 3.3 doesn't need the special driver; it will format the disk as a 720K or 1.44 Mb, depending on the type of 3.5-inch floppy drive installed.

Putting a 3.5-inch drive into a standard bay is no great problem. The smaller 3.5-inch case fits into an envelope case that fits the bay. You can use the same floppy controller for a low-density drive (720K) installed in an XT; on an AT, you already have a high-density floppy controller and can use either a low-density (720K) or high-density (1.44 Mb) drive. See the data pages for instructions on swapping floppy drives.

Chapter 5
Maintaining Hard Disks

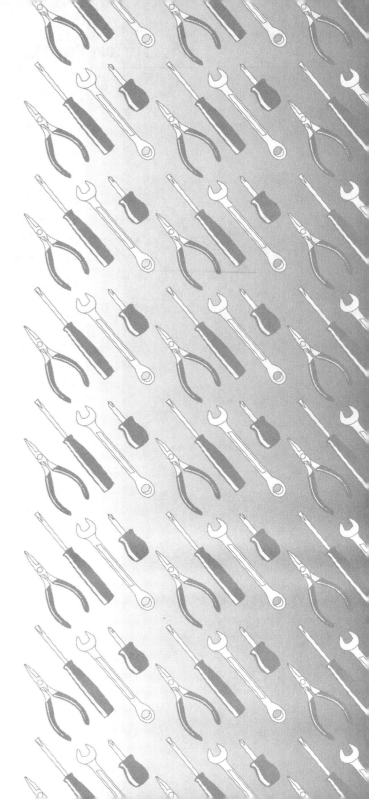

Everyone has to cope with hard disk problems now—hard disks are standard on new systems. It wasn't always this way; the clone chain we worked for sold two-floppy IBM compatibles for $2,000 in January 1985, when a 10 Mb hard disk would have boosted the price to $3,600. Today, $2,000 will buy you a 486 clone with a 120 Mb disk and a video graphics array (VGA) monitor, if you shop right.

Our owner used to say that the trick in the clone trade was marketing the hottest $2,000 machine. This was, and is, the ballpark price an average customer will pay for a new system. They may pay more for hotter features, but they start looking at the $2,000 range. This is true of both desktop and laptop machines. Hard disk prices have continued to drop, but the new cheap hard disks aren't as durable as they are convenient. This is true of all magnetic media, but hard drives seem so much more permanent to the unwary.

Hard Disk Life Span

Hard disks are sealed boxes. They can't be opened for routine service. Don't expect them to last for more than two years. Just as you expect to replace the tires on your car every few years, plan to replace a hard disk in two years. Accept the fact that your hard disk is a consumable item.

The most compelling reason for short hard disk life is the pressure on manufacturers to reduce costs. This forces them to use cheaper parts, to move assembly operations from the United States to countries with cheaper labor, and to tolerate more casual standards.

The surface of a hard disk platter is carefully polished, then a magnetic coating is sprayed on and the surface is repolished. Both base and coating must be nearly defect-free to reliably read and write data. Moreover, the hard drive heads are much smaller than the floppy drive's relatively large ones, and the disks spin at very high speeds. Any laxness in any one of the components means it's a short-lived piece of hardware. Both brand-name and no-name computers are assembled with identical hard disks, so the premium you might pay for a brand name computer is no guarantee of hard disk longevity.

In the quest for ever-lower prices, many hard disk manufacturers have ended up being embarrassed by the poor quality of their products. The issue is a familiar one in the computer business—price-sensitive buyers push the price down to the point where it is difficult to produce a quality product and still make a profit. Margins (the difference between dealer cost and sales price) on hardware have dropped from the 30 percent that dealer expected in 1985 to 20 percent in 1989 and to 8 percent in 1992. At that margin, a lot of equipment goes out the door with margins of 5 and 6 percent. As the market has become more price sensitive, quality has been swapped for low price.

Hard drives have improved enough that manufacturers now provide a year's warranty, which is hardly a long and healthy life. The dealer warrants the whole system for one year, expecting never to have to touch it. The hard drive will probably survive this period, but may show signs of trouble not long after. Drive rebuilders (companies who rebuild drives and guarantee them for 30 days) report many year-old brand-name drives arriving on their doorsteps quite dead.

Overall, the PC computer business is going through a quality crisis similar to the one the automobile industry went through during the 1970's. As a comparison, the price pressure in the computer business would make your 1993 Chevrolet cost $900 and last for nine months, instead of costing $15,000 and lasting for seven years.

Figure 5.1
An exploded hard disk. Photo courtesy of Microscience.

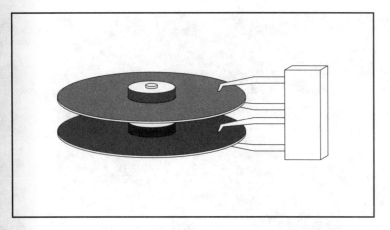

Figure 5.2
A hard disk with two platters has four recording surfaces, so the hard disk needs four read/write heads. The heads move together, in and out across the platter surface.

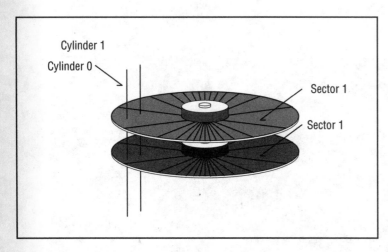

Figure 5.3
Each bit of data is located in a particular sector (pie slice), on a particular track (concentric data storage ring), on the top or bottom surface of a particular platter. The outermost track on every platter is Cylinder 0. The next track is Cylinder 1. Cylinder 2 is the third track from the outer edge, on both top and bottom surfaces, on all the platters.

With these warnings in mind, protect your data. Back up your hard disk regularly. Run utility programs, weekly if possible, that analyze your drive and ensure that the surface is reliable and any questionable areas are locked out. Your data is much more valuable than any mechanical device or application software, as every mainframe computer site knows. Mainframe shops have alter-native emergency sites, for which they pay whether or not they ever use them, and a multitude of backup and recovery routines. Studies show their data is ten times as valuable as the hardware. On a smaller scale, the same is true for you. So use and enjoy your fast, convenient hard disk, but be prepared to check it often and replace it. See Chapter 10 for more suggestions on how to guard your data.

The Structure of a Hard Disk

To best protect your data on a hard disk, you need to know how the data is stored on it. An "exploded" hard disk is shown in Figure 5.1 on the previous page.

Hard disks are physically made up of platters and heads, but logically made up of cylinders and sectors, as shown in Figure 5.2. A Seagate ST-238 drive, for example, has two platters with 614 cylinders. Each platter has two sides, so the drive has four heads to read these platters. The heads record data in concentric rings, called *tracks*. See Figure 5.3. Each track has a given number of sectors. Since the ST-238 is an RLL drive, it has 26 sectors per track, and holds 33 Mb of data. The Seagate ST-225, by comparison, is similar in construction, but has a less precise recording surface, so it can hold only 17 sectors per track for a total of 22 Mb of storage. Larger drives may have as many as 8 platters, 16 heads, and 1,024 cylinders, the maximum numbers that a PC BIOS can support.

Hard Disks

There are two popular ways to package information: modified frequency modulation (MFM) and run length limited (RLL) encoding. The first technique, MFM encoding, uses 17 sectors per track. RLL encoding uses 26 sectors per track and packs much more information into the same area, so a high-quality surface is required. Suitable hard disks are RLL-certified by the manufacturer. In each case, the data coding scheme is built into the controller hardware, not the hard disk. An MFM controller with an RLL-certified hard drive produces MFM data encoding on an over-qualified recording surface.

Within DOS, the hard drive platters appear to contain a continuous stream of information. In other words, what you see as two platters is seen by DOS as a long length of tape (see Figure 5.4). In DOS, the disk is a large string of clusters or, if this is an MFM drive, packets of four sectors. Some drives' clusters are packets of as many as 15 sectors—it depends on the drive type. DOS reads and writes to the disk in increments of sectors and allocates space by the cluster, not by the individual sector.

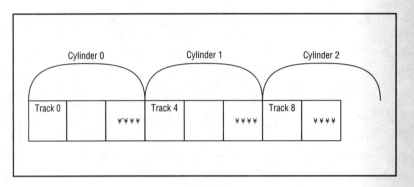

Figure 5.4

DOS sees the data as a continuous stream, like the music on a cassette tape. Tracks 0 and 1 are the outermost tracks on a platter. Track 0 is on the top surface, Track 1 on the bottom surface of the platter. Tracks 2 and 3 are also the outermost (top and bottom) tracks, but they lie on the second platter. This makes sense, because the read/write heads move together, moving head 0 into position to read. Track 0 also moves the other heads into position to read the outermost tracks on the other platters.

The boot sector and file allocation tables (FATs) are recorded on Track 0, and often the root directory starts on Track 0 as well. You can see why this track needs to be defect-free—it contains the index that DOS creates when it records data.

The first portion of the disk starting on Track 0 contains the boot sector, FAT1, and FAT2. Inside the boot sector is information that indicates how much, if any, of the disk belongs to DOS (DOS understands that it may have to share the disk with another operating system) and where the DOS boot files are located. FAT1 and FAT2 are simple arrays of numbers that indicate, for example, that Cluster X is linked to Cluster Y, Cluster Z is unusable, and Cluster W is free. The two FATs are copies of each other. The hard disk boot sector is shown in Figure 5.5 on the next page. Sector 01, the beginning of the FAT, is shown in Figure 5.6, also on the next page.

If the boot cluster is damaged, DOS will not be able to recognize the disk and will give you a message such as "Non-System Disk," if it can give any message at all. Usually the machine just locks up. If the FAT is slightly damaged, the DOS command CHKDSK or a data-recovery program

Hard Disks

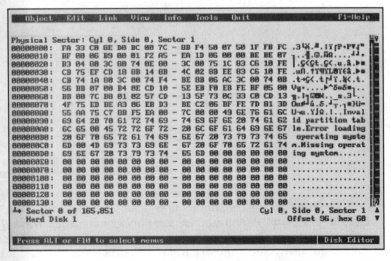

Figure 5.5
The hard disk boot sector (sector 00). Programs like the Norton Utilities (shown here) will allow you to examine the boot area, the FAT clusters, and the root directory on a hard drive.

Figure 5.6
Sector 01, the beginning of the File Allocation Table (FAT).

may be able to reconstruct the pointers (the directions to the next cluster in the chain). If the FAT is unreadable, the pointer information and whatever is on the disk are lost. Even though the information is actually still on the disk, there is no way to access it in any meaningful form. If you want to know about all this in greater detail, read *Advanced MS-DOS Programming*, by Ray Duncan (Microsoft Press, 1986, 1988).

The root directory begins at the beginning of Cluster 2. It contains the names of the files and subdirectories and indicates what pointer in the FAT is the marker for the first cluster of each file. If the root directory is badly damaged, data on the disk cannot be retrieved. Subdirectories are just files of file names, file sizes, dates created, file attributes, and first cluster numbers. In other words, a subdirectory is structured just like the root directory, but it is itself a file. When a file is erased, the first letter of the file name is changed to hex value E5 (E5H, in computerspeak) and the FAT pointer is zeroed out, but the data is not actually erased from the disk.

Hard Disks and Controllers

So far, we've assumed that your standard PC clone is equipped with a moderately sized MFM or RLL drive that fits in the same size bay as your 5.25-inch floppy drive. This was the standard configuration for several years. Recently, however, IDE, ESDI (Enhanced Small Device Interface), and SCSI (Small Computer System Interface) drives have become increasingly popular. These drives offer the advantage of placing the data separation circuitry (encoding and decoding) on the drive itself, not on the hard disk controller. The separation allows the manufacturer to use any encoding scheme he wishes. These encoding schemes also make it possible to manufacture very compact drives with high transfer rates, as well as mega-sized drives. And because so much more of the brains are on the drive, the controller is inexpensive.

If you are upgrading to a larger drive from your original configuration, you will undoubtedly be considering an IDE drive. These drives are emerging as the most popular, especially since the SCSI interface isn't standardized enough to let you easily daisy-chain other peripherals to the same controller, the supposed advantage of this interface.

Installing IDE, ESDI, and SCSI drives is no different from installing MFM or RLL drives. The difference in low-level formatting is taken care of by special software bundled with these drives (typically Disk Manager). Big IDE and ESDI drives are more expensive and often more reliable than the garden variety small 20 and 30 Mb drives. A 300 Mb drive currently costs $1,400; the buyer of such a drive wouldn't tolerate a failure in two years, which is the standard life span of the cheap drives.

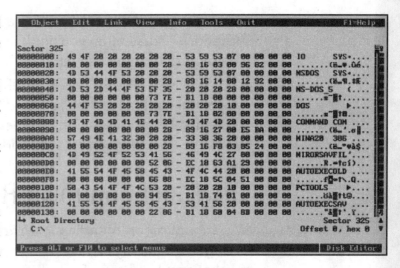

Figure 5.7
Sector 127 starts the root directory. This hard drive was formatted with MS-DOS 5.0.

SCSI drives have been around longer than ESDI drives. Many small minicomputers and Apple/Macintosh computers and workstations use SCSI. It would be nice to attach a CD-ROM (Compact Disk-Read Only Memory) player to the same controller, but getting a CD-ROM to work on a shared controller is difficult. The PC world is still too diverse for universal standards, we're sorry to say.

Whether your drive is an MFM, RLL, IDE, ESDI, or SCSI, the hard drive platters and heads are the same; the only difference is the controller board on the hard drive itself.

Hard Cards

Hard cards are nothing exotic—they're a regular 3.5-inch hard disk bolted onto a hard drive controller. The original HardCard was designed by Plus Development Corporation and is still a reliable buy. The card occupies two or three slots inside the machine. It functions like any hard disk, except that it's designed to be logically relocatable (can have its address reset) and can therefore be installed in a machine that already has a regular hard disk controller.

Getting the hard card to function as this second drive, however, can require setting and resetting jumpers because often you don't know the existing hard drive controller's I/O and ROM addresses. The hard card must use different I/O and ROM addresses. Making sure the addresses are unique to each controller can take some exasperating experimentation.

You're not likely to put a $400 hard card in a $200 machine, but if you choose to install a hard card as the first hard drive—as in an older Compaq, Corona, or other luggable—there is no such address problem. You simply plug it in and play.

Drive and Controller Recommendations

We are not recommending specific brand names of drives and controllers because the PC world changes so quickly. Today's hot buy is tomorrow's paperweight. Quality changes rapidly in the PC market as well. A run of bad drives and controllers can happen to any manufacturer. When you're ready to replace or upgrade your drive, talk to friends, computer support people at your company, the local users' group, and your dealer. Between them, they'll be able to recommend the best current combination. The best combination varies too much from month to month for us to give you any useful advice. Just be sure to match the drive to the appropriate controller.

In general, we recommend that you replace the hard drive controller when you replace the hard drive. It's often hard to know which part is the culprit when a problem surfaces. Many distributors bundle the two parts together and sell them as a kit.

Whenever you have a hard disk installed by a repair shop, it's a good idea to have the shop open the machine and show you the new drive. Look for the date of manufacture and don't accept the drive if it's more than a year old. Something is clearly wrong if the drive has been floating around for longer than that. Look to see if there are any stickers on the drive that are clearly not the manufacturer's—one of the authors had the misfortune to work at a shop that passed off rebuilt drives as new. Finally, make sure that a bad track table accompanies the drive. No drive is perfect, but low-level formatting locks out the bad tracks. The percentage of bad tracks should not exceed 5 percent of the total.

See Chapter 10 for more information on safeguarding your hard disk data. Data loss is the most serious problem for any computer user.

Chapter 6
Diagnosing Memory Problems

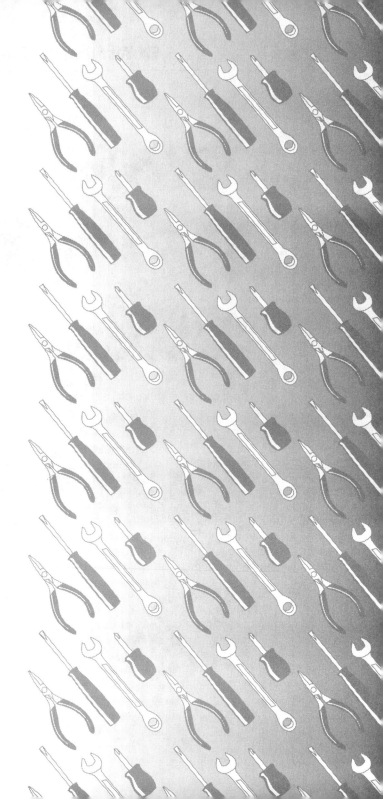

This chapter gives you a few hints for dealing with common memory problems and some clues for tracking down offending chips.

Only older machines have rows of memory chips and separate memory cards: 386s and up, and many 286s and laptops, generally use SIMMs (Single Inline Memory Modules) instead. You may have an older 386 that sports a special proprietary memory card—these were popular for a couple of years, and cost big bucks. Now memory is very cheap. Machines commonly arrive with 1 MB onboard, and can be upgraded in a typical 1-2-4-8-16 MB path.

Not all machines use the same word length. Some machines store a "word" (some multiple of 8 bits) as 8-bit, 16-bit, or 32-bit words. The longer the word length, the faster the memory talks to the CPU. You will need to buy upgrades in the correct configuration. The manual that came with your computer will be quite clear about what you need. Most places that sell RAM chips and SIMMs know what machine requires what strip. Once in a while, as with a MacIntosh Quadra upgrade, the

Figure 6.1
Closeup of memory chips stamped with identifying numbers.
Photo by Mel Chamowitz.

Figure 6.2
1 MB SIMM. With inexpensive, compact memory, modern
machines can hold 8Mb or more of RAM.

warehouse accidentally assigned the same number to two different strips. Only one of the four SIMM strips was the wrong part, yet the machine wouldn't even boot.

Memory problems can largely be traced to faulty memory chips and SIMMs. A photograph of memory chips, showing the alphanumeric codes that are etched on them, appears in Figure 6.1. One chip has standard numbering and one chip has nonstandard numbering. Memory chips are usually coded *LL4ZCXXXX-YY/P*, as detailed in Figure 6.2. SIMMs use a similar numbering system, such as *LL41XXXX*, as shown in Figure 6.3. A few manufacturers use other systems, but these are rare.

Let's look at what happens when your PC develops a memory problem. We assume that you're not interested at this point in learning how DOS handles memory or in other memory matters that concern programmers. For this reason, we'll focus only on fixing the suddenly forgetful machine.

The most common symptom of memory problems is the BIOS message "NMI error at [address]" or "Memory parity interrupt at [address]." If you have a Phoenix BIOS, the message continues "Type (S)hut off NMI, (R)eboot, (I)gnore."

Nonmaskable interrupt (NMI) occurs when the hardware, specifically the memory parity circuitry, detects an error. The exact wording of the message on your screen depends on your computer's BIOS. Generally, the BIOS will give an address in the NMI error message, but this address is rarely the faulty one. The computer refreshes the memory many times per second, but it does not keep track of the exact address it is refreshing at the moment. When the refresh process shows up a bad chip, you get an NMI error. But the machine has no idea what chip is the bad one. The CPU does know where the instruction pointer was pointing in the memory, so it writes that address on the screen. Unfortunately, the address has absolutely nothing to do with the actual bad chip.

If only an odd number of bits go bad, you're in luck. The computer is constantly making parity checks and will notify you if the bits don't add up correctly. If an even number of bits go bad, the computer can't detect the problem and doesn't report a memory error message to you. The result can be untraceable problems. For example, this kind of memory problem may result in files that are trashed when they're copied or word processing files that are saved as gibberish.

Be aware that some machines don't perform a parity check anymore. You can tell because they use SIMM strips with eight chips, not nine. Memory problems in these computers won't result in NMI messages, just weird symptoms, such as a screenful of smiley faces or a document that was saved in English and is retrieved in Indonesian. Look first for memory problems, not an exotic virus.

When to Pull and Test Memory Chips

Whenever you get an NMI message, press **S** to shut off the NMI and save your work. Then turn off the computer. The offending chip or SIMM may only be loose in its socket. Unplug the machine, open up the case, and press firmly on all the memory chips or on the SIMM strips.

Frequently, when an individual chip goes bad, corroded wires are the cause. There are tiny wires inside the memory chip, connecting the actual chip of silicon to the legs on the outside of the memory chip. Run QAPlus. If it says that a given chip or SIMM is bad, pop it and replace it.

Figure 6.3
Explanation of Alphanumeric Codes on Memory Chips

LL	Two-letter initial code of the chip maker
C	CMOS or low-power version of chip (may not **appear**)
P	Letter code for the package type
4Z	Number of bits
XXXX	Size of chip. Common numbers are:

Description	Number
64 for 64K by1	4164
256 for 256K by 1	41256 or 41257
1000 for 1000K or megas	411000 or 4100 or 41000

Some chips have more than 1 bit. These are:

Chip	Number
4 x 64K	4464 or 41464
4 x 256K	44256
8 x 1024K	48000 (SIMM)
9 x 1024K	49000 (SIMM)

YY	Speed in nano-seconds. Numeric equivalents are:

YY	Speed +/-20%
05	50 ns
06	60 ns
07	70 ns
08	80ns
10	100 ns
12	120 ns
15	150 ns
20	200 ns
30	300 ns

If your NMI message persists, have all your memory chips tested in a memory chip tester. Most dealer repair shops have such a machine. The charge should be less than $25. Have the chips tested at least 20 ns faster than the manufacturer of the mainboard recommends—the testing machine dials are somewhat difficult to read at a precise setting. Once in a while, chips pass the test, but still cause NMI errors. In this case, spray Freon on the chips to chill them before retesting. You might also heat them with a hair dryer and retest. This reveals if temperature variations are the cause of the problem.

The repair shop can use a similar tester on SIMMs to locate the faulty one. Unfortunately, you can't pull and replace an individual chip. The whole 1 Mb strip must be replaced, at $40-$50, a bargain compared with the days of the Great Memory Shortage when these things cost $50 per separate chip.

A few memory test programs do exist, but we can't recommend any of them because none are able to test the lowest 64K of RAM. QAPlus says it can test the lowest 64K of RAM by tricking the CPU into momentary stupidity. We'd still rather diagnose and solve a suspected or confirmed memory problem by pulling the SIMMs or chips and running them through a memory tester.

When to Replace the Mainboard or Card

When you have an XT with socketed memory chips on the mainboard, it is worthwhile to have the chips pulled and tested. On the average, this procedure takes 15 minutes. The time charge for testing all the chips and replacing one or two of them is less than the cost of installing a new board. If you have an older PC/XT clone with soldered memory chips and a persistent memory error message, replace the whole machine. It's dead. A new 386/SX mainboard can live quite happily in a former AT, though, and it makes sense to install a new mainboard if the rest of the components are fairly new. You *can* put a 386 mainboard in an XT case, but the power supply will need to be upgraded to 200 MW, and probably the 8-bit hard disk controller will be too slow to work with the faster chip. At this point, buy a new machine.

There are other parts of your computer besides the mainboard that use memory chips. These components include the video card and some hard disk controllers that use a *cache* (place to store data temporarily). The memory chips in these devices are usually soldered in, so if the memory goes bad, the board needs to be replaced. A few hard drive controllers, such as Corporate Systems Center (CSC) Fastcache 64, use SIMMs which can be replaced.

Upgrading Memory

Even though MS-DOS below V.5.0 can only address 640K of RAM, MS-DOS 5.0, DR-DOS 6.0, and Windows 3.1 can trick the machine into using a large amount of memory. Upgrade 386/486 machines by adding the appropriate number of 1 Mb or 4 Mb SIMMs.

Programs running under DOS 3.3 and earlier make use of expanded memory through a technique called *bank-switching*. Blocks of 16K are switched in and out of a 64K window in RAM. Up to 8 MB of extra RAM can be added in this manner on add-on cards. These expanded (bank-switched) memory cards are still popular, though their sales dropped when the cost of memory became irrational during the RAM chip wars. These cards are very easy to design, build, and install, but you need to make sure that the *driver* (a piece of software that tells the computer how to use the card) is written according to current LIM standards. In other words, buy a name-brand expanded memory card, such as Intel or AST. Some low-price imported cards provide badly-written drivers that produce erratic results. The LIM standard is periodically revised by the three vendors—Lotus, Intel, and Microsoft—who established the standard.

Some systems have odd memory configurations in which the system board memory stops at 512K and picks up again at 768K. Several vendors tried this, but we have never liked it. Clones also exist that can't ever be expanded beyond 512K of RAM because of the design of the mainboard. Stay away from these computers—you need every byte of memory you can get.

Chapter 7
Solving Printer Problems

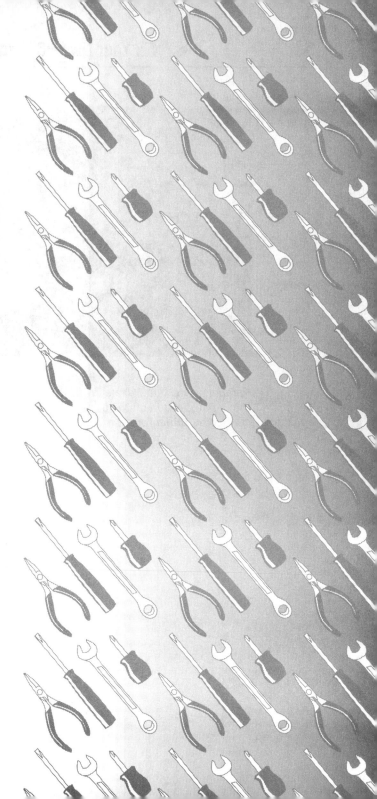

This chapter describes the three major types of printers: dot matrix, ink jet, and laser. It also gives you some tips for determining what's wrong with your printer and how to solve the problem. Printer and parallel cables are shown in Figure 7.1 on the next page.

We've dropped advice about daisy wheel printers from this edition. There are still a few heavyweights clanging away out there, but there is less and less software that provides the drivers for them. WordPerfect 5.1 still support them, but graphics-capable applications won't talk to them at all.

The printer is the major input/output device, besides the screen, that lets the computer communicate with us. It is the part of a computer that most of us relate to when the computer, in concert with word processing software, imitates a fancy typewriter. In a paper-oriented society, the printer output is your computer's most visible product. Attractive output is high-quality work in many people's minds. Did you pay more for your laser printer than for your computer? Many people do.

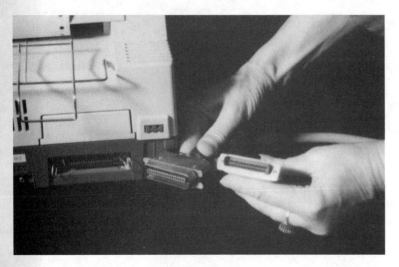

Figure 7.1
Parallel printer cable. Note the 25-pin DB25 connector, which plugs into a parallel port on the back of the computer, and the Centronics connector, which plugs into the printer.

At our clone chain, 60 percent of the computers sold were used solely as word processing machines. As a result, printer repairs are often a more intense subject than computer repairs.

Types of Printers and Their Associated Problems

Printers fall into groups: dot matrix, ink jet, and laser. Dot matrix printers are further classified as 8-, 9-, and 24-pin types. Most printers are still black and white, but color printers are dropping into the small-office and home-use range. They're usually ink jet types at affordable prices (thermal wax process printers are much higher).

Dot Matrix Printers

Although there are dozens of different brands of dot matrix printers, they divide into two major groups: they're either similar to IBM Proprinters or they're similar to Epsons. All manufacturers add extensions to these definitions, but your dot matrix printer will emulate either an IBM or an Epson. Dot matrix printers are classified by the number of pins in the print head. The difference between 8-, 9-, and 24-pin dot matrix printers is print quality. Print quality depends on the number of wires that make up the printhead—the more wires, the better the quality. The wires are so small in 24-pin printers that it's hard to see the dots. In fact, 24-pin dot matrix printers have the same resolution (dots per inch) as laser printers, and dot matrix printers are a far better value if you'll never need to produce commercial-quality photocopies. Almost all dot matrix printers are sold for home use now. Businesses almost always buy heavy-duty laser printers and put them on networks.

Ink Jet Printers

Ink jet printers squirt tiny droplets of ink in programmable patterns. The first ink jet printers required a special coated paper and cost about the same as the later "personal size" laser printers. The new ones use any smooth paper and are about the same price as a medium-quality dot matrix. Resolution is 300 dots per inch, the same as laser printers without Resolution Enhancement, and appears slightly fuzzier than laser output because of the droplet pattern. The output is entirely acceptable for business letters, spreadsheets, and some graphics.

Color jet printers are fun and not terribly expensive, giving attractive prints in three colors—cyan, red, and yellow. The fourth color, black, is necessary for top-quality color prints.

Laptop-sized printers use ink jet technology. They operate for about 40 minutes on battery, print one page per minute, and can handle Windows fonts. Amazing, isn't it? You can put a 386 laptop and its companion 2-pound printer on an airline tray (in business class, of course, not on the 5 x 7 trays in steerage) and have the same computing and printing power that would have required a hand truck, not so long ago. The cartridges for ink jet printers are pricey ($25), which isn't so astounding, considering the price of laser cartridges. Do you pay more for printer cartridges than software upgrades? Most of us do, gladly.

Laser Printers

Laser printers are as commonplace in the American office as copy machines. The differences between the two are not as great as you might think. You can think of a laser printer as a computerized copy machine, requiring the same kind of care. You shouldn't expect your laser printer to spit out pages as fast as the demo in the store, or at the advertised page-per-minute speed. These speeds are for all-text pages after the first page. Pages that mix text and graphics take more time and require extra RAM in the printer. Plan on adding at least 1 Mb RAM to the printer if you do much graphics.

Keep in mind, as well, that the software that drives laser printers is specialized and not always easy to configure to produce peak speed. Very slow laser output isn't entirely the printer's fault, it's also a function of computer power. It can take up to 45 minutes to compose an all-text newsletter page from an IBM PS/2 Model 30 trying valiantly to run PageMaker under Windows, for example, a task that warrants an upgrade to at least a 386SX machine.

Determining the Source of a Printer Problem

A printer port rarely breaks—regardless of whether it's a serial port or a parallel port. Simple tests can determine if your problem is an exception. First test your printer and cable. Hook up your printer to another computer using your own printer cable, fill the screen with any text (the DOS DIR command lists your files, for instance), and press **Shift/Print Screen (Prt Sc)**. If the printer prints the contents of the screen, the printer cable and printer are both okay, so it's time to turn to the troubleshooting charts in Section 3. Some laser printers won't print a partial page, so you may need to do a manual form feed.

You may need to make a trip to your computer dealer to hook up your printer to one of the floor machines (demo computers). Most clone dealers are accustomed to this. Our experience with national-brand dealers varies. Don't take in the printer during the busiest sales time (typically late morning on Saturdays, lunch hour during the week, or just before closing on weekends). It's a good idea to also call your salesperson and let her know that you're coming.

The serial connections on printers once caused many problems. RS1-1 232 was subject to interpretation by computer and printer manufacturers, some of whom created their own individual standards. We used to have a repairman who made $50 an hour for the shop rewiring serial cable pins. Today, however, almost all printers use the parallel connection; therefore, many printer problems (the serial port problems) have been eliminated. Even if you have a printer that must use a serial connection, you can minimize serial port problems by using a SmartCable (by IQ Technologies). We have never failed to get the connection right with one of these devices. See Chapter 8 for serial connection troubleshooting tips.

Printers vary in the way they handle carriage returns and line feeds and the way they interpret escape codes for fonts and print size. To accommodate these differences, you must install a software program called a *printer driver*. Modern word processing software is delivered on ten or more disks, due to the amazing number of printer drivers the software must provide. In comparison, PC-Write, the shareware word processing classic, used to be furnished on just one disk.

The most common reason for printer problems is an incorrect printer driver installation. This doesn't mean that you've installed the printer incorrectly, but that you've installed the wrong printer driver while setting up the software. The result can be some truly odd characters that appear when you print bold or underlined words. When you first use the software, you must select the correct printer driver to copy into the program. If you don't see the exact model number and guess wrong, or if you inadvertently type the wrong choice, you will install the wrong printer driver.

There are two reasons why printer repairs can be a problem. First, printers are mechanical, with dozens of wheels and gears; break one, and fail to locate a replacement, and you have a dead printer. The second reason is an industry problem: some manufacturers are much better at warranty repairs than others. Some warrant all of the parts. Others specifically exclude the printhead, the most expensive and delicate part of the printer. If your printer is under warranty, the dealer must ship it back to the manufacturer for repair. It must be in the original carton and foam packaging, to protect it from shipping damage. Some manufacturers will return your printer in a month; others may take three or four months to repair and return your printer. Before you buy a printer, check the warranty repair history of that brand. Check the warranty policy of the retailer. Many now exchange printers on the spot or give you a loaner.

bitsatatime.This¤16-bitõversus8-bittransferacc
muchofthespeed ´advantagesõof■anAToveran
TheEISA(EnhancedÛIndustryõStandardArchite
isthebigbrotherÛofâtheÄclassiℇCbus.Noticetha
connectorsarehigherâandÄaõslightlydifferentsʰ
acceptsbothstandardâandÄEISA — cards,withtʰ
thattellsthemachineówhatõkindofcardsareinsta
EISAcardsareon ´theâmarketõyetprimarilyahigh-
controllersandLANÇcards.ßSome■superfancyℇ
onthemarket,which¤won'tßinterestyouat$300
atIndustrialLightÇ&âMagicõdoinₘorphingandne

Figure 7.2

Don't panic if your printout looks like this. You have the wrong printer driver installed in your word processing program. This page had a Panasonic 1124 selected as the printer, but was printed on an HP Laserjet III.

Despite our enthusiasm for clone computers and their retailers, we think that you're usually better off to purchase your printer from a retailer who specializes in printers and who is a repair depot for the brand you choose. It's more likely that the part you need will be in stock with such a retailer. Computer dealers may tell you that they can only stand behind the system if all the peripherals are purchased from that dealership, but don't be persuaded by the sales hype.

The final point to keep in mind is that you usually can't fix your printer by yourself. In general, the most you can do is make certain that it is a mechanical problem—not a data communications (parallel or serial cable) or software problem.

Chapter 8
Serial Connection Problems

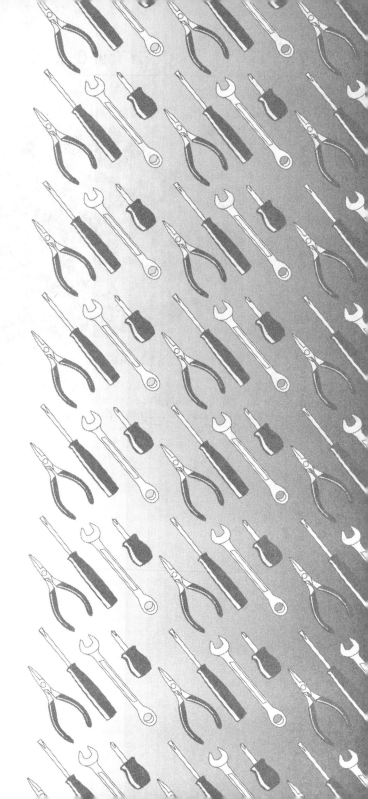

This chapter describes the serial connection and the problems that arise when add-on devices (peripherals) are attached to the computer via the serial port. It also offers a method to test the serial connection.

Making various add-on devices work with the PC can be a problem. Fortunately, only one of our customers persisted in trying to plug a serial device (a cash register) into the parallel port on his computer, because that's what his old machine's serial port had looked like. He fried several parallel ports in a row this way. Most serial connection problems are more straightforward.

Most clones now include both a parallel and serial card, a multi I/O card, or serial and parallel ports right on the mainboard. The serial port allows you to add many kinds of peripherals to add to your computer system. You may need an external modem or one of the other add-on devices you attach via a serial port—mice, plotters, digitizers, digitizing pads, and electric pencils, for example.

Figure 8.1
Try to identify the expansion cards in this typical AT/286 clone. The serial card is easy; it's the 25-pin male connector in the fourth slot from the right. The modem has two square RJ-11 connectors for telephone wire. The MPG video card with the 9-pin DB9 female connector for the monitor also has a 25-pin female parallel port connector.

Your PC has only a limited number of ways to employ add-on devices; the serial port is the most versatile. The major hurdle in diagnosing and repairing a serial communication problem is that computer manufacturers have interpreted the RS-232 standard in various ways and have altered the 25-pin connector to a 9-pin, perhaps to avoid our persistent customer's mistake in identifying the right port.

Printer manufacturers have further reinterpreted the standard, sometimes by hearsay, since they consider themselves more like typewriter manufacturers than electronics manufacturers. The results have been predictably interesting to untangle.

The Serial Port

Your computer may have a 25-pin male, 9-pin male, or a 25-pin female serial port. The physical connector was never defined by the Electronic Industry Association (EIA), because EIA assumed it would be a 25-pin female connection. After IBM equipped the AT/286 with a 9-pin male serial port, EIA was careful to define the physical connector for succeeding serial definitions, such as RS-422, and was also careful to specify what the pins communicate. When we have to, we patch the mismatches with gender menders and 9- to 25-pin pigtails—leaving interesting tangles hanging out the back of the machine.

Unless you're using a standard straight-through serial cable, we suggest that you buy a SmartCable (IQ Technologies, Inc.), shown in Figure 8.2. It is readily available at computer hardware and software stores, and costs little more than a standard straight-through cable. A custom-engineered serial cable can cost twice as much.

A SmartCable contains a device that monitors the serial cable lines and sorts things out for you, as long as you follow the directions on the back of the cable. Basically, you set the two switches to the most likely position, then follow the directions to fine-tune them—this doesn't take long.

Serial Problems

How to Test a Serial Connection

The first step in testing a serial connection is to check how many serial ports the computer believes it has. If you have two physical serial ports, but Norton's System Information program or QAPlus shows only one, then clearly the device addressing switches on one or the other are not set right.

When Norton checks the serial ports, it reads the equipment list—a list the BIOS assembles as it boots the computer. The BIOS checks serial port addresses, but doesn't compare each physical card with its address, so it is possible to set up two serial ports so they have the same address (both set to COM1, for instance). The BIOS will never catch this.

It is also possible to accidentally set the switches on a serial port so that its I/O address is one that DOS cannot recognize. The BIOS doesn't see this serial port, so it doesn't include it in the equipment list.

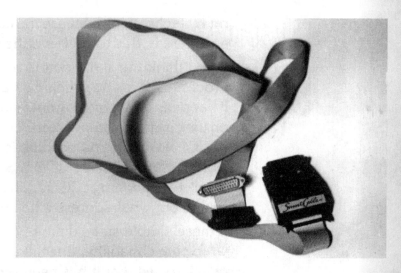

Figure 8.2
SmartCables are a serial port lifesaver. This one is designed to work with either a male or a female DB-25 serial port. AT versions, with 9-pin connectors are also available. Photo by Mel Chamowitz.

The BIOS can only talk to two serial ports: COM1 and COM2. Sometimes a modem, for example, may be set to COM3 or COM4, because some software can bypass the BIOS and address COM3 or COM4 directly. This is fine. Just be sure your software allows you to set the serial card to one of these nonstandard addresses.

Serial cards are packaged with instruction manuals that give suggested address switch (or jumper) settings. Remember, when you install a serial port you must give it a unique I/O address. On the card you just installed, the I/O address is a physical address set by switches or jumpers. DOS simplifies things for you at this point by dealing with the logical address: COM1, COM2, COM3, etc. Some serial port manuals refer to hexadecimal addresses instead of the DOS COMx names. COM1, for example, is the physical I/O address 03F8 and is paired with interrupt 4. COM2 is the I/O address 02F8 and is paired with interrupt number 3.

When you take delivery of a new computer, ask for all the instruction manuals for the parts. Manuals for serial ports are frequently flimsy, ill-printed, and misleading, but they're better than nothing. We installed an inexpensive serial card that functioned properly when it was set up right, but baffled

Serial Problems

many technicians because the addresses printed on the card and in the manual were both different and were both wrong. Nevertheless, ask for the documentation. It can't hurt.

If you think the serial port is properly addressed, but it still doesn't work, recheck your thought processes. Are you sending data to COM1 when the modem or the printer is connected to COM2? It happens pretty often. Communications software looks for a modem at the COM port you selected on the program setup screen. Communications programs ask you to specify COM1, COM2, COM3, or COM4. An internal modem is often preset to COM2, even if no additional serial port is present. Don't assume that it's COM1. Software configured to look for a modem at COM1 will not be able to talk to a modem at COM2. Check the jumpers on the serial card or the modem against the manual to find out what address it has been set to.

If these simple steps don't reveal an obvious problem, it's time to use a serial test program with wrap plug capability. CheckIt and QAPlus programs send data out the transmit data (TD) line and check to see that it has been properly received on the receive data (RD) line.

These programs require a wrap plug, which you can either purchase or solder up at home out of a spare RS-232 plug female or a DB9 plug female, both of which are inexpensive and available at electronic supply houses. See "Serial Ports" on page 000 in Chapter 16 for instructions. We promised you that you'd never have to solder to fix a computer, but if you already know how to solder and like to play with this kind of thing, you can look like a serial wizard.

If a serial port passes the wrap plug test, it's usually good. Look again for a mismatched COM port and interrupt, or for an incorrect MODE command. An almost-right MODE command will result in almost-right printing, which is the same thing as very odd printing.

See "Serial Ports" in Chapter 16 for additional details on the diagnosis and repair of serial ports.

Modems

Modems come in internal and external varieties, shown in Figures 8.3 and 8.4. Each style has some significant benefits. Some systems managers insist on external modems because problems are more easily diagnosed. It is also sometimes necessary to communicate with another modem of the same type, and perhaps the same brand. If the modem uses an optional data-compression standard such as MNP, you need another MNP modem to get the benefits of the data compression. Some very fast proprietary modems will only speak to another identical model. These high-speed modems are expensive, and an external modem is easier to share between two computers, easier to install, and easier to troubleshoot. You need to be sure to buy a modem that conforms to the CCITT V.32/V.32bis/V.42/V.42bis standards for data compression and error correction. V.32bis is the specification for 14,400 bits/second communication. V.42 addresses error control and V.42bis governs data compression. Some modems advertise that they can do 57,600 bits/second, if all the options are activated and conditions are ideal. You can probably get 19,600 bits/second if you have decent phone lines.

From the repairperson's point of view, the main problems with external modems are the serial port, the cable running from the serial port to the modem, and poor quality telephone connection. Solve these problems by testing the port with a wrap plug, using a SmartCable, and calling the phone company, respectively.

Internal modems have their own problems. When you install an internal modem, you must be sure to set the IRQ (interrupt jumpers) and the I/O address jumpers correctly. Test the machine before reinstalling the cover, since it's easy to make a mistake here. The I/O address must be unique—it must not interfere with another serial device already installed in the machine.

If your telecommunications software supports COM3 and/or COM4, set the modem to COM3—you are unlikely to have another serial device set to COM3. Be sure to set the IRQ for the I/O address you are using. Each I/O address is paired, by tradition, with a particular interrupt. See Appendix D for a list of common I/O addresses and their associated interrupts.

Whether you use an external or internal modem, your telecommunications software must be set up impeccably. Modems are not forgiving beasts. A minor baud rate error or the incorrect I/O

Figure 8.3
A 2400-baud external modem. Photo courtesy of Practical Peripherals.

Figure 8.4
This internal modem has two RJ-11 telephone wire connector sockets on the card end. One socket is for the phone line from the wall. Use the second socket to connect a regular telephone handset to the line. Photo courtesy of Swan Technologies.

address will make your perfectly good modem appear to be stone-cold dead (modems are that way; they either work fine or they won't work at all). SmartCom is probably the pickiest brand of telecommunications software we have encountered. It works reliably only with genuine Hayes modems, and often refuses to get along with Hayes-compatible modems that function well with other programs.

The most expensive modems use the Rockwell chip set. These chips are relatively immune to noise. If you have to use a modem over noisy long-distance lines, it's best to buy a well-made, and expensive, modem. Cheap modems cut off in the middle of a transmission if the line gets noisy.

Chapter 9
Upgrading your Machine for Windows and Other Uses

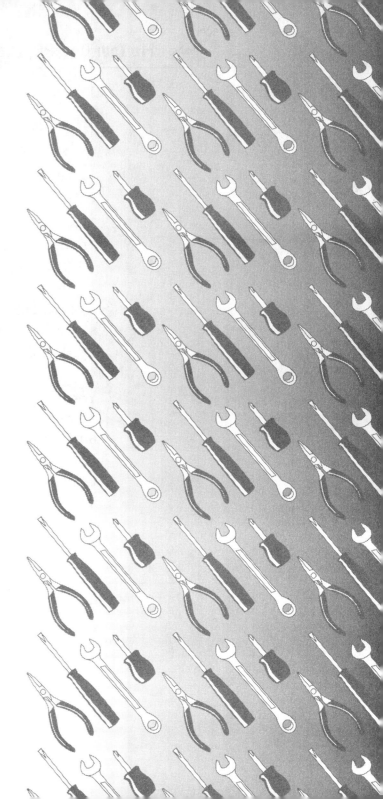

This chapter discusses how to upgrade your computer to run Windows 3.1. Specifically, we discuss what pieces of the machine to upgrade for your Windows application. Not everybody uses Windows, so we tell you other things you can do to upgrade your system.

Windows is a fact of computer life now—no longer a curiosity, after Microsoft sold 4 million copies of Windows 3.1. New users learn much faster with a Graphical User Interface (GUI), so businesses find it easier and cheaper to train new users on Windows than on DOS applications, despite the expense of upgrading. Then, newly purchased PCs arrive with MS-DOS 5.0 and Windows 3.1 already loaded leaving the experienced users on the older machines. The old hands don't tolerate this for long, so they move up to Windows, too.

You may need to upgrade your PC to run Windows, so let's look at what you need to run it.

- ✔ 386/SX processor, at a minimum
- ✔ 4 Mb of RAM (random access memory), preferably more

✔ High-resolution super video graphics array (SVGA) color monitor

✔ SVGA video card with at least 512 Kb of RAM, preferably 1 Mb

✔ Big, fast hard drive (Windows needs 5 Mb of disk space by itself; the applications often need 10 Mb or so)

The cost to upgrade an older PC completely is not trivial. In the Washington, D.C. area, Fall 1992 prices are:

386 motherboard	$200
RAM upgrade to 4 Mb	$150
Super VGA video card, if necessary	$200
SVGA color monitor	$400
Bigger hard drive, if necessary	$450
Total	**$1400**

You can buy a new 386 machine with a one-year warranty for the same price. It doesn't make a great deal of sense, then, to upgrade the machine. Use it as it is with the old software until it breaks, and then replace it. The new machine will probably arrive loaded with the software you want.

You may not need a total upgrade, though. You may only need to replace one component. Think what you want to improve. What exactly is driving you nuts? Is it a specific application, or the way it behaves in general? Different Windows applications make different demands on the system. Here are some suggestions about improving Windows life.

Refer to Figure 9.1 for a chart of PC upgrades and Figure 9.2 for a chart of upgrades to run Windows.

Slow Display

Windows applications make heavy demands on the computer, especially the video card. Waiting for the screen to catch up with you can drive you nuts, especially if you're using your word processor in graphics mode instead of draft mode. Graphics and WYSIWYG (What You See Is What You Get) publishing packages need the best video card you can afford. Look for SVGA cards with 1 Mb of memory, or better yet, the new graphics accelerator boards. These are based on several different standards—Weitek, S3, and TIGA, but all offer much faster display. They work by putting a graphics coprocessor on the video card. The price varies from not-bad to hair-raising, so see what

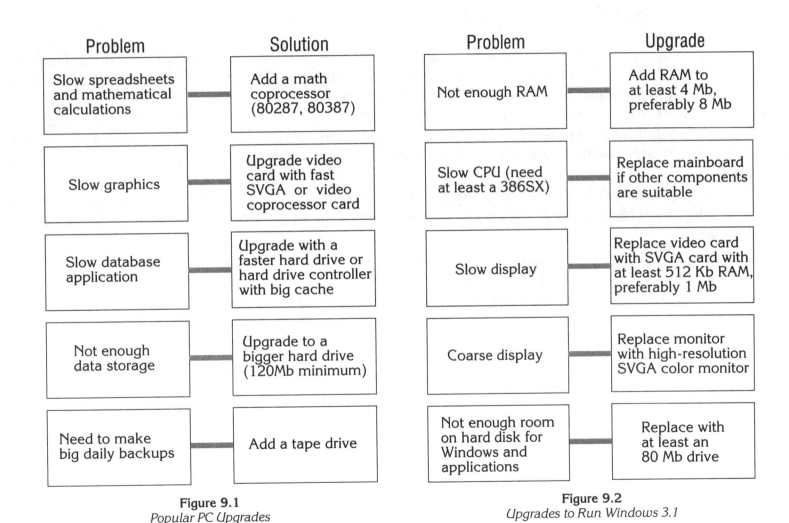

Figure 9.1
Popular PC Upgrades

Figure 9.2
Upgrades to Run Windows 3.1

your application really needs. Word processing, for example, makes different demands on the video than computer-assisted design.

Slow Spreadsheets

Spreadsheets run much faster with a math coprocessor chip, if you have a 286 or 386 machine. (486 DX chips have the math coprocessing functions built in, while 486SX chips do not.) Floating point calculations (that just means numbers after the decimal point) choke up an otherwise speedy microprocessor. Add an 80287 or 80387 chip, at prices from $60 to $200, for better performance. An 80287 chip makes an AT computer about ten times as fast on certain calculations as a 386 clone. Locate the empty socket on the motherboard when you're inspecting the computer's interior. It's clearly labeled, usually right next to the CPU. If you add an 80387 coprocessor chip, be careful. There are many little pins on the chip that bend and break easily. You might want your local repair shop to do the installation, if you have a tendency to mash delicate parts.

Slow Database Application

If you find yourself going for coffee while your computer cranks through a database sort, you may really want a faster hard drive, not a faster machine. Disk access times of 18 ms or less are a necessity for database programs. In fact, though, a drive cannot run faster than a seek rate of 16 ms—it takes that long for the disk to spin into position for a read. You can speed things up by configuring a bigger disk cache in MS-DOS, or invest in an upgrade hard disk controller that has built-in RAM. Talk to one of the mail order houses that specialize in hard drives for advice on what will work with your system. You will probably need to replace both drive and controller, but you'll save yourself innumerable blood pressure spikes during the day.

Upgrading your System for Other Reasons

The rest of this chapter describes several add-ons—extra devices you can add to the basic configuration of your computer. It also gives you advice about choosing add-ons to meet your needs.

Extended and Expanded Memory

The most common add-on is extra memory. Today extra memory refers to memory above 640K RAM, but it once meant memory above 256K. In ATs, expanded Lotus-Intel-Microsoft (LIM) memory is generally what you want to add. *Expanded memory,* also called EMS, is generically known as *bank-switched memory.* Spreadsheet programs such as Lotus 1-2-3 (up to version 3) and its clones can make use of LIM for giant spreadsheets, as can Ventura, PageMaker, dBase III+, some fax cards, and many other devices and programs. In order for LIM to work, the card must be accompanied by a well-written driver. In this case, it's the software that counts, since anyone can make the card.

Extended memory is memory above 1 Mb; a 286 or 386 in "protected mode" can address up to 16 Mb or 2 gigabytes, respectively. Special memory utilities trick DOS into using the area of memory called high memory to access the extended memory. QEMM and 386MAX use this method.

Figure 9.3
This card is a top-of-the-line Gammalink CP that turns your PC into a fax machine.

Fax Cards

Figure 9.3 shows a fax card. As with many add-ons, there are two types of fax cards: those designed for home use and those designed for industrial use. Even fax cards designed for home use are getting more and more sophisticated. The biggest problem with these cards, as with any add-ons, is setting up the I/O addresses You set the addresses with jumpers. There are always alternative settings, so it's important to make sure that the fax card you buy has documentation.

When you first run the card's setup program, you tell the software how you have set the jumper selection, but these I/O addresses can conflict with other hardware in your computer. If your computer won't work now, or the add-on board seems to be dead, you may have such a conflict. In severe cases, you may even lose your setup program. Take out the offending card, consult its documentation, set the jumpers to another selection, and try again. We remind you to use a diagnostics program to map the available I/O addresses.

Voice Mail Cards

Voice mail cards will answer your phone, give you the ability to program different responses to different callers, and record the answers. The fancier voice mail cards can handle up to sixteen lines, acting as a receptionist.

Some voice mail cards don't like to work with multitasking software, such as DesqView, Windows, or some terminate and stay resident (TSR) software. Inexpensive voice mail cards start at about $200. From there, the prices range from $700 for a single-line board to $2,000 for a four-line model. A high-end voice mail card can make a one-person office sound like a corporate headquarters.

MIDI (Synthesizer) Boards

If you're interested in synthesizers, you probably know what you want in terms of a MIDI board and how to hook it up. Be aware, however, that the same advice we gave in our discussion of fax cards also applies to MIDI boards: if you have a conflict, then change the I/O jumper selection.

Sound Boards

SoundBlaster is the brand name of the card that is becoming the standard for PC sound that you can add to spreadsheets, presentations, and games. These were a toy until Windows 3.1 included a sound capability that works well. Now sound boards are popular—ATI even makes a combined video and sound card. Other cards include a CD-ROM interface so you can listen to music while you work on your PC. To produce nice sound, you must add external speakers or earphones, if you're listening in your work cube at the office.

The same advice applies to these as all other add-ons—find out if the I/O jumper selection matches one of your available addresses, and make sure the card has adequate documentation so you can change the I/O address if necessary.

High-Power Communications Cards

The world of mainframe communications is not usually the home computer owner's concern, but in case you suddenly find yourself dealing with these cards, remember they are basically serial cards that let you tap into a bisync network. The IRMA card is a systems network architecture (SNA) card, for example, and although it's often called a 3270 card, 3270 terminal emulation is only a small subset of IBM's SNA. If you've read this far into the paragraph, you're way beyond home use by today's standards, but in five years we all may be linked up SNA-style. If you want to know something about this, read James Martin's SNA—*IBM's Network Solution* (Prentice-Hall, Englewood Cliffs, NJ, 1988).

Video Cards

Replacing your video display with a better one is probably one of the first upgrades you'll consider. The standard clone machine price often includes only a monographic card and a monochrome monitor. Brand-name clones are more often marketed without either, unless the video is built into the mainboard. Many clone buyers are back within a month of purchase to upgrade the monitor; many know they will want to upgrade and specify a video card, such as the varieties of ATI cards, that can be reset to work with many types of monitors.

If you're replacing a video card—either when you upgrade or because the old card has died—take a look at the ATI series. We liked ATI even when we had to open the computer and reset dip switches; some have external dip switches now, and others of the same type rely on software alone to tell the machine what to do. In general, we like separate video cards better than mainboard circuitry, for the obvious reason that it's far easier and cheaper to replace a card than a mainboard. Other good brands, in addition to ATI, are Video Seven, Orchid, and Everex.

Whatever you buy, there will be a better one available next year. The graphics accelerator boards we mention in the Windows section of this chapter are an example.

When you upgrade your video card, don't forget to re-run the setup program if you have a 286, 386, or 486 machine. You'll also have to edit your AUTOEXEC.BAT file to include any new video drivers, if the installation disk didn't do it automatically. You copy the drivers over from a disk included with the card.

Figure 9.4
Mice.

Mice

Mice are another fact of PC life now, even for confirmed DOS bigots. They're handy for many applications, and are essential for desktop publishing, CAD, and paint programs. Mice come in two basic variations: serial and bus versions. Serial mice simply attach to your serial port, although you may find you have a 9-pin serial port and a 25-pin mouse connection. Your dealer and Radio Shack carry 9-to-25 pigtails for $10 that solve the problem. Bus mice avoid the connection problem entirely. You just snap in the mouse board, connect the mouse, and you're done. In either case, you will need to alter your AUTOEXEC.BAT or CONFIG.SYS file to include the mouse driver.

Figure 9.4 shows different types of mice. Try any mouse you're thinking of buying with the software you intend to use it with before you actually make your purchase. You should also be aware that mice vary in their resolution and that computer graphics demand a high-resolution mouse.

Bigger Hard Drive

The data pages show how to replace a hard drive and controller. It's an easy job, except for transferring the data from the old drive to the new one. You'll need to run a complete backup and restore, of course. Don't upgrade from a 20 Mb drive to a 40 Mb drive—a 100 Mb drive fills up fast when applications take so much space.

Consider using a storage compression program like Stacker, SuperStor, or StorMore, if you need more hard disk space. The street price is $90, a bargain for another 80 Mb of hard drive. It installs and configures itself as easily as any we've ever seen, and works flawlessly. StorMore is another such program, included with DR DOS 6.0, but not tested by us.

Chapter 10
Data Protection and Recovery

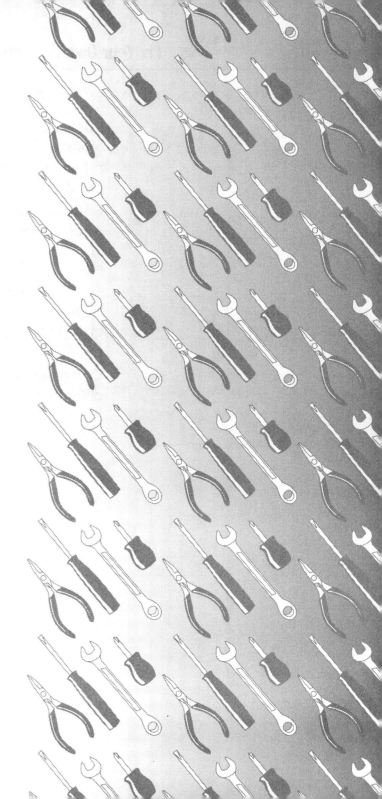

This chapter explains the best methods for protecting and recovering data. You can often rebuild and retrieve lost files, but it's easier to protect your data before there's a problem.

Lost data brings customers to the repair shop counter in tears of rage. Hardware failure accounts for a great deal of this lost data, but equally often, it was the customer who failed—not the drive. Our customers have included a writer who just lost the only copy of her forthcoming book (a friend accidentally formatted the hard disk, and there were no backups), an engineering company that just lost $100,000 of work on a hard drive that everyone thought someone else was backing up, and a law student who owned just three floppy disks and couldn't read a semester's worth of work from the abraded bit of Mylar. Failed hard disks with all a company's data and no backups are all too common. In all these cases, recovering the customer's data was far more urgent than repairing the computer.

Because DOS writes to hard and floppy disks in basically the same way, the procedures for guarding and recovering data from these two types of disks are similar. Before we discuss these procedures, however, we'd like to review some of the basics about hard and floppy disk structure. For a more complete explanation, see Chapters 4 and 5.

Both hard disks and floppies record the following information in the first (boot) section on Track 0: (1) media type information, (2) DOS version information, and (3) instructions telling the computer to read the system files if it's a bootable disk. Both floppy disks and hard disks are also formatted with the File Allocation Tables (FATs) starting at the beginning of the second sector on Track 0. The FATs vary in length depending on the version of DOS used to format a particular disk. Typical hard disk clusters are 2K. Remember, though, that cluster size is not fixed on either hard or floppy disks. In fact, hard disk programs like Disk Manager use the variable cluster size to finesse around the 32 Mb hard disk size barrier in older versions of DOS.

One difference between hard and floppy disks is the fact that a hard disk can be partitioned into different sections (one for DOS and one for Unix, for example). Floppies, on the other hand, can accommodate only one operating system per disk. If you want to boot from your hard disk—and most of us do—you'll need to record the address of the system files that start the bootup process in the boot sector on track 0.

Despite these differences, the data itself is laid down in much the same way on both floppy and hard disks, with surprisingly few adaptations necessary for the large size and increased speed of a hard disk. Chapters 5 and 14 include additional information about FATs, clusters, and how DOS organizes data on your disks.

Backups—Still the Simplest Solution

We'll start our discussion of data recovery with a few words about prevention. Most data loss can be prevented with good backup habits. Copy your important files to disk or tape every time you make significant changes and back up all your data regularly. How often is regularly? It depends on your nerves and the time it will take to recover from the inevitable disk crash.

Begin by backing up on-line with the automatic backup feature of your software—if it has this utility. When writing this book we all used the automatic backup feature of our chosen word processor. This method doesn't safeguard against a hard disk failure, but it does protect against loss of the

RAM (random access memory) contents while you're working. Your data resides precariously in RAM until it's saved to disk—a power flicker or dislodged cord can wipe RAM clean and you will lose everything you've done since the last time you saved. At a cost of five seconds while a "Please Wait" message is displayed, automatic backup every five or ten minutes is not burdensome.

In addition, install a data-recovery program such as PCTools MIRROR or Norton's IMAGE. DOS 5.0 includes MIRROR, licensed from PC Tools's publisher, Central Point Software. These programs place a third copy of the hard disk's FAT in a safe place on the disk so your files can be rebuilt if you ever lose DOS's copies of the FAT. Put a command in your AUTOEXEC.BAT file to run one every time you boot the computer. You may still have Disk Technician running in the background if you purchased it before 1992. We used to recommend it highly, and are sorry that it is off the market.

Backup Software

Specialized backup products are more convenient than the MS-DOS BACKUP and RESTORE. They use compression and speed-up routines and estimate in advance the number of disks you'll need. They also read the data straight through the DMA (Direct Memory Access) chip, thus speeding up the process dramatically.

A complete hard drive backup is only necessary twice: to have a full record of the contents, and when you need to reformat. This could be as a result of upgrading your DOS, or when you're warned to do an immediate backup by a disk repair utility.

The DOS BACKUP and RESTORE utilities are better than they used to be, but are still primitive, time-consuming, and require an amazing number of previously formatted disks. A DOS BACKUP file can only be restored by the same version of DOS—if you back up an old hard drive with DOS 3.1 and try to restore it on a hard disk running DOS 5.0, it won't work.

After the initial backup, the only items you really need to back up to floppy disks are important data files. Backing up software programs again really isn't necessary—you can reload your software programs from the originals if something happens to the hard disk—and it's probably not crucial that you back up your latest letter to Mom. In fact, it's a good idea to prune away unnecessary files from your hard disk regularly; a packed disk takes much longer to compress (reorganize the data for optimum efficiency).

The leading utilities (and a number of public domain and shareware programs) provide a user-friendly shell for file manipulation. You can mark as many files as you wish, then copy them all to a backup disk with a single "C" command. This eases the pain of typing in the names of a dozen files, which is the usual reason that users put off making backups.

Tape Backups

An alternative to disk backups is a built-in tape drive. These are very attractive to owners of large hard drives. The tape units are much cheaper now, too. A Colorado Jumbo 120 Mb tape drive discounts for $200, for example. Even with 150 Mb 1/4-inch cartridges at $25 apiece, that's cheaper than the cost of the diskettes required to back up a large hard disk. Besides, who wants to sit there and feed 30 diskettes into the machine?

Tape drives fit into a half-height slot and use small cassette cartridges. A standard floppy drive controller operates the tape drive, using one of its floppy drive channels. We only run into trouble assembling these machines if the customer also wants the full complement of floppy drive sizes built in. The Compaticard floppy controller from Micro Solutions allows you to install more than the normal number of floppy drives. The Compaticard supports up to 16 drives in an XT clone, and up to 14 floppy drives in AT/286/386/486 computers.

Most drives now conform to the streaming tape drive standard. If the drive conforms fully to the QIC standard, you can run either the manufacturer's backup software or third-party software. PC Tools CPBackup recognizes the tape drive and has the advantage of letting you back up to another machine even without your drive's software. This is an improvement over the past, when the manufacturers customized both the data organization on the tape and the data encoding scheme. If the built-in tape drive failed, the backup tapes could only be read by a drive of the identical type.

If you're running any kind of small-business software, especially accounting software with multiple modules, nightly tape backups are the only way to go. If your hard disk crashes, the data can be restored to a new hard disk with all the interrelated numbers still in the right place. Just remember to rotate the tapes, either by using Tape A and Tape B on alternate nights, or by using five tapes marked Monday through Friday. This method protects you from a tape drive going bad in mid-backup, thereby crunching your only copy of the data.

What To Do When You Mistakenly Delete or Reformat

This section tells you what to do if you accidently delete data or reformat a disk and thereby erase the data on it.

Undeleting

When you erase or delete a file, DOS does two things. First, it writes hex code E5 (written E5H in computerspeak) over the first character in the file name in the directory. The old filename and the file size are still there in the directory (they are not erased), but the DOS DIR command doesn't display this information because it's for a deleted file. After completing this first step, DOS zeros out the FAT entries to free up the physical space on the disk where the deleted file was stored. When DOS examines the FAT, it will now see the zeroed-out clusters as vacant space where it can write new data.

If you catch your mistake soon enough, you can use a diagnostic program with an undelete option—PC Tools or Norton Utilities, for example—to display the directory record. These utilities note a directory entry starting with E5H and flag it as an erased file. Norton Utilities Unerase and PC Tools Undelete display any erased files with a question mark as the first character in the file-name. You can manually change the first character of the filename back to the proper character, or simply select the file you want to undelete. The undelete program then fixes the FAT entries automatically. Remember that DOS 5.0 and DR DOS 6.0 include undelete utilities—a further reason to upgrade.

The most recent versions of PC Tools, DOS, DR DOS, and Norton handle delete protection with a multi-level scheme. All use small programs running continuously in the background to monitor your disk activity. Their manuals tell you how to install and activate the level of protection you desire. For maximum protection, deleted files can be placed in a "Trashcan" directory for later purging. The file is safe there until you decide you really want to purge it or that you want it back. Alternatively, PC Tools, DOS 5.0, and DR DOS 6.0 will maintain a running list of deleted files that you can retrieve if you change your mind.

This option keeps a copy of all the information from the boot record and the FAT, including the pointers that tell DOS where all the pieces of the file are. With delete tracking, undeleting an accidental "oops" is almost painless, as long as you recover the file before DOS writes over the sector. When will that be? It depends on how much work you're doing that writes to the disk. If you wait several days or do substantial writing to the disk, your chances for recovery diminish significantly. You should also avoid running COMPRESS or Norton Speed Disk if you need to recover a deleted file, at least until you've recovered the file. When you run defragmenting programs such as these, the files on your hard disk are all moved around, so the cluster chains stored in the deleted-file database are no longer valid.

Finally, you can try Undelete or Unerase on the fly, even if you didn't have a delete protection utility running. If you don't catch your mistake right away, though, your data recovery efforts may not be successful. Most undelete utilities run into trouble when confronted with fragmented files. When DOS deletes a file, as we mentioned above, it takes two actions—it writes hex E5 in place of the first letter in the file name, and it puts a null (hex 00) in every cluster record in the FAT table attached to that file. Once the FAT is zeroed, the linking information for that file is gone. In this case, an Undelete utility can look at the total original file length in the directory, but it can't determine the exact clusters on which the file was recorded—it can only assume that the file was contiguous and link a row of clusters that equal the file's original size. You have a better chance of recovering accidentally deleted files if the files are contiguous. For this reason, using defragmenting utilities regularly to compress your files is good insurance.

Recovering from Accidental Reformatting

A DOS floppy disk reformat overwrites each byte of data as it formats; once you format a floppy, your data is gone. A DOS hard disk reformat, on the other hand, is the same as deleting all files on the disk, since it zeroes out the FAT table and puts E5H at the beginning of each filename. Most DOS versions don't write blanks to the entire data portion of the disk, so even though your files are probably still there, you won't be able to find them without pointers in the FAT table. This also means that merely deleting an unwanted file on the hard disk doesn't protect your privacy. Security conscious users run a Norton's WIPEINFO or PCTools WIPE, which not only deletes the FAT pointers but also overwrites all data areas to erase the data itself.

Norton's old Format Recover saved the book we mentioned at the beginning of the chapter. The new Norton Utilities UnFormat program is even better. If it finds an IMAGE or MIRROR file,

Data Recovery

UnFormat refers to that while recovering the disk. Without an IMAGE or MIRROR file, UnFormat tries its best, but you can expect to lose some data. PC Tools UNFORMAT, like Norton's UnFormat, provides total recovery if you have been running MIRROR and only partial recovery if you haven't.

Protecting Your Data

This section describes other measures you can take—measures in addition to regular backups—to protect the data on your hard and floppy disks.

Using MIRROR or IMAGE

Most of the data loss prevention programs designed for hard drives are made up of two parts. The first part makes copies of the FAT and root directory. If your FAT or root directory gets corrupted, the second part of the program uses these copies to recover data from the disk. Two protection/recovery systems that perform well are the PC Tools MIRROR/DISKFIX combination and the Norton Utilities IMAGE/Disk Doctor team. These programs can be used to reconstruct either hard or floppy disks. Most users load the preventative half of the program only on their hard disk, preferring to take their chances with data loss on a floppy disk.

PC Tools MIRROR works by keeping a backup copy of the FAT and root directory in a special hidden file. When something goes wrong, you can run the corresponding DISKFIX program, which restores the disk to its original condition. If you haven't run MIRROR before, DISKFIX will attempt to reconstruct the data, but may not be able to reconstruct all files in their entirety. MIRROR also offers a Delete Tracking option that keeps a record of all deletes. With this option, retrieving the file is a simple matter.

You should install MIRROR on your hard disk so it loads automatically when you turn on your computer. When you run a program, start it with a batch file containing MIRROR so that MIRROR is loaded after the application. That way, MIRROR will run each time you exit the program.

Norton's IMAGE works roughly the same way as MIRROR, and reads DOS 5.0 (PC Tools) MIRROR files as well. The two competing utility packages have many of the same features, in fact, but we generally like PC Tools better, since it has more programs in the basic package, including the fine backup program.

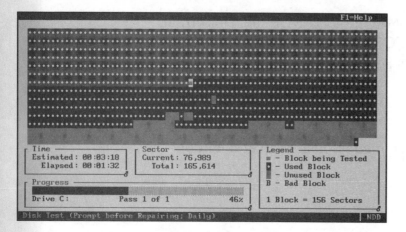

Figure 10.1
System utilities and diagnostic programs can probe the hard disk surface for bad spots and lock them out so data will not be written there. This quick surface scan by Norton Utilities took only three minutes to run. More rigorous tests run for many hours—set them up to run overnight, if possible.

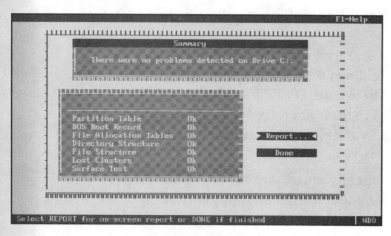

Figure 10.2
This hard disk received a clean bill of health after a quick surface scan. We would run a tougher test once a week or so, just to be sure.

Using Compression Utilities

If you want to have any success in recovering data, you should run a compression program regularly. Try Norton's Speed Disk or PC Tools COMPRESS. These defragmenting programs reorganize your disk by pulling scattered pieces of your files into contiguous clusters. Undeleting and unformatting is much easier when the utility doesn't have to jump all over the disk, tracing a web of pointers. In fact, if you run a compression program regularly, it is possible to ensure 100 percent data recovery from accidental file deletions (and substantial recovery from an accidental format), even if you haven't run MIRROR or IMAGE regularly.

Using Surface Analyzers

Surface analysis programs analyze your hard drive by performing a read/write test to see if the entire surface can reliably hold data. Using ingenious data-repair algorithms, they reconstruct the data in the suspect areas that DOS can't read. Your indication that DOS has found such a suspect area is the error message "Abort, Retry, Ignore."

Disk Technician was interesting (you may still have a copy, or run across a copy for sale). It's a resident surface analyzer that continuously runs in the background. In addition to running a preset read/write test when you ask it to, Disk Technician monitors the hard disk continuously, and uses your normal DOS reads and writes as its test program. Unfortunately, the first version of Disk Technician was far too complex to use unless you were willing to spend a lot of time learning it. The new version was considerably easier to use, but probably overkill for the typical non-business user, or even for many text-only business users.

SpinRite is very easy to use. Be prepared, however, to let it run overnight. It will take that long to run its tests. SpinRite also has the habit of removing the manufacturer's bad track table, which we don't like. Every hard drive is tested by the manufacturer to identify bad tracks. Most drives have a few bad tracks, which are not particularly significant. The manufacturer puts a list of these bad tracks on the outside of the hard disk. A technician then enters the bad track table as he or she is low-level formatting the disk, and DOS marks the affected sectors internally as unusable. You really need this bad sector information to remain on the disk, even if the analysis program has an equally effective lockout scheme.

Norton Disk Doctor and PC Tools DISKFIX perform virtually the same job as SpinRite. Any of these programs can be counted on to find bad spots, move the data to a safe part of the disk, and mark the bad spots so they won't be reused. They are easy to use and take less than an hour to run on an average-size drive. Their value is in catching bad spots before you lose data. We recommend running one of these programs at least once a week. Why not set up a batch file for disk-maintenance and backup, then run it weekly?

Saving Your Data from a Faltering Disk

If your drive begins to mislay files or report impossible-looking file sizes, assume that the problem is in the FAT. Get a copy of PC Tools or the Norton Utilities. They are both efficient, effective, and easy to use.

If neither PC Tools nor Norton will fix the trouble automatically, try the "Troubleshooter" Chapter in Norton's Disk Explorer manual (part of the Norton Utilities package). The techniques recommended aren't for the faint-hearted, but the manual is clear and comprehensible. It tells you how to fix a bad Track 0, fix bad directory entries, recover subdirectories from a bad directory, edit the boot record, and edit the partition table. It's worth buying Norton just to have this chapter on hand.

Those of us who don't have time, or skills, for home brain surgery send ailing disks to a commercial data-recovery service. If you absolutely cannot afford to lose your data, send the disk out without messing with it yourself. Your tinkering may make a bad situation worse. We particularly recommend using a commercial data recovery service if the disk has been damaged by fire or water.

A bad sector in the middle of a long file can cause the trickiest data recovery problems. If the sector is, in fact, totally unreadable, all the rest of the file can be lost. A tiny error, equivalent to an inkblot

Data Recovery

covering two bad characters on page 13, could make the hard disk lose the rest of this book. DOS can correct small errors itself—we're talking about errors the equivalent of one bad character. But no program can correct more than 11 bad bits (that's about one and a half 8-bit characters). Some programs can read through the bad place the way you or I read through an inkblot on the page of a book. We just skip over the blot and keep going. SpinRite II can do this. But you, the brains behind this file, will have to manually go into the file and reconstruct the missing information under the inkblot. This is practical with text, marginally practical with database and spreadsheet files, and impossible if you're dealing with a program file like WP.EXE. But you probably can reload your program files from backup disks, so it's not a big problem.

Reformatting the Hard Disk

If you regularly use a disk analysis program to detect bad clusters, you only need to consider reformatting the drive when the number of reported errors begins to increase. If you're not using a disk analysis program, be prepared to reformat your hard disk at least once a year. Over time, the hard drive head assembly drifts out of alignment with the tracks it originally laid down on the platters. As the misalignment increases, the heads begin to read and write data less accurately. When you reformat the disk, the heads are aligned with the new tracks it lays down and, although it's not quite the same as on a new drive, the alignment is internally consistent. SpinRite, Norton's Calibrate or PC Tools DISKFIX will non-destructively low-level format the drive—no tedious backup and restore!

If you specified a high-quality drive in your computer, you may not have to reformat once a year. Ask what type of head actuator the drive contains. Hard disk mechanical assemblies come in two forms. The most common is the stepper motor. Voice coil drives are less common—and far more expensive. A stepper motor drive depends on mechanical parts to keep the heads in the right place over the tracks. A voice coil drive, on the other hand, uses electronics to determine when the heads are in the right place. A voice coil drive cannot go out of alignment, so it never needs reformatting. The average PC clone is equipped with a stepper motor drive, though, and should be reformatted once a year. This means that you'll have to reformat just once in the drive's probable lifetime.

Summary of Data Protection Measures

Here's a summary of the measures you can take to protect your data on floppy and hard disks.

How to Protect Your Data on Floppies

✔ Make backup copies of important data.

✔ Buy lifetime guarantee disks. If something happens to Track 0 (where the directory and FAT are stored) send the disk back to the manufacturer to reconstruct the data.

✔ Learn how to use quality undelete utilities to rescue you when the inevitable mistake happens.

✔ If you format the floppy accidentally, the files are lost. No utility can recover the lost files.

How to Protect Your Data on Hard Disks

✔ Make backups.

✔ Run PC Tools MIRROR or Norton's IMAGE every time the machine boots and start all application programs from batch files that run MIRROR or IMAGE as the last step before returning to the root directory.

✔ Run PC Tools or Norton's UNFORMAT if you mistakenly format your hard disk.

✔ Run defragmenting (compression) utilities regularly.

✔ Run surface analyzers regularly.

✔ If your hard disk uses a stepper motor, reformat it once a year.

Finally, you should assume that the hard drive will crash and the floppy will die—and plan accordingly.

For more information on data recovery, refer to the Disk Explorer manual that comes with the Norton Utilities.

Section 2
The Data Pages

Chapter 11
Elementary Repair Skills

This chapter describes four basic repair procedures:

✓ Removing the system unit cover

✓ Removing an expansion card

✓ Installing an expansion card

✓ Telling the computer what you have just installed

    a. Setting switches on XT clones

    b. Running setup on a 286, 386, or 486 industry standard architecture (ISA) (AT-style) or extended industry standard architecture (EISA) computer

    c. Running the EISA configuration utility

    d. Using the boot reference diskette on a PS/2 computer with Micro Channel architecture (MCA)

Use these procedures as you perform the installations and repairs outlined in Chapters 12-16.

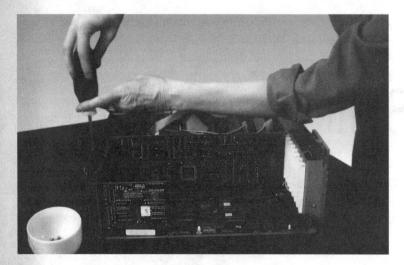

Figure 11.1
Remove the screw holding the expansion card bracket to the case.

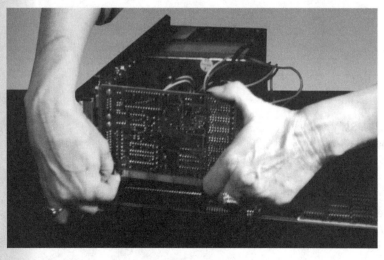

Figure 11.2
Lift the expansion card.

How to Remove the System Unit Cover

You've probably read Chapter 1 and have removed the system unit cover to look at the components inside the machine. If not, turn back to Chapter 1. Figures 1.1 through 1.3 on pages 16-17 and 1.8 through 1.11 on pages 21-23 show you how to remove the cover from the typical desktop or tower computer.

How to Remove an Expansion Card

An expansion card is electrically connected to the mainboard whenever its flat card edge connector is pressed into one of the plastic expansion slot connectors on the mainboard. The card is physically connected to the back wall of the system unit chassis with a single screw.

Removing an expansion card is quite easy. Begin by taking out the screw that attaches the card to the system unit chassis, (Figure 11.1). After you remove the screw, set it aside in a safe place—we often use an old coffee cup. Lift the card with both hands (Figure 11.2), and remove it (Figure 11.3). Don't worry, you won't hurt it with your bare hands.

Removing these cards doesn't take much force, but watch your fingers—the card bristles with prickly solder blobs and little metal legs. Put your fingers in comfortable places before lifting. It's also helpful to rock the card back and forth slightly from end to end to dislodge it from the slot.

The same techniques work with XT clones, AT-style ISA computers, and EISA computers. Look at our three-picture series illustrating card removal. Figures 11.1 and 11.3 show an MGP card being removed from an AT clone. Figure 11.2 shows a similar MGP card coming out of an XT clone. Some AT and

EISA cards have longer bus connectors, which makes it slightly more difficult to pull the card out of the expansion slot, but the moves are the same. For further information about the MGP card in these pictures, see "Monochrome Graphics Video Adapter" in Chapter 13, page 159.

How to Install an Expansion Card

Reinstalling the Original Card in Its Old Slot

Simply put it back where it came from. Carefully line up the card edge connector with the slot on the mainboard, then press down firmly. When the card is in place, the screw hole on the card lines up with the screw hole in the back of the chassis. Reinstall the screw and test the machine.

Installing A New Card to Replace a Bad Card

Most of the time the replacement card will look a lot like the bad card you took out. You usually want to replace an 8-bit hard disk controller with another 8-bit hard disk controller, an 8-bit video card with another 8-bit video card, and so forth. Compare the bus connectors on the two cards. If they are the same, just slap the new card into the old card's expansion slot.

If the bus connectors don't look the same, we have to ask "Why not?" Perhaps you're taking the opportunity to upgrade to a faster card with a different bus connector. SCSI host adapter cards, for example, are manufactured with 8-bit, 16-bit, and EISA edge connectors. So are network cards and many video

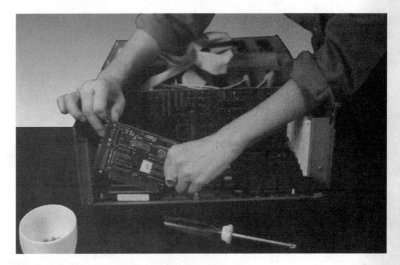

Figure 11.3
Remove the expansion card.

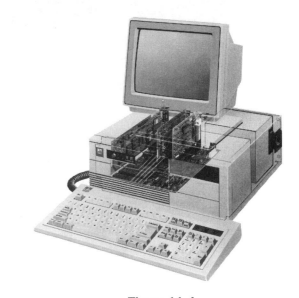

Figure 11.4
The mainboard is the large printed circuit board in the bottom of this com-puter. Three expansion cards (the vertical cards) plug right into the mainboard bus connectors. Photograph courtesy of DTK Computer, Inc.

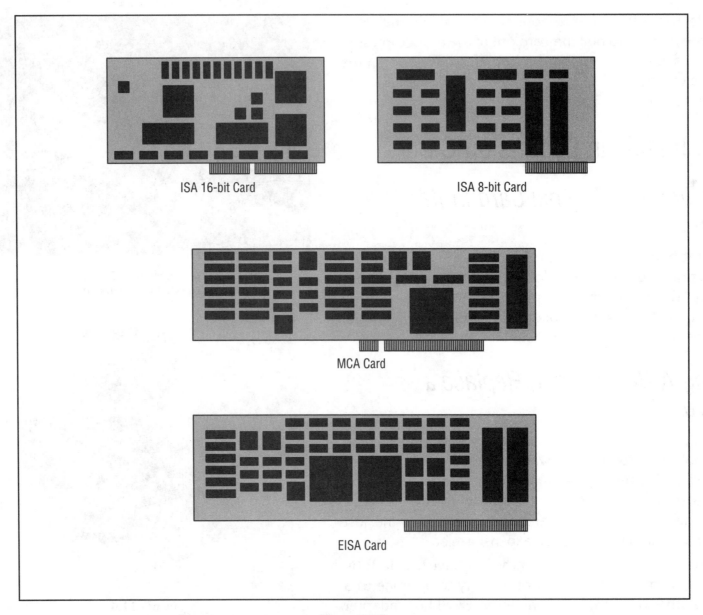

ISA 16-bit Card

ISA 8-bit Card

MCA Card

EISA Card

Figure 11.5
An expansion card's edge connector tells you what computers the card will fit.

cards. Some computers can accommodate more than one kind of bus connector. EISA computers, for example, accept both 8-bit and 16-bit ISA cards as well as EISA cards. Talk to your card vendor first to be sure the card and the bus are compatible before buying a new card.

Installing an Additional Card

Did you ever carry an air conditioner into the house, set it up carefully in the window, then find out that the air conditioner plug won't fit the electric outlet? Perhaps the air conditioner is 220 volts and the outlet is 110 volts. PC expansion cards, like electric appliances, plug right in when the card edge connector matches the mainboard bus connector. When the connectors don't match, no action.

To make it easier for you to distinguish 8-bit from 16-bit cards, and both of them from MCA or EISA cards, Figure 11.5 shows sample outlines of these four different cards. Don't pay attention to the general shape of these cards (rectangular, square, long and skinny, etc.)—the general shape is not important. Concentrate on the card edge connector—the place where the card plugs into the mainboard.

Choose the slot where you will install the new card:

✔ If you are installing an 8-bit card with the short, single bus connector, any bus expansion slot in any of the clones will do. These 8-bit cards fit in XT clones, in 286/386/486 ISA computers, and in EISA computers. Don't worry about long versus short slots on your 286/386/486 AT or EISA computer's mainboard—if the board will physically fit into the slot, it will work.

✔ If you have an ISA 16-bit expansion card it will fit in either a 286/386/486 AT-style computer or an EISA computer. You can't put EISA cards in your ISA computer, though—which is too bad, because EISA cards are very fast.

✔ EISA cards fit only in EISA mainboards, though ordinary 8-bit and 16-bit cards will fit in EISA mainboard connectors.

✔ MCA cards fit in high-end PS/2 computers with the MCA bus. Use only MCA cards in MCA computers—nothing else will fit.

Here's how to install your new card. Remove the screw at the back of the chassis which holds the slot cover to the case. The slot covers are slender metal strips (usually 3/4 of an inch wide) at the back of the chassis. You'll see one slot cover for each unused expansion slot. Remove the cover for the slot

Setup and Configuration

you want to use, and save the screw. Line up the card with a mainboard expansion slot and the empty slot cover. Press the card down firmly. When it bottoms out and the screw hole on the card lines up with the screw hole on the chassis, reinstall the screw. It's done.

How to Tell the Computer What You Have Just Installed

Your computer needs to know what devices (what pieces of hardware) are installed in it. All the computers in the PC family expect to find a keyboard, parallel ports, and serial ports. We don't have to tell them about those things. But after that the computer is dumb. When you install floppy drive(s), hard drive(s), or a video card and monitor, you must tell the computer what you've installed or the computer won't be able to use it.

Computers in the PC family are equipped with a basic input/output system read only memory (BIOS ROM) chip. The BIOS chip contains the nitty-gritty directions your computer needs to connect to a floppy drive, a video card, or another device. The BIOS ROM in the original IBM PC computer didn't know much (they didn't bother to put hard disk directions in the PC BIOS ROM because nobody thought ordinary users could ever afford hard disks). IBM XTs and their clones are a bit smarter. These computers know that they should search for additional ROMs (other ROMs besides the BIOS ROM—perhaps a hard disk controller ROM or a video card ROM). The BIOS chips in ATs and AT clones were smarter yet (they knew about hard disks, and actually had directions built in for the most popular hard disks then available). The AT computers (ISAs) kept the search-for-other-ROMs feature too. EISA computers are smarter yet. They know as much as the ISA computers. In addition, EISA computers can accommodate special EISA adapter cards, which transfer data at extraordinarily high speeds. But you, the installer, must tell the EISA computer which EISA cards are installed. MCA computers, like EISA computers, demand that you run a Micro Channel setup program from the reference disk shipped with your computer whenever you install a new card.

Each branch of the PC family uses slightly different techniques to tell the computer and the BIOS ROM what parts are installed:

✔ XT-style computers are the least flexible. XTs look at switches on the mainboard for an inventory of hardware devices. If you have an IBM PC or XT or an IBM XT clone, read the next section, "XT Clones," then go on to Chapters 12-16.

IBM AT computers and their offspring, the 16-bit computers with the ISA bus, are more flexible. ISA computers use a setup routine to tell the computer what devices are installed. Read "Running Setup on a 286, 386, or 486 ISA (AT-style) or EISA Computer," on the next page if you have a 286/386/486/AT computer.

EISA computers are compatible with ISA computers, so you must run the standard ISA setup routine ("Running Setup on a 286, 386, or 486 ISA (AT-style) or EISA Computer") whenever you add hardware devices to your EISA computer. In addition, EISA computers use an EISA configuration utility, so see "Running the EISA Configuration Utility" on page 109, as well as "Running Setup on a 286, 386, or 486 ISA (AT-type) or EISA Computer."

MCA is completely incompatible with ISA and EISA architecture. By the way, not all PS/2s are MCA computers. The PS/2 model 30 and the PS/1 are really modified ISA computers. If you have a PS/2 model 30 or a PS/1, read "Running Setup on a 286, 386, or 486 ISA (AT-style) or EISA Computer." If you have a model 50 or higher, read "Using the Boot Reference Disk on a PS/2 Computer with MCA," on page 110.

XT Clones

XT clones use switches to tell the computer how many floppy drives, how much memory, and what kind of video is installed. There is also a switch on the mainboard to set if you have installed an 8087 math coprocessor chip.

It's always best to set the switches according to the instructions shipped with the mainboard. If you have no instructions, you may use the generic switch table, Figure 11.6. Remember, though, not all clone makers designed these same generic

Figure 11.6
Table of Typical XT Switch Settings

Look for a bank of eight switches in a row. They will be either rocker switches or slides switches, eight in a row, and all in a little plastic case about 3/4 of an inch long. The switches may be marked ON, with or without an arrow pointing toward ON, or they may be marked OPEN, with or without the arrow. OPEN is the same as OFF. You will need a ballpoint pen, a toothpick, or a tiny screwdriver to change the switches. Set rocker switches by pressing the rocker down on the side of the switch you want. For example, press down on the OFF side of switch 1, since switch 1 should always be set OFF. Slide switches are different; move the lump on the slide switch toward the side you want. For example, move the little protruding switch lump on switch number 1 toward OFF.

Switch 1 Normally off

Switch 2 ON = no 8087 math coprocessor; OFF = 8087 installed

Switches 3 & 4 Used to set amount of memory installed — this varies from board manufacturer to board manufacturer

Example 1:
> 3 OFF & 4 OFF = 256K installed, using 4 banks of 64K chips.
> 3 ON & 4 ON = 256K or more installed, using 256K chips in bank 0 and bank 1 and 64K chips in banks 2 and 3. Chips may be installed only in bank 0; in bank 0 and bank 1; or in all four banks.
> 3 ON & 4 OFF = 192K, using 3 banks of 64K chips
> 3 OFF & 4 ON = 128K, using 2 banks of 64K chips

Example 2:
> 3 OFF and 4 OFF = 640K, using 256K chips in banks 0 and 1 and 64K chips in banks 2 and 3.
> 3 ON & 4 ON = 256K using a single row of 256K chips in bank 0.
> 3 OFF & 4 ON = 512K using 256K chips in banks 0 and 1.

Switches 5 & 6 Used to set the type of video display installed.
> 5 ON & 6 OFF = CGA color showing 80 characters per line (the normal CGA setting)
> 5 OFF & 6 ON = CGA color showing 40 characters per line
> 5 OFF & 6 OFF = monochrome
> 5 ON & 6 ON = a switch combination not used for anything

Switches 7 & 8 Used to set number of floppy drives installed.
> 7 ON & 8 ON = 1 floppy drive installed
> 7 OFF & 8 ON = 2 floppy drives installed
> 7 ON & 8 OFF = 3 floppy drives installed
> 7 OFF & 8 OFF = 4 floppy drives installed

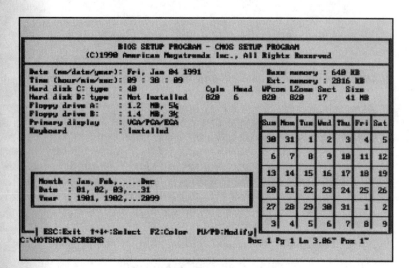

Figure 11.7
Typical setup screen.

switch settings into their XT mainboard. The wrong settings won't blow up the computer, but it won't work right either. Use our generic settings at your own risk.

Running Setup on a 286, 386, or 486 ISA (AT-style) or EISA Computer

As a general rule, software is more flexible than hardware, but hardware is faster. When IBM designed the AT they wanted to get the advantages of both, so they stored the configuration information in a battery-protected chip (the complementary metal oxide semiconductor [CMOS] chip) and they stored the actual how-to-operate-a-hardware-device information in the BIOS ROM. It's easy to change the settings in the CMOS chip with software (no grubbing around on the mainboard looking for switches). In addition, if your BIOS ROM becomes dated (that is, it knows only how to operate dorky old equipment) you can easily pry it out of its socket on the mainboard and replace it with a new BIOS ROM.

Early ATs and AT clones used a separate system setup disk. Running the system configuration software program (often called SETUP) allowed the user to edit the list of drives, memory type, video type, and so on in the CMOS chip. Since the CMOS chip is backed up with batteries, it remembers what hardware is installed in the computer, even when the power is off.

Many users lose or damage their setup disks. Typically, another computer's setup disk will not properly load the setup information into your computer. The manufacturers got smart and are now putting the setup program right into the BIOS ROM. These computers don't need a separate setup disk. They put a message on the screen: "Press **Del** if you want to run SETUP or DIAGS" or "Press <**Ctrl**> <**Esc**> for setup" or something similar. Press the keys they tell you to, then follow the directions on the screen. Figure 11.7 shows a typical setup screen. Don't experiment wildly, though you can easily recover from most mistakes you might make (is it so awful to go back to setup and tell it the correct day or mention that your B drive is a 1.44 Mb floppy, not a 720K floppy?). The only really dangerous spot is "hard disk type." Enter the wrong hard disk type and your data (along with the hard disk) disappears. It's still there somewhere, so don't panic. But you can spend a lot of time experimenting until you find the correct hard disk type again. Make a copy of the hardware con-figuration settings in your computers, then put it in a safe place.

Running the EISA Configuration Utility

EISA configuration utility (ECU) instructions come with all EISA computers. After installing a card, run the ECU, copy the EISA card configuration file for your new card into your computer, then use the ECU to configure your computer. EISA computers use these card configuration files to manage the expansion cards in your computer. ISA cards (the 8-bit and 16-bit AT-style cards) use jumpers and switches, and an ISA computer doesn't manage the card for you, you have to do it yourself.

What do we mean "manage the cards"? Expansion cards use resources, much like automobiles in a parking lot use up floor space. If the owners will be self-parking the cars, each owner must cruise until she finds a free space. In a lot with valet parking the owners can rely on attendants to arrange the cars efficiently. EISA is valet parking. Once the EISA computer knows what resources (floor space) your expansion card requires it shuffles the cards around, parking them here or there, until it finds a free space for your card. To do this, though, EISA must know each card's vital statistics. That's where the EISA configuration file comes in.

All new EISA cards come with an EISA configuration file disk. In addition, most EISA computer vendors provide a generic configuration file for ISA cards (which aren't usually sold with an EISA configuration file). On some EISA computers you don't have to use this generic ISA file, you don't have to tell

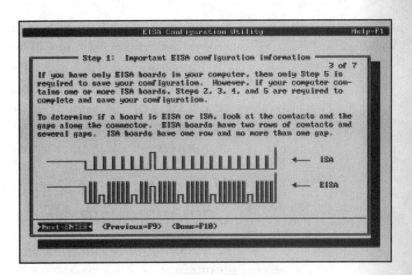

Figure 11.8
This EISA configuration utility screen compares ISA and EISA cards.

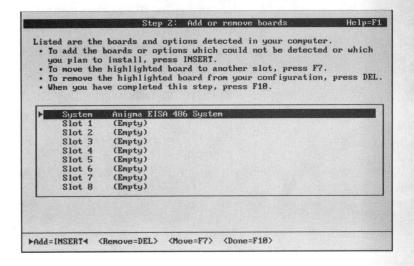

Figure 11.9
Configuration screen for 486 EISA computer with many ISA cards installed. No EISA cards are installed, so the configuration utility thinks all slots are "empty."

EISA about your ISA cards. Other EISA computers make it mandatory. In either case, ISA cards are not as convenient as EISA cards because you have to remove the computer cover and reset the jumpers on the ISA card if you want to change the resources it uses. The ECU will move EISA cards around for you electronically. On the other hand, ISA cards are much cheaper than EISA cards. Network servers often need high-speed EISA network cards and hard disk adapters cards, but ordinary workstations often run just fine with the ISA versions. That's the beauty of EISA computers—they're backward-compatible with ISA cards.

Using the Boot Reference Disk on a PS/2 Computer with MCA

PS/2 computers with the Micro Channel bus use a boot reference diskette to load and edit the configuration information for your computer. The reference diskette is self-booting. Simply put it in the A drive and reboot the computer with **Ctrl-Alt-Del** (that means hold down **Ctrl** and **Alt** keys, then hit the **Del** key once and release everything). You should ask the boot diskette to automatically reconfigure the computer whenever you add a new piece of hardware to an MCA computer. Some new expansion boards require a special configuration file, which is shipped on a diskette with the new board. Just follow the instructions that come with the board.

In PS/2s, the configuration is backed up with a lithium battery. The chips forget this configuration information slowly, so you can replace the lithium battery without losing the configuration information if you do it quickly. If you want to lose the configuration information (for example, you have installed a password and can't remember it anymore) you'll have to leave the lithium battery disconnected for at least 20 minutes, then reconfigure the computer with the reference diskette.

Now you're ready to go to Chapter 12, which describes the basic parts of a computer.

Chapter 12
The Basics

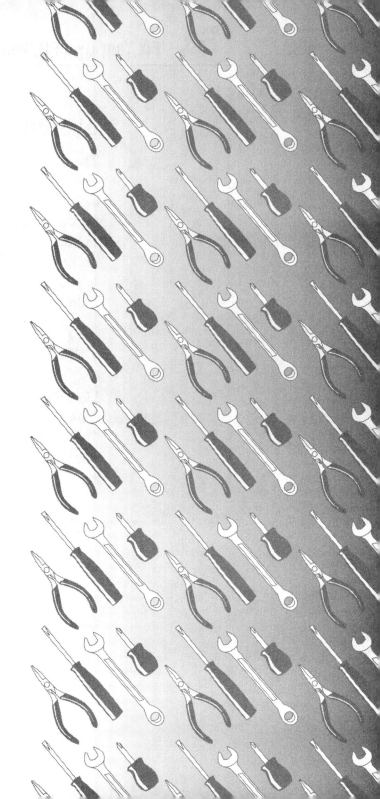

This section describes the following basic items:

- ✔ System unit case and cover
- ✔ Mainboard
- ✔ Power supply
- ✔ Keyboard
- ✔ Clock card

System Unit Case and Cover

The steel computer case provides both physical strength and electromagnetic insulation. In order to pass Federal Communications Commission (FCC) regulations, the case must be solid, with all openings (for example, empty expansion slots) covered to keep electromagnetic waves generated by the computer inside the chassis. Poor electromagnetic shielding does not harm the computer or cause it to malfunction, but it does tend to cause television interference problems whenever the computer is on. The stray electromagnetic waves that are broadcast by the crystals in a typical computer can also interfere with FM radios, cellular telephones, or any other equipment with an antenna. A 25 MHz crystal, for instance, broadcasts at 25, 50, 100, and other multiples of 25 MHz.

> **Warning:** If you are disassembling a computer with a plastic case, use caution. The screws are tightened into plastic threads in plastic posts. Avoid stripping the threads, and don't overtighten the screws because the plastic posts will break right off.

Lightweight laptop or portable computers have electromagnetic shielding too, even those with plastic cases. Compaq computers, for example, have aluminum plates embedded in the plastic. Other clone makers use aluminum paint over the plastic parts. This works fine, too, since fully enclosing the computer with any conductive surface will shield other sensitive electronic equipment from computer-generated interference.

How to Test the System Unit Case and Cover

In general, if the case looks all right, it is all right. Just remember to put all the covers back after you work inside the machine.

Believe it or not, though, even the case occasionally causes system troubles. A really poorly designed case (one with misshapen metal lugs in the wrong places) can cause intermittent shorts. We once had a shipment of these defective cases in our assembly shop. Part of the case sat very close to rough, soldered component leads on the bottom of the mainboard. Sometimes the mainboard actually touched the case, with only the black paint film on the case providing insulation. The mainboard didn't short out at first. Over time, though, the hard disk caused the mainboard to vibrate enough to rub away the paint on the case. When that happened, we started getting intermittent shorts and all kinds of symptoms. This problem was extraordinary, but we want to show that nothing, even the computer case, should be ruled out when troubleshooting.

How to Remove and Install the System Cover

First turn off the computer. It is not necessary to unplug the 110-volt power cord from the back of the computer, but cautious people feel reassured when they do this.

Desktop Models

The screws holding the cover in place are usually hidden on the back. Most computers have five machine screws: four at the extreme corners and one in the center top of the back surface. A few desktop models use four screws, two on each side of the case. You'll need a standard blade or Phillips screwdriver to remove the machine screws (see Figure 1.1 on page 16). Once you've removed the screws, pull the top cover forward and slightly up in front, then slide the cover off the chassis (see Figure 1.2 on page 16). The cover might be a bit sticky until it breaks loose, but once it starts sliding it should move smoothly.

> **Warning:** It's easy to catch the power supply wires or the floppy drive ribbon cable on the rough underside of the case cover. Be gentle and use good sense when removing or reinstalling the cover; ripping these wires loose will increase the diagnostic challenge.

Tower Models

Tower computers are often identical to the manufacturer's desktop models, but the disk drives are rotated to mount horizontally in the tower. A tower case looks different than a desktop case, and it usually has five to ten cover screws, rather than four or five. Many tower models are easier to work on if you lay them down on their side first. Remove the cover screws, then pull the cover forward and up. Others should stay upright so you can pull the cover off lengthwise, like a sock off a foot.

The tower case usually has a full-length plastic face plate with lights and cutouts for the floppy drives. Some models won't let you remove the floppy or hard disks until you snap this plastic cover off. Other tower models mount this face plate semi-permanently with screws and let you slip the drives out from the back. Examine your computer and use your own judgment.

Cover Reinstallation

Before you reinstall the cover, look down inside it and check to see if there are any pegs on the inside front surface. If there aren't any pegs, simply tip the cover up extra high in front as you slide it onto the chassis, then slide it straight back into place. Tighten the machine screws gently; force is neither necessary nor helpful. If there is a peg or two on the inside of the cover, installing the cover is a bit trickier; you must wiggle the cover up and down a bit to make it slide that last half-inch into position. Once in place, install the screws and test-boot the computer.

Mainboard

The *mainboard* is also known as the *system board* or the *motherboard*. Figures 12.1 through 12.4 show different types of mainboards. Figure 12.1 is an XT clone mainboard, Figures 12.2 (on page 116) and 12.3 (on page 117) show a 286 ISA (Industry Standard Architecture) mainboard and a 386 ISA mainboard, and Figure 12.4 (on page 118) shows a 486 EISA (Extended Industry Standard Architecture) mainboard. The glossary provides definitions for these terms, but don't panic yet. We're going to ease into the jargon slowly.

IBM PC/XT and AT mainboards contain the items listed on the following pages. Most clones follow the same plan, though a few put the memory and/or the microprocessor on separate cards and use the mainboard strictly as a bus board (an information transfer path). 386/486 computers with the ISA or EISA bus have these same basic components too.

Microprocessor (CPU Chip)

This is an 8088 or 8086 chip for PC/XT clones, an 80286 for AT/286 ISA clones, an 80386 for AT/386 (ISA) machines, and an 80486 for 486/AT computers with the ISA bus. EISA computers use either the 386 or 486 (the common shorthand for 80386 is "386"). The *microprocessor* is the single most important factor in your computer's performance. Many programs, for instance Windows 3.1, require at least a 286 or 386 microprocessor chip. Figure 12.5 on page 124 shows a 386 chip blown up so you can appreciate how complex these microprocessors are.

Figure 12.1

This photo of an XT-style mainboard shows five expansion slots in the upper right quadrant, and four vertical rows of RAM memory chips in the upper left quadrant. The row of memory chips closest to the expansion slots is permanently soldered onto the mainboard. If a chip in this row goes bad, you'll have to replace the whole mainboard. The remaining three rows of memory chips are socketed. Each row has eight data chips, with a ninth chip (the parity chip) near the edge of the mainboard above each row. The 8088 CPU chip is the large rectangle in the lower right hand corner. An empty socket of the same size for a math coprocessor chip is right below the CPU chip. Photo by Robert McLaughlin.

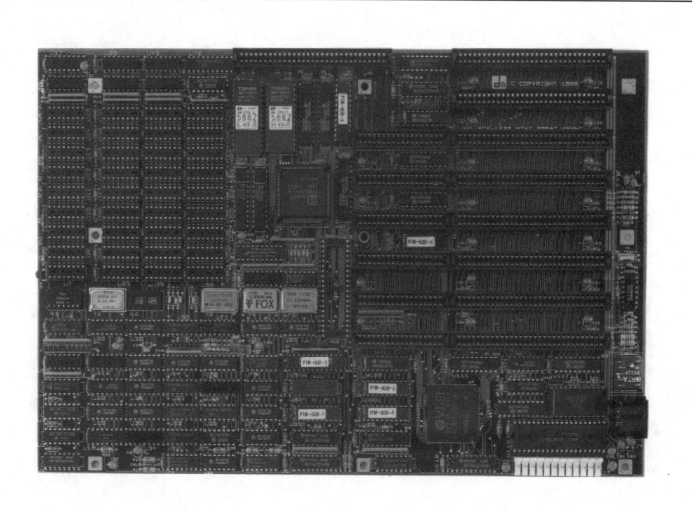

Figure 12.2

This photo of an AT-style mainboard shows eight expansion slots in the upper right quadrant, and four vertical rows of sockets for RAM memory chips in the upper left quadrant. Each row has space for eight data chips plus a parity chip. Two rectangular BIOS ROM chips (with square white labels) and the square 80286 CPU chip are located between the memory chip sockets and the expansion slots on this mainboard. With six long AT-style expansion slots and two short XT-style expansion slots, this mainboard can accommodate either 8-bit or 16-bit expansion cards. Photo courtesy of DTK Computer Inc.

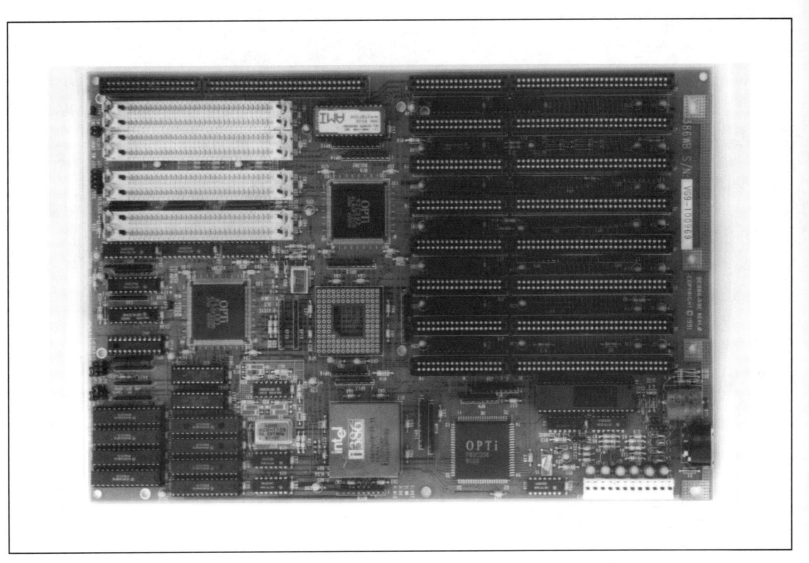

Figure 12.3

This is a 386/AT mainboard—note the square, gray microprocessor chip marked "Intel" and "i386." The white SIMM sockets provide space for up to 32 megabytes of RAM on the mainboard. The empty square socket next to the 386 microprocessor will hold an 80387 math coprocessor or a Weitek 3167 math coprocessor, which are particularly useful for math-intensive applications like spreadsheets or CAD. All eight of the black bus connectors are 16-bit slots, but one of the bus connectors has a second slot next to the SIMM sockets. If you need more memory than the mainboard will hold, you may plug in a proprietary 32-bit memory expansion card here on the end slot. Photo courtesy of JDR Microdevices.

Figure 12.4

This 486 EISA mainboard came out of a SWAN Technologies EISA computer. The EISA expansion slots in the upper right quadrant will accommodate ordinary 8-bit and 16-bit expansion cards from your old 286 or 386 computer, as well as ultra-fast EISA expansion cards. Like the 386 mainboard in Figure 12.3, this 486 mainboard uses SIMM memory modules. Two SIMM strips are installed; there is room to add six more. Recognize the big 80486 chip in the upper left hand quadrant? Photo by Robert McLaughlin.

BIOS ROM (System ROM)

The computer power-on self-test (POST) and the boot instructions are stored in the *BIOS* (Basic Input/Output System) *ROM*, a read-only memory chip. The ROM also provides the most basic level of hardware control while the computer is running.

RAM (Random Access Memory)

Also called *system memory*, *RAM* provides a temporary storage area for DOS, programs, and data. Under DOS, 640K of system memory can be used. Some machines are equipped with less than 640K. Other computers have more than 640K installed. The excess (over 640K) is expanded, XMS, or extended memory. If you want to upgrade memory or learn how to use the memory already installed in your computer more effectively, see Chapter 6.

The first 64K of memory is filled with housekeeping information (data the computer needs to operate itself). For example, consider the interrupt vector table. This table tells the microprocessor what instructions to follow if a particular piece of hardware requires the microprocessor's attention. This table must be correct. It must also be in place in order for the computer to do any work (including a memory test). Therefore, not all memory tests can read or write to the first 64K of memory without crashing the computer. Most memory tests start testing at 256K and verify the memory from 256K on up. The diagnostic programs that *do* test every bit of memory temporarily move this housekeeping information to another location.

DMA Chip(s)

DMA (Direct Memory Access) channels allow direct information transfer from a hard disk to system memory. These specialized chips are very efficient at a single job: taking information from one location and writing it to another. The CPU could do the same task (and the CPU did have to do it on some early clones without a DMA chip), but it is substantially slower. Normally, floppy drives do not use DMA channels; however, some proprietary backup programs, (such as FastBack) harness the DMA to speed up hard-disk-to-floppy-disk transfers. Network cards and SCSI host adapters often use DMA for really fast data transfer.

Mainboard

Bus

The *bus* is the main information path inside the computer. It connects the microprocessor, memory, ROM, and all expansion cards.

Bus Connectors for Expansion Cards

PC/XT clones use an 8-bit bus with a single 62-pin connector for each expansion card (see Figure 12.1 on page 115).

AT/286/386/486 computers have a 16-bit bus, with two connector sockets for each expansion card. This 16-bit AT bus is also called the *ISA* (Industry Standard Architecture) bus. The 62-pin socket on the ISA bus is identical to the PC/XT 62-pin socket; therefore, cards designed to use this single socket (in other words, 8-bit cards) will usually work in a 286, 386, or 486 ISA bus computer too. You'll often see one or two bus connector positions on ISA mainboards with only the single 62-bus socket. The single sockets sometimes make it easier to install one of the bulky old 8-bit cards. See Figures 12.2 (on page 116) and 12.3 (on page 117).

EISA computers use an amazing multi-purpose bus connector socket. This socket will hold ordinary 8-bit cards, ordinary 16-bit ISA-style cards, or (if you've got the bucks to buy them) EISA cards. Figure 12.4 on page 118 shows an EISA mainboard.

Dip Switches or CMOS Chip

PC/XT clones use *dip switches* to tell the BIOS ROM what hardware is installed on each individual machine. Technicians set the switches to reflect the amount of memory and number of floppy drives installed, the video type, and the presence or absence of a numeric coprocessor. Note the dip switches in the lower center of Figure 12.1. Figure 11.6 on page 107 is a table of generic XT clone switch settings.

All 286, 386, and 486 computers use a setup program to write system hardware information in the *CMOS* chip. Like the PC/XT dip switches, CMOS keeps track of the memory and number of floppy drives installed, the video type, and the presence or absence of a numeric coprocessor. It also contains the date, the time, the number and type of hard drives installed, and the type of floppy drives installed. The CMOS chip is protected by battery backup; so no configuration information gets lost while the power is shut down overnight.

EISA computers also use an extended setup routine called the *EISA configuration utility* (ECU). The ECU stores information about any expansion cards installed in the computer.

Clock and Clock Crystal

Both PC/XT clones and 286/386/486 computers have an internal clock, calibrated with a quartz crystal, to set the tempo for computer processes. In addition, 286/386/486 computers employ a real-time clock, with battery backup, that remembers the date and time whether the computer is on or off. The original PC/XTs and the first clones had no real-time clock on the mainboard. Many users installed a clock expansion card (see "Clock Card," on page 137). The clock was such a popular feature that XT clone manufacturers added it to their new mainboards.

Computer speed (the tempo of the internal clock) is measured in MHz. A higher MHz number equals a faster computer (all other things being equal). A 386/16 computer, for instance, uses a 386 microprocessor chip running at 16 MHz. A 486/33, like our Swan mainboard in Figure 12.4, should be substantially faster because (1) the Swan is a 33 MHz machine (the computer's internal clock is running twice as fast) so it's marching to a faster beat, and (2) it uses a 486 microprocessor (a smarter chip than the 386, the 486 does twice the work on each tick of the clock).

Clock/CMOS Battery

This 4.5–6.0 volt battery powers both the CMOS chip and the real-time clock/calendar chip whenever the computer is off. 286, 386, and 486 computers have this battery (or a wire carrying a current from the battery pack) right on the mainboard. Older PC/XT clones (using the 8086 or 8088 microprocessor chip) do not have a clock on the mainboard. If an expansion card with a clock has been installed, the battery is located on that expansion card.

Numeric Coprocessor Socket

This socket can accommodate an optional mathematics chip for heavy number-crunching work. All mainboards have the socket, but very few computers have numeric coprocessor chips installed. Since 486 microprocessor chips incorporate a numeric coprocessor inside the 486 chip, most 486 computers have a Weitek math coprocessor socket in case the user wants to install the Weitek chip (it's even faster than the math coprocessor built into the 486 chip).

Mainboard

Jumpers

As you can see in the mainboards shown in Figures 12.1 through 12.4 (on pages 115-117), each mainboard manufacturer uses jumpers and switches slightly differently. You must have the mainboard manual to know which function a particular jumper controls.

Integrated I/O Circuitry on the Mainboard

The original IBM XTs and ATs used expansion cards for parallel and serial ports, for floppy drive controllers, for hard disk controllers, for video adapters—for practically everything except the keyboard.

Sophisticated new 386 and 486 mainboards often contain the serial and parallel port circuits, floppy drive controller circuits, VGA video circuits, perhaps even IDE hard disk controller circuits. Integrated I/O (Input/Output) circuitry is cost effective (no need for a separate parallel card or video expansion card). The mainboard maker can also test all the components together and guarantee the complete product—no more worries about subtle incompatibilities between your floppy drive controller and your mainboard. Expect this trend to continue. As chips get smaller there is more empty real estate on the mainboard, so why not add another function or two?

Where to Find the Mainboard

To get to the mainboard, you must turn off the computer and remove the system cover. We tell you how to remove the cover on page 113. The mainboard will be on the bottom of the computer; it's the largest printed circuit board in the whole machine. Expansion cards fit vertically into mainboard bus connectors (the line of rectangular, plastic connectors across the top surface of the mainboard).

How the Mainboard Works

To build a computer from scratch, you would need memory and memory management chips, a BIOS ROM, a microprocessor, I/O devices, an internal clock and timer chips, a reliable source of power, and the electric circuits to connect it all together (the bus). Most of these important chips are mounted on the mainboard. I/O devices plug into the mainboard bus with expansion cards, and the power supply rests in its own box, but the rest of the computer is on this single board.

Mainboard

To understand how the mainboard components interact, consider what happens, step-by-step, when we power on a computer. The initial steps are hard-wired into the circuitry. The power supply comes up to speed, then sends a "power good" signal to the clock reset chip on the mainboard. The clock reset chip in turn sends a hard reset to the microprocessor (the CPU). The CPU resets and initializes (runs a self-test and prepares the bus for use).

The final, hard-wired step in the microprocessor reset procedure involves jumping to a very high address to look for further instructions. There is a redirect pointer at that high address, which sends the microprocessor to the starting address of the POST and initialization routine in the BIOS ROM.

From now on we are following instructions programmed into the ROM. ROMs are replaceable, and they don't all have the same POST/initialization routines. You may choose to change the ROM in your computer (because it has a bug or because it lacks some features available only in newer ROM versions). The computer will then obey different POST/initialization instructions from the new ROM. Therefore, any description of POST for clones must be fairly general, and perhaps not strictly accurate for your particular machine. Nevertheless, we'll give it a try.

The ROM POST initialization routines create a working computer from a pile of circuits. During this procedure, the ROM BIOS writes its name, date, and copyright signature on the screen; checks the keyboard (CapsLock and NumLock lights flash on and off); reads the dip switches (or CMOS if it is a 286, 386, or 486 computer) to learn what equipment the switches (or the CMOS) believe is installed; counts and tests the system memory; and puts a system memory message on the screen.

Consider "check the keyboard," a single step in this POST/Initialization process. XT clones make the CPU do keyboard testing and initialization. 286s, 386s, and 486s call on a keyboard controller chip. In either case, a stream of data from the keyboard is suspect. It provokes the screen message "Keyboard Stuck Key Failure." A disconnected keyboard produces a long hesitation, then the message "Keyboard Bad" appears, and the BIOS continues with the POST routine. Remember, all the error messages at this stage are coded into the ROM. Two different ROMs will complain about an error with slightly different screen messages. They may also deal with an error in slightly different ways. For instance, many 286 clones do not have any error message for a disconnected keyboard. Instead, the computer gets stuck at the keyboard test step in the POST, waiting eternally for the nonexistent keyboard to reply "All OK."

Don't let these screen error messages confuse you. Any differences between the messages on your computer, a friend's machine, and the examples given in this book, may not be as substantive as they seem.

Mainboard

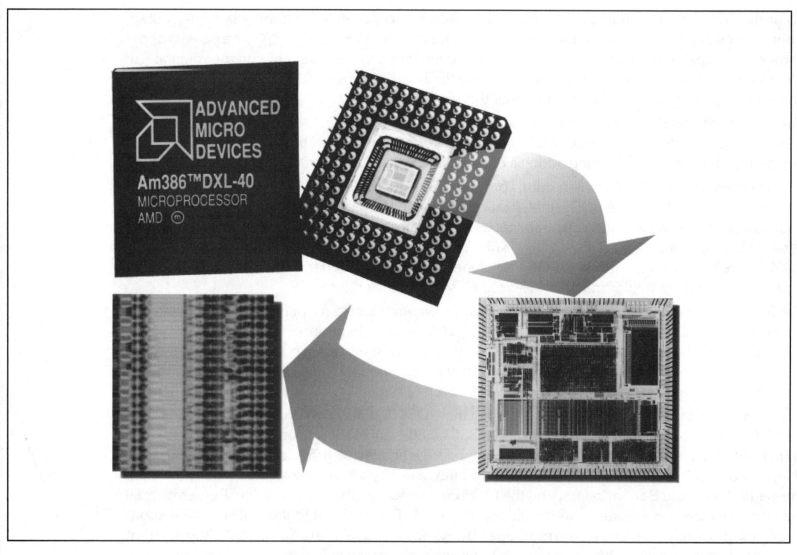

Figure 12.5

Slightly over an inch square, the 386 chip looks impressive from above (top left). A network of tiny wires connecting the microprocessor chip to the mounting pins becomes visible when we flip the 386 chip over (top right). Enlarged, the chip shows separate regions dedicated to addressing, registers, scratch pad memory, the arithmetic logic unit, etc. Enlarged again, it reveals individual circuits. Original photo courtesy of AMD. Montage by Lora McLaughlin.

Mainboard

In Section 4 we list common IBM BIOS, Phoenix BIOS, and look-alike BIOS error messages and tell you what to do about them.

The ROM checks other parts of the system during the POST/ Initialization routine, but you don't notice what it's doing—there's no visible response as the ROM finishes each task. Nevertheless, CPU registers must be cleared and loaded with initial information, the DMA system must turn on the RAM refresh cycle, and the interrupt vector table must be set up in very low memory.

The BIOS ROM checks the floppy drives (the floppy drive light flashes, and the drive spins as it's doing this) and initializes the printer (the printer lights flash, and the print head returns to the far left position as it's doing this). In addition, the ROM checks for ROM BIOS extensions—those extra ROMs installed on a hard disk controller or an EGA or VGA video card—and follows the initialization instructions in each of these ROM extensions in turn.

The ROM next tries to boot a disk in drive A, looking at track 0, sector 1—the DOS boot sector. If no disk is present, it tries drive C, the hard disk, again checking only track 0, sector 1.

The boot sector loads the two hidden DOS files, called IO.SYS and MSDOS.SYS. These files are dedicated to low-level hardware control. The IO.SYS contains resident device drivers (the software instructions for operating standard hardware devices, such as the keyboard, the disk drives, the printer, and the serial ports). The boot sector then looks for a CONFIG.SYS file (the file containing installable external device drivers for oddball equipment). Mice require an external device driver, as do 1.44 MB 3.5 inch drives with any DOS version below 3.3. Hard disk management programs like Disk Manager use a custom device driver to split the hard disk into bite-sized pieces for DOS.

As a final step, the computer loads a command-line processor or a shell (the interface between the keyboard/mouse and the DOS commands). Most people use COMMAND.COM from the DOS disk, but any shell can be used. If you find the familiar C> prompt of COMMAND.COM (the standard user interface) difficult, DR DOS and QUICKDOS provide easier access to DOS file management functions.

Windows is loaded on top of DOS, but it doesn't use most DOS functions. In fact, Windows is really an alternative operating system (which happens to be loaded on top of DOS) that accesses the CPU chip independently. That's why DOS will run on any of the 8088 family of CPU chips, but Windows 3.1 won't. Windows was written to take advantage of the improvements engineered into 286, 386, and 486 chips.

An XT clone boots up as an XT clone, but 286/386/486 computers don't boot up as 286s, 386s, or 486s. Instead they boot up in real mode, and impersonate XT clones. If you are using ordinary DOS, your computer will stay in real mode.

How to Test the Mainboard

Very few of the mainboard components are individually serviceable. Here's what you can do:

- ✔ The RAM and ROM chips can be replaced.
- ✔ The clock/CMOS battery is a simple slip-out/slip-in replacement.
- ✔ Both 8088 and 8086 CPU chips are also fairly easy to install, but 80286, 80386, and 80486 chips are tricky.

On most mainboards, the clock generator and timer chips, the clock crystal and clock reset chip, dip switches, the CMOS chip, the bus controller chip, the DMA controller chip (for direct disk drive to RAM memory information transfer), and all the chip sockets are soldered on. The board itself is a maze of printed circuits, none of which is readily repairable. Therefore, whenever the problem is stickier than bad RAM, bad ROM, a dead CMOS battery, or incorrect dip switch/jumper settings, it's often necessary to replace the entire mainboard.

Ironically, this soldered-chip design makes troubleshooting much easier. If the DMA controller chip is not individually replaceable, there is no need to trace a machine fault down to this particular chip. Instead, experiment with the easier solutions first. If they don't solve the problem, then replace the mainboard. Let's consider those NMI errors that happen while the computer is running as an example. When is an NMI error caused by a bad mainboard?

First of all, what is an *NMI*? NMI stands for Non-Maskable Interrupt. Intel designed internal hardware interrupts into the 8088/8086/80286/80386 family of chips. One of these—the NMI interrupt—occurs most often when the memory parity (a test for memory recording accuracy) shows a memory error. This interrupt is called nonmaskable because the hardware cannot mask (selectively ignore) this interrupt while processing another task. When an NMI occurs, the NMI error message goes up on the screen and everything is deadlocked until you address the NMI error—no matter what else is going on.

The memory parity test (probable source of the NMI error) is done strictly with hardware. There is no software or microprocessor involved. So there is no point thinking about a possible bad CPU or defective software code when you're considering the causes of an NMI error.

What causes a parity error? There are four possibilities: (1) a bad RAM chip, (2) a drop in voltage (below 4.5 volts) that causes the chips to forget the stored data, (3) malfunctioning address logic to the memory chips that causes one RAM chip to be mistaken for another, or (4) a bad parity logic chip that reports a parity problem when there is none. Causes 1 and 2 (a bad chip or low power) are the most likely to occur. Causes 3 and 4 are symptoms of bad (and nonreplaceable) chips or circuits on the mainboard.

Let's troubleshoot this NMI error a little further. What can you determine from the address on the screen that's part of the NMI message? Does it explain where the problem is located? No, it points to the place in memory where the program was working when it got that error, even though the error could have come from any place in memory.

Here are the steps you should take. Run a software memory test. If it finds bad chips, that's great—replace them. If the software test doesn't find anything, take all the RAM chips out of the mainboard and run them through a chip testing machine. If all the chips test good, it's time to consider cause 2, which is low power on the +5 volt line. Is it summer, and is there a heat wave? Perhaps a brownout is the source of your low power problems. If you have any doubts, test the line voltage (household current) into the computer. You'll need a voltmeter (under $20 at Radio Shack) and the accompanying instruction book. 104 volts is the minimum acceptable for error-free operation. The instructions tell you how to test the line voltage without ending up with a wet toe in a hot socket.

If you still have the NMI errors, replace the power supply. There is no way to test a power supply for those short-term voltage drops that produce intermittent NMI errors. If the problem doesn't go away after you replace the power supply, there are two other possible solutions, both expensive: replace the mainboard or replace all the RAM chips. Neither solution is more likely than the other to be the correct choice. So you can either replace the mainboard or replace all the RAM chips. If you still get NMI errors after you try one solution, try the other solution.

This approach doesn't sound very scientific—and it isn't—but it is the most cost effective way to handle the problem. Enormously expensive machines, capable of analyzing the current flow on every wire in the mainboard, could be built, but to what end? Someone would have to pay for the machine. And each time the mainboard was improved and redesigned, the machine would become

Mainboard

Figure 12.6
The CMOS backup battery pack (the little black cube) is plugged into the mainboard. Write down where the red and the black wires go or make a sketch before you unplug them. Photo by Robert McLaughlin.

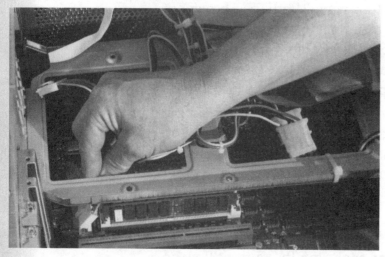

Figure 12.7
Remove the power supply connectors from the 486 mainboard. Note how they are installed—they must be installed the same way. Photo by Robert McLaughlin.

obsolete. Real technicians use the technique described, testing the cheapest and most likely solutions first. The troubleshooting charts in Section 3 will help you navigate this maze of possibilities.

How to Remove and Install the Mainboard

This section explains how to remove and install the mainboard. Before you begin, turn off the computer and remove the system unit cover. See Chapter 1 or page 113 here in Chapter 12 if you need help getting the cover off.

1. **Remove cards.** Remove all the expansion cards, marking any cables or wires you must disconnect in the process. Figures 11.1 through 11.3 on pages 102-103 illustrate this process.

2. **Mark and remove wires.** If there are wires connected to pins on the mainboard, mark them for reinstallation. Figures 12.6 through 12.9 show some of these wires. Mark them well, it's easy to mix them up or reinstall them backward. You should also take a moment to compare the new and old mainboards. Sometimes the new mainboard has slightly different jumper locations. It is easiest to plan any adjustments while the original mainboard is still fully wired to the chassis.

   Don't forget the power supply wires. In Figure 12.7 we're removing the power supply connectors from a 486 EISA mainboard. Figure 12.9 on page 130 shows the power supply connectors on an XT clone.

3. **Remove power supply?** The computer case is pretty crowded. You may choose to remove the power supply

screws and slide the power supply out of the case so you'll have some working room—see page 135 for details.

4. **Remove mounting screws and slide mainboard out— XT mainboard.** Most PC/XT mainboards have nine stand-offs (little metal or plastic legs) that attach the board to the bottom of the case. Look for screws on the bottom of the computer which correspond to the nine screws or nuts on the top of the mainboard. You can remove either the top nuts or the bottom screws. Other XT clones use two screws and a handful of insulated plastic pegs (Figures 12.10 and 12.11 on the next page).

   After you remove the nuts or screws, slide the mainboard out of the chassis (Figures 12.13 and 12.14 on page 131 give you a rough idea). Note the paper insulating washers on both the top and bottom of the mainboard at each of the nine stand-offs and/or screws. You will reuse these insulating washers, the stand-offs, and the screws to mount the new mainboard.

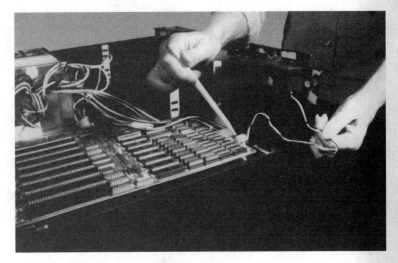

Figure 12.8
This XT clone mainboard has only a speaker wire connector and two power supply connectors.

   Remove mounting screws and slide mainboard out—286/386/486. Many new 386 and 486 mainboards are mounted with six to ten small screws, with the mainboard reinforced and electrically insulated at the screw holes (Figure 12.12 on the next page).

   Other 286, 386, and 486 mainboards are mounted with seven plastic stand-offs and two screws (Figures 12.14 to 12.16 on page 131). Look for an insulating washer under the screw heads. Remove the screws, then slide the mainboard 1/2-inch sideways, moving it away from the power supply, as shown in Figure 12.14. Lift it up and wiggle it out of the chassis. Sometimes it's easier to squeeze the tops of the stand-offs and lift the mainboard out, as in Figure 12.15. Save the washers and stand-offs to mount the new mainboard, as shown in Figure 12.16.

5. **Transfer reusable components and set switches.** Before you install a new mainboard, carefully check it and read its manual. In most cases, you'll transfer the RAM and numeric coprocessor from the old to the new mainboard. Take care not to bend the new mainboard

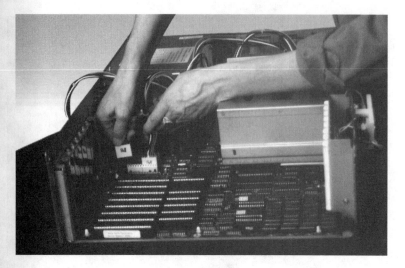

Figure 12.9
Remove the power supply connectors from the XT clone mainboard.

Figure 12.10
This XT clone mainboard has two screws holding it to the case.

Figure 12.11
A plastic stand-off used to mount the mainboard to the case.

Figure 12.12
This 486 EISA mainboard is mounted with many small Phillips screws. Photo by Robert McLaughlin.

Mainboard

Figure 12.13
Slide the mainboard over and lift it out of the case. Photo by Robert McLaughlin.

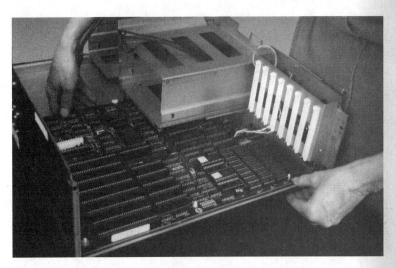

Figure 12.14
Some mainboards mounted on stand-offs will slide over 1/2-inch and then lift right out of the case.

Figure 12.15
Sometimes it's easier to squeeze the tops of the plastic stand-offs and lift the mainboard out.

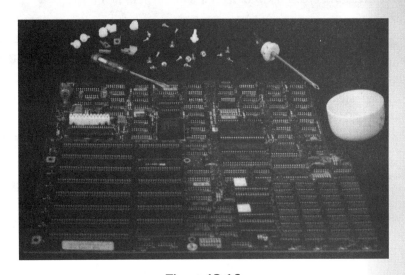

Figure 12.16
A 286/AT clone mainboard. The screws and stand-offs that we kept in the cup as we disassembled the computer are on the table.

Figure 12.17
To reinstall this AT-style mainboard, place the stand-offs in the slots, slide the board back into place, and press down so the pointed ends of the stand-offs snap into the holes in the mainboard.

and crack it while installing these chips. The microprocessor and ROM(s) should be already installed on your new mainboard. Set the dip switches and jumpers as instructed in your mainboard manual. Install the stand-offs on the new mainboard—using insulating washers where needed.

6. **Slide the new mainboard in.** Slip the mainboard into position and install the remaining screws, or try the push-down technique shown in Figure 12.17.

7. **Reinstall wires/cables/cards.** Plug in both power supply connectors and reconnect any miscellaneous wires. Reinstall the power supply and the expansion cards.

8. **Test the computer.** The computer should boot and perform properly and no longer show those symptoms which caused you to replace the mainboard. If it doesn't, double-check each of the memory chips and the ROM for misinstallation. It's very easy to bend a leg on a chip as you press it into the mainboard socket. If you still have problems, recheck each step you took, looking for a misinstalled card, cable, or jumper wire. If you have all the same symptoms that caused you to replace the mainboard, you now know that the mainboard is not causing the problem. Someone may have sold you a defective mainboard, but it's highly unlikely that it has the exact symptoms you started with.

If you're stuck, get a cup of coffee and find a friend to help you. Anyone can easily miss a detail. Experienced technicians will often ask another technician into their workroom when they are buffaloed. Together they go over the diagnostic reasoning and recheck the parts installation. It's amazing what a fresh pair of eyes can see.

Power Supply

The *power supply* is a transformer. It transforms household current (115 volts alternating) into appropriate voltages (5 and 12 volts direct) for the other computer components. An XT clone power supply appears in Figure 12.18. Figure 12.19 shows an AT-style power supply for a 286, 386, or 486 computer. Figure 12.20 on the next page shows a 4-wire power connector.

Where to Find the Power Supply

The power supply is inside the computer case. Turn off the computer and remove the cover. Complete instructions for removing the cover are provided on page 113. The power supply is the largest metallic box inside the computer chassis. If you have any trouble locating it, examine the back of the machine. The power cord from the 115-volt wall outlet plugs directly into the power supply at the point where the power supply extends through the back of the computer case.

Figure 12.18
An XT clone power supply. Photo courtesy of PC Power & Cooling, Inc.

Figure 12.19
An AT/286, 386, or 486 power supply. Photo courtesy of PC Power & Cooling, Inc.

How the Power Supply Works

Warning: The electronics inside the power supply are very sophisticated. THIS IS ONE OF THE FEW AREAS INSIDE THE PC WHERE YOU CAN GET HURT. *Do not* open the power supply!

The power supply has a very simple job: to provide clean smooth power at +12 volts DC, -12 volts DC, +5 volts DC, and -5 volts DC. It monitors its own power output on startup and sends a "power good" signal to the mainboard when the voltages have stabilized at their required levels. The microprocessor resets and bootup starts when the mainboard receives this signal.

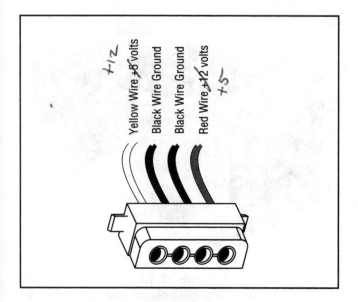

Figure 12.20
A four-wire power supply connector.

How to Test the Power Supply

Loss of CMOS setup in 286, 386, or 486 machines is often caused by a bad power supply. The CMOS chip requires at least 4.5 volts to reliably hold the configuration setup information (date, time, installed hardware). It is powered by batteries whenever the computer is turned off. When the 5-volt line climbs above 5 volts or the "power good" line to the mainboard is on, the CMOS battery backup disengages. If a defective power supply has sent the "power good" signal before the 5-volt line is high enough, the setup information is lost. Be sure to check the batteries first. They tend to wear out after a year of service. If you replace the batteries and run the CMOS setup routine, but the problem still remains, then you probably have a faulty power supply.

Power supplies are not serviceable in the field. Besides, replacements are cheap. If your power supply is not performing correctly, do not attempt to repair it, just throw it away.

You can easily test the voltages produced by your power supply with a hand-held voltmeter. To do this, you must hook the power supply up to 115 volts and to a load of some kind—a disk drive or the main-board will do. All the four-wire connectors are identical, so you can use any one of them to test your power supply while it is hooked into the computer. This is probably the best way to test the power supply since it should perform properly when fully loaded with all add-on boards, drives, etc.

If the DC voltages are low, consider the external circumstances before condemning the power supply. It's smart to test the AC line current. The electric company browns out our city, for example, on summer afternoons during a heat wave. 104 volts AC is the minimum acceptable standard. Frankly, 104 volts is pretty pathetic—if your line voltage is this bad, buy an uninterruptible power supply. We discuss UPS designs in our local area network (LAN) repair book, *Troubleshooting Your LAN* (MIS:Press, 1992).

Unfortunately, power supplies will occasionally fail for only a microsecond, perhaps on bootup or during drive access. In addition, a defective unit may send the "power good" signal prematurely, causing the microprocessor to reset while voltages are unstable. Premature reset can cause a problem in almost any part of the computer, since random errors may be introduced any place in memory. If you turn the computer power switch off and on again, the same problem may recur, or a different one, or no problem at all. The ordinary voltmeter does not respond rapidly enough to catch a momentary dip or surge in power. In this case substitute a known-good power supply and retest the machine to confirm the bad power supply diagnosis.

Occasionally, one of the four-wire power connectors will fail while the others remain functional. If you suspect a problem with one of the four-wire connectors—because disk drive B doesn't function at all, for instance—you can try switching the suspect power connector with the known-good one from drive A.

Figure 12.21
Remove the four screws holding the power supply to the case.
Photo by Robert McLaughlin.

How to Remove and Replace the Power Supply

Before you remove the power supply, unplug the 110-volt power cord and disconnect the four-wire power supply connectors from disk drives, tape drives, and other devices.

The mainboard receives power from a single long connector or from two multi-wire connectors. Examine these connectors closely before removing them. They must be reinstalled properly. If you jam the connectors on backward and turn on the computer, you will damage the mainboard.

Remove the four screws that hold the power supply to the back surface of the chassis (Figure 12.21). Slide the power supply forward 1.5 inches (to clear the lugs on the bottom of the case) and lift it up out of the case (Figure 12.22).

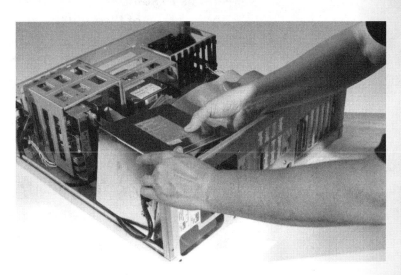

Figure 12.22
Push the power supply forward, then lift it up out of the case.
Photo by Robert McLaughlin.

To install a power supply, perform the steps in reverse order.

⚡ **Warning:** Make sure you reinstall the power connectors on the mainboard correctly.

Keyboard

When you press or release a keyboard key, the keyboard sends a signal to the computer via a keyboard port on the mainboard. If you look at the back of the chassis, you can see the cable connector. If you disconnect the keyboard cable, you can see the mainboard and the keyboard port through a hole in the chassis.

How the Keyboard Works

Beneath the keys on the keyboard is a grid of circuits. When you press a key, two wires on the grid are connected. These wires send a signal to the keyboard microprocessor, which converts the grid signals to standard scan codes (signals identifying which key was pressed or released). The scan codes are sent through the keyboard cable to the mainboard. In XT clones, the ROM converts the keyboard scan code into an ASCII character code (a number, letter, etc). AT clones use a keyboard controller on the mainboard to make this translation.

Because XT and AT clones map the five pins of the keyboard cable to different signals, many keyboards are manufactured with an XT/AT switch on the back. An XT keyboard plugged into a 286, 386, or 486 computer sends only gibberish. If the monitor displays a keyboard error message on bootup, this XT/AT switch is the first place to check.

How to Test the Keyboard

Before you try to correct a keyboard problem, give it some thought. Does the problem involve just one or two keys? If so, a bad connection at the key switch may be the culprit. Try spraying the keyboard with compressed air or with a good quality, non-corrosive electronic circuit cleaner to clean out the contamination.

If you have any working keys and a whole row or column of nonworking keys, the grid must be suspect. One of the wires may be broken or shorted out. A bad grid is too expensive to replace. If this is the problem, you'll have to replace the whole keyboard.

Sometimes no portion of the keyboard works properly. It's possible that there's a bad microprocessor chip in the keyboard, but before you discard the keyboard, check that the XT/AT switch is properly set and the keyboard tightly plugged in at the system mainboard. Also don't forget to check for a stuck key. I once thought I had a bad keyboard, when actually I had a book lying on a key while booting. When the computer checked the keyboard signals, it puts up the "Bad Keyboard" message.

How to Remove and Install the Keyboard

To remove the keyboard, simply unplug it from the system unit. Check the XT/AT switch on the new keyboard. Rotate the new keyboard's plug until the pins fit into the connector on the mainboard, then push it in firmly. The system may have to be rebooted to recognize a new keyboard.

Clock Card

Neither the IBM PC nor the IBM XT had a real-time clock on the mainboard, so neither did early clones. You can install a clock card in these computers, though, which adds a battery-powered clock that remembers the date and time, even when the computer is turned off or unplugged. All 286/386/486 computers have real-time clocks integrated into the mainboard circuitry, as do many XT-style computers built in the late 1980's and the 1990's. If you are interested in the clock/calendar function on a 286/386/486 computer, check the mainboard section, page 121.

Where to Find the Clock Card

Take off the system unit cover (instructions provided on page 113). Clock cards have a battery on the card. In most cases this battery is a silver, disk-shaped battery about the size of a quarter. A few clock cards use a cylindrical battery about 3/4-inch long and 1/2-inch in diameter.

A simple clock card is short, has no cables attached to it, and has very few chips on it. Some computer owners prefer to install a multi-function card, which includes a serial port, parallel port, clock, and sometimes even extra memory. When you troubleshoot a multi-function card, treat it like multiple cards that are functionally independent but happen to be located on the same circuit board.

How the Clock Card Works

The battery on the clock card powers the clock/calendar chip whenever the computer's power is below 5 volts. This enables the clock chip to continue calculating the date and time, whether the computer is running or not.

You need special software to read the date and time inside the clock card. Because there are a number of possible clock card addresses and date/time formats, you must use the correct software with each clock card. Mismatched software looks for the clock at the wrong address and returns a "no clock found" message, even if a fully functional clock is present.

How to Test the Clock Card

Before you test the clock card, make sure you are using the right software for your card. Set the date and time and leave the computer on. Wait a couple of minutes, then recheck the time and turn the computer off. Leave it for a few minutes, turn it back on, and make sure the clock continued running while the computer was off.

If the clock seems okay with the computer on but doesn't work with the computer off, replace the battery. Turn off the computer. You can easily slip disk batteries into place—sometimes without even removing the card. Soldered batteries can be replaced too, but be sure to test the battery with a voltmeter before bothering to desolder it. The battery must read 4.5 volts or higher for proper clock chip performance.

If the clock isn't working at all (if the date and time won't set, for instance) the software is probably wrong. Try other clock setting software and double-check the jumpers on the card before you condemn the card. You may be able to reconfigure the clock address so the clock is installed where your software expects to find it.

Keep in mind that clock cards are not very accurate. Losing even ten minutes a day is no cause for alarm. Just reset the clock card periodically with the clock setting software. Do not use the DOS DATE and TIME commands with an XT clock. These commands change the DOS clock (the temporary clock running in the computer while the power is on), but they do not store information in the real-time clock (the battery-powered clock), so any changes you make will be lost as soon as you turn off the computer.

How to Install a Clock Card

Turn off the computer. Remove the system unit cover (described on page 113 and in Chapter 1).

1. **Remove old clock card (if necessary).** If you need to remove an old clock card, remove the screw holding the card to the back of the chassis and save the screw. Then pull the card straight up out of the bus connector. These steps are illustrated in Figures 11.1 to 11.3, pages 102-103.

2. **Pick an expansion slot for the new clock card.** You can install your new clock card in any unused expansion slot. If you just removed an old clock card, you might as well put the new clock card in this same slot. If this is a brand new card, not a replacement, pick any unused expansion slot. Remove the screw at the back of the chassis that holds down the little metal cover for this slot, and throw away the slot cover. Save the screw.

3. **Install card.** Fit the card down into the expansion slot and press it into place. Reinstall the screw to hold the card tightly to the chassis, then turn on the computer and test the card using the clock software that comes with it.

Chapter 13
Video Options

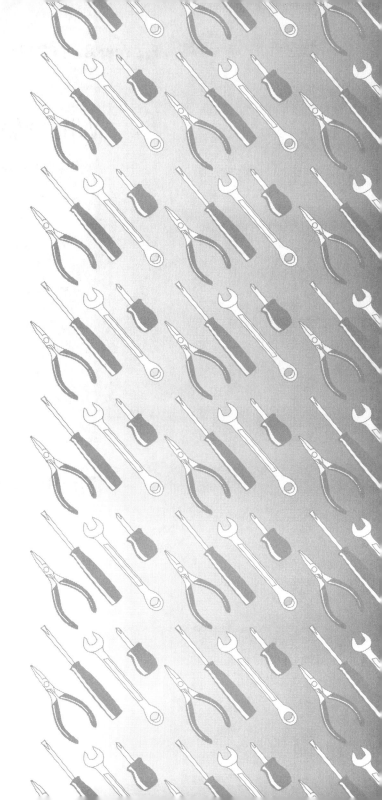

This section describes the following items:

- ✔ What makes for good video? MDA, MGP, CGA, EGA, VGA, 8515, and XGA compared
- ✔ Monitors
- ✔ Monochrome Text-Only Video Adapter (MDA) card
- ✔ Monochrome Graphics Video Adapter (MGP) card with Printer Port
- ✔ Color Graphics Video Adapter (CGA) card
- ✔ Enhanced Graphics Adapter (EGA) card
- ✔ Video Graphics Array (VGA) card—includes Super VGA and Extended VGA too
- ✔ 8514 Graphics Adapter card
- ✔ Extended Graphics Adapter (XGA) card
- ✔ Texas Instruments Graphics Architecture (TIGA) card

Video

What Makes for Good Video?

Good video is a function of:

- ✔ Resolution (the number of individually controllable dots of light on the screen)—more dots produce a finer-grained picture.

- ✔ Scan rate (how often the monitor rewrites the screen)—if there is too long a wait between rewrites the computer operator will notice flicker.

- ✔ Color and gray shades—it's possible to use gray shades and color shades to fool the eye so text characters or graphics look crisper than they would if you had only solid black or solid white to draw with.

- ✔ Speed (how fast text scrolls in a word processing program, or how fast the computer redraws a Windows screen)—slow video response is unpleasant and inefficient.

We'll talk about these four issues, comparing the popular video standards, then discuss each type of monitor and video card in turn. But first a quick how-it-works so the technical jargon will make sense.

The Video Card

The video card is the brains of the team and the monitor follows orders. If the video card is a chef, the monitor is the stove. The meals this team turns out are more limited by the ingenuity and creativity of the chef than by the stove. Better not match a chef who broils everything with a stove without oven or broiler—that team wouldn't work at all. But even the fanciest stove can't cook meals by itself; it requires a creative chef to exploit its potential. And even a fine chef will produce mediocre cakes in an oven with hot and cold spots or poor temperature control.

The video card controls the resolution, the scan rate, and the colors or gray shades available on a particular monitor. Of course, you must choose a monitor capable of following a given video card's directions—for example, choose a monochrome monitor for a monochrome video card, or a VGA-compatible monitor for a VGA card.

The inside of a monitor screen, like a television tube, is coated with phosphor compounds — which glow wherever an electron beam strikes them. The screen is treated as a grid of pixels (dots of light).

Each individual pixel may be excited by the electron beam, or passed over so that section of the screen stays dark.

Sometimes the computer's CPU figures out which pixels should be lighted. More often the video card receives a more general command (for example, "Display a capital letter *J*" or "Display a semicolon") and the video card must work out which pixels to light up to produce the glowing character on the monitor screen. Sophisticated high-resolution video cards with their own microprocessor require only general instructions from the computer's CPU ("Draw a square"); the microprocessor on the video card calculates which pixels to light.

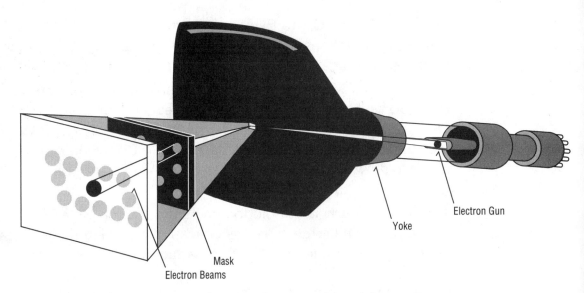

Figure 13.1
A monitor with the electron beam energizing the phosphor compounds on the video screen.

Video Resolution

The more individually controllable dots of light on the monitor screen, the crisper the image. Resolution is measured in horizontal dots on the screen by vertical dots on the screen. Some examples:

- ✔ 320 x 200 pixels for RGB color monitors using a CGA card, the original IBM color-monitor-and-video-card combination introduced in 1981
- ✔ 640 x 350 pixels for EGA color monitors and EGA cards, introduced in 1985
- ✔ 640 x 480 pixels for VGA color monitors and cards, introduced in 1987
- ✔ 800 x 600 for super VGA (now standard on all VGA cards except the cheapest)
- ✔ 1024 x 768 pixels for Extended VGA (also standard now on most VGA cards)

Video

The jump from CGA to EGA was dramatic, from 320 times 200 dots (64 thousand pixels per screen) to 640 times 350 dots (over 200 thousand pixels per screen). But the jump from EGA to VGA was dramatic too; VGA has almost 40 percent more pixels per screen than EGA.

Super VGA and Extended VGA show more columns in a spread sheet or more lines of text on the monitor, which provides a better overview of your work than an ordinary VGA card and monitor can give. But the characters on the 800 x 600 pixel or 1024 x 768 pixel monitor are smaller than the characters on an ordinary VGA monitor. Both video cards use the same number of individual pixels to draw a particular letter, but Super VGA and Extended VGA pixels are smaller (so the letter takes up less floor space on your monitor).

The column marked "Resolution" in Figure 13.2 on page 147 allows you to compare popular video standards. Don't forget to consider scan rate and interlacing, gray scales, and speed when you're choosing a new video card—all these factors are important.

Scan Rate and Interlacing

Vertical scan rate is the number of times per second the electron beam rewrites the monitor screen. Slow scan rates produce flicker. High scan rates produce a rock-solid image, but monitors capable of high scan rates are more expensive. A scan rate that is adequate on a 14-inch monitor will seem flickery on a big 17-inch or 20-inch monitor, so the high-resolution video modes often used on these large monitors need a higher scan rate.

The original IBM PC's monochrome card rewrote the monitor screen 50 times per second. A vertical scan rate of 50 Hz is too slow for most people's eyes, so IBM specified long-persistence phosphor compounds on the monitor screen. Once excited, these phosphors continue to glow for a while even after the electron beam has moved on to another part of the screen. This cures the flickering, but the monitor displays annoying ghosts when the user scrolls text.

An RGB color monitor, the color monitor paired with the CGA video card on the early IBM PC, refreshes the screen 60 times per second. High-resolution VGA and multiscanning monitors refresh 56, 60, 70, or 72 or more times per second.

See a pattern? A high vertical scan rate is better. Monitors that can handle super VGA (800 x 600) screen resolutions at 70 or 72 refreshes per second look good. The same super VGA resolution on a lower-quality "super VGA" monitor which refreshes the screen 56 times per second will look jumpy and flickery. That's why VESA, the Video Equipment Standards Association, has increased the vertical scan rate for super VGA video cards and monitors from 56 Hz to 72 Hz.

Searching for a free lunch, monitor designers came up with *interlaced* monitors (monitors that refresh only the odd-numbered row of pixels in one pass, then refresh the even numbered rows of pixels in a second pass). Interlaced monitors can display high-resolution video (many rows of pixels on the screen), yet they cost much less than noninterlaced monitors. Some people don't mind using interlaced monitors. But many others complain of headaches and eyestrain from the subliminal flicker inherent in the design. We neither use nor recommend interlaced monitors.

IBM has gotten a lot of grief for launching the 8514 and XGA standards as interlaced standards. Many non-IBM 8514-compatible cards are noninterlaced, though that means they will only work with very high-end multiscanning monitors capable of refreshing the screen 70 or more times per second.

See the column marked "Vertical scan rate" in the chart on page 147.

Color and Gray Shades

Color alone does not make the monitor display sharper, but it does make it easier to read. If you are having trouble quickly distinguishing the control features of a program (the mouse buttons, menus, commands, and error messages) from the work itself (the text, spreadsheets, or data-input screen), consider switching to VGA color or better. Your productivity will soar.

Sixteen colors are sufficient for text work and simple graphics. 256 colors make serious graphics look better. But we chose a 24-bit color video card with 16 million different colors to retouch the photos in this book. More colors usually produce slower screen redraws and generally slower video response.

If you want more colors you'll have to buy more video memory. But before you spend that extra $50-$100, think what you will be doing with this video card. Do you need 256 colors? Yes, if you are doing professional graphics or publishing. But most of us don't even own the kind of software you need to diplay 256 colors. Extra video memory, like a size 12 shoe on a size 10 foot, is no advantage. You can always add extra video memory later if you need it—simply install additional memory chips in the video memory sockets on your card.

Gray shades can make the display seem much sharper even though you are still working with the original number of pixels per screen. Clever font designers use gray shades strategically on the edges of characters to fool the eye, a technique called anti-aliasing. The user perceives noticeably crisper fonts with cleaner, smoother curves. Gray shades are available on EGA or better video cards: EGA, VGA, XGA, 8514, and TIGA cards—the same cards that provide good resolution and multiple colors.

Video Speed Issues

Raster graphics, the technique employed by MGP, CGA, EGA, and frame buffer VGA video cards, is CPU-intensive. The computer's CPU (the 8088, 286, 386, 486, or 586 chip) decides, pixel by pixel, which pixels to light and which to leave dark. This takes a lot of CPU time, and it's not particularly fast because the CPU is a multi-purpose microprocessor, not a video specialist.

By comparison, vector graphics (used by 8514 and TIGA video cards, and VGA cards with accelerators or coprocessors) relies on a customized microprocessor on the video card to make pixel-by-pixel decisions. The CPU issues hig- level commands: "Draw a circle," "Zoom," "Rotate," "Paint with color A." The video card's processor translates the general instructions into pixel-by-pixel directions for the monitor. Like an idiot savant, the video microprocessor does only one thing, but it does it very well.

Vector graphics speeds up video response for two reasons. First, it doesn't take long for the CPU to send the message "Scroll." So bottlenecks in the communications path between the CPU and the video card (for example, a slow 286 bus) are no longer a problem. Second, the coprocessor or accelerator on the VGA card is designed specifically to scroll, to draw figures, to move images around the screen quickly.

Vector graphics is not new. For years (the 1960's and 1970's) memory was expensive and processing power was comparatively cheap, so vector graphics was cost effective. When PCs were introduced the cost of memory began to fall, so raster graphics, a memory-intensive design, made economic sense. In the late 1980's specialized video microprocessors were invented to serve the CAD/CAM engineering design markets. As the price of these specialized video processors has fallen, vector graphics has come back into style.

Figure 13.2
PC Video Standards

Video Card Type	Resolution	Vertical Scan Rate	Colors/Gray Shades	Speed	Appropriate Monitor(s)	Connector for Monitor Cable	Other Comments
MDA	Text only 80 columns x 25 rows	50	None (monochrome)	Depends on computer's CPU	Monochrome or multiscanning	DB9	Original monochrome display for the 1981 IBM PC
MGP	720 x 348	50	None (monochrome)	Depends on computer's CPU	Monochrome or multiscanning	DB9	Also called a "Hercules graphics card"
CGA	320 x 200	60	16[1]	Depends on computer's CPU	RGB color or multiscanning	DB9	Original color display for the 1981 IBM PC
EGA monochrome	720 x 350	50	16 gray	Depends on computer's CPU	Monochrome or multiscanning	DB9	EGA monochrome emulates an MGP card
EGA color	640 x 350	60	256[2]	Depends on computer's CPU	EGA color or multiscanning	DB9	
VGA Super VGA Extended VGA	640 x 480 800 x 600[3] 1024 x 768[3]	60 or 70 56, 72, 76[4] 70 or higher[4]	16 or 256[5]	Depends on VGA card design, and driver, more than CPU speed	VGA color, multiscanning[4], or high-end multiscanning[4]	DB15	The minimum resolution we recommend if your're a new video card and/or monitor
8514	1024 x 768	87 but interlaced; 70, 72, or 76 if non-interlaced	16 or 256	Depends on card design and driver, more than CPU speed	High-end multiscanning	DB15	Though introduced in 1987, this video standard hasn't taken off; comes in interlaced and non-interlaced flavors
XGA	1024 x 768	87 but interlaced	16 or 256 or 65,536		High-end multiscanning	DB15	Requires a Micro Channel computer

[1] A CGA video card can produce 16 different colors, but it can only display 4 colors on the screen at any moment.

[2] An EGA card can produce 256 colors, but it can only display 16 colors on the screen simultaneously.

[3] You'll need a software driver written for this video card and the software you want to use if you wish to fire up the 800 x600 or the 1024 x 768 resolutions.

[4] A higher vertical scan rate is better — less flicker. The original Super VGA standard was 56 refreshes per second; it's now 72. New high-quality monitors support 72 refreshes per second, but older and/or cheap monitors may not. The standard for 1024 x 768 is 70 screen refreshes per second, but some vendors provide vertical scan rates of 72 Hz or 76 Hz for a better picture.

[5] A VGA card can produce 262,144 different colors (that's 256K). The number of colors it can display on the screen is a function of resolution and video memory installed on the VGA card. With 256K of video memory the card can show 640 x 480 resolution or 800 x 600 resolution, but the card will be limited to 16 colors on the screen at any one moment. Higher resolutions and/or 256 colors require more video memory on the card.

Monitor

We're really talking about a trade-off here: you can have video with lots of processing power and comparatively little memory, or you can provide lots of memory and skimp on the processor.

Windows accelerator cards take a slightly different tack. They have an area in video memory you load with fonts. Some cards, like ATI's line of Windows accelerator cards, use proprietary fonts (the ATI CRYSTAL fonts) or standard Windows fonts. Once loaded (once the card has stored the arrangement of pixels associated with each letter, number, and symbol) these fonts can be accessed very quickly. This allows Windows to say "Put a capital letter A at position x, y in font style Z." The video card will figure out which pixels should be lighted, and the video card will do it much faster than the computer alone could.

Monitors

Inexpensive monochrome monitors, the kind that were standard on PCs through the 1980s, are capable of displaying only one color—usually white, green, or amber against a black background. Look for a nine-pin connector linking the monitor cable to the video card inside the computer. Figure 13.3 on page 160 shows a typical DB9 (9-pin) video cable socket on a monochrome video card.

Higher-priced monochrome monitors, for example VGA monochrome monitors, are available with very high resolution and 16 shades of gray. Ultra-high-resolution, monochrome monitors with proprietary video systems intended for desktop publishing and computer-aided design, usually have extra-large screens, often designed to show two facing pages, or a vertical page in true proportions.

But high-resolution color video has really taken off in the 1990's. VGA color monitors are now standard equipment on PCs, and many users are upgrading to super VGA or one of the 1024 x 768 video standards because the monitor displays a much bigger visual field. Microsoft Windows, large spreadsheet, and desktop publishing users appreciate a full-page view of their work. In addition, high-level graphics users are choosing to manipulate photos, video, and animation with 24-bit color video cards capable of displaying millions of subtle color shades.

A Short History of the Search for Better Resolution

Monochrome Monitors

The next few paragraphs discuss monochrome monitor design, history, and technical jargon. If you're not interested, skip this section. "How to Test a Monitor" starts on page 154.

When IBM introduced the PC in 1981, a monochrome text-only video card, the Monochrome Display Adapter (MDA) board and a monochrome monitor were standard. The MDA video system could produce 25 lines of text, with 80 characters per line. This is still a readable display, even in the standard green and black. IBM simultaneously introduced the CGA video card, a much coarser, grainy display that bleared a lot of eyes. We liked the color and graphics and put up with the resolution.

Improvements in monochrome video cards began almost immediately. The Hercules card, also called a Monochrome Graphics Adapter (MGA) or Monochrome Graphics Adapter with Printer Port (MGP) card, provided monochrome graphics on a simple monochrome MDA-style monitor because it allowed pixel-by-pixel (dot-by-dot), as well as character-by-character, control of the display. The Hercules company designed the board to display Lotus 1-2-3 graphics while still allowing a high-resolution text display.

The next improvement was IBM's EGA in 1985. EGA features both color and monochrome modes, with pixel-by-pixel video control. EGA color was very popular, but hardly any software was written for EGA monochrome.

These three video adapter cards—MDA, MGA and EGA (in monochrome mode)—use the standard $60 monochrome monitor with a horizontal scan rate of 18.43 MHz and a vertical scan rate of 50 Hz (50 refreshes per second).

MDA, MGA, and EGA monochrome resolution (crispness of image) is 720 x 348 pixels (MGA) or 720 x 350 pixels (MDA and EGA). For an 80-character, 25-line screen of data, that means each character is allocated an area with dimensions of 9 x 14 pixels. Spacing between lines and between characters eats up some of these pixels, so the actual character is formed out of a 7 x 9 pixel rectangle (with two more rows of pixels available for letters with tails below the line, like *p* and *q*).

Beyond MDA, MGA, and EGA, the next higher monochrome resolution is VGA monochrome, which requires both a VGA card and a higher-priced VGA monochrome monitor. VGA provides 720 x 400 pixel resolution in text mode. That adds two horizontal rows of dots per character. In graphics mode, VGA works with a 640 x 480 pixel grid, which provides significantly more pixels per screen than the 720 x 348 pixels available with an MGA (Hercules) card. The distinguishing feature of VGA monochrome monitors, though, is their gray scales. These multiple shades of gray are displayed by an analog monitor with a 15-pin video data cable connecting the monitor to the computer system unit. VGA monitors use a horizontal scan rate of 31.5 KHz—well outside the operating range of simple MDA monochrome monitors.

Computers dedicated to desktop publishing can be equipped with ultra-high-resolution monochrome monitors which allow you to view two complete pages of text side by side. Many of these sophisticated monitors require a proprietary video card and special video drivers.

Color Monitors

The next few paragraphs discuss color monitor design, history, and useful technical terms. If you don't want to read this section right now, you can go directly to "How a Color Monitor Works" on page 152, to "How a Multiscanning Monitor Works" on page 154, or "How to Test a Monitor" on page 154.

The blurry, big-pixel color monitors, first found on IBM PCs in 1981, had 200 scan lines across the screen. These RGB color monitors, driven by CGA video cards, had a resolution of 320 x 200 pixels, which ain't so hot. Higher-priced color video systems (such as EGA, VGA, XGA, and 8514) have many tiny pixels on the screen, so subtle curves seem smooth, and individual pixels are unnoticeable. CGA video cards and the RGB monitor did introduce graphics to the PC world. CGA cards allow pixel-by-pixel control of the monitor screen. The PCs original monochrome display, by contrast, could display only preformatted characters in an 80 column x 25 row grid.

In 1985, IBM introduced EGA color with more pixels per scan line and more scan lines per screen than RGB monitors used. The highest resolution color EGA mode treats the screen as a 640 x 350 pixel grid. See "Enhanced Graphics Adapter (EGA) Card" on page 165 for more information about additional EGA video modes with different characteristics and different resolutions.

IBM's 1987 VGA video standard had a maximum resolution of 640 x 480 pixels. The VGA standard has four video modes, all with a horizontal scan rate of 31.5 KHz. Two different vertical scan rates are required though, so VGA monitors must be capable of either 60 or 70 Hz (60 or 70 complete raster refreshes per second).

Video card vendors soon launched a series of extensions to the VGA standard. Super VGA had 800 x 600 pixels per screen; Extended VGA had 1024 x 768 pixels.

The general pattern is more pixels per screen and more screen refreshes per second—in other words, we keep asking for faster monitors capable of displaying more pixels per second. In the early CGA/EGA/VGA days, people were content to buy a new monitor when they upgraded to a new video standard. Each new video standard used dramatically different technology—for example, different wires in the monitor-to-video-card cable, and different signals carried on those wires.

The improvement from VGA to super VGA and extended VGA was different. VGA and super VGA monitors use the same wires and the same signals. Super VGA monitors are simply capable of processing the video card's instructions faster (refreshing the screen more often and displaying more individual pixels on each screen). Therefore, multiscanning monitors compatible with multiple video standards became attractive to buyers who didn't want to lock themselves into a particular video standard when they bought a monitor.

NEC's Multisync was the first. The original Multisync was backward compatible with MGP, CGA, and EGA video cards. But many monitor vendors have written off the old MGP, CGA, and EGA standards—their new multiscanning monitors are compatible only with VGA video cards and above.

IBM's 8514 (1987) and XGA (1990) video standards are optimized for CAD and Windows, respectively. But 8514 and XGA do not demand a qualitatively different monitor. They both run on high-end VGA-compatible multiscanning monitors.

The VGA monitor design has been durable and flexible. We expect revolutionary improvements in the next few years in the video cards that drive this VGA family of monitors, but we suspect the monitors themselves will become faster without revolutionary changes in design.

How a Monochrome Monitor Works

Inside a monitor, an electron beam is aimed toward a phosphor-coated screen. The phosphor glows whenever the electrons hit it, producing lighted images on the screen. See Figure 13.1, page 143. When the monitor is plugged into a video adapter card, it receives a signal called the *scan frequency*. The monitor must lock in on the scan signal; in other words, the electron beam must cross the screen in synchronization with the scan signal.

The electron beam starts at the top left of the screen. It scans across the screen from left to right, exciting some dots of phosphor and passing by others. When the beam reaches the right side of the screen, it quickly returns to the left and scans another line directly below the first one. An ordinary monochrome monitor has 350 of these scan lines per screen.

When the electron beam reaches the bottom right of the screen, it leaps up to the top left corner and proceeds to trace the 350 scan lines from the top again. This set of 350 scan lines—which is often visible when the brightness control is turned up too high—is called the *raster pattern* (or *raster*).

An ordinary monochrome monitor refreshes the screen (rescans the complete raster) 50 times a second. The vertical scan rate is, therefore, 50 Hz. By comparison, the horizontal scan rate is 18,432 times per second (18.432 KHz). As the electron beam flies across the screen (18,432 times per second) it passes 720 pixels (dots of phosphor) per line. The video adapter card, located in the computer system unit, provides explicit directions to the electron gun in the monitor. As the electron beam scans across the screen, the video card calls for a burst of electrons here to excite this pixel or a burst of electrons there to excite that pixel.

How a Color Monitor Works

A color monitor creates color display by combining the three primary colors of light: red, green, and blue. Black is the absence of any color. Yellow is created by combining green light and blue light. White is created by combining all three light sources.

We discuss four types of color monitors in this section. An RGB monitor is the cheapest and provides the lowest picture quality. EGA, VGA, and multiscanning monitors are progressively more expensive, but each price jump provides a sharper picture (better resolution) and more colors. Each monitor must be paired with an appropriate video display adapter card (located in the computer system unit). The rest of this introduction discusses the technical details of these four types of monitors. If you aren't interested in these details right now, skip ahead to "How to Test the Color Monitor," then refer back to this introduction as necessary for specific facts about your monitor.

The cheapest color monitor, called an RGB monitor, has low resolution and the image is not very crisp. RGB color monitors have relatively few pixels. These pixels are also relatively large, and each contains a trio of phosphor dots: one red, one blue, and one green. There are three separate electron beams, each one dedicated to stimulating a single color of phosphor. As we mentioned earlier,

Monitor

other colors are made by mixing red, green, and blue light in the appropriate proportions. Red is displayed by exciting only the red phosphor portion of the pixel. Purple (or magenta) is produced when both blue and red dots are glowing. When all three phosphor dots in a pixel are excited, the three colors of light combine to show white on the screen.

To display a simple letter, for instance a capital *T*, the electron beam excites one horizontal row and one vertical column of pixels. Resolution (crispness of image) is not very good on an RGB color monitor; if you look closely you can see the individual pixels.

The three primary colors of light (red, green, blue) are controlled by simple TTL (on/off) signals; therefore, subtle color shadings are not available. RGB monitors can produce 16 colors. The monitor has a 9-pin connector on the cable running from the monitor to the video card, and it is compatible with the CGA video card.

EGA monitors also have a 9-pin cable carrying data from the video card to the monitor, but they must be paired with an EGA video card to work at all. EGA monitors are capable of substantially better resolution than RGB monitors, and they also have two intensity (brightness) signal levels available for each primary-color light source. These intensity variables allow more color selections; EGA monitors can produce 64 colors.

You can readily distinguish VGA monitors from CGA and EGA monitors because VGA monitors have a 15-pin video data cable. These monitors use an analog signal, which can be adjusted anywhere in a voltage range. If CGA and EGA monitors use simple on/off signals (like a light switch), analog monitors use a continuously variable signal (like a dimmer switch). This analog signal allows precise brightness control at each of the three primary-color light sources, yielding many delicate color shadings. A VGA monitor is capable of displaying millions of colors, but few video cards can push the monitor that far.

VGA, CGA, and EGA monitors are not interchangeable. A VGA monitor will not even plug into a CGA or EGA card, much less work properly with it. An EGA card attached to a CGA monitor produces snow. Even VGA monitors vary. Some can display only original VGA with 640 x 480 pixel resolution and a vertical scan rate of 60 or 70 Hz. Other VGA monitors can also display 800 x 600 pixel super VGA and/or 1024 x 768 pixel Extended VGA, which have a lot more pixels per screen and require 70, 72, or 76 Hz vertical scan rates. You can imagine how frustrated buyers get when rapid video changes make their expensive monitors obsolete. The multiscanning monitor (see the next page) overcomes this problem because it can function with multiple video standards.

Monitor

How a Multiscanning/Multisynch Monitor Works

Multiscanning monitors can lock onto multiple vertical and horizontal scanning frequencies, so a single multiscanning monitor is compatible with many different video cards.

Multiscanning monitors are continuously improving. The original version, the NEC MultiSync, was compatible with monochrome, CGA, EGA, and PGA (IBM Professional Graphic Adapter, a video standard that never caught on). Some newer multiscanning monitors can operate with all the standards above, plus VGA and super VGA (800 x 600) and Extended VGA (1024 x 768), which means they are also compatible with 8514 cards and TIGA cards. Most can deal with either 60 or 70 Hz vertical frequency (VGA family). Some of them can handle 50 Hz, so they're compatible with the IBM PC's original monochrome display adapters and EGA monochrome too. The best ones can refresh a high-resolution 1024 x 768 display at 72 Hz (72 times per second).

Most multiscanning monitors are shipped with both 9-pin and 15-pin cables, so you can easily hook them to any standard video card.

How to Test a Monitor

If your monitor has no video, it's best to start with a quick switch and cable check. Are both the computer and the monitor plugged in and turned on? Monitors develop a big electrostatic field in the first couple of seconds after they are turned on, so try this test: power off the monitor, then hold the back of your hand to the monitor screen and power it back on. The hair on the back of your hand will stand up as the electrostatic field develops. Check the video data cable from the video card to the monitor. It must be plugged in tight and screwed down at the video card end.

The next things to check are the brightness and contrast controls on the monitor. Many, but not all, monochrome monitors show a raster pattern when they are powered on and the brightness knob is turned all the way up—whether the monitor is connected to a computer or not. Don't adjust these controls and then accidentally leave them in the dim position. We've all done this. It can be very frustrating to finally fix a video problem without realizing you have fixed it because the monitor brightness is adjusted so low that no characters are visible. In general, full-stop clockwise is the brightest position.

No video can be caused by the video card, the monitor, or a multitude of problems in the computer system unit. The troubleshooting charts in Section 3 provide a plan to help you identify the culprit. Before jumping into the troubleshooting charts, though, do yourself a favor and try a couple of quick swaps if you have duplicate monitors or comparably equipped computers available. Try attaching the suspect monitor to a known-good computer. If the monitor works on a comparable computer (one with the same video adapter card), then test the suspect computer and the video card. For testing ideas, check the section of this chapter dedicated to your particular video card, as well as the troubleshooting charts in Section 3.

If you have snow (a fuzzy, random-dot effect) on your monitor, the most likely problem is an incompatible video card. The card is sending signals, but signals from a CGA card with a 15.75 KHz scan rate are gibberish to an MDA monitor with a scan rate of 18.43 KHz. Make sure that you've hooked up your monitor to a compatible card.

If your computer uses an 8088 or 8086 CPU chip (if it's an XT clone), and you have a flashing cursor and no other video at all, check the dip switch settings on the mainboard. Dip switches control the video address the mainboard is trying to use. The monitor is usually smart enough to put a cursor on the screen—even without any direction from the computer—but incorrect dip switch settings send the data to the wrong place in video memory (for instance to the nonexistent color video adapter). As a result, the actual video card gets absolutely no information from the computer and puts absolutely nothing, besides the cursor, on the video display screen. 286, 386, and 486 computers also need to have the video type set correctly in their CMOS setup memory chip, but these machines are smart enough to switch to the monitor's display mode long enough to display an initial error message, such as "Incorrect setup. Wrong video adapter."

If your problem is one or two incorrect characters in an otherwise good screen, the video memory located on the video card is at fault. Replace the card. If you feel like double-checking before buying a new video card, use QA Plus or CheckIt diagnostic software to test the video RAM (video memory).

Sometimes the screen will roll upward or downward. This is caused by an incorrect vertical sync adjustment. Most monochrome monitors have an external vertical sync knob. When you adjust it, first change the misadjustment to a slow upward roll, then try to stop the roll completely. If you go too far and the screen starts to roll downward, try to slow and then stop the downward roll.

Horizontal misalignment is usually slight, but occasionally it is so severe that the screen message appears to have rolled entirely around so that it is displayed as a mirror image of itself. If your computer has an external horizontal sync knob, use this knob to correct the problem.

Monitors are very similar to television sets. If you have a horizontal or vertical sync problem that seems too intimidating, or if the bottom line of letters is much larger than the top line (a sign of poor linearity adjustment), a good TV repair shop should be able to correct the problem. Monochrome monitors tend to be inexpensive, though, so more than an hour of repair work is not likely to be cost effective.

Color monitors are also susceptible to convergence problems. Each pixel is really a trio of phosphor dots. It is important to have these dots bunched closely together, or the display will be fuzzy, with one or more colors bleeding off the edges of white text. Television shops are able to adjust the convergence by slightly altering the angle of the three electron beams to bunch the trio of dots in each pixel closer together.

How to Remove and Install a Monitor

Turn off the monitor and the computer. Unscrew the two tiny screws holding the monitor data cable to the video card. Disconnect the video cable and power cables, then replace the malfunctioning monitor with an equivalent good one.

If you are replacing both the monitor and the video card, refer to the section that covers your particular video card for card installation hints. Remember, both the mainboard and the video card dip switches and/or jumpers may need to be reset if you are changing the video display type from monochrome to color, or even from MDA monochrome to EGA or VGA monochrome. Check your video card manual and your mainboard/computer owner's manual for details.

Monochrome Text-Only Video Adapter Card

This text-only monochrome card is also known as a Monotext Card, a Monochrome Expansion Card, and a Monochrome Display Adapter (MDA) card. We are talking about the original IBM PC display adapter here, NOT the MGA, MGP, or Hercules Card which soon replaced the Monochrome Text-only Video adapter as the standard video board. If you have an original IBM PC or XT (or a very early clone) and you computer was built in the early 1980's with monochrome video, you probably have an MDA card and should be here. The rest of you should check "Monochrome Graphics Video Adapter (MGA or MGP) Card" on page 159 for more information.

The monochrome text-only video adapter card is the least versatile and the least expensive video option available for PCs and clones. It is capable only of displaying 256 preformed characters—called the IBM PC character set—in standard positions on the screen. The card cannot draw free-form graphics images on the screen because it is not capable of pixel-by-pixel (dot-by-dot) control of the monitor screen. It is capable of driving only a monochrome monitor. Hooking it to an RGB color monitor will produce only snow on the screen, and may possibly damage either the monitor or the card.

The card treats the monitor screen as 80 columns by 25 rows of characters. Each of these positions may contain one of the preformed characters, nothing else. This text-only card is also capable of a 40-character-wide by 25-row format. Programmers rarely used this alternative format, but you'll occasionally see it in old programs and games.

Where to Find a Monochrome Text-Only Video Adapter Card

To locate the card, you must first remove the cover from the computer system unit, as described in Chapter 1 and in "System Unit Case and Cover" in Chapter 12. The video expansion card is often but not always on the far left, as far away from the disk drives and the power supply as possible. The monitor is attached to the video adapter card, so look on the back of the system unit to find the 9-pin female connector that your monitor plugs into. That 9-pin connector, called a DB9, is on the video card. If you're having trouble, refer to Figure 13.3 on page 160 which shows a DB9 female connector.

How a Monochrome Text-Only Video Adapter Card Works

The video card contains enough memory to store information for each character position on the screen. The monitor is continuously placing data from the video memory on the screen. A monochrome monitor will read the video memory and write it on the screen approximately 50 times per second.

When a program needs to write characters to the video screen, it may put data directly into video memory or it may ask the ROM to write the characters on the screen and rely on the ROM to put the necessary data in video memory. In either case, the video memory holds a record of the character (including the null character for blanks) to be displayed at each position on the video screen.

How to Test a Monochrome Text-Only Video Adapter Card

Many diagnostic disks provide video troubleshooting help. CheckIt and QA Plus, for example, include video test programs. These disks work if you have video on your screen, but the video is not quite right.

If you have no video at all, check for an incorrect match between the monitor and the video card. Don't use monotext cards with color monitors. If your computer uses an 8088 or 8086 CPU chip (if it's an XT clone), check for proper switch settings on the mainboard. 286, 386, and 486 machines also need to have the video type set correctly in their CMOS setup memory chip, but these machines are able to display an initial error message, such as "Incorrect setup. Wrong video adapter." See "How to Test a Monitor" on page 154 and/or the troubleshooting charts in Section 3 for additional troubleshooting hints if you have no video.

Customers sometimes complain that characters change on their video screen without an operator command. A Greek character, or a face, or a punctuation mark suddenly appears on the monitor in the midst of text, replacing the original letter of the alphabet. If the text is reloaded from the disk, it's fine. So what happened? The video memory on the video adapter card malfunctioned and the information stored on the video card changed. The video card—not the monitor—is at fault in this case. The monitor correctly displays each pixel as instructed; it just got incorrect instructions from the video card. Monochrome cards are cheap, so you could decide to slap a new one in, but maybe it's time to upgrade your video card and monitor. VGA and super VGA video cards and monitors are getting cheaper—do yourself a favor and trade up.

How to Remove and Install a Monochrome Text-Only Video Adapter Card

If you have to replace your monotext card, upgrade to an MGP (Monochrome Graphics Printer) card, at least. The graphics features on this card allow you to run much more software, and your monochrome monitor will work fine with it.

To remove the monotext card, first turn off the computer and monitor. Disconnect the data cable that runs from the video card to the monitor at the video card end. You will probably have to remove the two small screws that hold the cable connector tight. Remove the system unit cover, as described in Chapter 12.

The card itself is secured to the back wall of the system unit chassis with a single screw. Remove this screw, as shown in Figure 11.1 on page 102. Save the screw. Figures 11.2 and 11.3 (on pages 102-103) show you how to remove the card. The card should be lifted straight up, which shouldn't require much force.

Installation is the reverse of removal. Because MDA video cards are 8-bit cards, any bus connector in any of the clones is appropriate. Don't worry about putting the card in a long versus a short slot in your 286, 386, or 486 computer. If it will physically fit into either slot, it will work. Just line the slot connector (card edge connector) on the card up with the slot on the mainboard carefully and press down firmly. When the card is in place, the screw hole on the card will line up with the screw hole in the back of the chassis. Reinstall the screw and test the machine.

If you are installing a different type of video card (replacing the monotext card with a VGA or a color card, for example), be sure to set any switches or jumpers on the mainboard to reflect the new video adapter. See your mainboard manual and the section of this chapter dedicated to your new video card for more details. You don't need to change any switches if you are installing an MGP card.

Monochrome Graphics Video Adapter (MGA or MGP) Card

The MGA card is also known as a Hercules card, a Hercules Compatible Video Adapter, a Herc card, a Monographics board, and an MGP Card. An MGP video card is an MGA card plus a printer port. The MGA (or MGP) card is not the same as monochrome text-only video. See "Monochrome Text-Only Video Adapter Card" on page 156 for more information about that card.

The Hercules Corporation was the first to market the MGA card. It has the best aspects of both monotext and color video adapters: well-defined, crisp characters as well as pixel-by-pixel control of the monitor display. This feature was previously available only with color graphics adapters and an expensive color monitor.

MGP Card

Figure 13.3

A typical MGP card (Monochrome Graphics with Printer Port). The small connector is a DB9 (9-pin) video connector for the monitor cable. The large connector is a DB25 (25-pin) connector for a parallel printer cable. This happens to be a monochrome card, but many CGA color video cards look like this (compare Figure 13.4). Old monochrome cards and color cards from the early 1980's were longer (they ran the full length of the computer chassis, and every square inch was packed with chips). Each year computer manufacturers are able to compress more sophisticated functions into fewer and smaller chips. Compare the tiny VGA card in Figure 13.6. It's far more sophisticated than this monochrome card manufactured in 1989, but substantially smaller.

The Hercules card was a significant advance: so significant that many other companies copied it. There are now many brands of Hercules-compatible video adapters, and Hercules or Hercules-compatible video boards are the most popular form of monochrome. Most new MGA boards include a parallel port, and are thus called MGP boards.

Where to Find an MGA or MGP Card

To locate the MGP card, first remove the cover from the computer system unit, as described in Chapter 12. The video expansion card is often, but not always, on the far left, as far away from the disk drives and the power supply as possible. The monitor is attached to the video adapter card, so look on the back of the system unit to find the 9-pin female connector that your monitor plugs into. That 9-pin connector, called a DB9, is on the video card shown in Figure 13.3.

How the MGA or MGP Card Works

These MGA/MGP cards provide two video modes: text and graphics. In text mode the cards display clear, crisp, predrawn characters. This mode uses an 80 character x 25 character grid on the display screen. There is sufficient video memory on the MGA board to store a character for each of the 80 positions per line and for all 25 lines on the screen. The monitor reads data from the video memory and writes it to the screen 50 times per second.

When a program needs to write characters to the video screen in text mode, it can put data directly into video memory or it can ask the ROM to write the characters on the screen and rely on the ROM to put the necessary data in video memory. In either case, the video memory holds a record of the character—including the null character for blanks—to be displayed at each position on the screen.

The MGA or MGP card has surplus memory when operating in text mode. It has enough memory to hold four screens full of characters, so the card stores three additional pages (succeeding screens of data). This technique provides extremely quick page-down capability, since the information for succeeding pages is already in memory and ready to be displayed instantly. Some monochrome software uses this feature, but quick screen changes are not generally a high priority for monochrome applications.

In graphics mode, the MGA or MGP card controls each dot of light (each pixel) on the display screen individually. The screen is divided into 720 pixels horizontally and 348 pixels vertically. 720 horizontal pixels times 348 equals a quarter of a million individual dots on the screen, so it takes 64K (64,000 8-bit bytes of memory) to store a screen full of MGP resolution graphics.

Compare this to the CGA. CGA boards can show only half that resolution, having 320 pixels x 200 pixels. But CGA video cards store color information for each individual pixel in the video card's memory, and color uses up more space than monochrome information.

Characters can be displayed when the MGA or MGP card is in the graphics mode, but they are individually drawn onto the screen pixel by pixel. Pictures are also drawn pixel by pixel.

How to Test an MGA or MGP Card

Many diagnostic disks provide video troubleshooting help. QA Plus and CheckIt, for example, contain video test programs.

If you have no video at all, check for an incorrect match between the monitor and the video card. Don't attach MGA and MGP cards to color monitors. Mismatches between the video card and the monitor usually cause snow on the monitor screen.

If you have an XT clone computer, check the dip switch settings on the mainboard. Dip switches control the video address that the mainboard is trying to use. Incorrect dip switch settings usually produce a flashing cursor, with no additional video display. 286, 386, and 486 machines also need to have the video type set correctly in their CMOS setup memory chip, but these machines are able to display an initial error message, such as "Incorrect setup. Wrong video adapter." See "How to Test a Monitor" on page 154 and the troubleshooting charts in Section 3 for additional troubleshooting hints.

If you have one or two incorrect characters in an otherwise good screen, the video memory located on the video card is at fault. Replace the card. If you want, you can use the QA Plus or CheckIt diagnostic programs to test the video RAM before you buy a new card.

Figure 13.4
CGA card with printer port. Compare to Figure 13.3. Photo courtesy of Hercules Computer Technology, Inc.

How to Remove and Install an MGA or MGP Card

Before you remove the MGA or MGP card, turn off the computer and monitor. Disconnect the data cable from the video card to the monitor at the video card end. You will probably have to remove two small screws that hold the cable connector tight to the card. Remove the system unit cover, as described in Chapter 12.

The card itself is secured to the back wall of the system unit chassis with a single screw. Remove that screw as shown in Figure 11.1 on page 102. Save the screw. See Figures 11.2 and 11.3 (pages 102-103) for an illustration of card removal. Lift the card straight up; it shouldn't require extreme force.

Installation is the reverse of removal. Because MGA/MGP video cards are 8-bit cards, any bus connector in any of the clones is appropriate. Don't worry about putting the card in a long versus a short slot in your 286 or 386 machine. If it will physically fit into the slot, it will work. High-resolution (VGA or better) 16-bit cards must be installed in a long slot. Carefully line up the card edge connector with the slot on the mainboard, then press down firmly. When the card is in place, the screw hole on the card will line up with the screw hole in the back of the chassis. Reinstall the screw and test the machine.

If you are installing a different type of video card—if you're replacing your old MGA or MGP card with a VGA or a color card, for example—be sure to set any switches and/or jumpers on the mainboard to reflect the new video adapter. See your mainboard manual for more details.

Color Graphics Video Adapter (CGA) Card

A Color Graphics Video adapter drives an RGB monitor (named for the red, green, and blue glowing phosphors painted on the inside surface of the monitor's picture tube).

The CGA card was the first IBM PC video card capable of two new features: 16-color display and the pixel-by-pixel screen control necessary to display graphics. CGA adapters treat the screen as a grid that is 200 pixels tall and 320 pixels wide. When working with 320 x 200 pixels, the video card is able to display 4 of the 16 possible colors on the screen at any one time. Since it has relatively few pixels—and these pixels are quite large—a CGA card has much poorer resolution than a monochrome card. Nevertheless, color display and the potential to draw pictures or graphs dot by dot on the screen make the CGA board a popular item.

Color cards also offer a special high-resolution mode that provides two colors (for example, black and white) on the screen at a time. The two-color mode uses a 640 x 200 pixel grid. Even this high-resolution mode is much coarser than the 720 x 348 pixel resolution available with a monochrome MGP board.

Each pixel of a CGA-compatible color monitor is really a trio of phosphor dots. When excited by an electron beam, these dots glow red, green, or blue. Inside the monitor, three separate electron beams scan across the CRT screen. Each beam is responsible for exciting a single color of phosphor in each pixel. See "How a Color Monitor Works" on page 152 for more information.

The color monitor is a servant of the video adapter; it turns a pixel on or passes over it and leaves it blank at the explicit pixel-by-pixel direction of the CGA card. The CGA card provides an on/off signal to each of the three electron guns for each of the 64,000 pixels (320 x 200 pixels) on a screen.

There are many other video adapter cards capable of a color display, for example EGA, VGA, XGA, and 8514 video cards. These cards are quite different from the budget-priced Color Graphics Video Adapter board. If you have EGA, VGA, XGA, 8514, or a TIGA card, see the section later in this chapter that describes your board.

Where to Find a CGA Card

To locate the CGA card, you must first remove the cover from the computer system unit, as we described in Chapter 1 and in Chapter 12. The video expansion card is often, but not always, on the far left, as far away from the disk drives and the power supply as possible. The monitor is attached to the video adapter card, so look on the back of the system unit to find the 9-pin female connector that your monitor data cable plugs into. That 9-pin connector, called a DB9, is on the video card. See Figure 13.3 on page 160 for a close-up view of the DB9 on an MGP card, which looks identical to the DB9 on a CGA card.

How a CGA Card Works

A CGA board contains enough memory (16K) to store information for each pixel on the color monitor screen. All video data, whether it's text or graphics, is stored in the video memory, pixel by pixel. The monitor reads the video memory 60 times per second and places its contents on the screen. To display a simple letter, for instance a capital *T*, the electron beam in the monitor excites one horizontal row of pixels and one vertical column of pixels.

A program can display text either by creating the text font out of individual pixels or by asking the BIOS ROM to display text using its standard font. In the first case, the text is stored in the video memory as a collection of dots, not as a complete character.

To display a graphic (a picture composed of many little dots of color) the individual pixels are excited. Four colors can be used on the screen at any one time. There are always two palettes of four colors available, but the program can use only one of these palettes on the screen at a time (though the active palette can easily be switched). Three of the four colors in a given palette are predetermined by the video adapter circuitry. Any of the 16 basic colors can be chosen as the fourth color in either palette.

How to Test a CGA Card

Many diagnostic disks provide video troubleshooting help. CheckIt, QA Plus, and IBM Diagnostics provide test programs to demonstrate all 16 colors and both palettes. These disks will only work, however, if you have readable video.

If the problem is that you have no video at all, check for an incorrect match between the monitor and the video card. Don't use CGA cards with monochrome monitors. That mismatch causes snow on the monitor, since the video data transmitted for a line of color text is gibberish to a monochrome monitor.

If you have an XT clone, check for proper dip switch settings on the mainboard. 286, 386, and 486 machines need to have the video type set correctly in their CMOS setup memory chip, but these machines are able to display an initial error message, such as "Incorrect setup. Wrong video adapter."

See "How a Color Monitor Works" on page 152 and the troubleshooting charts in Section 3 for additional troubleshooting hints if you have no video.

If you have one or two incorrect characters in an otherwise good screen, the video memory located on the video card is at fault. Replace the card. You can use QAPlus or CheckIt diagnostic software to test the video memory before you get a new card. But CGA color cards are cheap, so it may be more cost effective to just replace the card.

How to Remove and Install a CGA Card

Before you remove the CGA card, you must turn off the computer and the monitor. Disconnect the data cable from the video card to the monitor at the video card end. You will probably have to remove two small screws that are installed to hold the cable connector tight to the card. Remove the system unit cover, as described in Chapter 12.

The card itself is secured to the back wall of the system unit chassis with a single screw. Remove that screw as shown in Figure 11.1 on page 102. Save the screw. Remove the card, as shown in Figures 11.2 and 11.3 (on pages 102-103). Lift the card straight up; it shouldn't require great force.

Installation is the reverse of removal. CGA video cards are 8-bit cards, so any bus connector in any of the clones is appropriate. Don't worry about putting the card in a long versus a short slot in your 286 or 386 machine. If it will physically fit into the slot, it will work. Carefully line up the card edge connector with the slot on the mainboard, then press down firmly. When the card is in place, the screw hole on the card will line up with the screw hole in the back of the chassis. Reinstall the screw and test the machine.

If you are installing a different type of video card—replacing the original CGA card with an EGA or a VGA card, for example—be sure to set any switches and/or jumpers on the mainboard to reflect the new video adapter. See your mainboard manual and the section of this chapter that covers your new video card for more details.

Enhanced Graphics Adapter (EGA) Card

Figure 13.5 on the next page shows an EGA card. This card provides medium- and high-resolution color or monochrome video display. It operates in either text mode (for word processing) or graphics mode (where charts and pictures can be drawn on the screen dot by dot). It is capable of producing 256 different colors when teamed with an EGA monitor, but the EGA card can display only 16 of those colors on the screen simultaneously. A data cable connects an EGA monitor to the EGA card, using a 9-pin (DB9) socket on the card.

Where to Find an EGA Card

To locate the EGA card, first remove the cover from the computer system unit, described in Chapter 12. The video expansion card is often—but not always—on the far left, as far away from the disk drives and the power supply as possible. The monitor is attached to the video adapter card, so look on the back of the system unit to find the 9-pin female connector that your monitor data cable plugs into. The 9-pin connector, called a DB9, is on the video card. See Figure 13.3 on page 160 for a close-up view of the DB9 female connector on an MGP video card.

Figure 13.5
EGA card. Photo courtesy of Swan Technologies.

EGA adapters and EGA monitors use DB9 connectors. Monochrome (MDA, MGA, and MGP) video cards and color (CGA) video cards also are equipped with a DB9 connector. Therefore, it is not easy to tell any of these video cards apart by looking at the outside of the computer. If you have doubts about your video card's identity, it's best to take off the system unit cover and look at the video card. Most EGA boards have dip switches to set the various possible EGA video modes. In addition, most EGA board manufacturers provide a prominent decal or other label on the EGA card.

How an EGA Card Works

An EGA video card is capable of multiple video modes. One mode, EGA monochrome, treats the screen as a 720 x 350 pixel grid. The grid has 720 pixels per horizontal line, and 350 lines per screen. In this monochrome mode, the EGA card drives a simple monochrome monitor to replicate the features of a Hercules graphics monochrome card. Many color modes are possible, ranging from 320 x 200 pixels (emulating a CGA video adapter) to 640 x 350 pixel screens with 16 different colors onscreen simultaneously. Extended EGA cards have two new video modes, both with 16-

color VGA-quality resolution. Most color modes will work either with an EGA color monitor or with a multiscanning monitor, but Extended EGA requires a multiscanning monitor.

Each pixel of an EGA-compatible color monitor is really a trio of phosphor dots. When excited by an electron beam, these dots glow red, green, or blue. Inside the monitor, three separate electron beams scan across the CRT screen. Each beam is responsible for exciting a single color of phosphor in each pixel. See "How a Color Monitor Works," page 152, for more information about monitor hardware.

The monitor is a servant of the video adapter; it turns a pixel on or passes over it and leaves it blank at the explicit pixel-by-pixel direction of the EGA card. EGA cards provide two on/off signals to each of the three electron guns. One signal is high intensity (bright) and one is low intensity. There are 256 different possible combinations of these six signals, thus 256 possible colors. At 640 x 350 resolution, the screen contains over 200,000 pixels. All this video information must be stored somewhere, so EGA cards have 256K of video memory right on the card. (Original IBM EGA cards had only 64K, but performance was limited, so 256K soon became the standard.)

The computer sends data to the video card. When the card is in text mode, the computer sends alphanumeric characters which are stored in video memory. The video card character generator changes each text character into a pattern of pixels and sends that data to the monitor pixel by pixel.

In graphics mode, the computer sends pixel-by-pixel instructions directly to the video card memory. The card then transmits that information to the monitor, which displays and redisplays the contents of video memory. The monitor refreshes the screen (re-energizes the pixels) 60 times per second; therefore, any change in video memory seems to appear on the screen instantly.

How to Test an EGA Card

Whenever you install a new EGA card or have doubts about an old one, you should test all the separate EGA modes—both monochrome and color. Luckily, EGA cards are usually sold with diagnostic software to make this testing easy.

But suppose you have no video display at all, or the screen is displaying snow or other gibberish. There are many possible causes for this type of problem. See "How to Test a Monitor," page 154. Usually you will find the problem there. If not, here are some other ideas.

EGA cards have many modes, with the initial bootup mode usually controlled by dip switches or jumpers. Make sure that the mainboard setting of these switches or jumpers matches the EGA card setting. Remember many 286, 386, and 486 computers have a jumper on the mainboard for color versus monochrome video, as well as setup information in the CMOS chip. Also make sure that the EGA card is set to work with the monitor you're using. Check your EGA card and computer mainboard manuals for the correct switch settings.

If you have one or two incorrect characters in an otherwise good screen, the video memory located on the video card is at fault. Replace the card. If you want, you can use QA Plus or CheckIt diagnostic software to test the video memory before you replace the card. See the troubleshooting chart in Section 3 for additional help.

How to Remove and Install an EGA Card

Before you remove the EGA card, turn off the computer and the monitor. Disconnect the data cable from the video card to the monitor at the video card end. You will probably have to remove two small screws used to hold the cable connector tight to the card. Remove the system unit cover, as described in Chapter 12.

The card itself is secured to the back wall of the system unit chassis with a single screw. Remove that screw as shown in Figure 11.1 on page 102 and save the screw. See Figures 11.2 and 11.3 (on pages 102-103) for an illustration of card removal. Lift the card straight up; it shouldn't require great force.

Before you install an EGA card, read the manual and set the dip switches as necessary. The mainboard dip switches may also need to be reset if you are changing from monochrome or from RGB color video to EGA.

Installation is the reverse of removal. Because EGA video cards are 8-bit cards, any bus connector in any of the clones is appropriate. Don't worry about putting the card in a long versus a short slot in your 286 or 386 computer. If it will physically fit into the slot, it will work. Just line the slot connector on the card up carefully with the slot on the mainboard and press down firmly. When the card is in place, the screw hole on the card will line up with the screw hole in the back of the chassis. Reinstall the screw and test the machine.

EGA Card

If you are installing a different type of video card—if you're replacing the original CGA card with an EGA or a VGA card, for example—be sure to set any switches or jumpers on the mainboard to reflect the new video adapter. See your mainboard manual for further instructions.

There are many video adapter cards capable of driving a color monitor, but don't confuse these cards with the EGA card. VGA, XGA, 8514, and TIGA cards are more expensive and have substantially higher resolution. CGA cards are cheaper and paint coarser pictures on the monitor. We have a separate section in this chapter for each of these video card standards.

Figure 13.6
VGA card. Notice how compact the VGA chip set has become. Many computer manufacturers put the VGA video controller right on the mainboard rather than using a separate video card. Photo by Robert McLaughlin.

Video Graphics Array (VGA) Card— Includes Super VGA and Extended VGA

Figure 13.6 shows a VGA card. This card produces a high-resolution, multi-color video display. Screen images are crisp, and as many as 256 different colors can be displayed on the screen at once. The VGA card uses analog (variable voltage) rather than TTL (simple on/off) signals; therefore, VGA-compatible monitors must also be analog. VGA cards and monitors use a 15-pin DB15 video cable connector instead of the standard 9-pin DB9 you expect on monochrome, CGA, or EGA monitors.

How a VGA Card Works

When IBM introduced VGA on its 1987 crop of PS/2 computers, VGA was a premium product—both original-IBM VGA and copy-cat VGA cards were pricey. By the mid 1990's VGA prices have dropped dramatically. VGA is now the "standard video" on most mail order PCs and most VGA cards now support 640 x 480 (the original IBM VGA resolution) plus 800 x 600 pixel (super VGA) and 1024 x 768 pixel resolution (Extended VGA).

If you are willing to limit yourself to 640 x 480 pixel VGA resolution, an inexpensive single-frequency VGA monitor will do. But you'll need a multiscanning monitor to run the higher VGA resolutions. Keep this in mind when swapping monitors to test a suspect computer and/or monitor.

Most software has 640 x 480 pixel VGA support built in—the software knows how to tell a VGA card using 640 x 480 pixel resolution what to put on the monitor screen. If you want to use the higher VGA resolutions, though, you'll need a software driver (a piece of software that tells your video card how to reinterpret the video instructions your software is sending to the card). Most video cards come with AutoCAD, Windows, Lotus 1-2-3, and WordPerfect drivers. Some card manufacturers provide many other drivers too—ask before you buy if you want to run a particular piece of software at high resolution on your hot new video card. Generic VGA drivers are also available from the manufacturer of your favorite software program, though these generic drivers are sometimes appreciably slower than drivers customized to a particular VGA card.

A well-written video card driver will increase the response speed of your monitor. Screens will scroll quicker, graphics will redraw faster, and you won't go gray watching the Windows hourglass. The popular magazines regularly bench test video cards and drivers. Since the magazines normally pan slow cards, a video card maker saddled with slow drivers will quickly rewrite their drivers to improve their card's performance. Be sure to install these new drivers when your video card maker issues them. You'll have to ask for the latest driver; video card owners are not automatically notified of updates.

Each pixel of a VGA-compatible color monitor is really a trio of phosphor dots. When excited by an electron beam, each dot glows red, green or blue. Inside the monitor, three separate electron beams scan across the CRT screen. Each beam is responsible for exciting a single color of phosphor in each pixel. See "How a Color Monitor Works" on page 152 if you want to know more about monitor hardware.

Since the monitor is a servant of the video adapter, it turns a pixel on or passes over it and leaves it blank at the explicit pixel-by-pixel direction of the video adapter card. The VGA card provides an analog signal to each of the three electron guns for each of the 307,200 (640 x 480) pixels, 480,000 (800 x 600) pixels, or 786,432 (1024 x 768) pixels on the screen.

Ordinary VGA cards can produce 262,144 (256K) different colors. But the video card doesn't have enough memory to store 262,144 different colors, so the card is run in 16-color mode (16 different colors displayed simultaneously) or in 256-color mode (256 different colors displayed at the same time). Even in 16-color mode your VGA card gives you a lot of color choices. You are allowed a maximum of 16 different colors, but these 16 colors can be chosen from the full palette of 262,144 colors that the VGA card knows how to create. Think of software programs you have installed recently, the ones with a choice of subtle color schemes. When you choose the "Desert Mist" or "Presidential Pomp" color scheme you're choosing one particular 16-color palette or another from the full 262,144 colors available.

High resolutions use up lots of video memory—remember the specifications for each pixel are stored in the VGA card's memory, and these high resolutions have lots of pixels. Color uses up video memory too. Sixteen-color modes require half as much memory as 256-color modes. If your VGA card has only 256K of memory, you're going to be stuck with 640 x 480 or 800 x 600 resolution and only 16 colors. 512K of video memory allows the highest resolution or 256 colors, but not both. 1 Mb of memory on the video card gives you both. To head off a common confusion, we're talking about video memory here (memory chips on the video card), not system memory (memory chips on the mainboard or on a memory expansion card).

Let's assume your VGA card has enough video memory to store instructions for the 307,200 or 480,000 or 786,432 pixels displayed on your monitor. It's time to redraw the monitor screen. How can the computer move that much information into the card fast enough to satisfy you?

Ordinary frame-buffer video cards don't give the computer's CPU any help. A 16-bit VGA card allows the CPU to shovel in more bits per microsecond than an 8-bit card, but these VGA cards sit passively, so video response is primarily a function of CPU speed. In addition, the CPU must figure out how each pixel should be displayed—which takes a lot of CPU time that could be better spent on other tasks.

By comparison, accelerator cards and coprocessor cards take over routine video tasks from the CPU. These VGA cards cost more, but they have the brains to recalculate what pixels should be lit as text or graphics scroll up the screen, to draw a shape on the screen by themselves, or to fill a shape with color. And they are much faster than the CPU. If you are routinely redrawing the whole screen (using Windows, scrolling WYSIWYG text, using draw and paint programs) you will be surprised how much faster an accelerated or coprocessed VGA card responds.

Where to Find a VGA Card

To locate the VGA card, you must first remove the cover from the computer system unit, as described in Chapter 12. The video expansion card is often—but not always—on the far left, as far away from the disk drives and the power supply as possible. Many computer manufacturers put video circuitry on the mainboard, so you may not have a separate video card. The monitor is attached to the video adapter card, so look on the back of the system unit to find the 15-pin female connector that your monitor data cable plugs into. The 15-pin connector, called a DB15, is the video port on the video card or on the mainboard.

How to Test a VGA Card

Many VGA cards come packaged with diagnostic software. This software is helpful if the video is working, but not 100 percent correctly. QA Plus and CheckIt will also test a mostly-working VGA card for subtle malfunctions.

When the computer has no video, first check the switches and cables. Make sure that the computer and monitor are both plugged in and turned on. Check the video data cable from the VGA card to the monitor. It must be plugged in tight and screwed down at the video card end. You should also check the brightness and contrast controls on the monitor, but don't adjust these controls and then accidentally leave them in the dim position. In general, the monitor is brightest when the knob is as far clockwise as possible.

A "No video" error can be produced by the card, the monitor, or a multitude of problems in the computer system unit. The troubleshooting charts in Section 3 provide a plan to help you identify the culprit. Before jumping into the troubleshooting charts, though, try a couple of quick swaps if you have duplicate VGA monitors or VGA-equipped computers available. Attach the suspect monitor to a known-good computer. If the monitor works on another VGA-equipped computer, the problem is clearly the system unit or the VGA card. Recheck the dip switches and jumpers on both the VGA board and the computer mainboard. Consult the computer and VGA card manuals for switch and jumper settings.

Try installing your suspect VGA card into a known-good VGA-equipped computer. The best test equipment is an identical working version of your dead machine. Swap the parts of the dead machine one by one into the working machine. When the symptom finally jumps from the dead computer to the good one, you know the last part you swapped is the culprit.

If you have one or two incorrect characters in an otherwise good screen, the video memory located on the video card is at fault. Replace the card. If you wish, you can use CheckIt or QA Plus diagnostic software to test the video memory before you replace the card.

See "How to Test a Monitor" on page 154 and the troubleshooting charts in Section 3 for additional help.

How to Remove and Install a VGA Card

Before you remove the VGA card, you must turn off the computer and the monitor. Disconnect the data cable (it runs from the video card to the monitor) at the video card end. You will probably have to remove two small screws that are used to hold the cable connector tight to the card. Remove the system unit cover, as described in Chapter 12.

The card itself is secured to the back wall of the system unit chassis with a single screw. Remove this screw as shown in Figure 11.1 on page 102 and save the screw. Remove the card, as shown in Figures 11.2 and 11.3 (on pages 102-103). Lift the card straight up; it should require only moderate force.

Installation is the reverse of removal. Most VGA video cards are 16-bit cards now, though 8-bit cards are still available. Look for a vacant double-length 16-bit slot on you mainboard. Line up the slot connector on the card with the slot on the mainboard, then press down firmly. When the card is in place, the screw hole on the card will line up with the screw hole in the back of the chassis. Reinstall the screw and test the machine.

If you are installing a different type of video card—if you're replacing the original monochrome card with a new VGA card, for example—be sure to set any switches or jumpers on the mainboard to reflect the new video adapter. If you have a 286, 386, or 486 machine, you may need to run the setup program in order to store the new hardware information in CMOS on the mainboard. See your mainboard and VGA card manuals for more details.

Don't confuse a VGA card with other color video adapter cards, such as CGA, EGA, 8514, and XGA. These color video standards are quite different from the VGA card, having significantly different prices, resolution, and monitor requirements. If you have a CGA, EGA, XGA, 8514, or (lucky you) a 24-bit color TIGA card, there is a separate listing for your board in this chapter.

Figure 13.7
ATI's 8514 Ultra video board. Photo courtesy of ATI Technologies.

8514 Video Card

IBM introduced 8514 in 1987 on PS/2 computers with the Micro Channel Architecture. The original IBM standard provided 1024 x 768 pixel resolution, but used an interlaced monitor. *Interlacing* (painting the monitor screen in two passes of the electron gun rather than all at once) allows high-resolution graphics on a moderately-priced monitor, but interlaced video tends to flicker.

The Video Electronics Standards Association (VESA) 8514 standard calls for non-interlaced monitors and a vertical scan rate of at least 70 screen refreshes per second. Many 8514 video cards provide 72 or 76 Hz scan rates for crisp, flicker-free pictures on large monitors.

How an 8514 Video Card Works

8514 uses the same monitor-to-video-card interface as super VGA and Extended VGA. In other words, a multiscanning VGA monitor that works fine with a high-resolution VGA card will work fine with an 8514 card. But your computer communicates with an 8514 card quite differently than with a VGA card.

Your computer tells the 8514 card "Please draw me a box" or "Rotate this box." This is vector graphics. The CPU issues a very high-level command and the 8514 video card figures out how to execute it. By comparison, monochrome graphics, CGA, EGA, and frame buffer VGA cards use raster graphics and rely on the computer's main CPU for most video processing. In raster graphics the computer's CPU figures out pixel by pixel what should be on the monitor screen.

8514 cards are much faster than raster graphics video cards, especially when running Windows and CAD software. TIGA cards (see page 177) also use vector graphics, but TIGA cards are built around a microprocessor from the Texas Instruments 34010 and 34020 family of video chips. TIGA is particularly fast for CAD applications. IBM's XGA video standard was designed particularly for the Microsoft Windows market. But any of these coprocessed video cards (8514, TIGA, and XGA) will be dramatically faster running Windows than the ordinary raster graphics VGA card.

Where to Find an 8514 Card

Remove the cover from the computer system unit, as described in Chapter 12. The video expansion card is often—but not always—on the far left, as far away from the disk drives and the power supply as possible. The monitor is attached to the video adapter card or to the video connector on the mainboard, so look on the back of the system unit to find the 15-pin female connector that your monitor data cable plugs into.

How to Test an 8514 Card

If the computer has no video at all, first check the switches and cables. Make sure that the computer and monitor are both plugged in and turned on. Check the video data cable from the 8514 card to the monitor. It must be plugged in tight and screwed down at the video card end. You should also check the brightness and contrast controls on the monitor, but don't adjust these controls and then accidentally leave them in the dim position. The monitor is usually brightest when the knob is as far clockwise as possible.

Some 8514 cards have VGA support built in. Other 8514 cards are designed for a computer with a separate VGA card or with VGA on the mainboard. In either case, the computer runs in VGA mode while booting, then switches over to 8514 mode. Do you have a VGA card installed? Does your 8514 card require a separate VGA card? Does the VGA card work?

See "How to Test a Monitor" on page 154 and the troubleshooting charts in Section 3 for additional help.

Extended Graphics Array (XGA) Card

IBM introduced XGA on its 486 PS/2 computers in 1990. The XGA standard requires a Micro Channel Architecture (MCA) computer (a high-level PS/2 or a PS/2 clone).

XGA cards provide very high resolution (1024 x 768 pixels per monitor screen) and the potential to display 65,536 colors onscreen simultaneously if you choose 640 x 480 pixel (standard VGA) resolution. In addition, XGA cards can be switched to emulate an ordinary VGA card with 16 colors and 640 x 480 pixel resolution.

XGA cards use a microprocessor on the card to do most of the routine work associated with screen redraws. 8514, TIGA cards, and VGA cards with accelerators (see pages 174, 177, and 169, respectively) also use video card microprocessors for fast video response.

How an XGA Card Works

XGA cards use the 32-bit MCA bus and MCA bus mastering (the card can take over the bus to speed up data transfer into the card). Therefore, they are surprisingly fast, but limited to the PS/2 family.

Each pixel of an XGA-compatible color monitor is really a trio of phosphor dots. When excited by an electron beam, each dot glows red, green, or blue. Inside the monitor, three separate electron beams scan across the CRT screen. Each beam is responsible for exciting a single color of phosphor in each pixel. See "How Color Monitors Work," on page 152, and "How Multiscanning Monitors Work," on page 154, if you want to know more about monitor hardware.

Since a monitor is a servant of the video adapter, it turns a pixel on or passes over it and leaves it blank at the explicit pixel-by-pixel direction of the video adapter card. The XGA card provides an analog signal to each of the three electron guns for each of the 307,200 (640 x 480) pixels or 786,432 (1024 x 768) pixels on the screen.

High-resolution monitors use up lots of video memory—remember the specifications for each pixel are stored in the XGA card's memory, and these high resolutions have lots of pixels. Color uses up video memory too. Sixteen-color modes require half as much memory as 256-color modes. To head off a common confusion, we're talking about video memory here (memory chips on the video card, or in the sockets on the mainboard dedicated to video memory if the XGA card is built right into the mainboard), not system memory (ordinary memory chips on the mainboard or on a memory expansion card).

Where to Find an XGA Card

Some PS/2s feature XGA integrated on the mainboard, while others use a separate XGA card. (And many mid-level or low-priced PS/2s feature VGA video, so don't jump to the conclusion that your PS/2 has XGA merely because it's a PS/2.)

Remove the cover from the computer system unit, as described in Chapter 12. The video expansion card is often—but not always—on the far left, as far away from the disk drives and the power supply as possible. The monitor is attached to the video adapter card or to the video connector on the mainboard, so look on the back of the system unit to find the 15-pin female connector that your monitor data cable plugs into.

How to Test an XGA Card

PS/2 computers come with diagnostic software. Use this to check your XGA card and monitor.

If the computer has no video at all, first check the switches and cables. Make sure that the computer and monitor are both plugged in and turned on. Check the video data cable from the XGA card to the monitor. It must be plugged in tight and screwed down at the video card end. You should also check the brightness and contrast controls on the monitor, but don't adjust these controls and then accidentally leave them in the dim position. The monitor is usually brightest when the knob is as far clockwise as possible.

See "How to Test a Monitor" on page 154 and the troubleshooting charts in Section 3 for additional help.

Texas Instruments Graphics Architecture (TIGA) Card

Texas Instruments has launched a graphics interface, called TIGA. These TIGA video cards use a Texas Instruments 34010 or 34020 video microprocessor chip and vector graphics. 8514, XGA, and VGA cards with accelerators (see pages 174, 175, and 169, respectively) also use video card microprocessors for faster video response.

Design professionals often choose TIGA cards with 24-bit photo-quality color. TIGA cards provide very high resolution (1024 x 768 pixels per monitor screen or better) and great speed. (Great speed is relative here. It is impressive to zoom in on a 24-bit, high-resolution photo. A TIGA card won't feel instantaneous, but very few video cards could do it at all.)

How a TIGA Card Works

TIGA cards use a VGA-style analog monitor, but a very fast high-end monitor. Each pixel of a color

TIGA Card

monitor is really a trio of phosphor dots. When excited by an electron beam, each dot glows red, green or blue. Inside the monitor, three separate electron beams scan across the CRT screen. Each beam is responsible for exciting a single color of phosphor in each pixel. See "How Color Monitors Work," on page 152, and "How Multiscanning Monitors Work" on page 154 for more information on monitor hardware.

The monitor turns a pixel on or passes over it and leaves it blank at the explicit pixel-by-pixel direction of the video adapter card. The TIGA card provides an analog signal to each of the three electron guns for each of 786,432 (1024 x 768) pixels on the screen. 1280 x 1024 pixel resolution has 1.3 million pixels, almost twice as many.

These high-resolution monitors use up lots of video memory—remember the specifications for each pixel are stored in the video card's memory, and these resolutions have lots of pixels. Color uses up video memory too, especially 24-bit color. It is not unusual to have multiple-megabytes of video memory on a TIGA card. We're talking about video memory here (memory chips on the video card), not system memory (ordinary memory chips on the mainboard or on a memory expansion card).

Though TIGA uses the same monitor-to-video-card interface as super VGA and Extended VGA, your computer communicates with a TIGA card quite differently than with a VGA card. Your computer tells the TIGA card "Please draw me a box" or "Rotate this box." This is termed vector graphics. Most other video cards use a pixel-by-pixel technique; the computer says "please turn on this pixel"—a technique called raster graphics. Frame buffer VGA cards (ordinary VGA cards without an accelerator), EGA cards, MGP cards, and RGB cards use raster graphics.

Most TIGA cards come with Windows drivers, so any program you will be running from within Microsoft Windows will use the TIGA card's fast video microprocessor. But other software may not have a TIGA driver, and your TIGA card may not have a video driver for your favorite non-Windows software. As always, ask before you buy.

Where to Find a TIGA Card

Remove the cover from the computer system unit, as described in Chapter 12. The video expansion card is often—but not always—on the far left, as far away from the disk drives and the power supply as possible. The monitor is attached to the video adapter card or to the video connector on the mainboard, so look on the back of the system unit to find the 15-pin female connector that your monitor data cable plugs into.

How to Test a TIGA Card

If the computer has no video at all, first check the switches and cables. Make sure that the computer and monitor are both plugged in and turned on. Check the video data cable from the 8514 card to the monitor. It must be plugged in tight and screwed down at the video card end. You should also check the brightness and contrast controls on the monitor, but don't adjust these controls and then accidentally leave them in the dim position. In general, the monitor is brightest with the knob turned clockwise.

Some TIGA cards have VGA support built in; others are designed for a computer with a separate VGA card or with VGA on the mainboard. In either case, the computer runs in VGA mode while booting, then switches over to TIGA mode. Do you have a VGA card installed? Do you need one? Does it work?

See "How to Test a Monitor" on page 154 and the troubleshooting charts in Section 3 for additional help.

Chapter 14
Data Storage on Removable Media

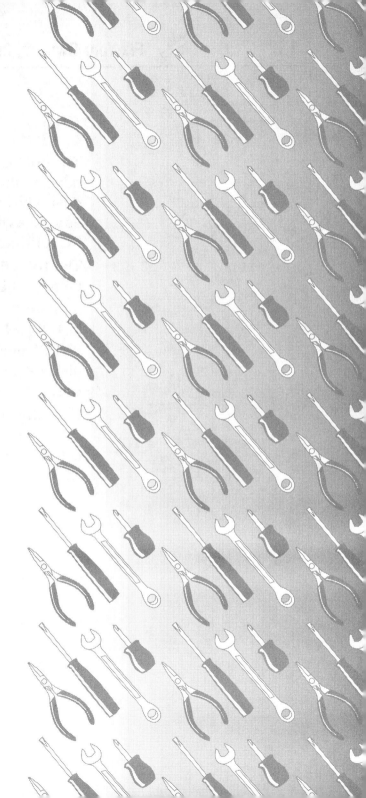

This chapter covers the following topics:

- ✔ Floppy disks
- ✔ 5.25-inch floppy disk drives and controllers
- ✔ 3.5-inch floppy disk drives
- ✔ Bernoulli drives with removable cartridges
- ✔ CD-ROM, WORM, and MO Optical Disk Drives
- ✔ Floptical drives
- ✔ Tape drives

Note: This chapter covers removable media. Look for hard disks in Chapter 15.

Floppy Versus Hard Disks: Removable Versus Fixed Media

The original IBM PC was capable of controlling two single-sided disk drives and a cassette tape drive. Both disk drives and cassette used removable media—you could replace the disk in your disk drive with another and insert a different tape in the cassette drive. The cassette drive became a joke as soon as it was released, but floppy disks became (and remain) the staple vehicle for distributing PC software. Disks are portable, comparatively cheap, and easy to operate.

The 180K floppy drives in the original IBM PCs weren't particularly fast (the new ones aren't much better). The floppy disks themselves were easily damaged and held too little data to satisfy either programmers or users.

In 1983 IBM introduced the XT, the first member of the PC family with a hard disk (or "fixed disk" as IBM preferred to call it to distinguish the new sealed medium from removable floppy drive diskettes). At the time, the XT's 10 Mb drive seemed the height of luxury—fast and capacious. It was, unfortunately, substantially more delicate than floppy disks and floppy disk drives.

Over the years this distinction between fixed and removable media has continued, though it's getting hard to pin the "more delicate," "larger capacity," or "faster access time" labels on one category or the other. Portable hard disks and hard cards with heavy-duty cushioning can take shocks that would have killed earlier hard drives. Iomega's 90 Mb Bernoulli cartridge, a removable medium, has twice the capacity (per cartridge!) and twice the effective speed of your average desktop computer sporting a 30 or 40 Mb fixed disk.

The fixed/removable distinction still makes sense, though, from a troubleshooting perspective. Fixed media are sealed. If anything goes wrong with either the media or the media-access machinery you'll have to replace the complete hard disk. If something is wrong with a floppy disk or a CD-ROM disk, but the drive itself is okay, simply throw away the bad disk. (Read Chapter 10 first, if you have a bad disk and you're hoping to salvage data.)

Magnetic Versus Optical Media

Tapes, floppy disks, and Bernoulli cartridges share a common recording process:

✔ Variable electric current fed into an electromagnetic recording head produces a variable magnetic field.

✔ The medium moves under the head, either spinning (the disks) or streaming past on rollers (tapes).

✔ Because the tape, disk, or cartridge is coated with a metallic coating, it preserves a record of the varying head current in a magnetic track on the disk or tape.

Later, the user can ask the drive to run the same section of the disk or tape under the head. As the changing magnetic field passes beneath the head it induces a variable current flow, recreating the original current flow used to write the data to the disk or tape. None of this technology is new; tape recorders read and write the same way.

In optical media, by contrast, the write and read processes are not necessarily mirror images of each other. CD-ROMs, for example, are read-only (ROM stands for Read Only Media). Manufactured in a CD stamping plant, then coated with aluminum to reflect light, the disks use a complex pattern of pits to store information. To read the disk, your computer's CD-ROM player focuses a thin laser beam on a section of the spinning disk. Light reflects from the flat surfaces but doesn't reflect from the pits. Inside the CD-ROM drive, a photo detector converts these on/off light flashes to electric signals intelligible to your computer.

Then there are the Floptical brand disk drives, a weird combination of both technologies. Flopticals use ordinary magnetic read/write techniques, but they cram over 700 tracks into the space where high-density 3-1/2 inch diskettes distribute 80 tracks. Flopticals use optical technology to position the magnetic read/write head accurately over the correct track.

Random Access Versus Sequential Media

Records and music CDs are both random access media; you can lift the needle or move the laser directly to a particular song, then play it. Music tapes, by comparison, are sequential. Though you may choose to fast-forward through songs, you still have to wade through the entire album to find your favorite part.

Floppy diskettes, Bernoulli disk cartridges, CD-ROM and WORM disks, and Floptical disks are all random access media. Data is easy to find. It's easy to write new data to an empty portion of the disk. And the drive read/write mechanism can quickly move from one location on the disk to another.

Floppy Disks

Like audio tapes, computer data tapes are sequential. Use tapes to archive the data on a hard disk or to ship mass quantities of data to other users. Tape drives are funny beasts, though. Because drive and tape standards are not universal yet, you can never be sure that a tape recorded on one manufacturer's drive will be readable on a different manufacturer's drive.

The next section, "Floppy Disks," is a general introduction to magnetic read/write technology on all the disk media (floppy diskettes, Bernoullis, Flopticals, even hard disks). New users should read "Floppy Disks" before turning to the section dedicated to floppy disk drives (page 188), Bernoulli drives (page 199), CD-ROM and WORM optical disk drives (page 200), Floptical drives (page 204), or tape drives (page 206).

Floppy Disks

Floppy disks are made of plastic (usually Mylar) coated with a ferric oxide capable of holding a magnetic charge. The plastic is flexible—hence the name floppy. You should be aware that the plastic and coating are very easily damaged. Although it is enclosed in a square protective jacket, bending, fingerprints, magnetic fields, dirt, dust, or egg salad will damage a 5.25 inch floppy disk.

3.5-inch floppy disks are sturdier, because they're fully enclosed in a stiff cover that prevents casual contamination. External differences are deceiving, though. Under their high tech cover, 3.5-inch disks use the same read/write technology as 5.25-inch floppies. Extra-high-density (2.88 Mb size) 3.5-inch floppy disks coated with barium ferrite use a patented perpendicular recording technology and twice as many sectors per track as high-density (1.44 Mb) floppy disks. The 2.88 Mb drive can read 1.44 Mb and 720K floppies as well, since it has a separate recording head to maintain compatibility with the older 3.5-inch disk. These 2.88 Mb drives are so new that most computer BIOS ROMs do not support them yet.

How a Floppy Disk Works

Imagine a circular stadium, with 40 or 80 concentric rows of seats (the tracks). The stadium has 9, 12, or 18 aisles radiating out from the center, which split the stadium seats up into sections (these are the sectors on your floppy). The stadium owners sell tickets only to groups, and only in multiple-sector-single-row blocks (clusters). If the group doesn't have enough spectators (bytes of data) to fill a complete block, that's tough, the rest of the seats in the cluster will just have to sit empty. To help visitors or late arrivals find their group, the stadium owners keep a master chart at the ticket office showing where each group has been seated. This chart also tells the stadium owners which clusters are still available, and which clusters are unusable because some seats in the cluster are broken. Now let's do the technical description.

Tracks and Sectors

When you insert a floppy into the drive and close the door, the disk centers on the drive spindle so it will spin true. At the same time, two read/write heads—one for the top surface of the floppy (side 0) and one for the bottom surface (side 1)—move into position, pressing very lightly on the disk. The heads are now prepared to read the magnetic marks on the disk or to write new ones.

The surface of the floppy is divided into circular tracks and then into sectors so data can be stored in a particular location and found again easily. Imagine the floppy rotating in the floppy drive, like a record on a turntable. Hold an imaginary felt tip marker 1/2-inch from the outer edge of the record and lower it gently onto the surface. The circle drawn out on the surface of the record is track 0. If you could accurately move the marker just 1/50-inch toward the center of the record, that new circle would be track 1.

Most of us imagine that information is written uniformly across the entire surface of a floppy disk. This is not true. 360K floppy disks, for example, have all 40 tracks packed tightly together in a band less than an inch wide near the outer edge of the disk. This makes sense because the longest (most spacious) tracks are near the outer edge of the disk. At 48 tracks per inch (TPI), these 360K disks are called *double-density*. By comparison, 1.2 Mb floppy disks jam 80 tracks in the same band less than an inch wide. These high-density 1.2 Mb floppies have 96 TPI. Both the 720K and the 1.44 Mb versions of 3.5-inch disks have 80 tracks and are 96 TPI.

A track is a very large space. On a 360K floppy, for instance, a single track holds more than 4,600 bytes of data. That's a lot of data. The track is divided up into 9 sectors. Each sector on a 360K disk holds 512 bytes of data—a more manageable size for the computer to deal with. 1.2 Mb disks have 15 sectors, each with 512K of data. 720K disks have 9 sectors, each with 512 bytes of data per sector. 1.44 Mb floppies record twice as much data per track, cramming 18 sectors onto each track.

If you multiply the number of tracks by the number of sectors by the number of bytes per sector by the number of sides of the disk, you'll get the total amount of data storage available. For

Floppy Disk

Figure 14.1
Physical disk configuration. This table lists the tracks per inch, tracks per side, and sectors per track for various types of floppy disks.

Floppy Drive Types					
Type	Size	Storage Capacity	Tracks per side	Sectors per track	Compatible DOS versions
Double density	5.25	360K	40	9	DOS 2.0 or newer
High density	5.25	1.2 Mb	80	15	DOS 3.0 or newer
Double density	3.5	720K	80	9	DOS 3.2 or newer
High density	3.5	1.44 Mb	80	18	DOS 3.3 or newer

example, for a 1.2 Mb floppy: 80 tracks x 15 sectors x 512 bytes per sector x two sides of the floppy = 1.2 Mb of data.

Figure 14.1 compares the TPI and sectors per track in double-density versus high-density disks for both 5.25-inch and 3.5-inch disks.

Directory and FAT

The disk formatting routine constructs a file allocation table (FAT) and a directory on track 0, so that stored data can be located on a disk. The directory contains the file name, size, date and time of last modification, file attributes, and physical location of the first part of the file. The FAT contains information about each cluster.

A cluster is a conveniently sized group of sectors used to store information. There are typically two sectors per cluster for a floppy drive and four sectors per cluster for a hard drive. All reading and writing on disks is done in whole-cluster increments. If only half a cluster is filled with data from File A, the rest of the cluster will be left blank.

We said that the FAT stores information about the contents of each cluster. The FAT is a numeric list of all the clusters, with space for a coded entry for each cluster. A zero in an empty cluster's FAT indicates that the cluster is available for use. Physically defective areas on the disk are marked bad by locking out the appropriate clusters in the FAT. Clusters with a nonzero FAT entry contain data.

A file appears to DOS as a chain of clusters. The first cluster is entered in the directory, along with the filename and other directory information. The FAT entry for that first cluster shows the number of the next cluster in the chain. The last cluster containing data for File A is marked as the end.

How to Test a Floppy Disk

Damaged floppy disks are a common problem. We know customers who are still keeping the books for an entire business on a two-floppy PC clone. They have their tax records on a single copy of a dusty floppy disk. If you're one of these fate-tempters, you might want to pick up a copy of Paul Mace's *Guide To Data Recovery* (Brady Books, 1988). It's a little dated, but crystal clear.

Chapter 10 covers floppy disk and hard disk data recovery options, particularly the many diagnostic programs to recover data from suspect floppies. These programs look at a floppy disk sector-by-sector, persistently reading and rereading the sector. They check the Cyclic Redundancy Code (CRC), a fancy mathematical algorithm that shows up any data corruption in the sector. A CRC number can be calculated from the data read, then compared with the CRC recorded in the sector when the data was originally written to disk. If the CRCs don't match, the data recovery program looks at the Error Correction Code (ECC). The ECC algorithm points to the specific bad bit(s) in a corrupted sector. Norton Utilities and PC Tools also contain data recovery utilities to help the frustrated user recover accidentally deleted files or whole directories. Please read Chapter 10 if you need to salvage data.

If you're not sure whether or not you have a damaged floppy, continue reading.

Check the suspect disk in a second floppy drive. Find a known-good disk drive of the same type as the suspect drive. If you're having problems reading the disk in a 1.2 Mb drive, for example, try another 1.2 Mb drive. If the disk works fine in one drive but acts poorly in another, then the problems are probably caused by malfunctions in the system unit hardware—the floppy drive, for example—rather than a bad disk. See the troubleshooting charts in Section 3 for diagnostic assistance.

A Known-Good Floppy

QA Plus, CheckIt, PC Tools DISKFIX, and Norton Utilities all have excellent floppy disk diagnostic routines. Each diagnostic uses slightly different algorithms to test the disk, so occasionally a floppy will slip past one test only to be flagged bad by the next diagnostic program. In most cases, however, it's unnecessary to run two tests.

If the suspect floppy passes these diagnostics we can consider it a known-good floppy disk.

Don't Use DOS CHKDSK to Repair Disks

We discuss and recommend diagnostic/repair utilities in Chapter 10. We don't recommend CHKDSK, the DOS disk-scanning and error-correction utility. It's neither as smart nor as gentle as any of the aftermarket diagnostic programs. No, that's too generous. CHKDSK is a maniac with a meat cleaver. If it finds anything wrong on a diskette it lops off the offending part and renames it FILE0000.CHK. The second offending part will be named FILE0001.CHK—you see the pattern.

This is not good. Better to gently repair a damaged file the way PC Tools DISKFIX and Norton's Disk Doctor do. If you run CHKDSK and it chops up a damaged file, these gentle alternatives won't be able to reconstruct it again.

> ⚡ Warning: Use a good aftermarket diagnostic program to repair damaged disks. If you have no other error-correction utilities, DOS CHKDSK is better than nothing. You won't have a second chance to repair the file, though, so don't use CHKDSK on really valuable data disks.

If you must use CHKDSK because you have access to nothing else, here are some suggestions:

Try to read or boot the floppy disk, then run CHKDSK. Don't run CHKDSK/F yet. CHKDSK analyzes both FATs (both copies of the FAT table stored on the disk) and reads the disk directory, looking for the most obvious data storage errors. This quick check reveals lost clusters and cross-linked file problems.

A cross-linked file has some portion of the data area shared by two files. It's smart to copy both the cross-linked files to different disks, then examine them to see which file is correct and which is saddled with an inappropriate tail-end of alien data. If you save both files before running CHKDSK/F, you will have more options (more copies to play around with) while you're trying to recover some useable data.

Now run CHKDSK/F. This message comes up on the monitor: "xx Lost Clusters Found in yy chains. Convert Lost Clusters to Files (Y/N)?" Press **Y** (Yes), then look in the root directory for files named FILE0000.CHK, FILE0001.CHK, etc. Examine these files. Save anything that looks useful. Delete anything that is clearly trash.

Nine times out of ten, the files created by CHKDSK are useless. DOS just left an extra bit lying around in the FAT table while it was erasing files. CHKDSK finds this extra bit and freaks out. You do not need to freak out. A few lost clusters every few months is not unusual, especially if you turn the computer off while running Microsoft Windows.

5.25-Inch Floppy Disk Drive (360K or 1.2 Mb) and Controller Card

The floppy drive reads and writes information on floppy disks. Much as a tape recorder stores music on a cassette tape, the drive uses a read/write head to store information in magnetic pulses on the disk.

The floppy drive contains all the physical machinery necessary to spin the disk and move the head to any desired track on the disk. It also has drive-door-closed and write-protect sensors. The brains of the disk reading and writing process are in the floppy drive controller.

The floppy drive controller is an interface (a connection-point) between the computer bus and the floppy disk drives. The controller gets DOS read/write instructions from the computer bus connector on the mainboard, then sends instructions down a ribbon cable—containing both control lines and data transfer lines—to one or more floppy drives.

286, 386, and 486 computers generally use combination cards that feature both floppy and hard drive controllers. XT clones use two separate cards, a floppy drive controller and a hard disk controller. In either case, the floppy and hard drive controller circuitry are independent, so one system might fail while the other continues to work properly. See Figure 14.3.

Where to Find your Floppy Drive and Controller Card

Floppy drives are easy to locate because you already know where to insert floppy disks. If you remove the system unit cover, as described in Chapter 1, you can easily see the floppy drive. It's the rectangular device (approximately 6 x 8 x 1.5 inches) located right behind the floppy drive door.

The floppy drive has a four-wire power cord from the power supply unit and a ribbon cable from the floppy drive controller. In the early 1980's, most personal computers used full-height floppy

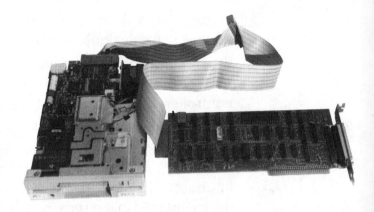

Figure 14.2
This is the floppy drive subsystem for an XT clone: a floppy disk drive, the floppy drive controller cable, and the controller card. Photo by Mel Chamowitz.

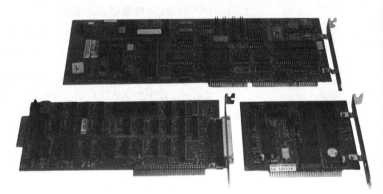

Figure 14.3
The top card is an AT-style drive controller with connections for both hard drives and floppy drives. XTs require two separate controller cards. The bottom left is an XT-style floppy controller. Bottom right is an XT-style hard disk controller.

drives. These drives were twice as tall (about 3 inches high) and came in either single-sided or double-sided designs. You are not likely to encounter full-height floppy drives in modern machines.

Figure 14.2 shows a typical XT clone floppy drive subsystem. If you wish, you can compare this to the AT-style floppy drive subsystem shown in Figure 4.1 on page 51. XT and AT floppy drive controllers are different, but the same cables and floppy drives will work in both machines.

The ribbon cable coming off the back of the floppy drive runs to the floppy disk drive controller. Other ribbon cables in the machine may go to a hard drive or to a separate serial port (but only the floppy drive cable plugs into the back of the floppy drive). See our line drawings of ribbon cables in Chapter 15 if you're unsure. Follow the floppy drive ribbon cable carefully. It runs to other floppy drives installed in the system, then terminates at the floppy disk drive controller.

How a 5.25-Inch Floppy Disk Drive and Controller Work

When you insert a disk, two read/write heads—one for the top surface of the floppy (side 0), and one for the bottom surface (side 1)—move into position and press very lightly on the floppy. The heads are now prepared to read the magnetic marks on the disk or to write new ones.

The drive moves these read/write heads according to commands from the controller card. In turn, floppy disk drive controllers get their read or write instructions from DOS. These instructions are quite explicit. For example, DOS might tell the floppy disk drive controller to instruct the floppy drive to move the read/write head to track 15, sector 5 and read the contents of that sector. If you're confused about tracks and sectors, see "How a Floppy Disk Works," on page 184; these terms are explained there.

It's apparent that the floppy disk drive controller is not a particularly sophisticated device. It doesn't have to keep track of the contents of a disk—DOS does that. It doesn't have to know what parts of the disk are empty and available to store new data—DOS does that. It doesn't have to decide which read/write head on the drive it is going to activate—DOS makes that decision; the controller just executes it. The floppy disk drive controller *does* have to change the DOS instruction "move to track 15" into on/off signals that control the stepper motor that moves the heads from track to track. It also has to know what sector of the floppy disk is under the read/write head at any moment.

The floppy disk drive controller uses an index hole, punched in the floppy disk jacket and also in the disk itself, to locate sectors. When a floppy disk spins, the two index holes line up once every revolution and an electric eye in the disk drive sends a signal to the floppy disk drive controller. The controller then counts the sector markers until the desired sector is under the read/write head. The controller reads the data in the sector, separating housekeeping bits from the actual data, then returns a clean stream of data to the microprocessor on the bus.

Formatting a Floppy Disk

New floppy disks must be formatted, one of the hardest jobs a floppy drive must do. While formatting a floppy disk, the drive writes to each byte on the disk—which is why formatting destroys any data previously stored on the disk. If a floppy drive can format a disk correctly, it is probably working okay. The exception to this rule is when the floppy drive is misaligned. A misaligned drive will read disks it has written without any problems, but will have difficulty reading disks formatted and written on another disk drive. Nevertheless, disk formatting tests many key floppy drive functions. A step-by-step explanation of the formatting process reveals important information about floppy drives and how they work.

Formatting begins when you insert an unused floppy disk into the drive and type the DOS FORMAT command. The drive first checks that the door is closed, then it positions the read/write head on track 0. Track 0 is the outermost (largest) track on the floppy disk. The drive writes sector marks (9 sectors for 360K disks and 15 sectors for 1.2 Mb floppies) on track 0, then moves the head to the next track to write sector marks. It continues this process until the last track has been prepared.

360K disks have 40 tracks, so the last track is number 39. 1.2 Mb disks have 80 tracks, so the last track is number 79. In both cases, the last track is the innermost (and smallest) track. Both 360K and 1.2 Mb disks are 5.25 inches in diameter, but not all the surface is covered with data. The drive actually writes on a donut-shaped band less than an inch across on each side of the disk.

The disk formatting routine also constructs a FAT and a directory on track 0, so that stored data can be located on the disk. The directory contains the filename, size, date and time the file was last modified, file attributes, and physical location of the first part of the file. The FAT contains information about each cluster.

How to Test a 5.25-Inch Floppy Drive and its Controller Card

First make sure the drive can boot a known-good floppy (if it's the A drive) or read a known-good floppy (if it's the B drive). See "How to Test a Floppy Disk," page 186, for the definition of a known-good floppy. If the drive can't read a known-good floppy, go to the troubleshooting charts in Section 3. Begin at the START chart and work your way through until you locate the problem.

A technician who is out in the field with no test parts will sometimes use this cable-switching trick to check whether the problem is in the floppy drive alone or in the cable-controller-mainboard end of the chain: If you have a second floppy drive of the same type (e.g., both drives are 5.25-inch 360K drives), you may be having trouble with only one drive. Try switching the floppy drive cable from drive A to drive B. Put the twisted end on drive B and try to boot from your new drive A (the old drive B). If the old drive B works as a drive A, the original drive A is the only problem.

If the drive boots a floppy, try formatting the disk. If this works, but you have doubts about the drive, many diagnostic programs are available to help. Mace Utilities, for instance, contains a floppy drive diagnostic that you can run for an unlimited period. CheckIt, QA Plus, PC Tools COMPRESS, and Norton Utilities all do roughly the same job, though in slightly different ways. These diagnostics read and write to our test disk, repeatedly checking data accuracy at every point on the data storage surface.

If you are having more and more data errors with a drive—especially with disks written on another machine or with older files that you recorded a year ago—your floppy drive may be going out of alignment. The only way to test this is to buy the kind of diagnostic program that comes with a pre-formatted test disk. To test for misalignment, you must judge the drive against a known-good standard disk: that's where the prerecorded test disk comes in. Misalignment is not adjustable with hand tools, though, so it may be easier to take the machine to a reputable service facility and have them test alignment and adjust it as necessary. Early PC drives frequently went out of alignment. Since the late 1980's alignment problems have become noticeably less common, in part because the floppy drives get much less wear in computers with hard drives.

Test the floppy disk drive controller the same way you test a floppy drive. First make sure that the drive formats disks properly, then use a diagnostic program to see if the drive reads and writes properly for hours at a time. If the drive functions properly, then the drive controller must be working okay.

The controller is not likely to be at fault when one floppy drive works and the second one doesn't. Conversely, both drives bad usually means a bad controller, not simultaneous drive failure. The same circuits are used to control both floppy drives, but the hard disk controller has separate circuitry. Therefore, a working hard disk tells us nothing about the state of the controller card, even if the same card controls both floppy and hard drives (the 286/386/486 design).

If the disk drive is still not working properly, see Chapter 4 for additional information about floppy disk system problems. The troubleshooting charts in Section 3 should also help.

How to Install a Floppy Drive Controller

Note: See also "How to Install the Floppy Drive Cables" and "How to Install a 5.25-Inch Floppy Drive" on the next two pages.

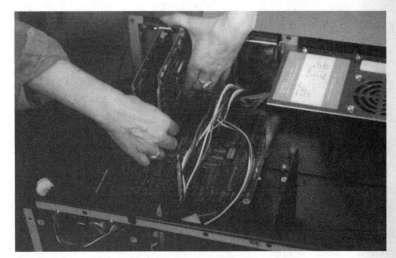

Figure 14.4
Removing an XT clone's floppy drive controller.

1. **Remove old controller card.** Remove the system unit cover (described in Chapter 1). Carefully examine the floppy drive ribbon cable; it's installed so the red (or blue) stripe is toward pin #1 on the controller card's cable-connection pins. Many controllers, especially the ones in 286/386/486 machines, have the number 1 silk-screened on the controller next to the connector pins. Plan now, before you take the cable off, to reinstall the cable so the red or blue stripe faces the end with the number 1. Other controllers, especially in PC and XT clones, have a notch cut in the connector on the controller card. The end with this slot is pin #1, and again you will reinstall the cable with the colored edge toward pin #1. Now remove the cables.

   Remove and save the screw fastening the controller card to the system unit chassis, then pull the card straight up out of the bus connector (Figure 14.4).

2. **Choose the right controller card.** Ordinary XT-style controllers are designed for 360K (low-density) drives. If you are installing a high-density (1.2 Mb) floppy drive in an XT or PC clone, you will need a special high-density floppy drive controller. Of course, only 8-bit controller cards with the single bus connector work in XT clones. ISA computers, the 16-bit and 32-bit 286/386/486 machines, use AT-style controllers.

3. **Put the card in the slot.** Installation is straightforward. Press the card down into the mainboard bus connector. Put 286/386/486 cards with a long bus connector in any

Figure 14.5
The floppy drive control cable. This is drive A on a 286/AT clone. The red edge of the ribbon cable is facing the notched end of the edge connector.

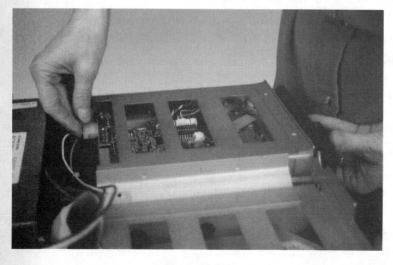

Figure 14.6
The four-wire power cable.

convenient long connector on the mainboard. In 8088 and 8086 (PC/XT) clones any slot will work. After you install the card, connect the ribbon cable and reattach the screw that holds the card to the system unit chassis. Test the machine. If it's working, replace the cover and you're done. If not, recheck the cable—the next section tells you how.

How to Install the Floppy Drive Cables

Note: See also "How to Install a Floppy Drive Controller" (page 193) and "How to Install a 5.25-Inch Floppy Drive."

The wide, flat gray cable running from the floppy disk controller to each floppy drive is called a *ribbon cable*. You should examine the ribbon cable connections and routing before you remove any parts. Even if you forget, there are enough clues on the cable, the drive, and the controller card to reinstall it right.

Note the red stripe on one edge of the ribbon cable. That red stripe signifies pin #1. The floppy drive has a flat, gold-colored cable connector, called an edge connector. There is a notch cut in one end of this connector. The end with the notch is pin #1 on the drive. When you reinstall the cable, the red edge of the ribbon cable must face toward the notch (Figure 14.5).

Notice that one section of the ribbon cable is split off at the connector and twisted. When you reinstall the cable, the twisted end must be on the A drive. The B drive is hooked to the straight-through connector in the middle of the cable. See our line drawings of ribbon cables in Chapter 15 if you're confused.

Reconnect the four-wire power connector (Figure 14.6). Any of the four-wire power supply cables will do, they are all alike. Please note that these connectors are not rectangular; two corners have been cut off on a diagonal. Examine the socket on the floppy drive before installing the connector. Determined technicians have been known to force these things in upside down and smoke the drive.

How to Install a 5.25-Inch Floppy Drive

Note: See also "How to Install a Floppy Drive Controller" (page 193) and "How to Install the Floppy Drive Cables."

1. **Remove old drive.** It is often easier to remove the cables (a ribbon cable and a four-wire power cable) after the drive is loose. Do as you wish. In any case, examine the cables carefully (maybe even mark them) before you disconnect them so you will be able to reinstall them properly.

   On most XT clones, the floppy drives are mounted directly on the chassis. To remove the drive, you must remove the machine screws on the sides of the drive. Occasionally the screws are installed from below. In this case, turn the computer on its side and look for holes in the bottom of the chassis to access these screws.

   On most 286 and 386 computers, the floppy drives are installed with rails. Locate the small metal clip that is screwed onto the front surface of the chassis next to the drive. Remove this clip. You should now be able to slide the drive out of the chassis on rails (much as a drawer slides out of a cabinet), see Figure 14.8.

2. **Set switches/jumpers on the new drive.** Floppy drives have jumpers (or, occasionally, dip switches) to set the floppy's drive selector and terminating resistor op-

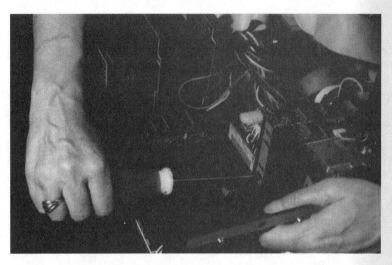

Figure 14.7
Removing the floppy drive mounting screws on an XT clone.

Figure 14.8
Sliding the floppy drive out of the AT/286 clone chassis.

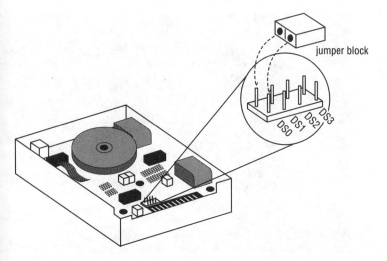

jumper block

Figure 14.9
Sometimes the drive selector jumpers are numbered DS0, DS1, DS2, DS3 on the circuit board of the floppy drive. Other manufacturers number them DS1, DS2, DS3, DS4. In either case, put the jumper on the second lowest set of DS pins.

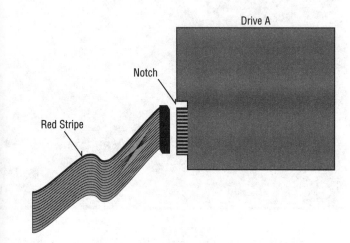

Drive A

Notch

Red Stripe

Figure 14.10
Installing the floppy drive cable on drive A. Note the twist in the cable, the stripe (top of cable), and the notch in the driver's edge connector.

tions. DOS machines require that the drive selector (DS) on both drive A and drive B be set to the second drive. This may not seem to make sense, but the machine won't confuse the two drives when they're set to the same DS—the twist in the ribbon cable straightens everything out.

The floppy drive cable has three connectors: one for drive B (which is straight-through), one for drive A (which has part of the ribbon cable twisted at the end), and one for the floppy drive controller card. The cable, not the DS jumper, determines which drive is seen by the machine as drive A and which as drive B.

3. **Check terminating resistors.** Not all floppy drives have a terminating resistor. You should have received an installation sheet describing the switch/jumper settings and the terminating resistor (if so equipped) on your new drive. If you didn't, ask an experienced person whether your floppy drive has a terminating resistor and, if so, where it is located. If the drive doesn't have a terminating resistor, you can ignore this step. If it does have a terminating resistor, you must configure the drives so that the resistor is on drive A. Drive B needs no resistor.

4. **Slide in drive, connect cables.** Once you configure the drive, you can install it. Reuse the rails and machine screws from the drive that you are replacing. Screw the new drive down firmly, but not too tightly; the screws are easy to strip. After you secure the drive in the chassis, connect the ribbon cable and the four-wire power cable from the power supply. If you need help, "How to Install the Floppy Drive Cables" starts on page 194.

After you install the new drive, turn on the machine and test the drive rigorously. If it passes all the tests, you're done. If not, recheck everything carefully, looking especially for incorrect switch settings and incorrect/ loose cables.

3.5-Inch Floppy Drive (720K or 1.44 Mb) and Controller Card

3.5-inch drives are very similar to 5.25-inch drives. Read "How a Floppy Disk Works'" page 184, and "How a 5.25-inch Floppy Disk Drive Works," page 190, for general floppy drive theory. The next few paragraphs highlight some differences between 5.25-inch and .5-inch technology.

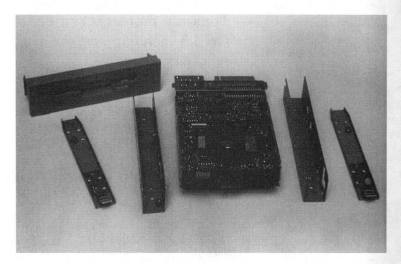

Figure 14.11
A 3.5-inch floppy drive with mounting hardware.
Photo by Susan Sasser.

When you remove the system unit cover you can easily see the little 3.5-inch floppy drive. It's the rectangular device (approximately 4 x 5.5 x 1 inch) located right behind the floppy drive door. It has a four-wire power cord from the power supply unit and a ribbon cable from the floppy drive controller. 3.5-inch floppy drives are mounted in a bracket approximately 6 x 8 x 1.5 inches so that they can fit into the standard opening provided for a 5.25-inch floppy drive (see Figure 14.11).

The 3.5-inch floppy diskette is smaller, less delicate, and contains more information than its 5.25-inch counterpart. Double-density 3.5-inch floppies contain 720K of data arranged on 80 tracks, with 9 sectors per track. The high-density floppy packs 1.44 Mb of data into 80 tracks by using 18 sectors per track. By comparison, double-density and high-density 5.25-inch floppy diskettes hold 360K and 1.2 Mb of data, respectively.

5.25-inch high-density (1.2 Mb) drives have trouble working with double-density (360K) disks. The disks are prone to errors, especially if the user switches a 360K diskette back and forth between high-density and double-density drives, reading and writing indiscriminantly in both. The 3.5-inch drive manufacturers have avoided these problems. Both 720K drives and 1.44 Mb drives read, format, and write to 720K floppies without errors.

The write-protect scheme of a 3.5-inch drive is the opposite of the 5.25-inch write-protect notch. On 3.5-inch floppies, the disk is write protected if the notch is open. When the notch is covered, recording is enabled.

How to Test a 3.5-Inch Floppy Drive

As with 5.25-inch drives, 3.5-inch drive diagnosis requires a good system floppy to test bootup, a second floppy to format, a diagnostic program capable of continuous read/write testing, and (if misalignment is suspected) alignment testing software packaged with its own preformatted test floppy. These tests are described more fully in "How to Test a 5.25-Inch Floppy," page 186.

How to Install a 3.5-Inch Floppy Drive

We covered the basics of disk drive removal and installation in "How to Install a Floppy Disk Drive Controller," page 193, "How To Install Floppy Drive Cables," page 194, and "How to Install a 5.25-Inch Floppy Drive," page 195. In this section, we point out those features that are unique to the 3.5-inch floppy disk drive.

The installation steps for 3.5-inch and 5.25-inch drives are similar—the cables, physical installation, drive select configuration, even the terminating resistor requirements. Nevertheless, 3.5-inch drives do have some idiosyncrasies. When you buy a new 3.5-inch floppy drive, be sure to get a mounting bracket, face plate, and adapter kit. With these adapters, the 3.5-inch drive is a plug-compatible replacement for any 5.25-inch drive.

Not all DOS versions support 3.5-inch floppy drives. Only DOS 3.2 or above supports them. DOS 3.2 supports 720K drives, but not high-density 1.44 Mb drives. DOS 3.3 and above can handle either 720K or 1.44 Mb drives. DOS 5.0 can handle 2.88 Mb floppy drives, plus all others.

The BIOS chip in 286, 386, and 486 computers has the ability to operate either high- or low-density 3.5-inch floppy drives—as long as you store correct drive configuration data in the CMOS chip with the setup program. 8088 and 8086 computers, on the other hand, were designed before the 3.5-inch drive became popular. These types of computers need a software device driver to tell DOS that the 3.5-inch drive exists. If you need to use a device driver, copy it into your boot directory. You will also need to change your CONFIG.SYS file to include the line: **DEVICE = EXDSKBIO.DRV** (or the name of your driver).

Ordinary XT clone floppy controllers can handle low-density (720K) 3.5-inch drives with a software device driver. High-density (1.44 Mb) drives require a special high-density XT-style controller.

Bernoulli Drives

A Bernoulli drive uses a flexible disk mounted in a protective cartridge. The drive stores data magnetically on this disk in closely spaced concentric tracks. Currently, Iomega manufactures Bernoulli drives that store up to 90 Mb of data on a disk.

Bernoulli disk cartridges are expensive, but data access time is comparable to a hard disk speed, so Bernoulli drives are better for discrete units of interactive data than for archiving or dead storage. An accounting firm might, for example, keep the financial records for individual small businesses on separate Bernoulli cartridges. When not in use, cartridges can be locked in a fireproof vault— important for security conscious users.

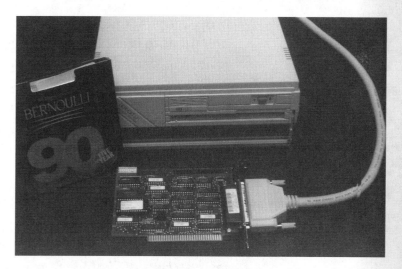

Figure 14.12
External Bernoulli drive, cable, and SCSI host adapter card.
Photo by Robert McLaughlin.

How Bernoulli Drives and Their SCSI Adapter Cards Work

Bernoulli disk cartridges use a flexible disk with a metal particle coating. Unlike most other magnetic disk media, Bernoulli drives write only on the top surface of the disk using a single read/write head. At rest, the disk curves downward, hanging below the head. This space between the head and the disk makes Bernoulli cartridges tough (Iomega says they can withstand an 8-foot drop to a hard surface without damage).

When the cartridge is installed in a Bernoulli drive the flexible disk spins up to speed and raises up very close to the read/write head. If the power fails, the disk "loses lift" and falls back down away from the head.

Bernoulli drives are SCSI devices. Bernoullis use a SCSI host adapter (either generic SCSI or proprietary Iomega SCSI) to connect as many as seven SCSI devices to the PC. The Iomega proprietary adapter connects only Iomega products on its SCSI bus. Generic SCSI cards will drive any mixture of SCSI devices such as CD-ROM, hard disk, Bernoulli drive, DAT tape drive, and so forth. We discuss the SCSI bus at length in Chapter 15. Check there for more details.

Because SCSI interfaces are available on PC family computers (XTs, ATs, 286/386/486 ISA computers, and EISA computers) and also on Macintosh and PS/2 computers, Iomega provides adapters and proprietary file exchange software. This allows you to move a portable Bernoulli drive from computer to computer and still access your data.

How to Install and Test Bernoulli Drives and Their SCSI Adapter Cards

If you're using a generic SCSI host adapter card, use standard SCSI device troubleshooting and installation techniques, described in Chapter 15. Review your host adapter manual before you install a Bernoulli drive. Some host adapter cards reserve certain SCSI device addresses for special functions. The Adaptec 1540 series, for example, reserves SCSI devices 0 and 1 for SCSI hard drives.

For the Bernoulli drive itself and Iomega's proprietary SCSI host adapter card, read Iomega's straightforward installation and troubleshooting pamphlets. Internal drives should be mounted in the computer with screws or rails, like hard disks, and connected to the SCSI adapter with a standard 50-pin SCSI ribbon cable.

SCSI host adapters have an external drive connector on the back; depending on the adapter board, this is either the 50-pin SCSI connector or the Centronics-type SCSI connector shown in Figure 15.5 on page 218. You'll find a Centronics-type SCSI connector on the back of Iomega's Bernoulli drive.

Make certain you have the appropriate software package before attempting installation. When we tried Iomega's proprietary-adapter software with a generic SCSI host adapter the drive choked. Worked fine with Iomega's generic-SCSI software.

Don't forget to format the disk before you try to use it.

CD-ROM, WORM, and MO Optical Disk Drives

Music CDs use a pattern of pits and "lands" (the flat spots between pits) to record sound, and the reflected light of a laser to "read" the pits and lands. CD-ROM and WORM drives use similar disks to record data and similar lasers to read the CD-ROM or WORM disk.

CD-ROM disks are read-only media. CD-ROMs are not cheap to produce. Yes, a factory can stamp out copies of a master CD for pennies, but the original master costs a lot to produce, much like the master tape for a record or the plates for a book. So CD-ROMs are really an alternative medium for commercial publishing, particularly for publishing data in computer-readable form, not for data storage by an individual user.

WORM drives and disks, by comparison, are particularly suitable for private archiving and permanent storage. WORM stands for Write Once, Read Many times—the classic role of backup media. Because WORM disks are not erasable, they provide an audit trail. You can accomplish some storage tasks better with this audit trail—for example, recording financial transactions at a bank.

Figure 14.13
CD-ROM drive with 50-pin SCSI interface cable and CD-ROM cartridge. Photo courtesy of JDR Microdevices.

MO (Magnetic-optical rewriteable) disks are erasable; they may be erased and rewritten many times. MO disks make good storage for the huge CAD and graphics image files that would otherwise fill your hard disk.

CD-ROMs, WORM disks, and Magnetic-Optical disks are sturdy, with much longer shelf life than tapes or ordinary diskettes. The data is stored optically; magnetic fields cannot erase or damage CD-ROMs, WORM disks, or MO. Because the optical pits are covered with clear plastic, accidental abrasion damage is also unlikely. Since all three optical disks remain readable more than 15 years after being written, most computer people consider them "permanent" storage.

How CD-ROM, WORM, and MO Drives Work

Both CD-ROM drives and WORM drives share a common disk read technology—they shine a laser onto the disk surface and measure the reflected light level. Pits scatter the beam. The lands of the CD (that's the areas where there are no pits) reflect the beam back to the drive's photodetector. The photodetector converts the variable light levels into a variable electric current, which is, in turn, decoded into usable data.

Unlike other disk media, CD-ROMs and some WORM disks use one long spiral groove, like an LP record groove, to record data. This is called Constant Linear Velocity (CLV) recording. To maintain

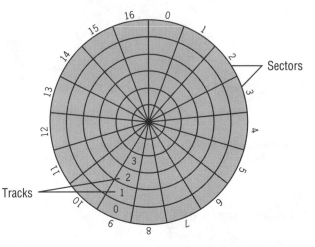

Constant Angular Velocity

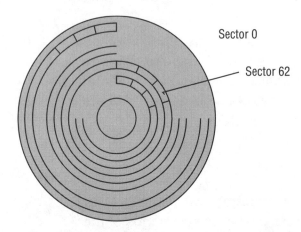

Constant Linear Velocity

Sector 0

Sector 62

Figure 14.14
A standard hard or floppy disk with sectors and tracks records data with the CAV method (Constant Angular Velocity, top picture). Compare the spiraling CLV method (Constant Linear Velocity, lower picture) used by CD-ROM drives.

constant linear velocity (a constant number of inches per second), CD-ROM drives and CLV WORM drives use sophisticated drive-spinning mechanisms that spin the drive slower and slower as the read/write head gets closer to the outer edge of the disk. See Figure 14.14.

Other WORM drives and most magnetic-optical disks record data in multiple concentric rings (in tracks) arranged like rows of seats in a stadium rather than a single long spiral. Most other disk media (floppy disks, hard disks, Bernoulli cartridges, Floptical disks) use this track system too, recording data in concentric circles. This track-and-sector system is called CAV (Constant Angular Velocity) recording.

Because the outermost edge of a CD is the hardest area to manufacture accurately and the most easily damaged, a CD-ROM data groove starts at the inside of the disk and spirals out toward the outer edge. Ordinary magnetic disk media (hard disks, floppy disks, etc.) record on the choice outer tracks first, gradually working their way in toward the crowded central tracks.

WORM disks are not standardized yet—manufacturers can't even agree on CAV versus CLV recording. Many WORM disks use a thin, reflective film of metal imbedded in the CD disk. A laser "writes" to the disk by melting holes in the film, making bubbles, or otherwise disturbing the reflections from the metal film. This creates bright/dark patterns for the laser and photosensors to pick up in the read phase of the cycle.

MO disks are not standardized yet, either, but most drives use a combination of a weak magnetic field and a laser beam to record data on the disk. The medium is resistant to magnetism at ordinary temperatures. When the laser beam heats a tiny spot on the disk, though, that spot easily becomes magnetized. Unlike CD-ROM and WORM disks, the MO disk doesn't become less reflective at the lasered spots. To read the disk, the MO drive shines a gentle polarized laser beam onto the disk. When polarized light hits a magnetic field it rotates very slightly. The drive photodetectors are sensitive enough to pick up the slight rotations in the laser beam bouncing off the magnetized spots on the disk.

CD-ROM, MO, and WORM drives are SCSI devices. The optical drive need not be the only SCSI device installed—a single SCSI host computer can connect as many as seven devices to the PC via its SCSI bus. Most optical drives now use generic SCSI adapters (generally the better choice), though some still require a proprietary SCSI adapter (an adapter not capable of supporting SCSI devices from another manufacturer). We discuss the SCSI bus at length in Chapter 15. Check there for more details.

How to Install and Test CD-ROM, WORM, and MO Drives and Their Adapter Cards

SCSI Adapter Cards

To install or test the adapter card, use standard SCSI device troubleshooting and installation techniques, described in Chapter 15.

Drive Installation

For the CD-ROM, WORM, or MO drive itself you'll have to rely on the manufacturer's installation and troubleshooting pamphlet and on their technical support lines. Internal drives should be mounted in the computer with screws or rails, like hard disks.

Software Considerations

Device drivers tell the computer how to interact with an oddball piece of equipment. From the computer's perspective all these optical drives are odd. Your WORM and/or MO drive will require a device driver, or a hardware interface that makes the computer think it's dealing with an ordinary hard disk rather than an optical drive. If you're installing a CD-ROM drive, don't forget to install Microsoft's MSCDEX extension drivers for CD-ROM plus a device driver for your particular drive.

Testing the Drive

Ironically, CD-ROM and WORM technology is very sensitive to dust—not dust on the CD disks, but dust on the lenses inside the drive that guide the laser beam to the photodetector. Many new optical drives use self-cleaning lenses.

Optical disks can, of course, go bad—though they're supposed to be virtually indestructible. If one disk won't work in your drive, but others will, the disk is likely to be bad, not the drive. Conversely, if a disk works fine in comparable drives, but won't work in your drive, better call the drive vendor for help. You'll have to take the drive in for factory service.

Floptical Disks and Drives

Floptical brand disks look much like ordinary 3.5-inch diskettes. Like 2.88Mb floppy diskettes, Floptical diskettes are made of Mylar with a barium ferrite magnetic coating. Like ordinary 720K, 1.44 Mb, and 2.88 Mb 3.5-inch diskettes, Floptical diskettes store data magnetically. In fact, many Floptical drives are both read and write compatible with ordinary double-density (720K) and high-density (1.44 Mb) 3.5-inch floppy diskettes.

Unlike ordinary 3.5-inch diskettes, Floptical disks provide optical feedback to the drive so the drive can accurately position the read/write head over the chosen track, even if that track has become slightly eccentric. Because data-recording tracks can be much closer together than on an ordinary 3.5-inch diskette, each Floptical disk stores over 20 Mb of data.

How Floptical Disks and Drives Work

The Floptical disk manufacturer stamps very closely spaced concentric rings into the surface of ordinary 3.5-inch barium ferrite disks. These rings (1,250/inch) will guide the read-write heads as they position themselves over the appropriate track on the disk. Light from an LED (light emitting diode) on the read/write head shines onto the disk, reflecting back to a photodetector which converts the light energy to electrical current. As the head moves across the disk, the light (and current) drops off over a groove and gets stronger over the flat, reflective "land" between the grooves. Therefore, the drive can distinguish one track from the next.

Using ordinary magnetic disk reading/writing technology (but using a very small read/write head suitable for the skinny tracks), the Floptical drive writes data on the flat tracks between the optical guidance grooves. Most Floptical drives are "variable mode." Their read/write head contains both a small head to write tiny magnetic marks on Floptical diskettes and an ordinary read/write head used to read and write to ordinary 720K and 1.44 Mb floppy disks.

Floptical drives are SCSI devices. They require a SCSI adapter in the computer. Since the SCSI standard allows up to seven devices chained to a single SCSI host adapter, your Floptical drive could share the adapter with a WORM or CD-ROM drive or a SCSI hard disk. We discuss the SCSI bus at length in Chapter 15. Check there for more details.

How does the computer know that the Floptical drive is installed in place of an ordinary floppy drive? Special software redirects interrupt 13h (the interrupt the computer uses to send commands to the floppy disk) so commands routed from the computer to the ordinary floppy drive go to the Floptical drive instead.

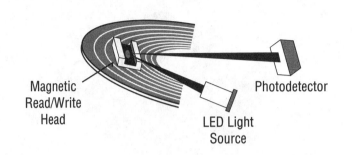

Figure 14.15
The read/write head has two recording surfaces: one reads and writes conventional 3.5-inch floppy drives, the other reads and writes very tiny tracks on a Floptical diskette. Using an LED, which shines infrared light onto the Floptical diskette, the Floptical brand drive can accurately locate the read/write head over the correct track.

How to Install and Test Floptical Drives and Adapter Cards

SCSI Adapter Cards

Floptical adapter cards are SCSI host adapter cards. We discuss the SCSI bus and SCSI host adapter cards (including troubleshooting and installation) in Chapter 15.

Software Considerations and Compatibility Issues

Floptical diskettes need to be partitioned with DOS FDISK, much like a hard drive. Floptical technology works transparently with DOS 3.x or higher. If you want to stay with an earlier version of DOS you'll need to use special Floptical utility programs in place of some DOS commands.

Figure 14.16
Install this QIC tape drive in your computer the same way you mount a floppy drive, then connect the floppy drive ribbon cable to the tape drive's edge connector. QIC tape drives use the floppy drive controller and floppy drive ribbon cable, so you'll need to remove your second floppy drive (or install a special four-floppy controller) to make space for the tape drive. Photo courtesy of JDR Microdevices.

SCSI hardware standards are quite detailed, so SCSI hardware is very compatible. But SCSI software is not. Therefore, it makes sense to talk to your SCSI host adapter manufacturer, your Floptical drive manufacturer, and the makers of any other SCSI equipment you intend to hang onto the SCSI bus—not all adapters will work with all drives, and software drivers are not yet available for all possible combinations of SCSI devices. Do your homework before you purchase, and ask for a money-back guarantee from your vendor. In a couple of years these things will all be plug-compatible, but right now it ain't necessarily so.

Read the Installation Pamphlet

As we've said before, read and follow the installation directions shipped with your new hardware. We are trying to supplement these instructions, not replace them.

Tape Drives and Their Adapter Cards

After disks, magnetic tape is the most common backup medium. Disciplined users will (reluctantly) shuffle through 20 high-density diskettes to back up a 30 or 40 Mb hard disk, but they balk at backing up bigger drives on diskette. Because magnetic tapes as large as the biggest hard disks are readily available, magnetic tape drives allow unattended hard disk backup. Unattended backups are likely to get done, disk shuffling won't.

There are many tape drive standards to choose from, but the major players break down into two families.

QIC (Quarter-Inch Cartridge)

Available either as DC-2000 minicartridges or full-size DC-6000 cartridges, both quarter-inch standards feature relatively inexpensive tape drives. The DC-2000 systems cost about half what the DC-6000 system drives do, but store substantially less data per tape. Quarter-inch tape has been around since the early 1970's.

Helical Scan Tapes

Both 4-mm DAT drives and 8-mm helical scan tape drives are expensive, but 4- and 8-mm tapes generally hold far more data than quarter-inch tapes. Figure 14.17 shows you why. It should be no surprise that the 8-mm tape holds roughly twice as much data as the 4-mm tape, and 8-mm tape drive systems are roughly twice as expensive as 4-mm tape drive systems. Both these helical scan standards were developed in the late 1980's.

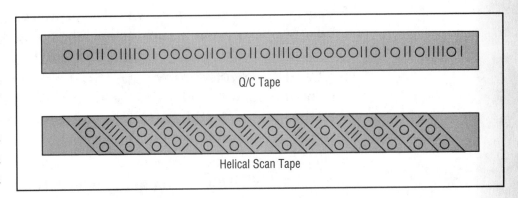

Figure 14.17
QIC tape versus Helical Scan tape.

How Tape Drives and Their Adapter Cards Work

QIC Tape Drives

Some QIC tape systems use proprietary data storage formats, while others use the QIC-40 or QIC-80 standards. A QIC-80 drive should theoretically be completely compatible with all other QIC-80 drives—they should be able to read and write to each other's tapes without difficulty. If this feature is important to you, be sure to buy a drive that is QIC-80-certified (one that has been tested and certified by the industry's test agents), not merely a QIC-80-compatible drive.

QIC tape drives record data in ordinary linear tracks laid down parallel to the edge of the tape.

Most QIC-80 and QIC-40 drives use the computer's floppy drive interface to connect to the bus. Cheaper drives simply plug the unused B drive connector on your floppy drive cable into the back of the tape drive. Other QIC tape drives use an interface board to connect the tape drive cable to the bus, but again the tape drive appears to the computer like another version (albeit a weird one) of a floppy drive. One external QIC tape drive connects to the parallel port, but reroutes signals inside the computer so the floppy drive interface signals come out through the parallel port pins. A few high-speed QIC systems use a proprietary IDE or SCSI interface.

Helical Scan Drives (DAT and 8-mm)

Really big hard disks require helical scan tape backup. Though the next generation of quarter-inch tape drives may jump to substantially higher capacities, in the early 1990's helical scan tape has been the backup medium of choice for huge (gigabyte-level) hard drives.

DAT and 8-mm drives use rotating heads mounted on a slight angle to the tape. The head records a slanted magnetic trail of data at an angle to the tape, which allows much higher data densities than the ordinary lengthwise track used on quarter-inch tape media, see Figure 14.17. But the rotating heads and sophisticated tape advance mechanism used in helical scan tape drives are expensive.

Most DAT drives are SCSI devices, often using the high-speed SCSI-2 version of the standard. We discuss the SCSI bus at length in Chapter 15.

How to Install and Test Tape Drives and Their Adapter Cards

QIC Tape Drives

Follow your tape drive vendor's installation and troubleshooting directions. When troubleshooting a QIC tape drive that uses the floppy drive interface, consider the common causes of floppy drive failure: incorrect drive select settings, incorrect termination, or plugging the wrong floppy drive cable connector onto the drive (e.g., plugging the A drive connector to a tape drive that is supposed to be impersonating drive B). These same mistakes can choke a QIC tape drive. So can a bad floppy drive, especially if the tape drive shares cables and/or a floppy drive controller with the bad floppy drive.

Not all QIC drives work with all floppy drive controllers. Problems are rare, but it's worth calling the tape drive vendor if you suspect hardware incompatibilities.

Helical Scan drives (DAT and 8-mm)

Follow the vendor's installation directions for your new tape drive. We can give you some general hints, but most vendors use proprietary software and/or interface cards. Therefore, each drive is installed and tested somewhat differently.

Since DAT and 8-mm tape drive adapters are usually SCSI cards, check out the SCSI installation pointers listed in Chapter 15 before you start installation. As always, follow the vendor's installation pamphlet.

Chapter 15
Hard Disks

T his chapter covers the following topics:

- ✔ Hard disk design: SCSI, IDE, ESDI, and ST506 compared
- ✔ Ribbon cables
- ✔ SCSI drives and host adapter cards
- ✔ IDE drives and adapter cards
- ✔ ESDI drives and controller cards
- ✔ ST506 MFM and RLL drives and controller cards

Mechanical parts wear. Eventually your hard disk will fail. We discuss hard disk maintenance in Chapter 5 and data protection and recovery in Chapter 10. We recommend you read those chapters *before* you need them. Read them now if you're hoping to salvage useful data stored on your ailing hard disk. In Chapter 15 we cover hard disks and their controller cards (how they work, how to test them, and how to install or replace them), not data recovery techniques. Read this chapter after you've saved everything you can save, when you're ready to test and replace the bad parts.

Hard disks are similar to floppy disks, but the technology is upgraded in every way. Hard disks spin faster, pack in more data per inch, move from track to track more quickly, and accommodate multiple platters in each drive unit. Both hard drives and floppy disk drives record magnetic signals on a disk, then read those signals back when requested. A 5.25-inch half-height floppy disk can hold either 360K or 1.2 Mb of data. A hard disk with 8 platters, 16 heads, and 10 times the read/write speed fits into the same space and holds over 200 Mb of data.

Like other electronic items, from calculators to digital watches, each generation of hard disks is smaller, faster, and more powerful. Half-height models are replacing the full-height hard disks of the early 1980's, and hard drives with 3.5-inch platters (for a smaller, lighter drive) are replacing the 5.25-inch styles. More precise voice coil servo mechanisms are replacing cheap stepper motors in high-density, high-capacity hard drives. Perhaps most significant, new hard disk interface standards let data flow faster between the hard disk drive and its host computer.

Nevertheless, all of these hard disks share the same basic design. Polished aluminum disks, called *platters*, spin inside the hard drive. The platters are coated with oxides of magnesium, chromium, and/or iron. On each side of each platter, a read/write head glides on a cushion of air very close to the platter, but not quite touching it. The read/write heads record data as magnetic marks on the platters. Figure 5.1, on page 55, is an exploded view of a Microscience hard disk showing the head assembly and the platters. Because the hard drive platters are not removable like floppy disks, hard drives are also called *fixed disks*.

There are hundreds of hard disk and controller models, each with idiosyncratic switch settings and jumpers. If you intend to install hard drives professionally, or simply want to know more, get a copy of *The Hard Disk Bible* from Corporate Systems Center, (408) 737-7312.

Treat your hard disk gently. It is a delicate, precision-tooled mechanical device and is easily damaged. Dropping a hard disk might crash a read/write head into the platters. Even if the head is not damaged, the data underneath the head could get scrambled.

Hard drives in good quality notebook and laptop computers are designed to take more shocks and wear and tear than ordinary hard drives. Feel free to slap your notebook computer down on the airplane tray table, but don't drop it out of the overhead luggage bin onto the floor. Surprisingly, hard disks and floppies survive X-rays well, but the radio waves generated by airport metal detectors can destroy the data.

Why Do We Care About SCSI, IDE, ESDI, and ST506?

Computers communicate with hard disks through an *interface* (a set of rules describing the adapter card, the cable, the electronics on the hard disk itself, and the electrical signals running between the hard disk and controller). SCSI, IDE, ESDI, and ST506 are the four significant interfaces in personal computers.

Think of each interface as an independent contractor. Each of these hard drive interfaces offers to:

✔ Provide a standard controller/adapter card which plugs right into the computer's mainboard bus.

✔ Talk to DOS and the computer's BIOS ROM through this adapter card.

✔ Store data on the hard disk and retrieve it when necessary.

Each hard drive interface handles the actual data storage in its own way. SCSI, for example, uses a separate bus (separate data and control signal path) to carry the data signals and control signals from adapter card to hard disk and back again. The SCSI bus is so separate, in fact, that you should tell your computer there are "no hard drives installed." SCSI doesn't want the computer messing around with its bus, its data, or its hard disk.

By comparison, ST506 expects the computer's ROM BIOS to know how many heads and cylinders are on the hard disk, which read/write head should read what data, and what track on the hard disk this head should read. ST506 may be an independent contractor, but it requires a great deal of supervision.

IDE drives allow ordinary computer bus signals on the cable running from the IDE adapter card to the IDE hard drive. But the IDE interface lies to the computer about the hard drive actually installed, cleverly convincing the host computer that a non-standard hard disk is obeying its commands as an ST506 drive would.

These hard drive interfaces all do the same basic job (store and retrieve data, and connect to the computer mainboard), but in such different ways that none of the parts are interchangeable. ESDI hard disk controller cards won't work with SCSI, ST506, or IDE drives. SCSI cables or adapter cards won't work with anything but a SCSI drive. In addition, the troubleshooting and installation techniques vary from interface to interface. Therefore, we have divided this chapter into SCSI, IDE, ESDI, and ST506 (MFM and RLL) units. Each unit contains customized *How It Works*, *How To Test*, and *How To Install* sections for each interface.

Comparing the ST506, ESDI, IDE, and SCSI Interfaces

How does your computer talk to its hard disk? If you're lucky, you already know which hard drive interface you have in your computer. If not, pondering this brief history may help you guess. A quick warning: whenever we hit an acronym we'll follow it with its full name, but honestly you're better off forgetting the long name—no one uses it.

Almost all pre-1987 PCs used Seagate's ST506/ST412 interface, named for Seagate's popular ST506 hard disk. ST506 drives are also called MFM (Modified Frequency Modulation) and RLL (Run Length Limited) drives. The MFM data encoding technique was used on the first IBM XT hard drives (and is still used on small, inexpensive hard drives). Barely adequate in the low end 20-40 Mb hard disk market, the ST506 interface is slow. To increase speed and data storage capacity, drive manufacturers started using RLL encoding with the ST506 interface. Because RLL encoding stores roughly 1.5 times as much information in the same space, it requires high-quality RLL-certified hard disks and a special RLL hard disk controller.

Since 1987 ST506 has faced stiff competition from the ESDI standard (pronounced "ezz-dee"). ESDI drives transfer data two, three, or four times as fast as ST506 drives do, and they're readily available in the 200-1,000 Mb storage range.

In the 1990's IDE (Integrated Drive Electronics) took off, replacing ST506 and ESDI in the small-to-medium-capacity hard drive market. After 1990, many new 286/386/486 computers with hard drives capable of storing 60-200 Mb of data contained IDE drives.

The largest and fastest hard drives use the SCSI interface (pronounced "skuzzy"). ESDI is also popular for very big drives. And a few big IDE drives (for example, Connor's CP3504 and CP3554) weigh in at 500 Mb or more.

How to Identify the Hard Drive Interface by Examining Your Ribbon Cables

If necessary, you can open your computer to examine the drive, its controller/adapter, and their associated cables. Remove the cover and find the hard drive—a solid, rectangular, metal device, about 6 x 8 x either 1.5 or 3 inches, with an indicator light on the front faceplate. There will be a 4-wire power cable and one or two ribbon cables attached to the back of the hard disk. Your floppy disk drive(s) also have a 4-wire power cable and a ribbon cable, but it is easy to tell floppy disk drives from hard drives: each floppy drive has a door in front to insert the floppy disks—a hard drive doesn't.

Once you have found the hard disk, look at the ribbon cable(s) attached to it. Compare them to the descriptions below and to Figures 15.1 and 15.2 on the next two pages.

SCSI and IDE both use a single ribbon cable running from the hard drive adapter card to the back of the hard disk. SCSI ribbon cables have 50 wires in the ribbon. IDE ribbon cables have 40 separate wires in the ribbon. Neither of these interfaces use ribbon cables with a "twist" in the middle. By comparison, the floppy drive cable has a "twist" with seven wires split off from the rest of the ribbon, flipped over, and clipped into the next connector (see Figure 15.2 on page 215).

ST506 and ESDI interfaces both use two ribbon cables. One is 34 wires wide (the controller cable) and the other is 20 wires wide (the data cable). You can follow the ribbon cables back to the hard disk controller card. If you have two cables and your hard disk is under 50 Mb you probably have an ST506 interface. The tiny Micropolis 1352 and 1352A ESDI drives, which were 30 and 41 Mb, respectively, Rodime's ESDI Cobra 40AT, and Microscience's ESDI 5040 at 46 Mb are the only exceptions we know. If the hard disk is over 200 Mb and has two cables, you have an ESDI drive. Between 50 and 200 Mb is a gray area, since both ST506 drives (also called MFM and RLL drives) and ESDI drives have been manufactured in this size range. Since ESDI is simply a faster (but incompatible) version of the ST506 interface, ESDI and ST506 drives and cables look the same. It makes sense to call your computer dealer or the hard drive manufacturer if you have any doubts.

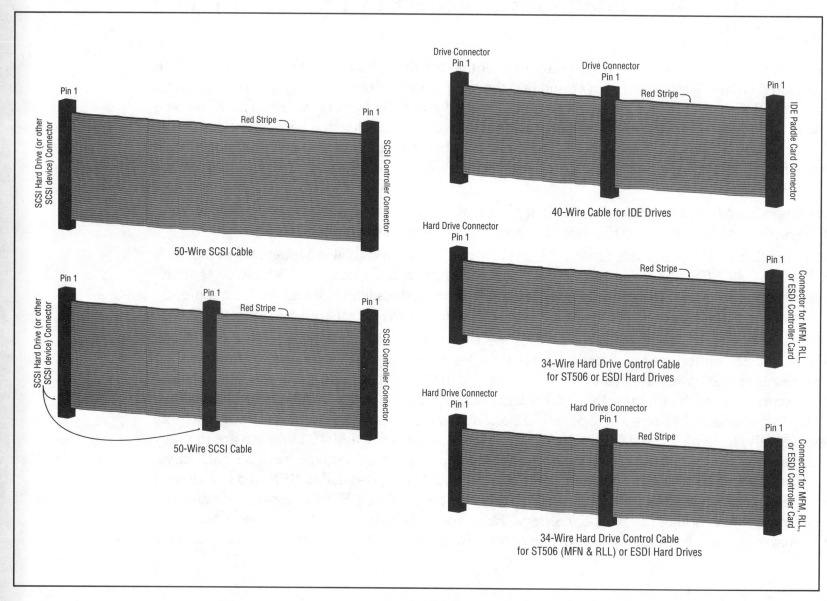

Figure 15.1
Straight-through ribbon cables.

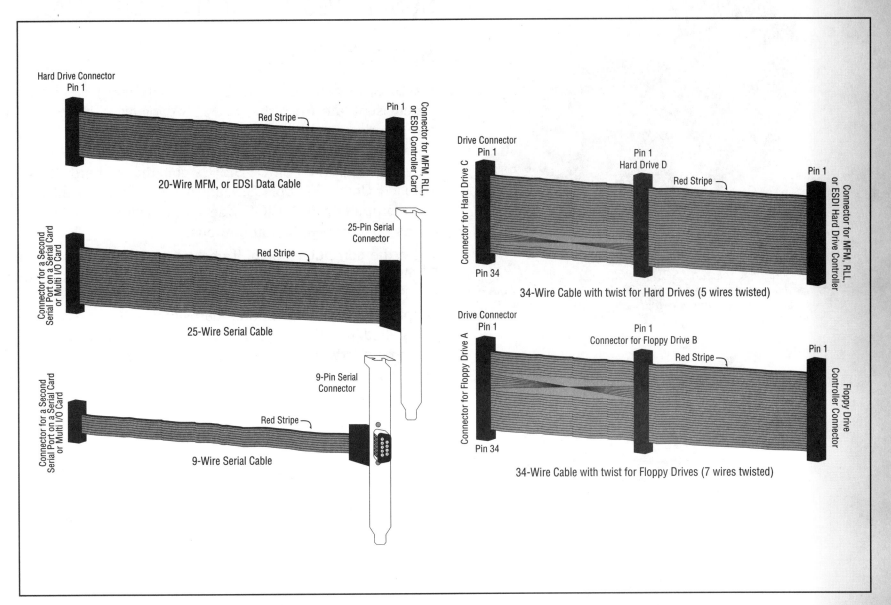

Figure 15.1a
Straight-through ribbon cables.

Figure 15.2
Ribbon cables with a "twist."

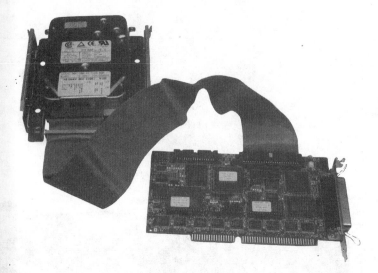

Figure 15.3
SCSI drive, cable, and SCSI host adapter card. This ISA SCSI card was installed in a Swan EISA 486 computer; the EISA bus is backward-compatible with ISA cards. Photo by Robert McLaughlin.

Figure 15.4
We could install this EISA SCSI host adapter to speed up data flow into and out of the SCSI hard disk shown in Figure 15.3. The original SCSI drive and cable go back into the computer, and the EISA host adapter would fit right into the EISA bus.

SCSI Drives and Host Adapter Cards

How SCSI Works

The SCSI (Small Computer Systems Interface) bus is completely separate from the ISA, EISA, or MCA bus on your computer's mainboard, so your desktop computer doesn't need to know any details about the SCSI hard disk. In fact, we tell your computer's CMOS SETUP chip that no hard disks are installed. Unlike ST506, ESDI, and IDE drives, which all rely on your computer's ROM BIOS to send read/write directives, SCSI drives are completely autonomous.

When the computer boots, it checks for additional hardware ROMs (the chips that tell your computer how to interact with each piece of oddball hardware). When it finds the SCSI host adapter ROM, your computer learns that a SCSI host adapter is installed, but it doesn't discover any details about the SCSI equipment attached to the SCSI host adapter. You could have as many as seven hard disks, tape drives, Iomega Bernoulli drives, optical drives, or other SCSI devices out there—the computer doesn't have a clue.

The SCSI host adapter card keeps track of data flow across the SCSI bus. Each SCSI item on the bus, whether host adapter card, hard disk, optical disk, or whatever needs a unique SCSI bus address (also called SCSI address and SCSI target address). By convention, the host adapter card is SCSI device #7. Any two of these SCSI devices can converse on the SCSI bus, without help from your desktop computer or its microprocessor. In fact, two SCSI devices can converse without the desktop computer's knowledge.

SCSI

How to Test SCSI Drives and Their Host Adapter Cards

The American National Standards Institute (ANSI) has developed a set of standard SCSI error codes. This is not as helpful as it could be, because the English error messages displayed onscreen in response to a particular error code have not been standardized. Error code 0204, for example, means the drive is not ready; it has not yet spun up to operating speed. Different SCSI controller manufacturers might display different error messages on screen when the controller receives an error 0204.

If you can read and write to your SCSI drive, but it won't boot, check the standard DOS screw-ups. Do you have clean copies of COMMAND.COM and the DOS hidden files on your SCSI drive? If you partitioned the drive, are you trying to boot from the active partition? You did, of course, remember to make one of the partitions active?

When installing a SCSI drive in an AT-style ISA computer or an EISA computer, tell the system SETUP that the hard drive is "not installed."

Poorly shielded SCSI cables can cause data corruption, or even prevent the computer from booting off the SCSI drive.

If the SCSI device won't read or write at all, check for proper installation, especially if you have just been working inside the computer. Perhaps you knocked a cable loose or have just added a conflicting piece of equipment. A second SCSI device sharing your boot disk's SCSI bus address would definitely choke things. So would incorrect termination. Read the section called "Check termination," page 219.

SCSI may be a standard, but they haven't worked the kinks out yet. Some older AT-style mainboards don't function properly with fast, 16-bit SCSI adapters. And not all host adapter cards work well with all SCSI drives. If you're still having problems, call the adapter manufacturer to be sure their card functions well with the drive and mainboard you have. (Yet another reason to buy drives and adapters together, from vendors who guarantee their products.)

Not all SCSI devices use the same SCSI software command set to communicate on the SCSI bus. If you have two SCSI devices that cannot seem to get along, you may have to speak to both of the hardware manufacturers to find a common language. Theoretically, the new SCSI II standard will take care of this problem.

SCSI

Figure 15.5
Two XT clone SCSI controller cards. The front one is both a floppy drive controller and a SCSI controller. The rear card is a plain SCSI controller. Note the 50-pin internal SCSI connectors on both cards and the 50-pin external SCSI drive connector on the card end bracket. Photo courtesy of Qume.

Figure 15.6
Two SCSI controllers with the 16-bit 286/386/486 ISA double bus connector. As in Figure 15.5, one controller is a SCSI controller only; the other regulates both SCSI and floppy drives. Photo courtesy of Qume.

In addition, many of the Big Nine computer makers use proprietary extensions to the SCSI standard. Compaq and Apple, for example, commission modified SCSI drives from the major drive vendors. Unlike generic SCSI drives, these proprietary variants have Compaq or Apple firmware installed on the drive. You must purchase special software which fools the computer into thinking you've installed a proprietary SCSI drive if you want to substitute a lower-priced generic SCSI for "the real thing."

Iomega's OAD and the Common Access Method (CAM) address the problem of incompatible SCSI software and devices by providing a common interface. SCSI hardware is standardized now, but it may take another year to fully standardize the software interface.

How to Install a SCSI Host Adapter Card

1. **Remove old SCSI adapter.** If you must remove a defective SCSI adapter, begin by examining the cables attached to the card. Mark them or take notes before you disconnect them so you will be able to reinstall them properly. Remove the screw holding the card to the rear of the computer chassis, as shown in Figures 11.1 through 11.3 on pages 102-103. Then pull the card straight up out of the bus connector.

2. **Set switches.** These adapter cards are often shipped ready to roll, straight out of the box, but just to be on the safe side, read the manufacturer's installation instructions. You probably won't have to set any switches unless you have another SCSI device that insists on being device #7 (the default SCSI bus address for the host adapter card).

3. **Check termination.** The SCSI bus must be terminated in two places, at the far ends of the SCSI cable(s). Figuring that most people will be using either an internal SCSI device or an external one, most SCSI adapter manufacturers ship their product with a terminator installed on the SCSI host adapter board. This works great if you have one or more internal SCSI drives: the host adapter (one end of the bus) is terminated, and you can terminate the last drive on the internal SCSI cable. The same argument applies when you install only external SCSI devices. If you have an internal SCSI drive, though, and decide to add an external device (perhaps a Bernoulli drive) you'll have to take the terminator off the SCSI host adapter card (it's in the middle of the bus now) and install a terminator on the last external SCSI drive. Each manufacturer uses their own termination technique. Read the installation booklet for your particular SCSI device or host adapter card.

4. **Install SCSI host adapter card.** Press the card firmly down into a slot on the mainboard. Install the screw that holds the card in place. If you have a 286, 386, or 486, run the setup program, and choose the hard disk type. For SCSI choose hard drive "not installed." If you're adding a second SCSI drive or replacing both your hard disk and controller, see also "How to Install a SCSI Drive."

5. **If you have an EISA computer.** The fastest SCSI cards are EISA SCSI cards running in an EISA computer. EISA computers also support ISA (non-EISA, AT-style) SCSI cards (see Figures 15.3 and 15.4). If you're installing an ISA SCSI host adapter you may not have to use the EISA configuration utility to tell your computer about the SCSI card—it depends on the computer manufacturer. If you are installing an EISA SCSI adapter, use it. EISA computers must be reconfigured with the EISA configuration utility whenever you add or remove an EISA card. See Chapter 11 for more details.

How to Install the SCSI Cable

SCSI uses a straight-through 50-wire ribbon cable for internal SCSI devices (those devices mounted inside the computer). External SCSI drives and the external connector on the back of a SCSI host adapter card use either a 25-pin connector which looks a lot like the parallel printer port on the back of your computer or a 50-pin Amphenol connector which looks like a longer version of the Centronics cable connector on the back of a parallel printer. These external cables are easy. You can't install them upside down or backward.

SCSI

The internal SCSI cable will be either gray with a red or blue line along one edge to identify pin #1 of the cable connector or multi-colored with a brown wire for pin #1. You must find pin #1 on your SCSI adapter, then install the cable with the #1 wire going to pin #1. If you're lucky, you can look up the pin #1 location in the manufacturer's installation pamphlet for this SCSI adapter. If not, maybe the manufacturer marked pin #1 with a silk-screened 1. It's worth a phone call to be sure you get this right. Cavalierly installing the cable backward ("if it's not right I'll just flip it around") can blow a fuse in the drive when you turn on the power. Figure 15.1 on page 214 shows SCSI ribbon cables.

How to Install a SCSI drive

1. **Remove old SCSI drive (if necessary).** First remove the system unit cover, as described in Chapter 12. Examine the ribbon cable on the back of the hard disk, noting the red-marked edge which should face toward pin #1 on the drive. Disconnect the 4-wire power cord and this ribbon cable from the hard disk.

   Most AT style computers (286, 386, and 486 machines) use rails screwed to the side of the hard disk which allow the disk to slide in and out of the chassis like a drawer. In these 286, 386, and 486 computers, look for the clips on the front of the chassis which hold the hard disk. Remove the screws holding the clips in place or squeeze the spring-loaded clips and slide the hard disk out. Save these rails and clips; you will need them for the new hard disk.

2. **Set switches.** In some ways the SCSI bus is like a small local area network (LAN) with many individual computers speaking to each other over a shared bus. As with LANs, each device on the SCSI bus must have it's own device number (its own bus address).

   Device #7 is traditionally reserved for the SCSI host adapter card. You may pick any unused address for your hard disk. Just make certain that your host adapter card hasn't reserved special relationships with particular SCSI bus address numbers. The Adaptec 1542, for example, treats devices 0 and 1 differently than all the rest, so you might run into difficulty if you set a particular drive to device 0. Read your SCSI adapter installation manual. It will reveal the idiosyncracies of your particular controller. Insist on installation instructions with every card you buy, and read them.

3. **Check for correct termination.** See the "Check termination" section in "How To Install a SCSI Host Adapter," page 218.

4. **Slide in drive and connect cables.** Most 286, 386, and 486 computers use rails (flat bars screwed onto the side of the hard disk) to hold the hard disk in place. If your computer requires rails, install them on the SCSI drive and slide it back into the chassis.

   Connect the ribbon cable. Be sure to connect pin #1 on each ribbon cable to pin #1 on the hard drive. Plug in any 4-wire power cable from the power supply. Note that the power supply cable connectors are not rectangular. Look at one carefully; two corners have been cut off on a diagonal. Examine the socket on the hard drive carefully and be sure to install the power connector correctly.

   Install screws to hold the drive into the chassis.

5. **Format SCSI drive.** SCSI drives are already low-level formatted at the factory, so they do not have to be initialized like the old ST506 MFM and RLL drives were.

   SCSI drives do have to be partitioned with the DOS FDISK command, then formatted with the DOS FORMAT command. Directions for these commands are in any DOS manual. If you are using DOS version 3.3 or earlier, it makes a lot of sense to upgrade to DOS 5.0 or DR DOS 6.0. These new operating systems handle large disks more gracefully.

IDE Drives and Adapter Cards

How IDE Works

IDE (Integrated Drive Electronics) puts all the brains on the hard disk. The adapter (also called a paddle card) merely sends signals from the drive across the bus. The adapter, unlike ST506 or ESDI hard disk controllers, does no data encoding or decoding; that's done in the circuit board on the disk. The adapter sends no control signals to the read/write heads on the disk; the circuit board on the drive takes care of that.

IDE drives are simple to install, and faster than the equivalent ST506 drive. Since most computers don't have a drive type pre-configured in the BIOS that matches the IDE drive, if you want to use all the storage space available on your IDE drive you'll have to tell the CMOS (the computer's list of installed equipment) that the IDE drive is a "user definable" drive type. Though DOS software doesn't have a problem with these user-definable drive types, some network operating systems

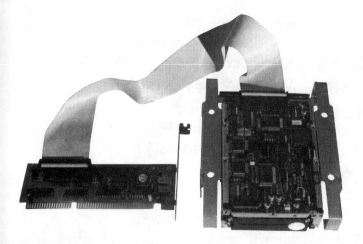

Figure 15.7
*An IDE drive with cables and adapter. This particular adapter
doubles as a floppy drive controller. Photo by Robert McLaughlin.*

hate them. If you're planning to use an IDE drive in your network server, discuss all the issues with your drive vendor before purchasing the hard drive.

How to Test IDE Drives and Their Adapter Cards

IDE drives either work or they don't. They don't slow down as they fail or lose storage capacity to bad sectors as they fail.

It's not unusual, though, for do-it-yourselfers to call up the IDE drive manufacturer complaining that their drive has only a fraction of the storage capacity they were promised. The problem lies in the computer's BIOS ROM and/or incorrect CMOS setup, not the IDE drive itself. The computer tries to access the logical sectors in this hard drive, as many logical sectors as the CMOS says there are in the drive. If you tell the computer there are fewer sectors in this IDE drive than actually exist, it will believe you—and report a smaller drive. See installation instructions below.

If the drive won't read or write, and this is a new installation (or you have just been mucking around in the computer), recheck the drive jumpers and the cables. If the drive doesn't even spin up you may have a bad power connection or you may have put the ribbon cable on upside down so the red stripe is away from pin #1.

If you can read and write to your IDE drive, but it won't boot, check the standard DOS screw-ups. Do you have clean copies of COMMAND.COM and the DOS hidden files on your IDE drive? If you partitioned the drive, are you trying to boot from the active partition? Did you remember to make one of the partitions active? If you have two IDE drives in the system you must boot from the master drive, not the slave.

How to Install an IDE Adapter Card (the Paddle Board)

1. **Remove old adapter card.** If you must remove an old IDE adapter, begin by examining the cables attached to the card. Mark them or take notes before you disconnect them so you

IDE

will be able to reinstall them properly. Remove the screw holding the card to the rear of the computer chassis, as shown in Figures 11.1 to 11.3, on pages 102-103, and pull the IDE paddle card straight up out of the bus connector.

2. **Select adapter board.** Since IDE paddle boards are so simple, you would think all adapter boards would work with all IDE drives. Unfortunately, this is not true. Buy the adapter and drive together, or check with your vendor before replacing only one of the set.

    XT-style 8-bit adapter boards with a ROM on the paddle board go in XTs and XT clones, of course. They drive XT-style IDE drives. Install 16-bit adapters and their corresponding AT-interface drives in 286/386/486 AT-style ISA bus computers and in EISA machines.

3. **Insert board in slot.** Line up the adapter board edge connector with an appropriate slot on the mainboard. Press the paddle board down, then secure it to the back of the case with a screw. Plug in the cable (see directions below).

How to Install the IDE Cable

IDE cables, simple straight-through 40-pin cables with three identical connectors, are hard to install wrong because the cable ends are keyed. In addition, most controllers (and some drives) have a *1* stenciled next to the pin #1 end of the cable connector. The cable has a red or blue stripe along one edge. Put this edge toward pin #1 on the drive and the controller. Figure 15.1 on page 214 shows an IDE cable.

How To Install an IDE Drive

1. **Choose the right IDE drive.** If you are installing a new drive/controller package, simply buy the drive and controller together from a reputable dealer. If you are adding a second IDE drive or are planning to replace only the drive, not the drive and paddle card together, you must do a little research.

    Not all IDE drives work with all adapters. And not all IDE drives function properly in a computer when a second IDE drive has been installed. Switches on the IDE drive tell the drive if it is (1) the only drive installed in this computer, (2) one of two drives, and the first drive (the master), or (3) one of two drives, and the second drive (the slave). As you might

IDE

imagine, two drives from the same manufacturer have no difficulties. If you are adding a second drive to your system, discuss the situation with your drive vendor. You want to end up with compatible drives, and be able to boot off the drive of your choice—not all drives can be slaves to another drive's master, or vice versa.

2. **Remove old IDE drive (if you're replacing a bad drive).** First remove the system unit cover, as described in Chapter 12. Study the 40-wire ribbon cable at the back of the hard disk so you'll be able to reinstall it properly, then disconnect it. Disconnect the 4-wire power cord from the hard disk.

   Remove the screws holding the hard disk to the chassis. PC/XT computers usually have screws threaded into the side of the hard disk. There may also be a screw or two that is accessible through holes in the bottom of the computer chassis. AT-style computers (286, 386, and 486 machines) usually use rails screwed to the side of the hard disk. These rails allow the disk to slide in and out of the chassis like a drawer. Look for clips on the front of the chassis. Remove the screws holding the clips in place or squeeze the spring-loaded clips and slide the hard disk out. Save the rails and clips; you will need them for the new hard disk.

3. **Set switches.** Because IDE cables are straight-through, with no differentiation between drives, we must set the switches on the drive itself to distinguish the first drive (called the master) from the second drive (the slave). Look for switches, too, to tell the master drive that it is the only drive in the computer or that there is a second drive, a slave drive, installed.

4. **Slide in drive, connect cables.** Slide the hard disk into the chassis. Most 286/386/486 computers use rails (flat bars screwed onto the side of the hard disk) to hold the hard disk in place. If your computer requires rails, install them on the hard disk and slide it back into the chassis. It's not unusual to put the rails on wrong (too high, too far forward, etc.) the first couple times. If you play around with them long enough you'll eventually get them right.

   Connect the 40-wire ribbon cable. Be sure to connect pin #1 on the ribbon cable to pin #1 on the hard drive. If you have two IDE hard disks in your system they will share the ribbon cable. Figure 15.1 on page 214 shows an IDE cable.

   Plug in any 4-wire power cable from the power supply. Note that the power supply cable connectors are not rectangular. Look at one carefully; two corners have been cut off on a diagonal. Examine the socket on the hard drive carefully and be sure to install the power connector correctly.

Install any screws that hold the drive into the chassis.

5. **Use SETUP to tell your computer about this hard disk.** When you enter the SETUP program you'll see a list of supported hard disks, complete with number of cylinders and heads. This list was stored in the BIOS ROM when it was manufactured. It is unlikely that the exact IDE drive configuration that you have will be in this hard disk list, especially if the BIOS ROM was manufactured before mid-1990. Until then, computer manufacturers didn't think the IDE drive would become popular, so they omitted popular IDE drive configurations from the list of drives their ROM BIOS supported.

But many IDE drives wouldn't fit into any standard drive list anyway. They may, for example, break a cardinal rule of BIOS-supported hard disks by putting more sectors on the large outer tracks than on the small-diameter inner tracks. Luckily, the CMOS drive you select doesn't have to match the physical configuration of the IDE drive, just the logical configuration. Multiply heads times cylinders times sectors per track to get the total number of ~~cylinders~~ *sectors* on a hard disk (this is the logical size). An 84 Mb IDE drive with 6 heads, 832 cylinders, and 33 sectors per track would have 164,736 sectors. If you select a hard drive type from the BIOS list that contains the same 164,736 sectors (or fewer), the drive will work. It will work even if the drive you picked has 8 heads and 624 cylinders (a different physical configuration) because the IDE drive electronics translates your computer's instructions to read a particular logical sector (in the drive the computer believes is installed) to the actual head-and-cylinder situation in the IDE drive.

If you must choose among a limited list of drive types, pick one as close as possible to your actual IDE logical size (total number of sectors), but pick one a hair smaller rather than a hair too large. Newer BIOS ROMs now support a user-definable drive with user-defined cylinder and head counts. Thus you can easily match the logical size of your IDE drive to the logical size of your user-defined drive by picking an ordinary number of heads (like 8, for example) and an ordinary number of sectors per track (17, 39, or 53 are typical values) and calculating the oddball number of cylinders you need to make the total number of sectors on the drive less than or equal to the actual number of sectors on your IDE drive.

Unfortunately, we have run into software (for example, Novell NetWare 3.10) that refuses to run properly on user-definable drives. If you don't have a reasonable size match to choose from, and you don't have (or can't use) a user-definable drive type, it makes sense to get a newer BIOS rather than wasting a quarter or a third of your IDE drive's capacity by entering too small a drive in your computer's CMOS setup.

6. **Format the IDE drive.** IDE drives are low-level formatted at the factory. You need not, and should not, attempt to reinitialize them.

   Use the DOS FDISK command to partition the drive. If you have an older version of DOS, you may want to use Disk Manager to partition this disk, since DOS versions below 4.01 limit each hard disk partition to 32 Mb or less (a big drag).

   Format the disk with the DOS FORMAT command. If you intend to boot from this drive, use the /S switch or the DOS command SYS C: to copy COMMAND.COM and the DOS hidden files to the boot partition.

   Directions for FDISK, FORMAT, and SYS are in any DOS manual.

ESDI Drives and Controller Cards

How ESDI Works

ESDI looks like the ST506 standard. The cables and connectors are identical to ST506 cables and connectors. But ESDI is much faster than ST506.

ESDI drives put the data separation circuitry (the data encoding/decoding circuits) on the hard disk; ST506 puts it on the hard disk controller. ESDI drives send clean data to the ESDI controller, not the weird drive-writing signals that actually encode the data on the disk platters. Therefore, ESDI drives don't have to be as carefully synchronized with their controllers, and higher data transfer rates are possible. The ESDI interface transfers two, three, or four times as much data per second as the old ST506.

DOS can't talk to more than 1,024 cylinders on a hard drive. To get around this limitation, many ESDI controllers allow "translation"—they lie to DOS about the physical configuration of the drive.

Theoretically, the ESDI interface can accommodate eight ESDI drives, but few controllers are designed for eight drives. If you're planning to connect more than two ESDI drives, get a special controller, then cable the drives and jumper as per the directions shipped with the controller.

How to Test an ESDI Drive and ESDI Controller

See "How to Test an ST506 Drive and Controller," page 232, for details. Since the interfaces are so similar, most troubleshooting techniques work for both ESDI and ST506.

How to Install an ESDI Controller Card

1. **Remove old controller card.** Begin by examining the cables attached to the controller card. Mark them or take notes before you disconnect them so you will be able to reinstall them properly. Don't forget the little two-wire cable to the remote hard drive light on the front panel of your computer case. It pulls right off the controller card and will slide back onto the equivalent pins on the new card. Remove the screw holding the card to the rear of the computer chassis (shown in Figures 11.1 through 11.3 on pages 102-103). Then pull the ESDI card straight up out of the bus connector.

2. **Choose the right controller.** Not all ESDI drives and controllers work with each other. Buy them together—or check that both drive manufacturer and controller manufacturer believe they work together. A slow ESDI drive will work with a fast controller, for example, but a fast drive won't work with a slow controller.

3. **Insert board in slot.** Line up the controller card's edge connector with an appropriate expansion slot connector on the mainboard. Press the board down, then secure it to the back of the case with a screw. Plug in the cables. Because ESDI and ST506 cables are the same, see the directions for installing ST506 cables (page 236) if you can't just copy the way the cables were hooked up to the old ESDI controller.

4. **Use SETUP.** Ordinarily we use SETUP to tell the computer what kind of drive is installed, so the computer's BIOS can issue intelligent read/write commands to the hard disk controller (which, in turn, issues its own read/write signals to the hard disk). Since ESDI

hard disk controllers lie to the computer about the ESDI drive's configuration, you don't have to enter the correct number of heads and cylinders in the CMOS.

The ESDI controller does, however, require you to enter a preliminary lie, so the computer knows that a hard disk is installed, and the ESDI controller and the computer can start a conversation. Most ESDI controllers ask you to set the drive type to type 1 with the CMOS SETUP routine. To be certain your drive will work properly, read and follow your ESDI drive's installation pamphlet.

How to Install the ESDI Cables

Physically, ESDI is a souped-up ST506 interface. ESDI uses the same cables and the same hook-up rules as ST506 (the old MFM and RLL hard drives). We have a section on ST506 hard drive cabling on page 236. Read that section, then return here when you have finished installing the cables.

How to Install an ESDI Drive

Steps 1-4. ESDI drives are installed like ST506 MFM and RLL drives. We have complete directions, starting on page 237, in the section called "How to Install an MFM or RLL Hard Disk with the ST506 Interface." Read that section, BUT COME BACK TO THIS SECTION before you format your ESDI drive.

5. **Format the ESDI drive.** The hard drive controller will have a low-level format routine built into the ROM on the ESDI card. Follow the directions in the controller's installation pamphlet. Remember, most ESDI drives want you to set the drive type to 1 with the CMOS SETUP program—again, read your installation pamphlet.

Use the DOS FDISK command to partition the drive. If you have an older version of DOS you may want to use Disk Manager to partition this disk, since DOS versions below 4.01 limit each hard disk partition to 32 Mb or less.

Format the disk with the DOS FORMAT command. If you intend to boot from this drive, use the /S switch or the DOS command SYS C: to copy COMMAND.COM and the DOS hidden files to the boot partition.

Directions for FDISK, FORMAT, and SYS are in any DOS manual.

ST506 MFM and RLL Drives and Hard Disk Controller Cards

Let's look at some photos of typical ST506 hard drives and controllers. Figures 15.8 and 15.9 show the hard disk subsystem, complete with cables, in an XT and an AT clone. The hard disk, you'll notice, is not directly connected to the computer. All signals from the disk travel through cables to the hard disk controller card. The controller card plugs into a mainboard expansion slot, making the connection to the rest of the computer.

Notice the 8-bit (single connector) controller card for the XT; the XT mainboard has short single-connector bus expansion slots. The AT controller is a 16-bit (double connector) card to match the double-length bus expansion slots on an AT mainboard. The controller must "match" the mainboard it plugs into. The hard drive must "match" the controller card. Since ST506 is not a particularly sophisticated interface, the ST506 hard disk and controller rely upon DOS for explicit "read here" or "write there" directions. Therefore, you must tell DOS how many heads and how many cylinders are in the hard drive you have installed. All these relationships (computer-to-controller, controller-to-cable, cable-to-hard drive, hard drive-to-controller, and DOS-to-hard drive) must be set up right, or the drive won't work. The installation section on page 237 clarifies these relationships.

Figure 15.8
This is the hard disk subsystem for an XT clone. It includes a hard disk, hard disk cables, and an 8-bit hard disk controller. Photo by Robert McLaughlin.

Figure 15.9
This is the hard disk subsystem in a 286/AT, 386/AT, 486/AT clone. It includes a hard disk, hard disk cables, and a 16-bit disk controller. Photo by Robert McLaughlin.

Where to Find the ST506 MFM or RLL Hard Disk and Its Controller in Your Computer

First take the cover off your computer, as described in Chapter 12. Typically, the hard disk controller card is installed close to the power supply and the hard disk(s). It has at least two ribbon cables attached to it (often three or four, if you have two hard disks in the machine and/or the controller also functions as the floppy drive controller).

To be sure that you've identified the hard disk controller correctly, find the hard disk (a solid rectangular device, about 6 x 8 x 1.5 or 3 inches, with a light on the front faceplate). There are also two ribbon cables on the back of the hard disk. One is 34 wires wide (the controller cable) and the other is 20 wires wide (the data cable). Follow the ribbon cables back to the hard disk controller card. The data cable goes there directly. The controller cable starts at the controller and runs to each hard disk in turn. If you have two hard disks, for instance, the controller cable has three connections: at the controller, at hard disk 0, and at hard disk 1.

How ST506 (MFM or RLL) Hard Drives and Controllers Work

Hard Disk

Under the ST506 interface standard, the hard disk does none of the data recording brain work. The hard disk controller (following DOS instructions) tells the drive where to move the read/write heads, when to write, and when to read. The hard disk is limited to following the controller's directions—it's not a very sophisticated device, but it obeys the controller's commands very quickly.

Controller

The ST506 hard disk controller mediates between DOS and one or two hard drives. DOS decides what information should be recorded and exactly where it should go on the platters, demanding a read/write action at a particular sector and track on the hard disk. The controller translates these instructions into electrical signals to the stepper motor, which moves the heads inside the hard drive. 286, 386, and 486 computers generally use combination cards, with both floppy and hard drive controllers located on the same card (see Figure 14.3, page 189). XT/PC clones almost always use two separate cards. In either case, the floppy and hard drive controller circuitry is independent, so one system might fail while the other continues to work properly.

Data Storage

Here is how information is stored on the hard disk, whether you're using DOS, Unix, Novell NetWare, or OS/2:

The microprocessor sends an I/O write signal down the bus (the major internal information path), along with the address of the hard disk controller. Address logic chips on the controller, which are responsible for monitoring the bus and recognizing the controller's address code, tell the controller to pay attention to the next bus signals.

Next, DOS sends the where-to-write instruction. DOS keeps track of the information on the hard disk. It knows what file has been recorded where, which sectors are empty and available to store information, and which sectors on the hard disk are locked out because they are not suitable for safe data storage. Then DOS requests a read/write operation by track and sector number. It tells the hard disk where (to what track) to move the head assembly and what sector on the track should be used to store the upcoming data.

Finally, DOS sends the data it wants to record. For more information on tracks, sectors, and disk recording basics, see Chapter 14. The information (the data DOS wants to store on the hard disk) cannot be recorded directly. Various housekeeping bits—clock bits and error correction code bits, for example—must be added. The hard disk controller is responsible for packaging (encoding) the data before the hard disk records it. When the data is read back, everything recorded on the hard disk is sent to the hard disk controller. Data separation circuits, located on the controller, sort out this raw information, discard the housekeeping bits, and send a clean stream of stored data back to the microprocessor through the bus.

There are two popular ways to package information on ST506 hard disks: MFM (Modified Frequency Modulation) and 2,7 RLL (Run Length Limited) encoding. MFM encoding uses 17 sectors per track, and the magnetic marks on the hard disk are spaced relatively far apart. 2,7 RLL data encoding uses 26 sectors per track and packs many more magnetic marks on each track, so an extremely precise hard disk is required. ESDI, SCSI, and IDE drives use newer versions of RLL encoding that compress the data tighter than 2,7 RLL does and allow far more sectors per track. It's not unusual to have 36, 54, or 108 sectors on an IDE, SCSI, or ESDI hard disk.

Suitable hard disks are RLL-certified by the manufacturer. In each case, the data encoding scheme is built into the controller hardware, not the hard disk. In other words, an MFM controller with an RLL-certified hard drive produces MFM data encoding on an over-priced, over-qualified recording surface.

How to Test an ST506 Hard Disk and Controller

Occasionally, a hard disk will break down and make so much noise while self-destructing that there is no doubt that the hard disk, and only the hard disk, is causing the malfunction. For instance, only one of the hard disks on a two-hard-disk computer may be making a grinding, bad-bearing noise. This noise usually starts out as a scraping, squeaking sound and eventually gets much louder. If hard disk 0 is fine, but hard disk 1 is noisy and is beginning to get louder and to exhibit read/write errors, then it makes sense to replace only hard disk 1.

Unfortunately, most troubleshooting situations are not so clear. Typically the single hard disk in a computer is malfunctioning, but silently. It's hard to tell whether the hard disk itself is causing the problem in this case.

Neither hard disk nor hard disk controller can be tested alone. We test these devices by seeing how well they do their jobs, and both must be installed before either will do any work at all. Therefore, substituting a known-good hard disk or a known-good controller, then observing if the symptom is gone, is the ideal way to determine which part is failing. This substitution technique has some limitations. A bad part can kill the good test part you've just swapped into the machine. This is not typical, but it is a major problem when it happens. In any case, not many people—other than computer dealers—have known-good hard disks and controllers lying around.

Despite these limitations, here are some troubleshooting suggestions.

Remove the system unit cover, as described in Chapter 12. First check that the hard disk platters are spinning when the power is on—they should be. Put your hand on top of the hard disk. Listen and feel as you turn off the computer, let the disks spin down, then turn the computer back on again. Most of the time you'll feel and hear the hard disk spinning. If you're not certain, try a slightly more aggressive test. While the computer is on, but not doing any work, unplug the four-wire, hard disk power connector, then plug it back in. You should hear and feel the hard disk slow down, stop spinning, then start up again as power is reapplied. Only one hard disk in a thousand will fail this test. If yours does, check the power connector with a voltmeter (+5 volts and +12 volts) before condemning the hard disk. If the power connector voltage is okay, replace the hard disk.

If the hard disk does spin when connected to power, check the ribbon cables running between the disk and the disk controller. These cables should be connected snugly to the pins on the controller card and to the flat edge-connectors on the back of the hard drive.

If this is a new installation, or if other technicians have been working on the machine recently, double-check the cables, looking for a backward connection or a floppy drive cable mistakenly installed on the hard disk. See "How to Install an MFM or RLL Hard Disk with the ST506 Interface," on page 237, if you have any questions. If it's a new installation, you should also recheck the configuration of the jumpers on both the drive and the controller. Misinstallation, rather than bad parts, is likely to be the problem, even though the error message on your screen is an intimidating "Error Reading Fixed Disk" or "Hard Disk Failure" or "HDD Controller Failure."

If the hard disk won't boot, try booting from a floppy to see if you can read some or all of the data on the hard disk. If you can, most likely neither the hard disk nor the hard disk controller is bad. Perhaps a voltage spike has destroyed the information stored in the boot sectors on track 0 of the hard disk. Recopy COMMAND.COM and the two DOS hidden files (using the DOS command SYS), then retest.

If you have just installed and formatted this drive, you are probably using DOS 3.3 or newer. Use FDISK to examine the drive partition setup. Did you forget to make one of the partitions "active"— one of our favorite mistakes.

If the hard disk still won't boot, or it boots but is beginning to produce read or write errors, consider using a hard disk analysis and maintenance program. We describe the most popular maintenance programs in Chapter 10.

If none of the suggestions discussed solves your problem, you may have to face losing some data in order to restore your hard disk to working order. When your hard disk won't boot or read, and it's generally malfunctioning, you may have to reformat. "XT Clones—How to Format a Hard Disk with the ST506 Interface," on page 241, and "286/386/486 AT Clones—How to Format a Hard Disk with the ST506 Interface," on page 245, give separate directions for XT or 286/386/486 clones. Before you reformat, however, read Chapter 10 carefully to make sure you haven't missed any tricks. Once you low-level format the hard disk, your data is gone.

If the computer won't format the hard disk, you'll have to replace both the hard disk and the controller. We do not recommend replacing only one unit, since a malfunctioning controller can burn out a good hard disk. It's better to replace both than to guess wrong, blow up the new disk, and end up buying two hard disks and a controller. If you absolutely need to try the cheapest solution, replace the controller first, then the hard disk.

How to Install an ST506 Hard Disk Controller

1. **Remove old controller card.** Removing a hard disk controller is the same as removing any other card. Begin by examining the cables connected to the card. Mark them or take notes so you will be able to properly reinstall them. Remove the screw holding the card to the rear of the computer chassis, as shown in Figures 11.1 to 11.3 on pages 102-103, and pull the card straight up out of the bus connector.

2. **Choose the right controller.** Before you install a hard disk controller, you should be familiar with the differences between the various types of controllers. One major division is 8-bit versus 16-bit cards. Figure 14.3, on page 189, shows 8-bit and 16-bit hard disk controller cards side by side. 8-bit cards are for PC/XT clones and have the short, single bus connector. These 8-bit controller cards usually regulate only hard disks. Typical 16-bit controller cards, by comparison, manage both the hard and the floppy drives. These dual-purpose controller cards are designed with two separate sets of circuits; they just share a single card and use only one card slot. 16-bit cards can be easily recognized by the two-part bus connector located on the base of the card, where it plugs into the computer mainboard.

As PC/XT computers near extinction, we don't see 8-bit controller cards as often. Don't confuse these 8-bit ST506 hard disk controller cards with 8-bit SCSI cards. If you're in doubt, compare your hard disk ribbon cables to the drawings on pages 214-215. ST506 uses two ribbon cables to each hard disk, while SCSI uses only one.

The other major division between the various types of hard disk controllers is the data coding scheme; this feature is also built right into the hardware. Both 8-bit and 16-bit cards come in MFM and RLL designs. Both MFM and RLL cards are hard-wired to produce MFM or RLL data coding respectively. They cannot be reconfigured or adjusted to use a different data packaging technique.

The hard disk should be certified for the chosen controller's data packaging method. Whatever data coding scheme you choose, use a matched set of hard disk and hard disk controller. Don't connect an RLL controller to an MFM-type hard disk. The combination will appear to work for the first couple of weeks, then will rapidly start losing data. On the other hand, an RLL-certified hard disk will work fine with an MFM controller, but the extra quality in the hard disk will be wasted because it is under-utilized to record data in the MFM format. Nevertheless, no data loss will follow from this mismatch.

3. **Set switches on XT controllers.** Once you select an appropriate hard disk controller card, you are ready to install it. 8-bit (PC/XT clone) controller cards have jumpers or dip switches to tell the controller and DOS what kind of hard disk(s) are attached. The controller manual, which you must read to learn how to set these jumpers, lists approximately 10 hard disk options. These include 4 heads and 306 cylinders, 4 heads and 615 cylinders, 2 heads and 612 cylinders, and so on. Use the option for your particular hard disk—if it's listed. If you have a non-standard hard disk, choose an option slightly smaller than the actual size of the hard disk. For instance, you can approximate a hard disk with 5 heads and 620 cylinders by setting the controller for 4 heads and 615 cylinders. Some of the hard disk area (the part accessed by the fifth head and the innermost tracks) won't be used, but no read/write problems will result. Of course, buying a new controller—one that's able to manage 5 heads and 640 cylinders—would allow you to have access to the full storage capacity of your hard disk. Either solution works fine technically, so it's mostly a question of economics. If you don't know how many heads and cylinders your hard disk has, call the drive vendor's technical department and ask.

4. **Put the card in the slot.** Press the card into a slot on the mainboard. Install the screw that holds the card in place.

5. **AT controllers—use SETUP.** 16-bit (286, 386 and 486) controller cards do not have jumpers to configure the controller for different hard disks. The information is instead stored on the mainboard in the CMOS chip. If you have an AT-style 286/386/486 computer, run the setup program once you've installed the card. Choose an appropriate hard disk type from the list in the mainboard ROM BIOS. Choose a drive type smaller than the actual hard

ST506

drive if the choices in the setup program don't match your hard disk perfectly. Newer ROM BIOS versions have more drive types to choose from, so consider upgrading your old BIOS ROM if your drive or something close isn't listed. Your computer manufacturer's technical support department will know what new BIOS versions are available and whether a new BIOS will help here. We discuss the role of SETUP and the EISA configuration utility in Chapter 11.

6. **Format the hard disk.** Unless you have replaced a bad controller with the identical hard disk controller, you'll have to reformat the hard disk so this new controller and the hard disk can talk to each other. You will need to low-level format the drive, run FDISK, then high-level format the drive. This three-step process is covered in "XT Clones—How to Format a Hard Disk with the ST506 Interface," on page 241, and "286/386/486 AT Clones—How to Format a Hard Disk with the ST506 Interface," on page 245. If you're adding a drive or replacing your present hard disk and controller, see "How to Install an MFM or RLL Hard Disk with the ST506 Interface," below, for tips about drive select jumpers and terminating resistors.

How to Install Cables for ST506 (These Directions Also Work for ESDI)

A separate data cable (20-wire ribbon cable) goes from the controller to each hard drive. The red or blue edge of the cable is for pin #1. On the controller card find the number 1 (usually stenciled next to the data cable connector pins). Hard disks have flat card edge connectors, with a notch cut close to the pin #1 end of the connector. Put the colored edge of the data cable toward the slot when connecting the cable to the hard disk.

All the hard disks share a single controller cable. It's a wide, 34-wire ribbon cable. Pay attention to the red/blue edge, so the cable correctly mates to pin #1 at each connection. Hard disk 0 (DOS calls it drive C) is at the end of this controller cable. The middle connector attaches to the second hard disk (if there is one). If you have only one drive and a short, straight-through ribbon cable with only two connectors, put one connector on the hard disk and the other on the controller card, making sure you put the color-coded edge toward pin #1 at each connector. The examples in Figures 15.11 to 15.14 (on pages 238-239) should make this clear.

On 16-bit (AT-style) controller cards, you also need to attach the floppy drive controller cable. Luckily, most of these cards have "to floppy drive" stenciled on the card at the appropriate connector pins. Since both floppy cable and hard disk control-ler cable have 34 wires, new technicians often mix them up. Be sure you have the floppy cable on the floppy connector and the hard disk cable on the hard disk connector.

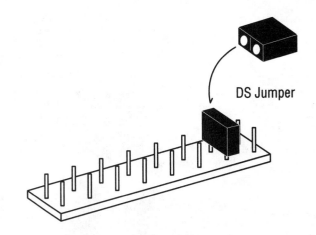

DS Jumper

Figure 15.10
A DS jumper on the second position. This is one of many DS setting methods; other manufacturers use switches or jump-ers on top of the drive.

How to Install an MFM or RLL Hard Disk with the ST506 Interface (These Directions Also Work for ESDI)

1. **Remove old hard disk.** First remove the system unit cover, as described in Chapter 1. Examine the two ribbon cables at the back of the hard disk, mark them for reinstallation, then disconnect them. Disconnect the four-wire power cord from the hard disk.

   Remove the screws holding the hard disk to the chassis. PC/XT computers usually have screws threaded into the side of the hard disk. There may also be a screw or two that is accessible though holes in the bottom of the computer chassis. Many AT-style computers (286, 386, and 486 machines) use rails screwed to the side of the hard disk. These rails allow the disk to slide in and out of the chassis like a drawer. To remove a 286 or 386 hard disk, look for clips on the front of the chassis. Remove the screws holding the clips in place or squeeze the clips to release them, then slide the hard disk out. Save the rails and clips; you will need them for the new hard disk.

2. **Set switches/jumpers on the new drive.** Before you install a new hard disk, you must set the drive select (DS) and terminating resistor. Hard drives have jumpers (or, occasionally, dip switches) to set the drive select number. Figure 15.10 shows a typical hard drive with the DS jumper in the second position.

   Some hard disk manufacturers use a 0,1,2,3 numbering system for the drive select jumpers on their hard disks. In this case the first hard disk is number 0. Others use 1,2,3,4 numbering, so the first unit is #1, and the second is #2. See the manual shipped with your hard disk for details about your drive. We will give you general principles, but this is no substitute for a manufacturer's sketch of the jumpers on the particular drive.

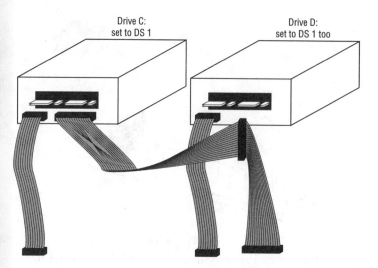

Figure 15.11
Cable routing for two ST506 (MFM or RLL) or ESDI hard drives. Note the cable twist at drive C. Both drives set to DS 1. Use a separate 20-wire data cable for each drive.

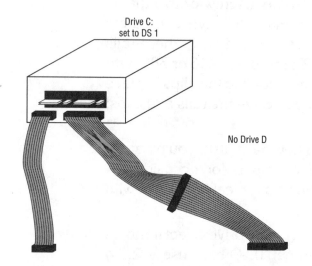

Figure 15.12
A single ST506 or ESDI hard drive with a 20-pin data cable and a 34-pin control cable. Because the control cable has a twist, set the drive to DS1.

If you have a cable with a twist and two hard drives (Figure 15.11). Set the DS jumper on both drives to show that each drive is the second hard drive in the computer. This doesn't make much sense, but the computer won't confuse the drives when they're set to the same DS. The twist at the end of the cable, where it plugs into the C drive, flips the DS signals back around so the controller thinks the C drive is set to DS 0. Arcane, isn't it? However, this is the same technique used to distinguish Floppy Drive A from Floppy Drive B, so it must have made sense to somebody at some point.

If you have a cable with a twist and only one hard drive (Figure 15.12). Set the DS jumper on this drive to make it the second hard drive in the computer. The twist at the end of the cable, where it plugs into the C drive, flips the DS signals back around so the controller thinks the C drive is set to DS 0. Don't try setting the drive to 0 and using the straight-through connector in the middle of the cable. Though it sounds plausible, you'd end up with a pigtail of cable (the end with the twist) not connected to anything, which would make weird electronic echoes on the cable whenever the drive and controller tried to talk to each other.

If you have one drive and a straight-through cable (Figure 15.13). Clone makers save money when they install a straight-through, one-hard drive-only, controller cable on single-drive systems. If you have this cheaper controller cable (with one connector on each end, no third connector, and no twist in the middle) set up the hard drive as if it were the first (and only) drive in the computer system. Set the drive select jumper on the first set of pins—not the second.

If you have two drives and a straight-through cable (Figure 15.14). You should never have two drives and a straight-through cable. Please recheck yourself—did you mistakenly identify an IDE or SCSI cable as an ST506/ESDI cable? If there's no mistake, set the first hard disk to DS0 (set the drive select jumper on the first set of pins—not the second). Then set the second drive to DS1 (the jumper on the second set of pins). Shrug your shoulders and go on. It's weird, but it should work fine.

3. **Check terminating resistor(s).** The first drive (the drive at the end of the hard drive controller cable) should have a terminating resistor (see Figure 15.15 on the next page). Any second hard drive, if installed, must not have one. Look for the terminating resistor in a socket on the bottom of the hard drive. Very few hard disk components are socketed, most often only the terminating resistor, so it should be easy to identify.

If necessary, remove the terminating resistor from your second drive with your fingers or by sliding a small screwdriver between the resistor and the socket. Occasionally someone has already removed the resistor before you buy the drive. Be sure to use a terminating resistor on the drive at the end of the controller cable, but not on the drive in the middle of the controller cable.

4. **Slide in drive, connect cables.** After you configure the hard disk, slide it into the chassis. Most 286 and 386 computers use rails (flat bars screwed onto the side of the hard disk) to hold the hard disk in place. If your computer requires rails, install them on the hard disk

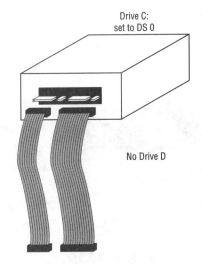

Figure 15.13
A single ST506 or ESDI hard drive with a 20-wire data cable and a 34-wire control cable. The control cable is straight-through, so set the drive to DS0.

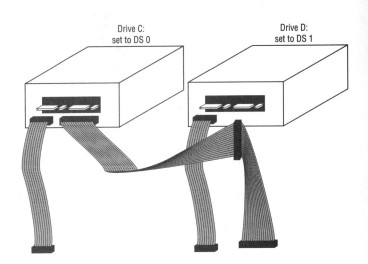

Figure 15.14
Two ST506 or ESDI hard drives connected with a 34-pin control cable with no twist at the C drive. Set drive C to DS0 and drive D to DS1. Use separate 20-wire data cables for each drive.

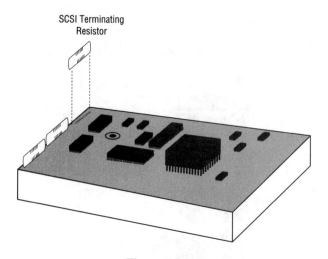

SCSI Terminating
Resistor

Figure 15.15
Terminating resistor on a hard drive.

and slide it back into the chassis. It's not unusual to put the rails on wrong (too high, too far forward, etc.) the first couple of times. If you play around with them long enough you'll eventually get them right.

Connect the two ribbon cables to the flat edge connectors on the back of the hard disk. Be sure to connect pin #1 on each ribbon cable to pin #1 on the hard drive. The red (or sometimes blue) edge of the cable is the #1 end. The gold-colored hard drive edge-connectors have a notch cut into the connector on one end. The end with the notch has pin #1, so put the red edge on the ribbon cable toward the notch.

If you have two hard disks in your system they will share the 34-wire hard disk controller cable, but each disk will have its own 20-wire data cable.

Once you've connected the ribbon cables, plug in any four-wire power cable from the power supply. Note that the power supply cable connectors are not rectangular. Look at one carefully; two corners have been cut off on a diagonal. Examine the socket on the hard drive carefully and be sure to install the power connector correctly. Then install screws to hold the drive into the chassis.

Warning: If you're working on an ESDI drive, it's time to jump back to the ESDI formatting instructions on page 228.

5. **Format drive.** After you install your new hard disk, you must format it. There are three steps in this process: low-level formatting, FDISK, and DOS FORMAT. Disk Manager automates much of the process. If you are using Disk Manager, follow the directions that come with the program disk. If you want to format your hard disk manually, read the directions in either "XT Clones—How to Format a Hard Disk with the ST506 Interface," on page 241, or "286/386/486 Clones—How to Format a Hard Disk with the ST506 Interface," on page 245.

XT Clones—How to Format a Hard Disk with the ST506 Interface

This section tells you how to format the hard disk in XT clones. You can do this manually or you can use a semi-automated hard disk format program called Disk Manager (from Ontrack, 800-752-1333).

How to Use Disk Manager to Format an XT Clone Hard Disk

It's not easy for the casual user to format one hard disk every two years. Even technicians who format many hard disks each week find manual formatting a big hassle. Disk Manager, a semi-automated hard disk format program, rescues us all. It's inexpensive, accurate, and efficient. We included manual hard disk format directions below, but we highly recommend that you use Disk Manager.

How to Manually Format an XT Clone Hard Disk

Formatting a hard disk manually involves three steps: low-level formatting, FDISK, and high-level formatting.

Step 1: Low-Level Formatting

A PC/XT clone mainboard knows nothing about hard disk hardware. 286, 386, and 486 machines, on the other hand, are engineered quite differently. If you want to compare designs, read "286/386/486 AT Clones—How to Format a Hard Disk with the ST506 Interface," on page 245. In XTs, all hard disk physical control is supervised by the hard disk controller ROM, not the CPU or the clone's ROM BIOS. Low-level formatting examines the hard disk for bad spots, locks out the bad spots so they cannot be written to, and writes the sector address marks on the hard disk. In other words, it is the most hardware-specific, preliminary level of hard disk preparation.

The details of low-level formatting are completely dependent on the hard disk controller. For this reason, the low-level formatting program is stored in the hard disk controller ROM. You can access the ROM format routine with the DEBUG command. To do this, type: **DEBUG <CR> g=c800:5**

ST506

<CR> (or whatever address the hard drive controller manual says). After doing this, answer the questions on the screen. By the way, debug means use the DEBUG utility. G=c800:5 means jump to the address c800:5 and follow the instructions at that address.

Most hard disk controller ROMs have the low-level formatting utility at the address c800:5, but a few use other locations. C800:6 and c800:ccc are occasionally used. The latter is only for RLL controllers. The conservative technician insists upon documentation whenever he or she buys a new hard disk controller, but one of these three addresses will usually work. You know right away if you have picked an incorrect address; the screen is full of gibberish.

Entering the correct address produces a screen of English language questions—not necessarily intelligible questions, just English. When faced with these controller questions, keep your wits about you. Those controllers that require answers in hexadecimal numbers will say so; don't worry, most don't. Some controllers use a 0,1,2,3 numbering system for the hard disks. In this case the first hard disk (usually drive C) is number 0. Others use 1,2,3,4 numbering, so the first unit is number 1, and the second is number 2.

When you're prompted to input an interleave factor, enter 3 for a PC/XT clone. You'll be prompted to enter a write precompensation cylinder factor. If you have no documentation with the drive you'll have to guess—one-half of the total number of cylinders is a reasonable rule of thumb. Both interleave and write precompensation are listed in the glossary if you want more details.

Most Western Digital XT hard disk controllers ask "Are you dynamically configuring the drive?" A "No" response means "Don't ask me any questions, just follow the jumpers on the card." A "Yes" response allows you to answer detailed questions about the hard disk design—in other words, to customize the installation. Unfortunately, many Western Digital XT controllers ask this question, then ignore your answers, and proceed to format the hard drive according to its switch and jumper settings. To ensure that your card is set up the way you want it, find out the correct jumper settings for your model of hard disk and physically configure the card correctly before you install it.

If you have to "dynamically configure" the drive, here are some hints. Landing zone is the track where the drive will park the head when you run a disk park program before moving the computer. When you're prompted for a landing zone, enter a track number equal to the number of tracks on the hard disk, plus one. If absolutely no outside guidance is available about any of these questions, try using the defaults in the controller's low-level format program. They won't hurt anything and might work out well.

Often the low-level format program prompts you for a list of known-bad areas. Check the top of your hard disk for a bad track label. It is important to enter all these bad tracks. The tests done by the hard disk manufacturer are more rigorous than those done by the low-level formatting program. Some tracks that failed at the factory, after long testing, might slip through the low-level formatting program's tests, get recorded on, and eventually lose your files.

When you have answered all the questions and pressed the final carriage return, the formatting routine starts working. As the head assembly moves from cylinder to cylinder, it makes a rhythmic ticking sound. It will take a few minutes, since the entire hard disk surface area must be scanned for defects. Ten to twenty minutes is not an unusually long low-level format time for a 40 Mb disk. Larger disks will, of course, take longer.

Step 2: FDISK Formatting

Step two of the hard disk formatting process—FDISK—prepares one or more DOS partitions (areas on the hard disk suitable for DOS files). This is a very quick process, taking about 30 seconds per partition. Up to four partitions per drive are allowed.

Unlike low-level formatting, FDISK is software-dependent. The low-level format program is stored inside the hard disk controller ROM, so changing controllers changes the screen messages and low-level format process. By comparison, FDISK is a DOS utility. Changing DOS versions changes the FDISK screen messages and, to some extent the FDISK process, but changing the hard disk controller doesn't affect FDISK at all.

DOS versions below 2.0 are unable to deal with hard disks at all. A few DOS versions above 2.0 are limited to 20 Mb hard disks, but DOS versions 2.0 to 3.2 can partition a hard drive as large as 32 Mb. MS-DOS 3.3 can partition larger drives, but each partition is limited to a maximum size of 32 Mb. MS-DOS versions 4.01 and above allow partitions of any size. Hard disk control programs like Disk Manager are designed to transcend the hard disk limitations imposed by older DOS versions.

Consider the case of an XT clone owner who wants to install a 40 Mb hard disk. She is using MS-DOS 3.1, a version that is unable to deal with hard disks larger than 32 Mb. Disk Manager makes the physical 40 Mb disk appear to DOS to be two smaller disks. Here is how it works: because DOS never communicates with the hard disk directly, it's easy for Disk Manager to make DOS think that the hard disk is set up in a way it's not. On an XT clone, DOS and the mainboard ROM BIOS have nothing to do with hard disk hardware. Using the FAT to keep track of empty versus written-on parts of the disk, DOS issues a read/write command by sector number. It subcontracts all physical hard disk management to the hard disk controller. The controller moves the read/write head from track to track to find the right sector.

To read or write anything on a hard disk, DOS sends interrupt 13 to the CPU, which in turn transfers the read/write process to the supervision of the hard disk controller ROM. This process works fine for the first 32 Mb of a hard disk. Unfortunately, DOS cannot send sector addresses above 32 Mb, so it has no way to call for information in the last 20 percent of a 40 Mb hard disk. The drive is physically capable of reading and writing to the last 8 Mb, but this data is inaccessible to DOS.

Disk Manager provides a device driver that contains a software interface between DOS and the physical hard disk controller. When DOS looks at the device driver, it believes there is a second physical hard disk inside the computer. It addresses the hard disk, through the device driver, and receives appropriate responses from drive D.

Meanwhile, the device driver is showing an entirely different face to the hard disk controller. When it gets a DOS request to read a sector on drive D, Disk Manager's device driver reprocesses that request so it will make sense to the hard disk controller. The controller then finds the requested data on the second half of the actual hard disk and sends it to DOS.

MS-DOS 3.3 was rewritten to eliminate the 32 Mb barrier. It allows you to divide up a very large hard disk into a number of smaller logical drives. As with Disk Manager, MS-DOS 3.3 has a maximum first partition size of 32 Mb. With Disk Manager, subsequent partitions may be any size, and may be a single logical drive or subdivided into multiple logical drives. MS-DOS 3.3, on the other hand, limits subsequent partitions to 32 Mb each.

If you wish, you can divide your 60 Mb hard disk into two partitions. DOS will then call one partition drive C and the other drive D and treat them as two separate drives, even though there is only one physical hard disk installed on the machine. One of these partitions must be selected as the active partition (the boot partition). The size of each partition is flexible, as long as it is less than 32 Mb. For example, an 80 Mb hard disk formatted with Disk Manager could be divided into one 30 Mb primary DOS partition (drive C) and one 50 Mb extended DOS partition (drive D). The 50 Mb partition could be subdivided into two or three logical drives (drives D, E, and F) if desired—with the sizes at your discretion—or not subdivided at all. If you're using DOS 3.3, however, you must divide the 80 Mb drive into at least three partitions to respect the 32 Mb partition size limit.

Step 3: High-Level Formatting (FORMAT C:/S)

High-level formatting (FORMAT C:/S) is covered in any DOS manual. Remember, if you've decided to partition your hard drive into two or more logical drives, you'll have to format each logical drive individually before writing data to it.

On DOS versions through 3.2, be sure to put the DOS system files (the two hidden files plus COMMAND.COM) on the first partition. That's the only place DOS looks for boot files. MS-DOS versions 3.3 and above allow you to specify an active partition, the one the computer will boot from. This active partition need not be the first partition. Of course, it must have the DOS system files installed.

High-level formatting is another slow process. Allow 3-5 minutes for a 20 Mb drive; the computer must examine each track for bad sectors. A typical screen message displays cylinder number after cylinder number as each one is completed. Some DOS FORMAT programs then count back up through the cylinder numbers a second time before declaring the formatting complete.

286/386/486 AT Clones—How to Format a Hard Disk with the ST506 Interface

This section tells you how to format the hard disk in AT-style 286, 386, or 486 clones. You can do this manually, or you can use Disk Manager (from Ontrack, 800-752-1333).

How to Use Disk Manager to Format a 286/386/486 Clone Hard Disk

It's not easy for the casual user to format one hard disk every two years. Even technicians who format many hard disks each week find manual formatting a big hassle. Disk Manager, a semi-automated hard disk format program, rescues us all. It's inexpensive, accurate, and efficient.

We have included manual hard disk format directions below, but we highly recommend that you use Disk Manager.

ST506

How to Manually Format a 286/386/486 Clone Hard Disk with ST506 Interface

Formatting a hard disk manually involves three steps: low-level formatting, FDISK, and high-level formatting (FORMAT C:/S).

Step 1: Low-Level Formatting

286, 386, and 486 computers were designed in the age of hard disks; therefore, hard disk control functions were designed right into the mainboard ROM BIOS. To start a low-level format on an AT 286/386/486, use the AT diagnostics disk (the low-level format option) or the low-level format utility that's part of your computer's setup program. Choose the appropriate drive type, matching cylinders, heads, and so forth. Slower ATs should have an interleave of 2. Fast 286s, most 386s, and all 486s can use an interleave of 1.

If your drive does not match a drive type exactly, you may choose a similar, but smaller, drive and lose access to the balance of your disk.

Hard disk management software programs like Disk Manager are very helpful in this situation; they allow you to install hard disks that are not supported by the mainboard's ROM BIOS. In order to do this, the disk management software has to inform DOS that the hard disk is smaller than it actually is. Here's how it's done: you use Disk Manager, for example, to perform all three steps involved in formatting the hard disk (low-level formatting, FDISK, and high-level formatting). Disk Manager looks at the nonstandard drive, then selects a standard drive (one supported by the computer's ROM BIOS) that is smaller than the actual hard drive you have installed. Disk Manager then writes information about this smaller drive in the computer's CMOS configuration record. When the computer boots, it goes through POST (Power-On Self-Test), believing the small drive is installed. This is necessary because the AT BIOS must move the hard disk head assembly to the last cylinder as part of the POST testing process.

After POST, the computer loads a special device driver for the hard disk. The device driver provides a software interface between DOS and the physical hard disk. All hardware has device drivers; many of them are automatically installed as part of the hidden DOS boot files. These device drivers insulate DOS from hardware details. The Disk Manager device driver is special, though; it is able to present one set of information to DOS and another set of information to the hardware.

The driver shows DOS a phantom second hard disk (the same size, not coincidentally, as the extra unusable part of the nonstandard hard disk). When DOS tries to store or retrieve information on this second hard disk, the device driver translates read/write commands for the second drive into sector by sector instructions to the controller to access the unusable part of the hard disk. The controller then finds the requested data on the hard disk and sends it to DOS.

Step 2: FDISK Formatting

Step two of the hard disk formatting process—FDISK—prepares one or more DOS partitions (areas on the hard disk suitable for DOS files). It is a very quick process, taking about 30 seconds per partition. If you're using MS-DOS version 3.3 or newer, be sure to make one of the partitions "active" if you want to boot from this hard disk.

Unlike low-level formatting, FDISK is software-dependent—it's a DOS utility. Changing DOS versions changes the FDISK screen messages and, to some extent, the FDISK process, but changing the hard disk or the hard disk controller doesn't affect FDISK at all.

DOS versions below 2.0 are unable to deal with hard disks at all. A few DOS versions above 2.0 are limited to 20 Mb hard disks, but DOS versions 2.0 to 3.2 can partition a hard drive as large as 32 Mb. MS-DOS 3.3 can partition larger drives, but each partition is limited to a maximum size of 32 Mb. MS-DOS versions 4.01 and later allow partitions of any size.

Though MS-DOS 3.3 was rewritten to eliminate the 32 Mb barrier and it allows you to divide up a very large hard disk into a number of smaller logical drives, it doesn't provide the same flexibility as a hard disk formatting utility. Both Disk Manager and MS-DOS 3.3 have a maximum first partition size of 32 Mb. With Disk Manager, subsequent partitions may be any size, and may be a single logical drive or subdivided into multiple logical drives. MS-DOS 3.3, on the other hand, limits subsequent partitions to 32 Mb each. This difference isn't all that relevant with a 40 or 60 Mb drive. If you wish, you can divide your 60 Mb hard disk into two partitions. DOS will then call one partition drive C and the other drive D and treat them as two separate drives, even though physically there is only one hard disk installed on the machine. One of these partitions must be selected as the active partition (the boot partition). The size of each partition is flexible, as long as it is less than 32 Mb.

In the case of an 80 Mb hard disk, however, Disk Manager can divide the disk into one 20 Mb primary DOS partition (drive C) and one 60 Mb extended DOS partition (drive D). The 60 Mb partition can be subdivided into two or three logical drives (drives D, E, and F) if desired—with the sizes at your

ST506

ST506

discretion—or not subdivided at all. If you're using DOS 3.3, however, you have to divide this 80 Mb drive into at least three partitions to respect the 32 Mb per partition size limit.

Step 3: High-Level Formatting (FORMAT C:/S)

High-level formatting (FORMAT C:/S) is covered in any DOS manual. If you have decided to partition your hard drive into two or more logical drives, remember that you will have to format each logical drive individually before writing data to it.

On DOS versions through 3.2, be sure to put the DOS system files (the two hidden files plus COMMAND.COM) on the first partition. That's the only place DOS looks for boot files. MS-DOS versions 3.3 and later allow you to specify an active partition, the one the computer will boot from. This active partition need not be the first partition. Of course it must have the DOS system files installed.

High-level formatting is another slow process. Allow 3-5 minutes for a 20 Mb drive; the computer must examine each track for bad sectors. A typical screen message displays cylinder after cylinder as each one is completed. Some DOS versions then count back up through the cylinder numbers a second time before declaring the formatting complete.

Chapter 16
Peripherals

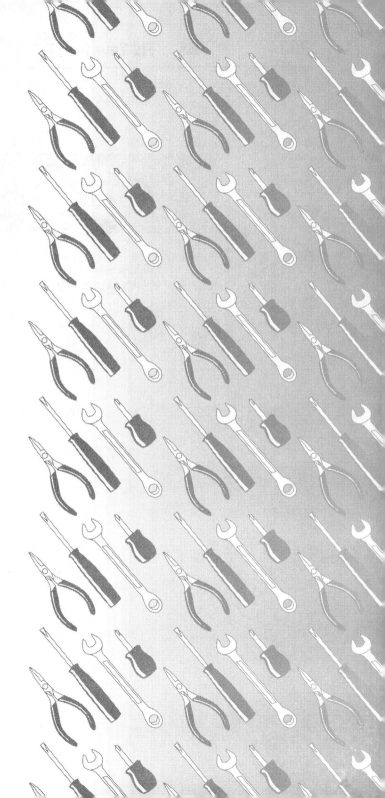

This section describes the following items:

- ✔ Parallel port
- ✔ Serial port
- ✔ Mouse
- ✔ Scanner
- ✔ Sound board

Parallel Port

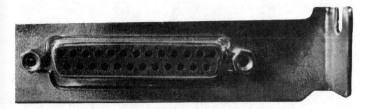

Figure 16.1
DB25 female connector on parallel card.
Photograph by Mel Chamowitz.

The original parallel port had a single function: to send data in one direction, from computer to printer. This parallel card sent data 8 bits at a time to the printer. If the computer received an out-of-paper or printer-busy signal from the printer, it held up data transmission. For years the parallel port was called the printer port—few other parallel devices existed.

New computers have honest two-way parallel ports so data can flow freely into and out of the computer. The two-way parallel port has spawned a whole raft of parallel-interface peripherals. You can now buy network adapters, CD-ROM drives, Bernoulli boxes, even external hard disks and tape backup units, which communicate with the host computer through a parallel port.

The new parallel-connection peripherals require true two-way parallel ports. A pocket Ethernet parallel-port adapter, for example, will connect new computers to a network without a hitch. When we tried the pocket adapter on our venerable GridCase 3 laptop, though, the old Grid computer's one-way parallel port wouldn't receive data from the network adapter.

Despite the flashy new parallel peripherals, printers are still the most common peripheral on a parallel port. Most printers sold in the last five years have been parallel printers, but printers come in two forms—serial and parallel—so you can't assume the port with the printer cable is a parallel port. If you don't know whether your printer is serial or parallel, we'll help you sort out the cables and connectors in the next few paragraphs.

How a Parallel Port Works

Because computers store information in 8-bit bytes, the simplest way to send a byte of information to a printer is in parallel form. Using eight separate wires from computer to printer, each of the 8 bits is sent on its own wire (on a separate data line).

Three signal lines on early parallel ports were assigned to the printer to send out-of-paper, printer-busy, and data-acknowledgement signals back to the computer. The parallel port could transmit signals on the 8 data lines, but not receive them. New parallel ports can either send or receive on all lines.

A standard parallel printer cable, often named a Centronics cable for the 36-pin Centronics connector at the printer end, connects the parallel card to the printer. Unlike serial ports, all parallel ports send the same signals on each particular pin, so no custom parallel cables are needed. Figure 16.2 is the pinout diagram for parallel ports.

Unfortunately, parallel cables are only guaranteed to be accurate for short runs of 12-15 feet, though users sometimes successfully employ cables as long as 25 feet. Each case is different. If it works, it works. If a longer run does not function reliably, you can always use a serial cable coupled with a serial-to-parallel converter box at the printer end of the cable, or try one of the long-distance signal-regenerating parallel cables.

Where to Find the Parallel Port

Look at the back of your computer. If you have a printer, follow the printer cable back to the computer and examine that connector first. Parallel ports use 25-pin connectors (called DB25 connectors) like the one in Figure 16.1. There are two types of DB25 connectors: male and female. Male connectors have protruding pins. One end of your parallel printer cable is a DB25 male connector. The corresponding socket, a female DB25 connector, is the parallel port. Look for this 25-pin female connector on the back of the computer system unit chassis. It's often right on the video card. Figure 16.1 shows a plain parallel card. By comparison, Figure 13.3 on page 160 shows a parallel port on an MPG video card, and Figure 16.4 on page 254 is a combination serial and parallel expansion card with floppy drive controller.

Serial ports also use a DB25 connector on the back of the serial card—which caused confusion in the early 1980's when some

Figure 16.2
Signals on a 25-pin parallel port connector.

Pin	Name
1	Strobe ✓
2	Data bit 0 ✓
3	Data bit 1 ✓
4	Data bit 2 ✓
5	Data bit 3 ✓
6	Data bit 4 ✓
7	Data bit 5 ✓
8	Data bit 6 ✓
9	Data bit 7 ✓
10	Acknowledge ✓
11	Busy ✓
12	Paper out
13	Select
14	Auto line feed
15	Error
16	Initialize printer
17	Select input
18	Ground
19	Ground
20	Ground
21	Ground
22	Ground
23	Ground
24	Ground
25	Ground

serial ports used female DB25 sockets identical to the parallel port socket on the back of the parallel card. For the past decade, all clone serial ports have been male (either 9-pin male DB9s or 25-pin male DB25s). Because parallel ports are always female, it's been impossible to mistakenly plug a parallel cable into a serial port, or vice versa. IBM is now shipping a female DB25 serial port on some PS/2 computers. We anticipate more confusion. Information on serial ports starts on page 254.

A computer may have up to three parallel ports. One may be on the video card. The other parallel ports are often located on multi-function cards (cards with serial and parallel ports, perhaps also a floppy drive controller or a clock or additional memory). Separate parallel cards—short cards with only a few chips installed—are also sold, but many people don't want to waste an expansion slot on a parallel port alone.

Once you locate the parallel port from the outside, take off the system unit cover (described in Chapter 1) and examine the actual parallel card inside the unit.

How to Test a Parallel Port

Parallel ports do not often stop working. It is most unlikely that the parallel port broke down overnight. More likely, you changed the software, installed a new parallel port, or knocked your printer cable loose. And don't forget that the printer itself may have failed.

If you're having parallel printer troubles, you should first figure out whether the problem is the printer, the port, or the cable. Take the printer and the cable to another machine that has a working parallel port. If the printer and the cable work, then start testing the suspect parallel port. If the printer and the cable don't work, turn to the troubleshooting charts in Section 3 for more hints.

If both the printer and the cable are good, use a diagnostic disk to see what parallel ports the computer thinks are installed. If you have two physical parallel ports, but Norton's System Information program, CheckIt, or QA Plus shows only one, the switches and interrupts on one of the ports are not set correctly.

Some video-with-parallel port cards have a port enable/disable jumper. Check the card manual for such a jumper. In addition, the physical port address and the interrupt assigned to the card are set with jumpers on some parallel cards. Check the manual. As with serial ports, you must be careful to give each parallel port its own unique hardware address. DOS refers to these different addresses as LPT1, LPT2, and LPT3. Be sure that your software is set up correctly to send information to the appropriate parallel port. The printer cabled up to LPT1 won't print your document if the word processor is sending the text to LPT2.

If you find no obvious problems, investigate the parallel port further. Try the CheckIt or QA Plus printer port tests. They require a wrap plug, which you can construct out of a spare male RS232 plug (available at electronic parts supply houses). Figure 16.3 identifies which signal pins must be soldered to other signal pins. Use short jumper wires or clean solder bridges to connect the pins together electrically. You must make five solder connections. If you'd rather buy a ready-made wrap plug, JDR Electronics and Jensen Tools sell wrap plugs for approximately $25 (see Appendix E for vendor phone numbers).

Figure 16.3
To make a plug for a parallel port, solder these pins together on a DB25 male connector.

Solder pin	to pin
2	15
3	13
4	12
5	10
6	11

If the parallel port passes the wrap plug test, the port is probably good. Check again for mismatched LPT port and interrupt, or for mismatched word processor output parameters. If you still can't find the problem, try the troubleshooting charts in Section 3. They have complete, step-by-step, parallel port diagnostic/repair procedures.

How to Remove and Install a Parallel Port

1. **Remove cables and computer cover.** Before you remove a parallel port, turn off the computer and monitor. Disconnect the printer cable (the cable from computer to printer) at the parallel port end. The cable will probably have two long, threaded knobs on the card end to hold the cable connector tight to the card. If so, unscrew these knobs by turning them counterclockwise. If the parallel port is on the video card, remove the video cable too. Loosen the two little screws that hold it to the card. Once you've disconnected the cables, remove the system unit cover (described in Chapter 1).

2. **Remove old card.** The card itself is secured to the back wall of the system unit chassis with a single screw. Remove that screw, as shown in Figure 11.1 on page 102, and save it. To remove the card, follow illustrations in Figures 11.2 and 11.3 (on pages 102-103). Lift the card straight up; it shouldn't require too much force.

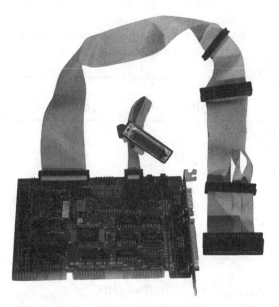

Figure 16.4
A multi-function (multi-I/O) card, with both serial (a DB9 male connector) and parallel port (a DB25 female connector) on the card, plus pins on the card to connect a floppy drive (the 34-pin ribbon cable) and a second serial port (the 9-pin ribbon cable to the DB25 serial port connector). Photo by Robert McLaughlin.

3. **Install new card.** Installation is the reverse of removal. Because parallel, video-with-parallel, and multi-function cards are 8-bit cards, any bus connector in any of the clones is appropriate. You don't have to decide between short (8-bit) and long (16-bit) expansion slots on the mainboard. If the card fits in the slot, it will work.

Carefully line up the edge connector on the card with the slot on the mainboard and press down firmly. When the card is in place, the screw hole on the card will line up with the screw hole in the back of the chassis. Reinstall the screw and test the machine.

Serial Port or Serial Adapter Card

A serial port provides a two-way channel for data. Information flows either from the computer to an external device or from the device back to the computer. Serial ports are used for external modems, for serial mice, and for plotters and scanners. Some printers use serial ports, but most use parallel ports. Because serial cables can reliably run 200 feet between devices (compared to the 15-25 foot maximum for parallel cables), they are often used for remote printers.

How a Serial Port Works

An 8-bit byte of information is carried in parallel form on the computer bus; in other words, all 8 bits are transmitted from place to place simultaneously. This information must be repackaged for serial port transmission. The byte is broken into 8 separate data bits, given 1 or 2 stop/start bits to bracket the package, and provided with a parity checking bit. This complete package is transmitted sequentially to the external serial device.

Unfortunately, many different package designs are allowed. There are a number of parameters that can be set in various ways. Either 7 or 8 data bits may be sent at a time, and either 1 or 2 stop bits may be appended. The serial device may use either even or odd parity, or use no parity checking at all. In addition, many different transmission speeds—ranging from 110 bits/second to 19,600 bits/second—are allowed. The data package is comprised of start bits, data bits, and stop bits. The data transmission standard for 110 baud transfer calls for a total of 11 bits in a data package. Any speed above 110 baud requires only 10 bits per data parcel.

Before any two serial devices can communicate, the parameters mentioned above must be set. Both devices must expect the same kind of data package and they must be working at the same speed. Many serial port problems can be traced to incorrect parameter setup. At the computer end, parameters are set with software, using the DOS MODE command or communications software for a modem. Sometimes a serial printer has variable speed or parity parameters, which may be set with dip switches. More often, the external serial device has a pattern of parameters designed into its hardware. In this case, you must read the manual and then instruct the computer to conform to the parameters that the serial device demands.

Although there are 25 pins on the big serial port socket, only 9 pins are ever used, and most implementations use less than that. Since one pin sends data and another receives data, no serial cable can be a straight-through design, connecting pin #1 to pin #1, pin #2 to pin #2, pin #3 to pin #3, etc. At a minimum, the wires must be crossed so that "data out" (TX) from the computer end of the cable is connected to "data in" (RX) at the external serial device. To send information back to the computer, "transmit data" (TX) from the serial device must be connected to "receive data" (RX) at the computer.

Commissioning custom serial cables to match the various configurations of computer and serial devices can be expensive. There is no longer any need to purchase custom cables. A SmartCable, manufactured by IQ Technologies, will solve most serial cable problems.

We have covered parameters and cables, which are two tricky parts of serial port setup. The last consideration is serial port address. Early DOS versions allowed two serial ports, called COM1 and COM2, each at a different address. New DOS versions allow COM3 and COM4 as well as COM1 and COM2. Each of these DOS serial ports has an associated physical address (a place where DOS will send data that it's trying to shove out the serial port). Use switches or jumpers on the serial card or modem to set up the card to use a particular physical address. Once the port address (the physical address) is set, use the MODE command to tell DOS where to send serial output. It makes sense to set the first serial port in a computer to COM1, since that's the default setting for the DOS MODE command.

Serial Port

Figure 16.5
25-pin serial port pinouts, male or female.

Pin	Name	Abbreviation
1	Chassis ground	
2	Transmit data	TX
3	Receive data	RX
4	Request to send	RTS
5	Clear to send	CTS
6	Data set ready	DSR
7	Signal ground	SG
8	Carrier detect	CD
20	Data terminal ready	DTR
22	Ring indicator	RI

Figure 16.6
9-pin serial port pinouts, male.

Pin	Name	Abbreviation
1	Carrier detect	CD
2	Receive data	RX
3	Transmit data	TX
4	Data terminal ready	DTR
5	Signal ground	GND
6	Data set ready	DSR
7	Request to send	RTS
8	Clear to send	CTS
9	Ring indicator	RI

Each serial port must have a different address. If you don't do this, your modem software will send dialing instructions to your mouse. Each physical port also has a corresponding interrupt number. Appendix D, the list of standard I/O addresses and their associated interrupts, will help you choose the interrupt that matches the physical address you selected. Serial cards, modems, and other serial devices are shipped with installation manuals. Read them.

Where to Find the Serial Port

There are three styles of serial port connectors: the XT-type DB25 male connector with 25 pins, the AT-style 9-pin serial connector fitted with a DB9 connector, and a new 25-pin female serial port connector shipping on some IBM PS/2s.

If you're not familiar with the term "DB9 connector," remove your video cable and look at the end. This cable has a male DB9 connector (unless you are using a video graphics adapter [VGA] or super VGA with a 15-pin DB15 connector). Now look for a similar socket on the back of the PC; not a female DB9 like the video card where the cable attaches, but a male DB9 like the video cable end. If you don't find a 9-pin serial port, look for a 25-pin male connector (with protruding pins) in the rear of the computer. Not all computers are equipped with a serial card, so you may find neither socket. If you find a single DB25 female connector on the back of the computer it's probably parallel, since most clones are equipped with a parallel port.

For years, all clone serial ports have been male (either 9-pin or 25-pin). These male serial ports make it impossible to mistakenly plug a parallel cable into a serial port, or vice versa. In the early 1980's, though, serial ports had 25-pin (DB25) female connectors, visually indistinguishable from modern parallel port connectors. Users were always plugging parallel printers into the serial ports of old Kaypros, for example—then complaining that the printer didn't work. IBM has reintroduced this female serial port on its PS/2 line, again baffling users.

Figure 16.7
To make a serial port wrap plug, solder these connectors.

Solder this signal	to this signal	and this signal
TX	RX	
RTS	CTS	CD
DTR	DSR	RI

How to Test a Serial Port

First find out what serial ports the computer thinks are installed. If you have two physical serial ports, but Norton's System Information program, CheckIt, or QA Plus only show one, then clearly the switches and interrupts on one of the ports are not set correctly.

Next, rethink the links between physical address, interrupt, DOS MODE command, software setup, etc. Make sure you're not doing something silly like sending data to COM1 when the printer cable is connected to COM2. Such mismatches happen fairly often. Communications programs must also be configured to search for a modem at the relevant COM port.

If these steps do not reveal an obvious problem, use a serial test program with wrap plug capability. CheckIt and QA Plus both have a test program that sends data out the "transmit data" (TX) line and checks to see that it has been properly received on the "receive data" (RX) line.

These tests require a wrap plug. You can construct one at home out of a spare female RS232 plug or a female DB9 plug, both of which are inexpensive and available at electronic supply houses. You will have to make three soldered connections. Figure 16.7 tells you which signal pins must be soldered to other signal pins(s). Use short jumper wires or clean solder bridges to connect the pins together electrically. If you'd rather buy a wrap plug ready-made, JDR Electronics and Jensen Tools sell them for approximately $25 (see Appendix E for supplier phone numbers).

Figure 16.5 is a pinout diagram for DB25 serial ports showing which pin carries which signal. Figure 16.6 is the pinout diagram for the most common (modern) DB9 serial ports. There were a few nonstandard 9-pin designs in the early 1980's, but they are not currently manufactured.

If a serial port passes the wrap plug test, there's a 99 percent chance it's good. Look again for mismatched COM port and interrupt, or for an incorrect MODE command. The troubleshooting charts in Section 3 will lead you, step-by-step, through our serial port diagnostic/repair procedures.

How to Remove and Install a Serial Port

1. **Remove cables and computer cover.** Disconnect the serial cable (if installed), and remove the system unit cover (described in Chapter 1).

2. **Remove old card.** Remove the single screw holding the card to the back of the system unit chassis (Figure 11.1 on page 102). Pull the old serial card straight up out of its slot.

3. **Set switches and jumpers.** Before you install a serial card, read the manual that comes with the card. If you have any questions, reread "How a Serial Port Works."

4. **Install new card.** The serial card is an 8-bit card, so it will fit in either a long or a short slot on 286, 386, and 486 computers. It will also fit in any of the slots on an XT clone. Line the card up with the expansion slot connector, then press it down firmly. When the card has settled into the bus connector on the mainboard and the screw hole lines up with the hole on the top or back of the chassis, reinstall the screw.

5. **Test new serial card.** Test the machine with the cover off first. Just be careful not to touch anything inside the machine while it's on. It's not unusual to find you have not set the switches exactly right on the first try. If the computer tests well, reinstall the cover and screws. If you have problems getting the new card to work properly, the troubleshooting charts in Section 3 should help.

Mouse

A mouse changes small hand motions into cursor motion onscreen. There are two ways for a mouse to communicate with the computer. Serial mice use a standard serial port (see Figure 16.8). Bus mice, on the other hand, have a unique address of their own and a dedicated bus mouse controller card—they don't use the serial port, its address, or its interrupt. Figure 16.9 shows a bus mouse.

How a Mouse Works

When you slide a mouse across the desktop or a special mouse pad, the mouse detects this motion, both in horizontal and in vertical directions. The mouse sends this information to the computer, typically along a cable to a serial port or to a dedicated mouse card installed in an expansion card slot. A few cordless models use infrared or radio signals to communicate between mouse and computer. Inside the computer, a device driver (a software program designed to interface the mouse to the computer) translates the mouse signal into instructions the computer can read.

There are many ways for mice to detect hand motion. Some mice use a track ball, which rolls as your hand slides the mouse across a flat surface. These are called either *mechanical mice* (if the ball motion is detected by rollers and mechanical motion encoders inside the mouse) or *optomechanical mice* (if the ball motion is translated into an electrical signal by an optical device). Two other designs are used. *Wheel mice* have two wheels at right angles—one to measure horizontal movement, the other to measure vertical movement. *Optical mice* use a special mouse pad, a flat surface imprinted with a grid pattern. When the mouse is moved on this surface, photosensors detect motion across the grid and send appropriate signals to the computer.

Not all mice have the same resolution. Some mice recognize a motion of 1/200 inch. High-resolution models recognize 1/1200 inch. A high-resolution model sends more motion signals to the computer per inch of hand motion.

Serial mice are serial devices. They require a unique serial port address and a unique interrupt number. Your mouse manual should help you set these parameters. A serial mouse requires a unique address because it gets control signals from the bus. The microprocessor speaks to a device by sending an address down the bus. All the devices are looking at the bus, waiting for their distinctive address. When a device recognizes its own address on the bus, it pays attention to the subsequent data signals. In order to receive these signals, a mouse must have its own address. Party line telephones use a similar system; the phone ring pattern is different for each household.

Figure 16.8
Serial port mouse with cable and 9 to 25-pin serial port adapter. Photo courtesy of Logitech.

Figure 16.9
Bus mouse with cable and bus card. Photo courtesy of Logitech.

Mouse

Most of the time, the mouse is trying to send, not receive, information. When a mouse is ready to transmit data it sends an interrupt to the microprocessor. The microprocessor looks up the interrupt number in the interrupt vector table, which tells the microprocessor to start using mouse-specific routines to accept the incoming data. The mouse and a modem cannot share an interrupt number. If they did, the microprocessor would be trying to interface with the mouse as if it were receiving telephone data communications via the modem.

Bus mice also need a unique address and a unique interrupt. Because they do not use a serial port, though, there is no possible interference with a serial device such as a modem or a serial printer. Bus mice, therefore, do not get assigned a COM port. The way bus mice communicate varies from manufacturer to manufacturer. Each makes a bus mouse controller card with a proprietary chip that is responsible for communications between the mouse and the CPU. The mouse card requires its own interrupt, and interrupt interference is the only place where mouse cards might conflict with the other hardware installed in the computer.

IBM PS/2s come with a mouse port built in, so other manufacturers are building a mouse port into their computers too. These mouse ports use serial mice with a funky, non-standard serial connector.

How to Test a Mouse

If you have trouble with a mouse attached to a serial port, try testing the serial port alone first. See "How to Test a Serial Port," for testing suggestions. If you don't find a problem with the serial port, check the mouse setup (address, interrupts, driver, etc.) to make sure that another serial device in the machine doesn't conflict with the mouse. If you suspect a conflict, test the mouse with the other device pulled out of the computer temporarily.

If you are having trouble with a bus mouse, double-check the setup. Make sure that the mouse driver is installed in the CONFIG.SYS or AUTOEXEC.BAT file, that it's the right driver, and that the interrupt is correct.

An optical mouse will not work without the special optical pad. The pad must be properly oriented as well.

If an optomechanical or a mechanical mouse works but seems jerky and less fluid than it should be, check the roller ball for contamination. These mice can be cleaned. Pop the ball out of the bottom of the mouse; it's usually held in with a snap ring. You can then clean the ball (and rollers, if there are any) with alcohol and a lint-free rag.

How to Install a Mouse

Mice come packaged with mouse device drivers and test software. Be sure you are using the correct mouse driver. A Microsoft mouse must have a Microsoft mouse driver; it won't work with the Logitech mouse driver. Install the mouse driver in the CONFIG.SYS or AUTOEXEC.BAT file. Most mice are shipped with two drivers, one suitable for the CONFIG.SYS file and one for the AUTO-EXEC.BAT file. You can use either.

Read the installation manual for your mouse. See "How A Mouse Works," for information about addresses and interrupts.

Scanner

Small scanners come in two specialized forms: graphics scanners for pictures and optical character readers (OCRs) for text. Larger desktop scanners often do both jobs. They read and recognize text characters (and store them in ASCII or standard word processing format) and they also scan, edit, and store graphic images (often in PC Paintbrush PCX or Aldus TIFF formats).

How a Scanner Works

Scanners bounce light off a target—which may be either a picture or text—and measure the amount of reflected light. Color scanners shine three separate lights (red, green, and blue) on the image. Black-and-white scanners use a single light. Most of this light is reflected from white paper, less from halftones in a photograph, and almost none from black text characters. The scanner sends this information to a scanner interface card in the computer, where either OCR or graphics software takes over.

The software processes the light level measurements. OCR software converts light gray shades to white, and dark gray to black. Then, using this two-color image, the OCR software tries to identify the letter written on the paper. Character recognition software uses one of two techniques: font matching and feature recognition. Font matching compares the character against all memorized fonts; as when using tracing paper to match an unknown shape against stored standard patterns. Feature recognition uses logic and piece-by-piece analysis of a character to deduce what letter it really is. Feature recognition relies on questions such as "Is there an extender protruding below the line of type?" (P, q, g, y, and j all share this characteristic feature.) By asking itself successive questions the software is able systematically to eliminate characters. Pattern recognition software is more flexible, since proportional spacing and new fonts are less likely to throw it off stride. It is also more expensive.

Graphics software retains the middle range of signal values, the ones which represent gray tones in an image. Some scanners convert the intermediate gray tones to dithered patterns (prepared patterns of black and white dots which match the approximate light/dark ratio of the gray tone). Other scanners retain up to 64 levels of gray tones in the stored image (this is called *gray scaling*). Gray scaling is more expensive, and requires a lot of memory to store an image.

How to Install and Test a Scanner

1. **Remove computer cover and old card (if so equipped).** The scanner itself is external to the PC, whether it is handheld or desktop in design. Inside the computer, though, you'll find a scanner interface card. Follow the scanner data cable back to the interface card in the computer then take the cover off the computer system unit, as described in Chapter 1, to see the whole card.

   A scanner interface card is similar to other expansion cards. It is held firmly into the computer with a machine screw. If you need to remove an old scanner card, remove the screw (Figure 11.1 on page 102) and pull the card straight up out of the bus connector on the mainboard (Figures 11.2 and 11.3 on pages 102-103).

2. **Set switches and jumpers on scanner interface card.** Some scanner manufacturers hook the scanner up to an ordinary SCSI host adapter card. We tell you how to install a small SCSI host adapter card in Chapter 15.

   Other scanners use a proprietary interface card sold only by the scanner manufacturer. Before you install your new scanner card, consider possible interference from the equipment already in the computer. The interface board must have a unique interrupt number and a unique address. Unfortunately, many scanners use the interrupts assigned to parallel or serial ports. Most of these interface boards allow you to choose among a number of possible interrupts and a number of addresses. Nevertheless, careful planning, with scanner manual in hand, is required. Diagnostic software (we discuss a number of brands in Chapter 2) can scan the peripheral equipment in your computer, then report what address and interrupt each peripheral is using. This information can really help.

3. **Install card.** Select a suitable expansion slot. If necessary, remove the slot cover. Line up the card with the expansion slot connector and press down firmly. The card should slip into the connector. Reinstall the screw, so the card is snug in the computer case.

4. **Plug in the scanner and test it.** The installation manual tells you how to set the scanner switches and how to hook up the cables. The scanner manufacturer will give you test software or troubleshooting information customized for your particular scanner.

Sound Board

Windows 3.1 allows sound recording, and playback from within documents, using the Windows Packager program. To take advantage of this, you'll need a sound board with the Windows 3.1 driver.

Some of these sound boards pipe music and voice to your stereo. Others allow recording as well —they have a microphone jack on the board. Top of the line sound boards provide multiple interfaces (CD-ROM, CD player, microphone, joystick, portable speakers or AUX jack on your stereo, and MIDI).

How a Sound Board Works

When recording sound, the board feeds audio from the in jack (microphone, CD player, whatever) through an analog to digital converter (ADC). To play sound, the sound board converts digitized audio stored in a document or file to analog sound. Speakers use analog; audio data is stored on the computer in digital form. The digital to analog converter is called a DAC. In raw form, digitized sound takes an incredible amount of space. But sound can easily be compressed to one-quarter size if your sound board contains a compression chip (an ADPCM chip).

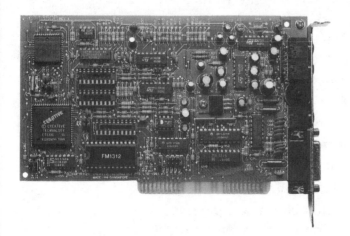

Figure 16.10
The SoundBlaster Pro has MIDI, CD-ROM interface, game port, microphone input, and line-out for speakers. Photo courtesy of Creative Labs, Inc.

How to Install and Test a Sound Board

Like all expansion boards, sound boards use an address and an interrupt. Each device in a computer must have a unique address (the place where the microprocessor can send information for that device). And each device in an ISA computer (that's an XT clone or a 286/386/486/AT clone) must have a unique interrupt (that's the signal from the device that it needs the computer's attention). EISA sound boards use level-sensitive interrupts, so an EISA sound board in an EISA computer could theoretically share an interrupt with another EISA device, but most sound boards are ISA and require a unique interrupt.

Your sound board will not work if it has an address or interrupt conflict with another card. Use a diagnostic program (we discuss many in Chapter 2) to figure out what addresses and interrupts are already being used. Then set the switches and jumpers on the sound board as per the manufacturer's installation instructions.

Make sure that your new sound board will work with Windows 3.1 and your CD-ROM. Not all of them will. It's best to buy a CD-ROM and sound board together, but if you're adding one or the other later, talk to your CD-ROM vendor and your sound board vendor before you purchase.

Use DiagSoft's QA/WIN diagnostic program to test sound boards and MIDI synchronizers.

Section 3
The Troubleshooting Charts

Introduction to the Troubleshooting Charts

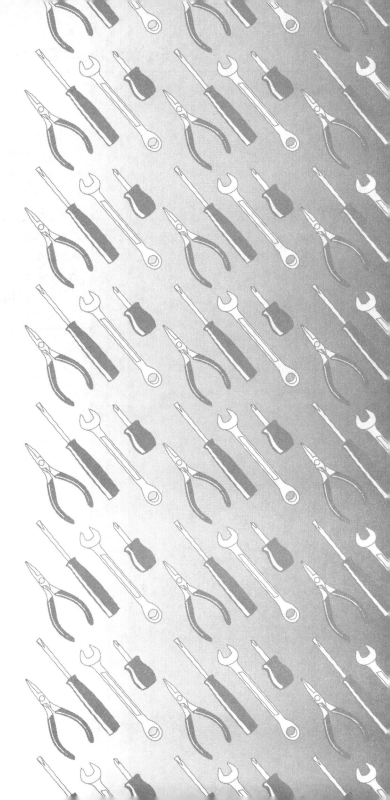

Welcome to the Troubleshooting Charts.

These troubleshooting charts illustrate our thought pattern as we diagnose a non-working computer. We use a step-by-step technique which is effective even for inexperienced non-technical computer owners. We have taught this same reasoning process to many new technicians who were learning on the job or attending pre-professional classes.

Our technique was developed in a computer store where replacement parts are always available. If you're using the charts at home, without any duplicate parts to swap in, can you use a friend's or colleague's computer to test your printer, monitor, or keyboard? If you are repairing machines at work, do you have access to known-good parts from equivalent machines in the office? If no loaner is available, you'll just have to put in a new card or disk when you get to a point in the troubleshooting charts where we suggest swapping in one of these parts. If the new part doesn't fix the problem, don't give up in despair. Even in repair shops, the technician has to bite the bullet and replace the most likely part. One of the things you pay for (at $50 or $75 an hour) is the right to rent the repair shop's parts for diagnostic purposes.

Despite buying an occasional extra good drive or card, you'll still save a lot of hassle and a lot of money doing your own simple repairs. Some of you will not want actually to perform the repairs, preferring instead to establish the most likely bad part by reading the troubleshooting charts and then take the computer to the repair shop for the actual screwdriver work. Either way, we think this simple (though, to be fair, sometimes tedious) system will work for you.

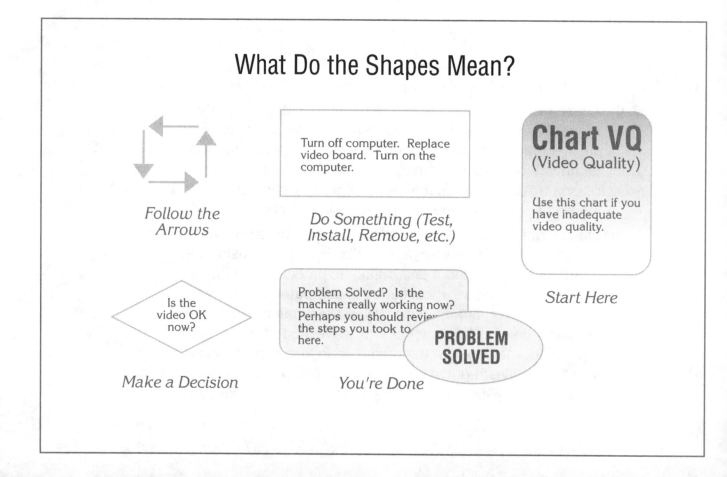

What Do the Shapes Mean?

Follow the Arrows

Turn off computer. Replace video board. Turn on the computer.

Do Something (Test, Install, Remove, etc.)

Chart VQ
(Video Quality)

Use this chart if you have inadequate video quality.

Is the video OK now?

Make a Decision

Problem Solved? Is the machine really working now? Perhaps you should review the steps you took to here.

PROBLEM SOLVED

You're Done

Start Here

Take these precautions before you begin working through the charts:

1. Always turn off the computer before removing or installing any components.

2. If you have a hard disk, make sure it is backed up before you do anything, even fixing your serial port. At the computer store we strongly recommend backing up the hard disk before a computer comes in for any repair, and make each prospective customer sign a release accepting full responsibility for her own data.

3. When professional technicians repair computers with multiple problems they start with one problem, fix it, then tackle the next. You might have to loop through these troubleshooting charts a second or third time to catch all the bad parts in a particularly sick computer.

4. Always deal with screen error messages first, before trying to diagnose any additional problems. Appendices A, B, and C list these screen error messages and our recommended fix for each problem. Appendices A and B cover error messages printed on your monitor, with the IBM-style numeric messages (e.g., "1701") covered in Appendix A and the English-like text messages (e.g., "Disk Drive 1 Seek Failure") in Appendix B.

5. Note where and how cables and wire connectors are attached before you begin disassembling your computer. You will be astonished by the poor documentation in this industry. If you don't write the details down while tearing apart the computer, you may well have to re-engineer the computer yourself during reassembly.

6. If at any point you think the monitor and/or keyboard you are using to test your computer might be bad, check them by connecting them to a known-good computer.

7. Before attempting major repairs, consider the cost of replacing this computer. Ask yourself whether it's worthwhile to repair the beast. Remember, you can buy twice as much computing power for half the money you had to spend two or three years ago.

With these points in mind, turn to the Start Chart on the next page. Subsequent charts appear in alphabetical order.

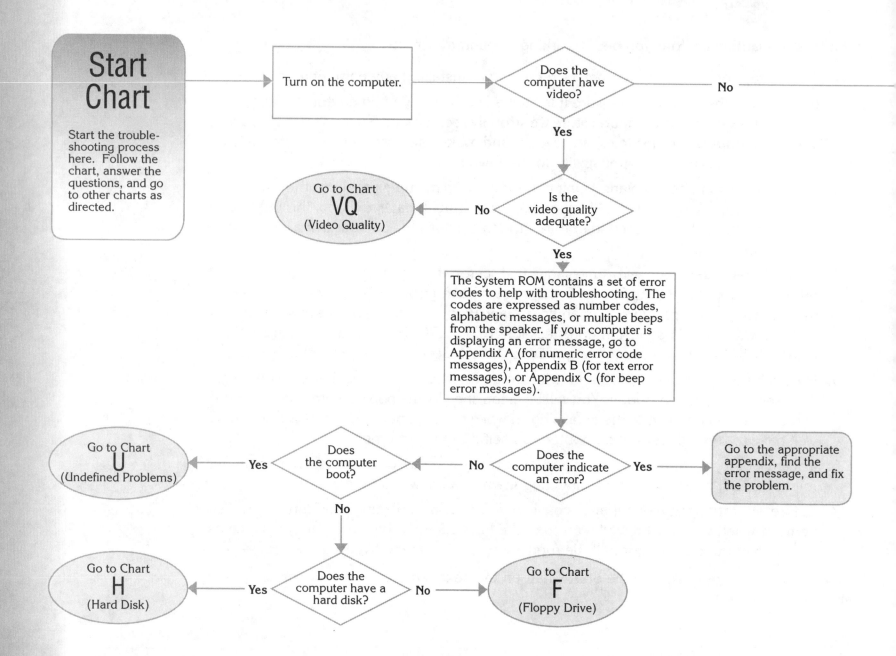

Start Chart

Start the trouble-shooting process here. Follow the chart, answer the questions, and go to other charts as directed.

Turn on the computer.

Does the computer have video? → **No**

Yes

Is the video quality adequate? → **No** → Go to Chart **VQ** (Video Quality)

Yes

The System ROM contains a set of error codes to help with troubleshooting. The codes are expressed as number codes, alphabetic messages, or multiple beeps from the speaker. If your computer is displaying an error message, go to Appendix A (for numeric error code messages), Appendix B (for text error messages), or Appendix C (for beep error messages).

Does the computer indicate an error? → **Yes** → Go to the appropriate appendix, find the error message, and fix the problem.

No → Does the computer boot? → **Yes** → Go to Chart **U** (Undefined Problems)

No

Does the computer have a hard disk? → **Yes** → Go to Chart **H** (Hard Disk)

→ **No** → Go to Chart **F** (Floppy Drive)

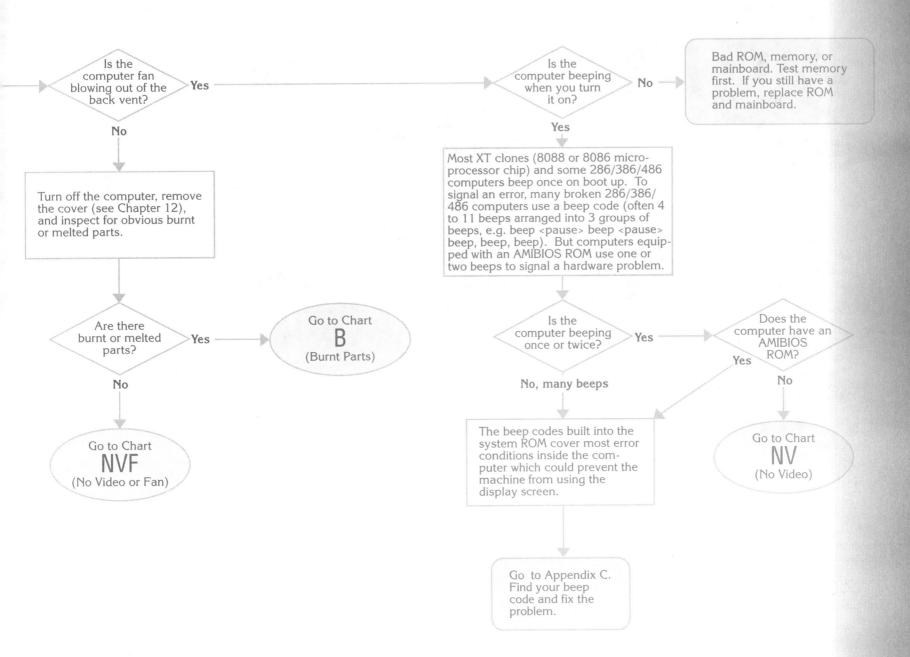

Is the computer fan blowing out of the back vent?

Yes

No

Turn off the computer, remove the cover (see Chapter 12), and inspect for obvious burnt or melted parts.

Are there burnt or melted parts?

Yes

No

Go to Chart
B
(Burnt Parts)

Go to Chart
NVF
(No Video or Fan)

Is the computer beeping when you turn it on?

No

Yes

Bad ROM, memory, or mainboard. Test memory first. If you still have a problem, replace ROM and mainboard.

Most XT clones (8088 or 8086 micro-processor chip) and some 286/386/486 computers beep once on boot up. To signal an error, many broken 286/386/486 computers use a beep code (often 4 to 11 beeps arranged into 3 groups of beeps, e.g. beep <pause> beep <pause> beep, beep, beep). But computers equip-ped with an AMIBIOS ROM use one or two beeps to signal a hardware problem.

Is the computer beeping once or twice?

Yes

No, many beeps

Does the computer have an AMIBIOS ROM?

Yes

No

The beep codes built into the system ROM cover most error conditions inside the com-puter which could prevent the machine from using the display screen.

Go to Chart
NV
(No Video)

Go to Appendix C. Find your beep code and fix the problem.

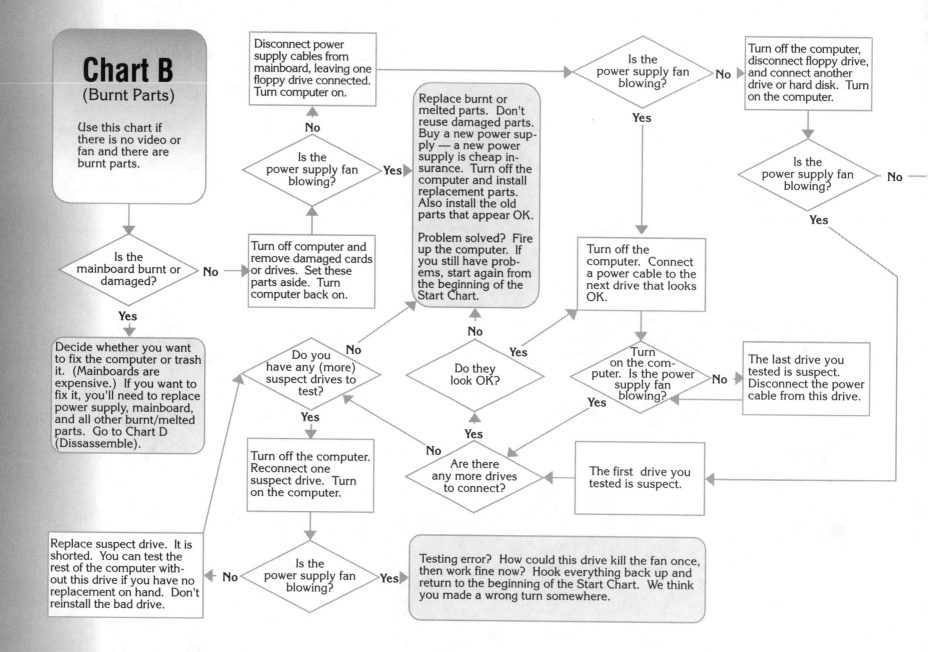

Chart B
(Burnt Parts)

Use this chart if there is no video or fan and there are burnt parts.

Is the mainboard burnt or damaged? — No →

Yes ↓

Decide whether you want to fix the computer or trash it. (Mainboards are expensive.) If you want to fix it, you'll need to replace power supply, mainboard, and all other burnt/melted parts. Go to Chart D (Dissassemble).

Turn off computer and remove damaged cards or drives. Set these parts aside. Turn computer back on.

Disconnect power supply cables from mainboard, leaving one floppy drive connected. Turn computer on.

Is the power supply fan blowing? — Yes →

Replace burnt or melted parts. Don't reuse damaged parts. Buy a new power supply — a new power supply is cheap insurance. Turn off the computer and install replacement parts. Also install the old parts that appear OK.

Problem solved? Fire up the computer. If you still have problems, start again from the beginning of the Start Chart.

Do you have any (more) suspect drives to test?

No →

Yes ↓

Turn off the computer. Reconnect one suspect drive. Turn on the computer.

Do they look OK?

No →

Yes ↓

Are there any more drives to connect?

No ↑

Turn off the computer. Connect a power cable to the next drive that looks OK.

Turn on the computer. Is the power supply fan blowing? — No →

Yes ↓

Is the power supply fan blowing? — No →

Yes ↓

Turn off the computer, disconnect floppy drive, and connect another drive or hard disk. Turn on the computer.

Is the power supply fan blowing? — No —

Yes ↓

The last drive you tested is suspect. Disconnect the power cable from this drive.

The first drive you tested is suspect.

Replace suspect drive. It is shorted. You can test the rest of the computer without this drive if you have no replacement on hand. Don't reinstall the bad drive.

Is the power supply fan blowing? — No →   Yes →

Testing error? How could this drive kill the fan once, then work fine now? Hook everything back up and return to the beginning of the Start Chart. We think you made a wrong turn somewhere.

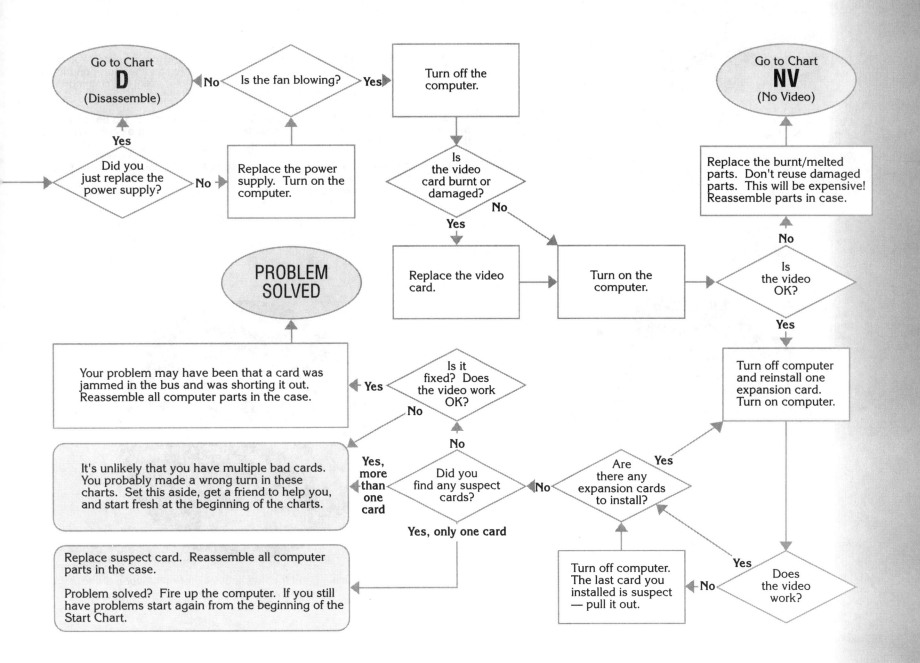

Chart D
(Disassemble)

Use this chart if your computer is showing such severe problems that it makes sense to disassemble it, removing all parts from the case.

When your computer has a really weird problem and it's braindead, the only solution may be to rebuild the computer piece by piece from the beginning. As the computer begins to show signs of life, diagnosis gets easier.

For this exercise, remove all the parts of your computer from its case. You will build up the computer on a wood or plastic table top (or another non-conducting surface). There is no danger to you — only 12 volts of current are running through these computer parts. (See photo on the left below.)

Though a short can't hurt you, it would damage the computer. Do not short out the parts by placing them on a metal table top or by dropping a screwdriver onto the computer parts while the power is on.

Do not short one card or board to another (don't let them touch) and don't short out a drive to mainboard (don't lay a drive down on the mainboard) — especially when the power is turned on. (See photo on the right below.)

Do work on a non-conducting wood or plastic surface.

Don't short things out! Piing the floppy drive on the mainboard like this would ruin the drive, the mainboard, or both if the power were on.

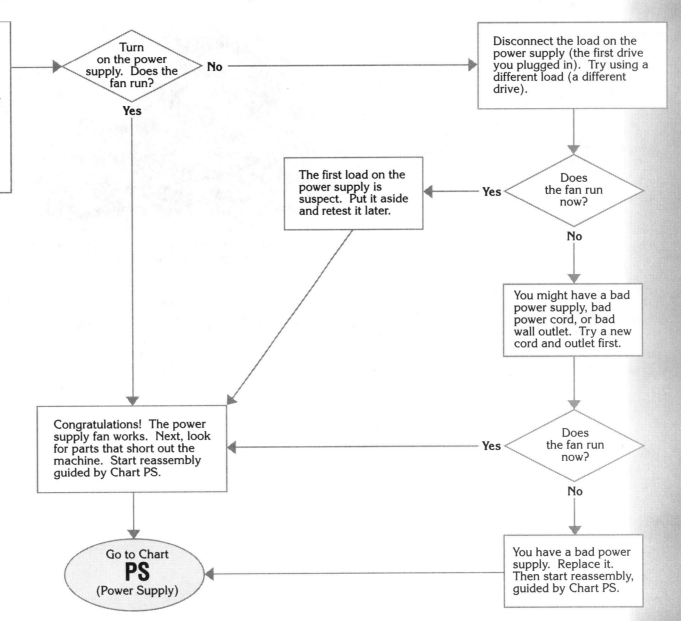

Chart D

- Test the wall outlet with a lamp or another electrical appliance.

- Plug in the power supply — just the naked power supply and no other parts.

- Attach a load to one of the power supply's four-wire connections (e.g. a floppy drive or a hard drive).

Turn on the power supply. Does the fan run?

No → Disconnect the load on the power supply (the first drive you plugged in). Try using a different load (a different drive).

Yes

Does the fan run now?

Yes → The first load on the power supply is suspect. Put it aside and retest it later.

No

You might have a bad power supply, bad power cord, or bad wall outlet. Try a new cord and outlet first.

Congratulations! The power supply fan works. Next, look for parts that short out the machine. Start reassembly guided by Chart PS.

Does the fan run now?

Yes

No

Go to Chart **PS** (Power Supply)

You have a bad power supply. Replace it. Then start reassembly, guided by Chart PS.

Chart F
(Floppy Drive)

Use this chart if the computer won't boot from the floppy drive.

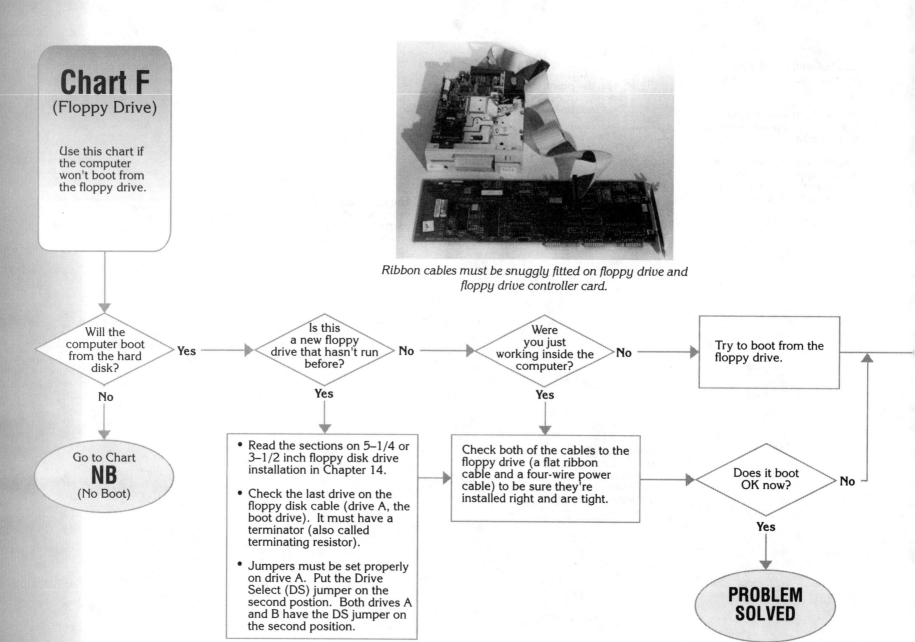

Ribbon cables must be snuggly fitted on floppy drive and floppy drive controller card.

Will the computer boot from the hard disk? — **Yes** →

No ↓

Go to Chart **NB** (No Boot)

Is this a new floppy drive that hasn't run before? — **No** →

Yes ↓

- Read the sections on 5–1/4 or 3–1/2 inch floppy disk drive installation in Chapter 14.

- Check the last drive on the floppy disk cable (drive A, the boot drive). It must have a terminator (also called terminating resistor).

- Jumpers must be set properly on drive A. Put the Drive Select (DS) jumper on the second postion. Both drives A and B have the DS jumper on the second position.

Were you just working inside the computer? — **No** →

Yes ↓

Check both of the cables to the floppy drive (a flat ribbon cable and a four-wire power cable) to be sure they're installed right and are tight.

Try to boot from the floppy drive.

Does it boot OK now? — **No**

Yes ↓

PROBLEM SOLVED

Your boot disk probably has a bad Track O. Try a different bootable disk, one you know is good.

Yes

Is there an error message on the screen?　**No**

Yes

Go to Appendix A (numeric error code messages), Appendix B (text error code messages), or Appendix C (beep error codes). Look up your error and follow the instructions.

• Boot from the hard disk.

• If you have a 286, 386, or 486 computer, check the SETUP. Be sure you have the correct number and types of floppy drives listed in the CMOS SETUP chip.

• Older computers use a SETUP floppy disk. Newer computers flash a message on screen during bootup giving the keys you must press to interrupt the normal cold boot and enter the setup mode instead.

• Try to read a floppy disk in the suspect drive. Try a second floppy disk. Make it a low-density (360K or 720K) disk, these are easier to read than high-density disks.

Will the computer read or write to disk at all?

No

Go to Chart
NB
(No Boot)

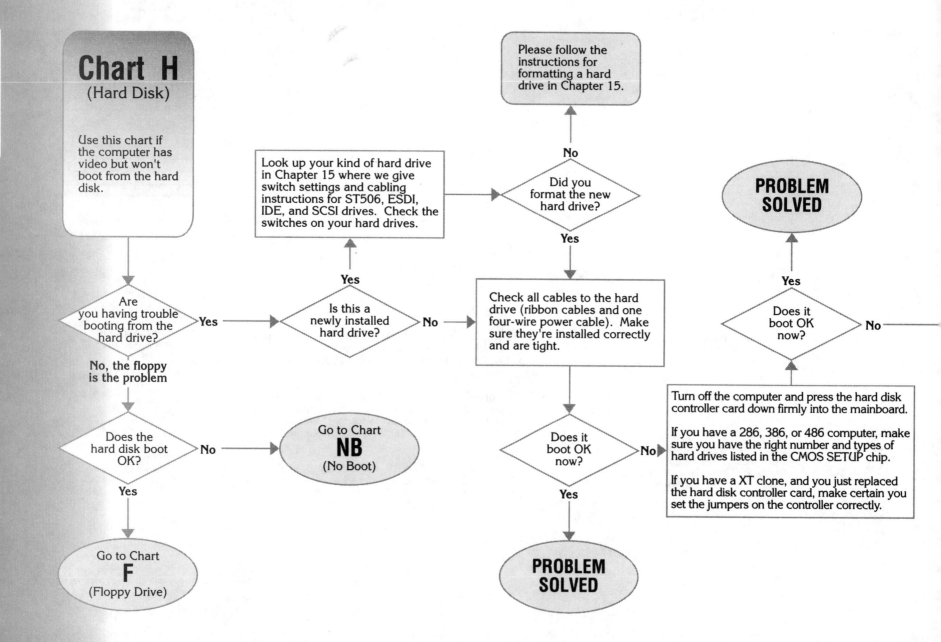

Chart H
(Hard Disk)

Use this chart if the computer has video but won't boot from the hard disk.

Please follow the instructions for formatting a hard drive in Chapter 15.

Look up your kind of hard drive in Chapter 15 where we give switch settings and cabling instructions for ST506, ESDI, IDE, and SCSI drives. Check the switches on your hard drives.

No ↑

Did you format the new hard drive?

PROBLEM SOLVED

Yes ↓

Are you having trouble booting from the hard drive? — **Yes** → Is this a newly installed hard drive? — **No** → Check all cables to the hard drive (ribbon cables and one four-wire power cable). Make sure they're installed correctly and are tight.

Yes ↑

No, the floppy is the problem

Does it boot OK now? — **No** →

Yes ↑

Does it boot OK now? — **No** →

Does the hard disk boot OK? — **No** → Go to Chart **NB** (No Boot)

Turn off the computer and press the hard disk controller card down firmly into the mainboard.

If you have a 286, 386, or 486 computer, make sure you have the right number and types of hard drives listed in the CMOS SETUP chip.

If you have a XT clone, and you just replaced the hard disk controller card, make certain you set the jumpers on the controller correctly.

Yes ↓

Go to Chart **F** (Floppy Drive)

Yes ↓

PROBLEM SOLVED

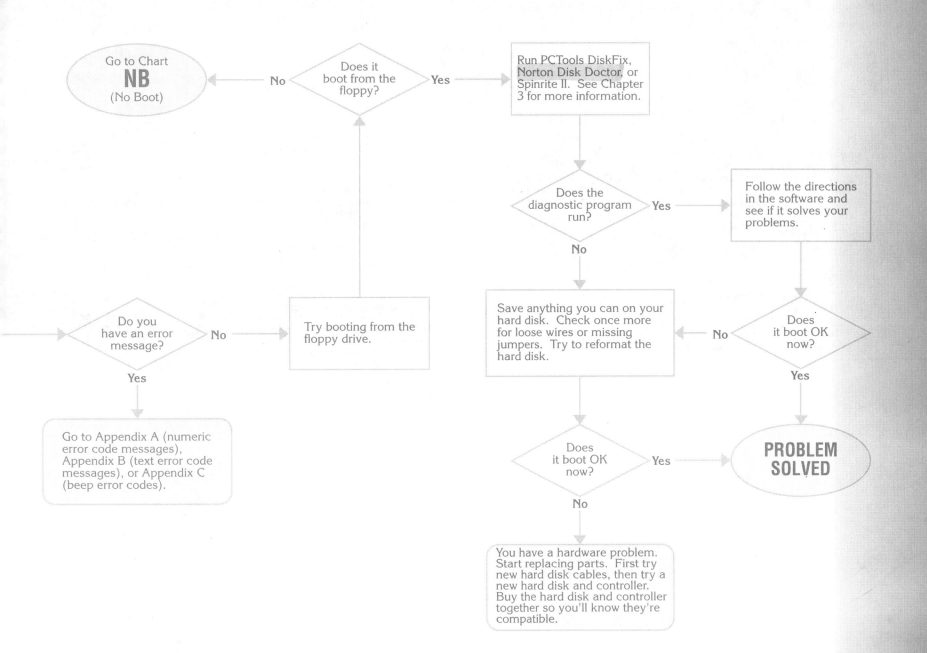

Go to Chart
NB
(No Boot)

No ← Does it boot from the floppy? → Yes → Run PCTools DiskFix, Norton Disk Doctor, or Spinrite II. See Chapter 3 for more information.

Does the diagnostic program run? → Yes → Follow the directions in the software and see if it solves your problems.

No

Do you have an error message? → No → Try booting from the floppy drive.

Yes

Save anything you can on your hard disk. Check once more for loose wires or missing jumpers. Try to reformat the hard disk.

No ← Does it boot OK now? → Yes → **PROBLEM SOLVED**

Go to Appendix A (numeric error code messages), Appendix B (text error code messages), or Appendix C (beep error codes).

Does it boot OK now? → Yes → **PROBLEM SOLVED**

No

You have a hardware problem. Start replacing parts. First try new hard disk cables, then try a new hard disk and controller. Buy the hard disk and controller together so you'll know they're compatible.

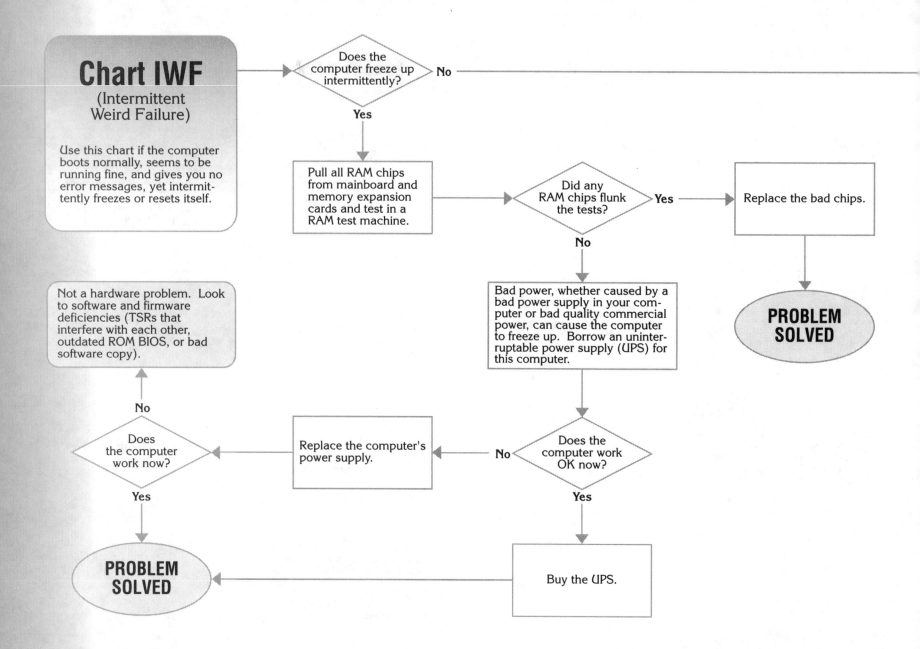

Chart IWF
(Intermittent Weird Failure)

Use this chart if the computer boots normally, seems to be running fine, and gives you no error messages, yet intermittently freezes or resets itself.

Does the computer freeze up intermittently? — No

Yes ↓

Pull all RAM chips from mainboard and memory expansion cards and test in a RAM test machine.

Did any RAM chips flunk the tests? — Yes → Replace the bad chips. → **PROBLEM SOLVED**

No ↓

Bad power, whether caused by a bad power supply in your computer or bad quality commercial power, can cause the computer to freeze up. Borrow an uninterruptable power supply (UPS) for this computer.

Does the computer work OK now? — No → Replace the computer's power supply. → **Does the computer work now?**

Yes ↓ Buy the UPS. → **PROBLEM SOLVED**

Does the computer work now? — No → Not a hardware problem. Look to software and firmware deficiencies (TSRs that interfere with each other, outdated ROM BIOS, or bad software copy).

Yes ↓ **PROBLEM SOLVED**

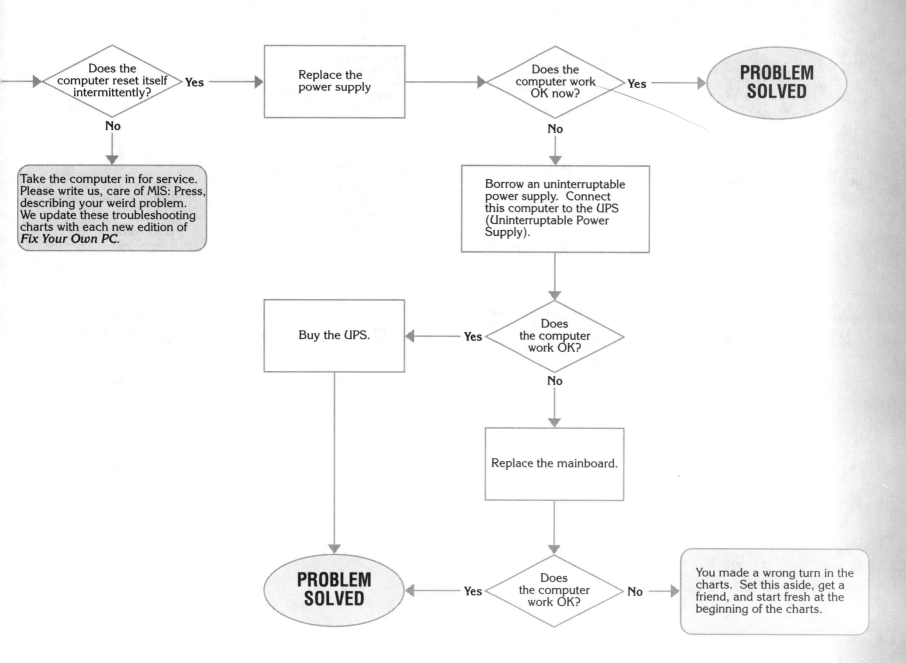

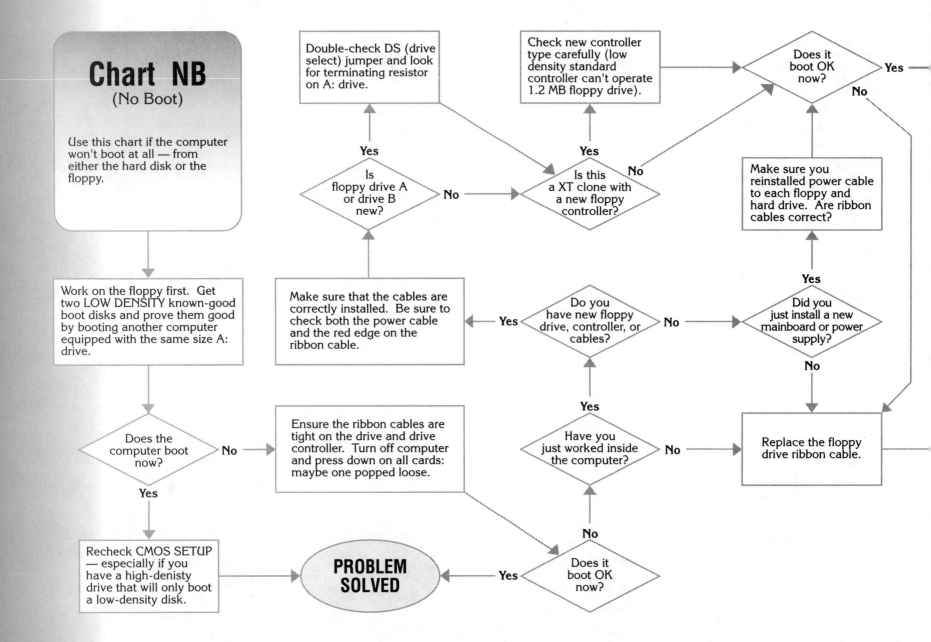

Chart NB
(No Boot)

Use this chart if the computer won't boot at all — from either the hard disk or the floppy.

Work on the floppy first. Get two LOW DENSITY known-good boot disks and prove them good by booting another computer equipped with the same size A: drive.

Does the computer boot now?

No →

Recheck CMOS SETUP — especially if you have a high-denisty drive that will only boot a low-density disk.

Yes

Ensure the ribbon cables are tight on the drive and drive controller. Turn off computer and press down on all cards: maybe one popped loose.

Make sure that the cables are correctly installed. Be sure to check both the power cable and the red edge on the ribbon cable.

Double-check DS (drive select) jumper and look for terminating resistor on A: drive.

Is floppy drive A or drive B new?

Yes / **No**

Is this a XT clone with a new floppy controller?

Yes / **No**

Check new controller type carefully (low density standard controller can't operate 1.2 MB floppy drive).

Does it boot OK now?

Yes / **No**

Make sure you reinstalled power cable to each floppy and hard drive. Are ribbon cables correct?

Do you have new floppy drive, controller, or cables?

Yes / **No**

Did you just install a new mainboard or power supply?

Yes / **No**

Have you just worked inside the computer?

Yes / **No**

Replace the floppy drive ribbon cable.

Does it boot OK now?

Yes →

PROBLEM SOLVED

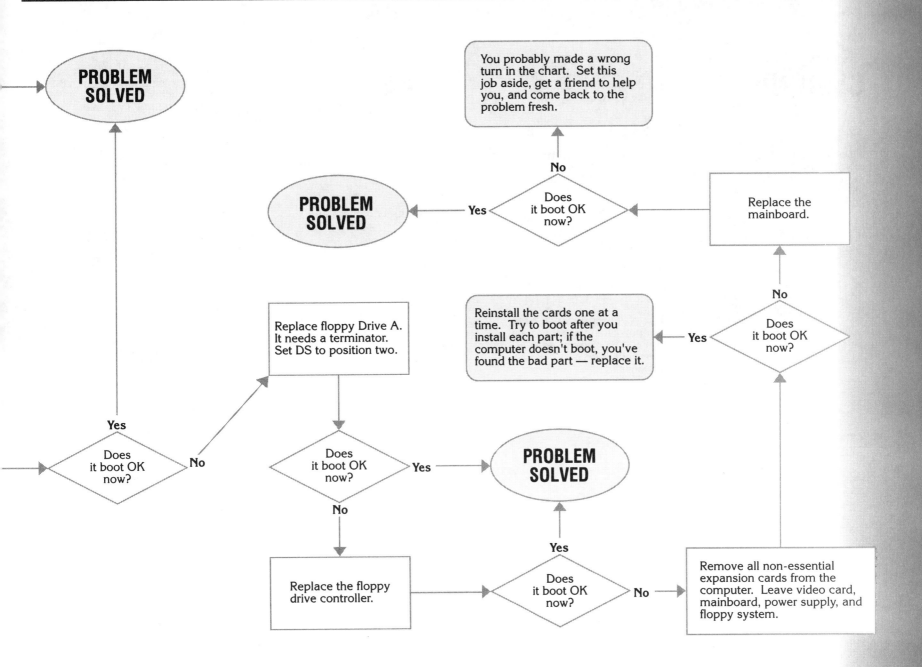

PROBLEM SOLVED

You probably made a wrong turn in the chart. Set this job aside, get a friend to help you, and come back to the problem fresh.

No

PROBLEM SOLVED

Yes

Does it boot OK now?

Replace the mainboard.

No

Does it boot OK now?

Replace floppy Drive A. It needs a terminator. Set DS to position two.

Reinstall the cards one at a time. Try to boot after you install each part; if the computer doesn't boot, you've found the bad part — replace it.

Yes

Does it boot OK now?

Yes

Does it boot OK now?

PROBLEM SOLVED

No

No

Replace the floppy drive controller.

Yes

Does it boot OK now?

No

Remove all non-essential expansion cards from the computer. Leave video card, mainboard, power supply, and floppy system.

Yes

No

Does it boot OK now?

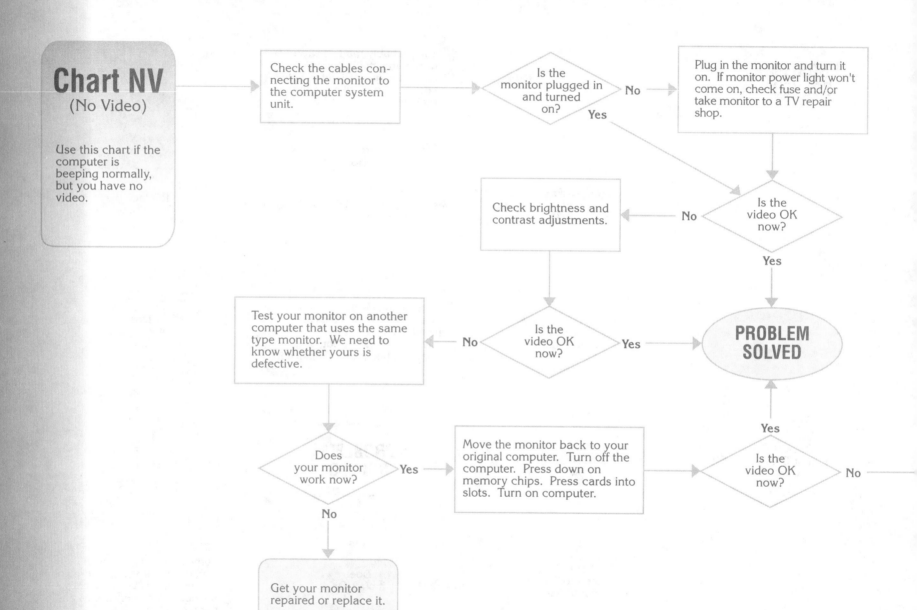

Chart NV
(No Video)

Use this chart if the computer is beeping normally, but you have no video.

Check the cables connecting the monitor to the computer system unit.

Is the monitor plugged in and turned on?

No → Plug in the monitor and turn it on. If monitor power light won't come on, check fuse and/or take monitor to a TV repair shop.

Yes

Is the video OK now?

No → Check brightness and contrast adjustments.

Yes

Is the video OK now?

Yes → **PROBLEM SOLVED**

No → Test your monitor on another computer that uses the same type monitor. We need to know whether yours is defective.

Does your monitor work now?

Yes → Move the monitor back to your original computer. Turn off the computer. Press down on memory chips. Press cards into slots. Turn on computer.

Is the video OK now?

Yes → **PROBLEM SOLVED**

No →

No → Get your monitor repaired or replace it.

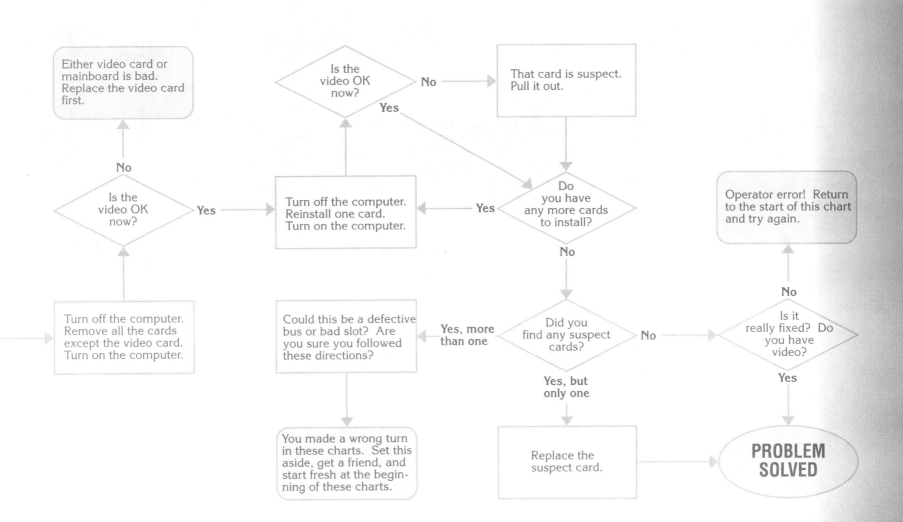

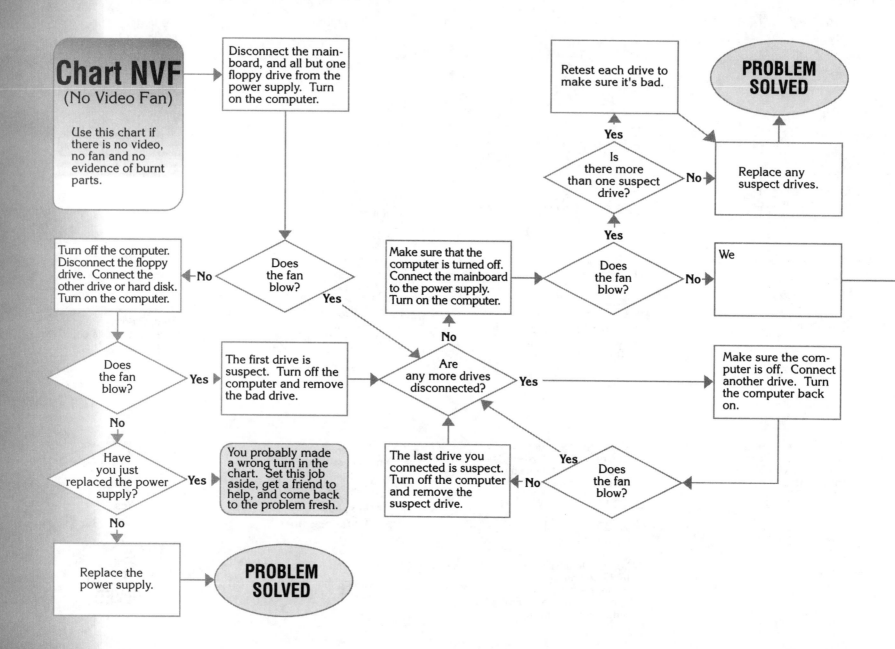

Chart NVF
(No Video Fan)

Use this chart if there is no video, no fan and no evidence of burnt parts.

Disconnect the mainboard, and all but one floppy drive from the power supply. Turn on the computer.

Retest each drive to make sure it's bad.

PROBLEM SOLVED

Is there more than one suspect drive?

Replace any suspect drives.

Turn off the computer. Disconnect the floppy drive. Connect the other drive or hard disk. Turn on the computer.

No — Does the fan blow? — Yes

Make sure that the computer is turned off. Connect the mainboard to the power supply. Turn on the computer.

Does the fan blow? — No → We

Does the fan blow?

Yes

The first drive is suspect. Turn off the computer and remove the bad drive.

No

Are any more drives disconnected? — Yes

Make sure the computer is off. Connect another drive. Turn the computer back on.

Have you just replaced the power supply? — Yes

You probably made a wrong turn in the chart. Set this job aside, get a friend to help, and come back to the problem fresh.

The last drive you connected is suspect. Turn off the computer and remove the suspect drive. — No → Does the fan blow? — Yes

No

Replace the power supply.

PROBLEM SOLVED

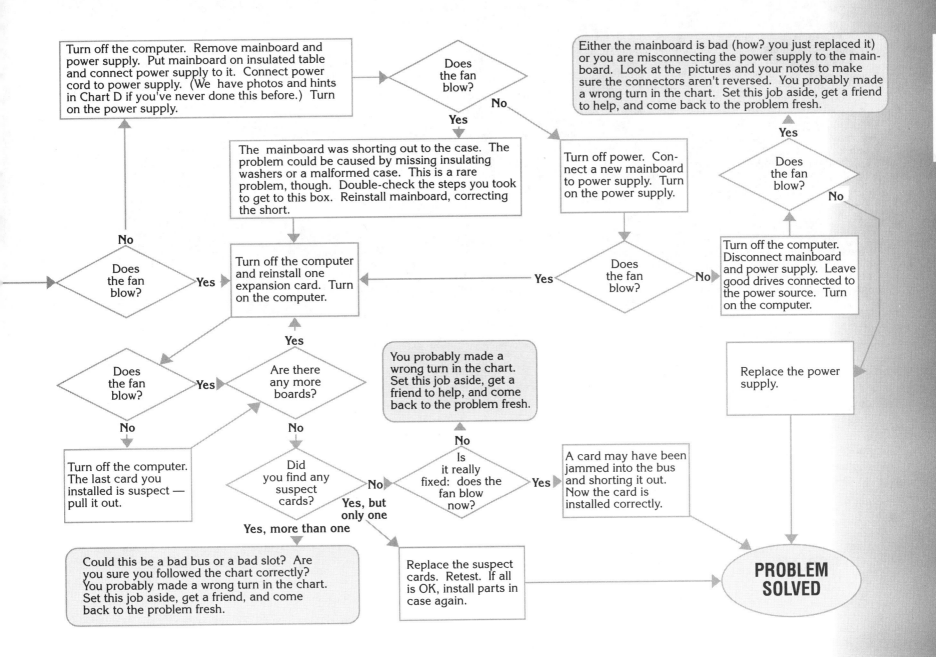

Turn off the computer. Remove mainboard and power supply. Put mainboard on insulated table and connect power supply to it. Connect power cord to power supply. (We have photos and hints in Chart D if you've never done this before.) Turn on the power supply.

Either the mainboard is bad (how? you just replaced it) or you are misconnecting the power supply to the mainboard. Look at the pictures and your notes to make sure the connectors aren't reversed. You probably made a wrong turn in the chart. Set this job aside, get a friend to help, and come back to the problem fresh.

Does the fan blow?

No

Yes

The mainboard was shorting out to the case. The problem could be caused by missing insulating washers or a malformed case. This is a rare problem, though. Double-check the steps you took to get to this box. Reinstall mainboard, correcting the short.

Turn off power. Connect a new mainboard to power supply. Turn on the power supply.

Yes

Does the fan blow?

No

No

Does the fan blow?

Yes

Turn off the computer and reinstall one expansion card. Turn on the computer.

Yes

Does the fan blow?

No

Turn off the computer. Disconnect mainboard and power supply. Leave good drives connected to the power source. Turn on the computer.

Yes

Does the fan blow?

Yes

Are there any more boards?

You probably made a wrong turn in the chart. Set this job aside, get a friend to help, and come back to the problem fresh.

No

No

Does the fan blow?

No

Turn off the computer. The last card you installed is suspect — pull it out.

Did you find any suspect cards?

No

Is it really fixed: does the fan blow now?

Yes

A card may have been jammed into the bus and shorting it out. Now the card is installed correctly.

Replace the power supply.

Yes, but only one

Yes, more than one

Could this be a bad bus or a bad slot? Are you sure you followed the chart correctly? You probably made a wrong turn in the chart. Set this job aside, get a friend, and come back to the problem fresh.

Replace the suspect cards. Retest. If all is OK, install parts in case again.

PROBLEM SOLVED

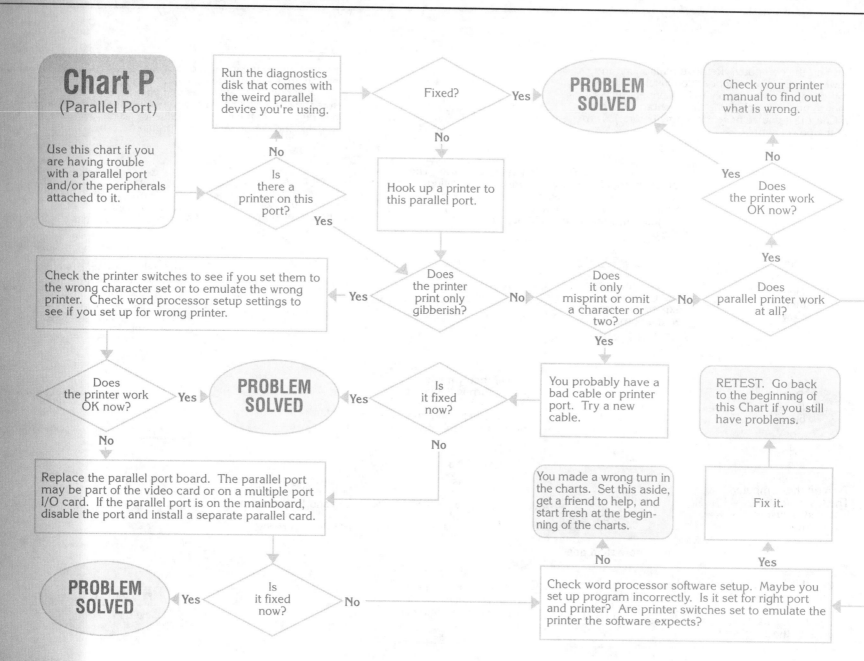

Chart P
(Parallel Port)

Use this chart if you are having trouble with a parallel port and/or the peripherals attached to it.

Run the diagnostics disk that comes with the weird parallel device you're using.

Fixed? — Yes → **PROBLEM SOLVED**

No

Is there a printer on this port? — No → (back to diagnostics)

Yes

Hook up a printer to this parallel port.

Check your printer manual to find out what is wrong.

No

Does the printer work OK now? — Yes

Yes

Does the printer print only gibberish? — No → Does it only misprint or omit a character or two? — No → Does parallel printer work at all?

Check the printer switches to see if you set them to the wrong character set or to emulate the wrong printer. Check word processor setup settings to see if you set up for wrong printer.

Yes

Does the printer work OK now? — Yes → **PROBLEM SOLVED** — Yes → Is it fixed now?

No

No

Yes

You probably have a bad cable or printer port. Try a new cable.

RETEST. Go back to the beginning of this Chart if you still have problems.

Replace the parallel port board. The parallel port may be part of the video card or on a multiple port I/O card. If the parallel port is on the mainboard, disable the port and install a separate parallel card.

You made a wrong turn in the charts. Set this aside, get a friend to help, and start fresh at the beginning of the charts.

Fix it.

PROBLEM SOLVED — Yes — Is it fixed now? — No → Check word processor software setup. Maybe you set up program incorrectly. Is it set for right port and printer? Are printer switches set to emulate the printer the software expects?

No

Yes

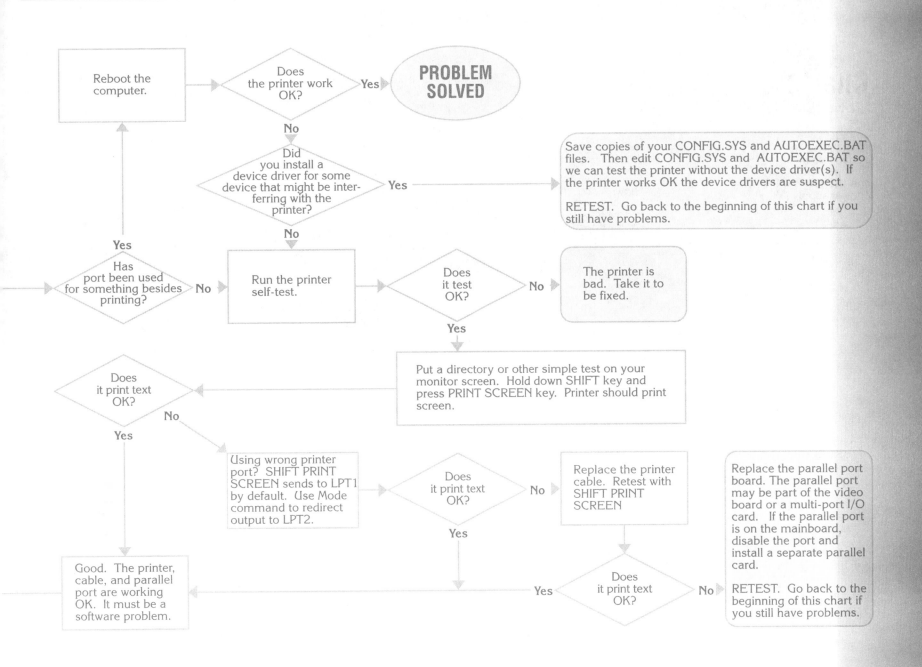

Reboot the computer.

Does the printer work OK? — Yes → **PROBLEM SOLVED**

No ↓

Did you install a device driver for some device that might be interferring with the printer? — Yes → Save copies of your CONFIG.SYS and AUTOEXEC.BAT files. Then edit CONFIG.SYS and AUTOEXEC.BAT so we can test the printer without the device driver(s). If the printer works OK the device drivers are suspect.

RETEST. Go back to the beginning of this chart if you still have problems.

No ↓

Yes ↑
Has port been used for something besides printing? — No → **Run the printer self-test.** → **Does it test OK?** — No → The printer is bad. Take it to be fixed.

Yes ↓

Put a directory or other simple test on your monitor screen. Hold down SHIFT key and press PRINT SCREEN key. Printer should print screen.

Does it print text OK?

No →

Yes ↓

Using wrong printer port? SHIFT PRINT SCREEN sends to LPT1 by default. Use Mode command to redirect output to LPT2. → **Does it print text OK?** — No → Replace the printer cable. Retest with SHIFT PRINT SCREEN

Yes ↓

Good. The printer, cable, and parallel port are working OK. It must be a software problem.

← Yes — **Does it print text OK?** — No → Replace the parallel port board. The parallel port may be part of the video board or a multi-port I/O card. If the parallel port is on the mainboard, disable the port and install a separate parallel card.

RETEST. Go back to the beginning of this chart if you still have problems.

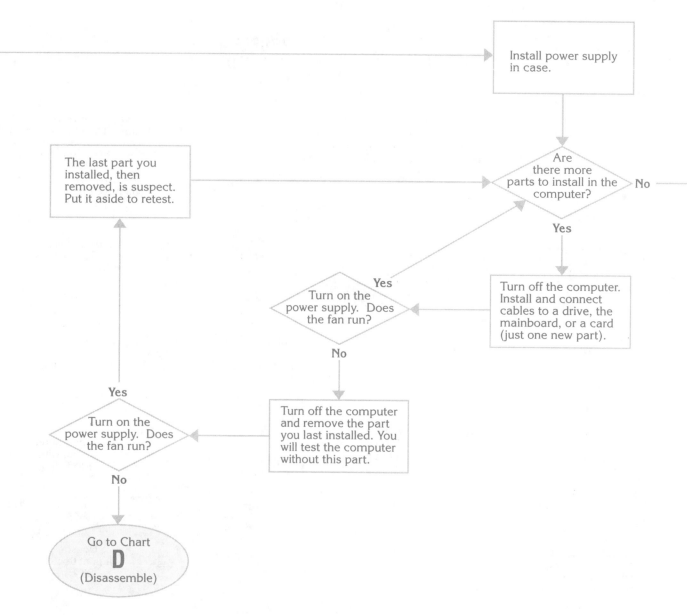

Chart PS
(Power Supply)

Use this chart when you need to test parts that may be shorting out the power supply.

Install power supply in case.

The last part you installed, then removed, is suspect. Put it aside to retest.

Are there more parts to install in the computer?

No

Yes

Turn on the power supply. Does the fan run?

Yes

No

Turn off the computer. Install and connect cables to a drive, the mainboard, or a card (just one new part).

Turn off the computer and remove the part you last installed. You will test the computer without this part.

Turn on the power supply. Does the fan run?

Yes

No

Go to Chart
D
(Disassemble)

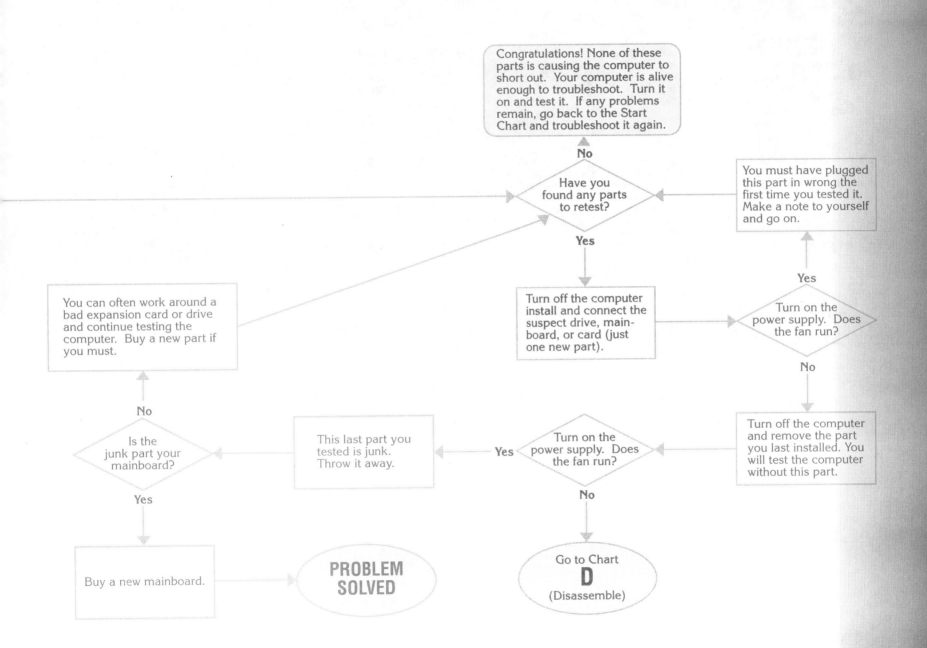

Congratulations! None of these parts is causing the computer to short out. Your computer is alive enough to troubleshoot. Turn it on and test it. If any problems remain, go back to the Start Chart and troubleshoot it again.

No

Have you found any parts to retest?

You must have plugged this part in wrong the first time you tested it. Make a note to yourself and go on.

Yes

Turn off the computer install and connect the suspect drive, main-board, or card (just one new part).

Yes

Turn on the power supply. Does the fan run?

You can often work around a bad expansion card or drive and continue testing the computer. Buy a new part if you must.

No

No

Is the junk part your mainboard?

This last part you tested is junk. Throw it away.

Yes

Turn on the power supply. Does the fan run?

Turn off the computer and remove the part you last installed. You will test the computer without this part.

Yes

No

Buy a new mainboard.

PROBLEM SOLVED

Go to Chart **D** (Disassemble)

Chart S

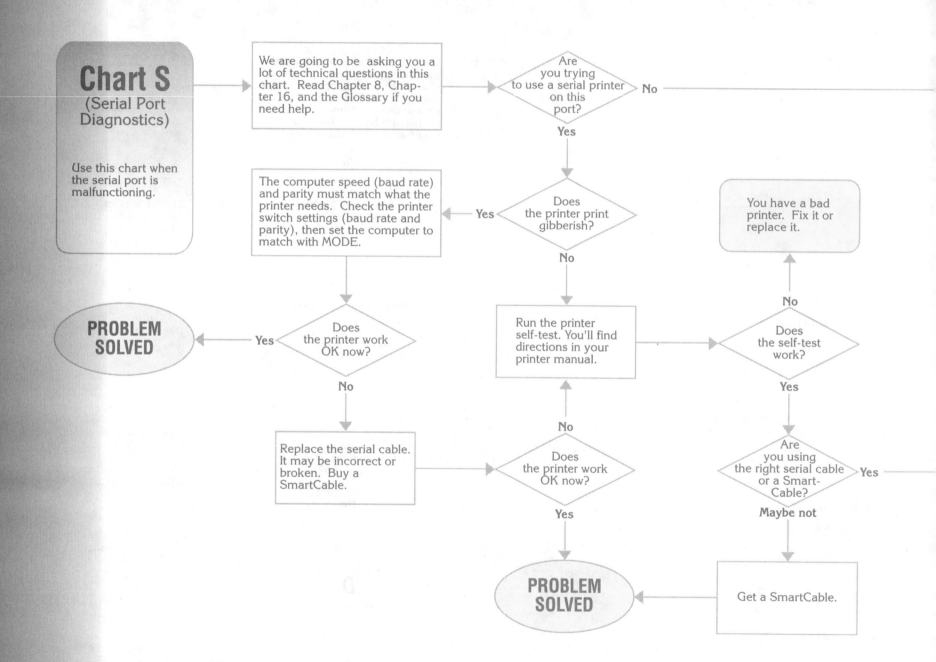

Chart S
(Serial Port Diagnostics)

Use this chart when the serial port is malfunctioning.

We are going to be asking you a lot of technical questions in this chart. Read Chapter 8, Chapter 16, and the Glossary if you need help.

Are you trying to use a serial printer on this port? — No

Yes

Does the printer print gibberish? — Yes

The computer speed (baud rate) and parity must match what the printer needs. Check the printer switch settings (baud rate and parity), then set the computer to match with MODE.

No

You have a bad printer. Fix it or replace it.

Does the printer work OK now? — Yes — **PROBLEM SOLVED**

No

Run the printer self-test. You'll find directions in your printer manual.

Does the self-test work?

No

Yes

Replace the serial cable. It may be incorrect or broken. Buy a SmartCable.

Does the printer work OK now?

No

Yes

Are you using the right serial cable or a Smart-Cable? — Yes

Maybe not

PROBLEM SOLVED

Get a SmartCable. — **PROBLEM SOLVED**

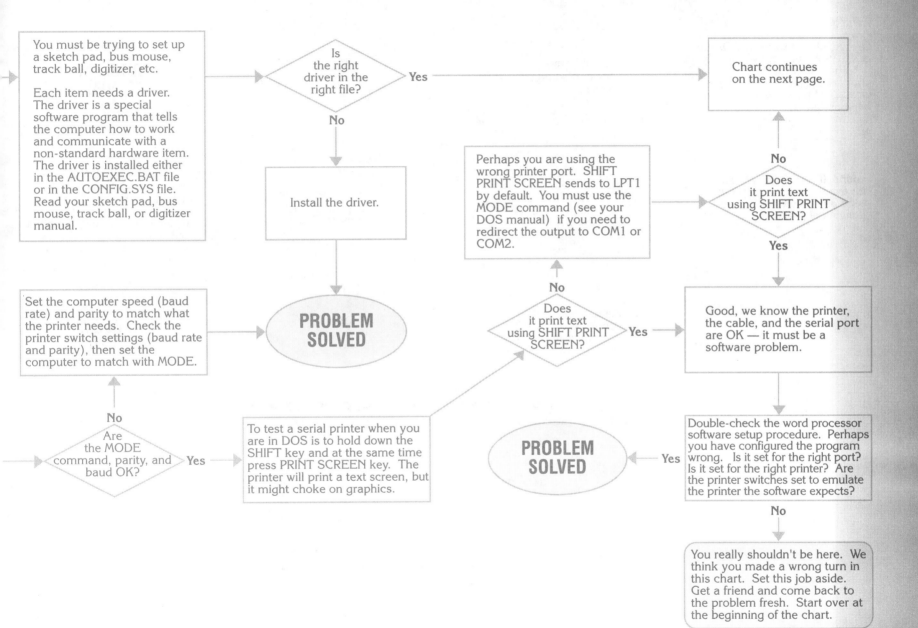

You must be trying to set up a sketch pad, bus mouse, track ball, digitizer, etc.

Each item needs a driver. The driver is a special software program that tells the computer how to work and communicate with a non-standard hardware item. The driver is installed either in the AUTOEXEC.BAT file or in the CONFIG.SYS file. Read your sketch pad, bus mouse, track ball, or digitizer manual.

Is the right driver in the right file?

Yes → Chart continues on the next page.

No

Install the driver.

PROBLEM SOLVED

Set the computer speed (baud rate) and parity to match what the printer needs. Check the printer switch settings (baud rate and parity), then set the computer to match with MODE.

No

Are the MODE command, parity, and baud OK?

Yes → To test a serial printer when you are in DOS is to hold down the SHIFT key and at the same time press PRINT SCREEN key. The printer will print a text screen, but it might choke on graphics.

Perhaps you are using the wrong printer port. SHIFT PRINT SCREEN sends to LPT1 by default. You must use the MODE command (see your DOS manual) if you need to redirect the output to COM1 or COM2.

No

Does it print text using SHIFT PRINT SCREEN?

Yes → Good, we know the printer, the cable, and the serial port are OK — it must be a software problem.

Does it print text using SHIFT PRINT SCREEN?

No

Yes

PROBLEM SOLVED

Yes → Double-check the word processor software setup procedure. Perhaps you have configured the program wrong. Is it set for the right port? Is it set for the right printer? Are the printer switches set to emulate the printer the software expects?

No

You really shouldn't be here. We think you made a wrong turn in this chart. Set this job aside. Get a friend and come back to the problem fresh. Start over at the beginning of the chart.

Chart S (continued)

Diagnositic software, like QAPlus or CheckIt, can help you figure out what interrupt (IRQ) each of your serial ports is using and what COM port address each has been assigned.

Your software (word processor, for example) must be set up to send and receive data at the right serial port using the right interrupt.

Set the COM port to the correct IRQ. Retest.

Does it work ok now?

Yes → **PROBLEM SOLVED**

No

Does the software send to this COM port?

Yes →

Does the COM port use the correct interrupt?

No

Yes →

In a computer repair shop, the technician would now test the serial port with diagnostic software and a wrap plug. See Chapter 16 for more information about wrap plugs.

No

Fix it. If the printer is connected to COM2, then the software must send to COM2. Retest.

No

Does it work OK now?

Yes → **PROBLEM SOLVED**

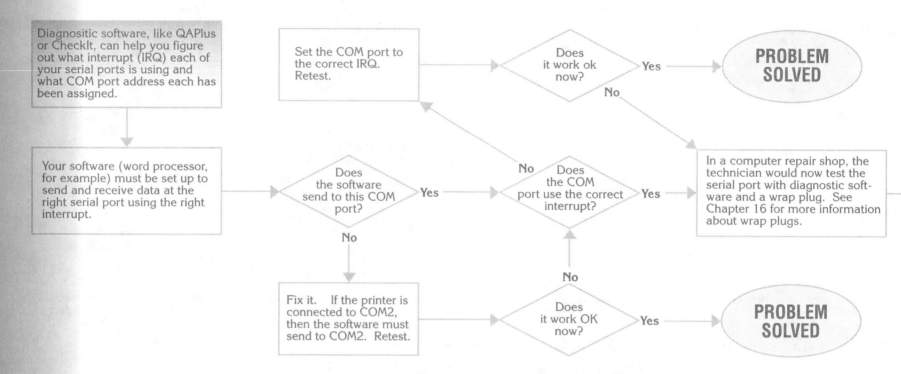

Norton's System Info program shows two serial ports in this computer. COM1 uses Interrupt 4. The serial mouse plugged into COM2 uses Interrupt 3.

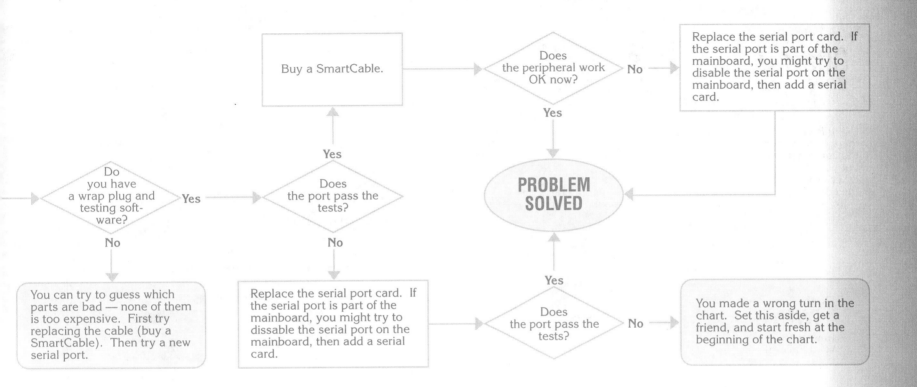

Buy a SmartCable.

Does the peripheral work OK now?

No → Replace the serial port card. If the serial port is part of the mainboard, you might try to disable the serial port on the mainboard, then add a serial card.

Yes

PROBLEM SOLVED

Do you have a wrap plug and testing software? → Yes → Does the port pass the tests?

No

You can try to guess which parts are bad — none of them is too expensive. First try replacing the cable (buy a SmartCable). Then try a new serial port.

Yes → Buy a SmartCable.

No → Replace the serial port card. If the serial port is part of the mainboard, you might try to dissable the serial port on the mainboard, then add a serial card.

Yes

Does the port pass the tests?

No → You made a wrong turn in the chart. Set this aside, get a friend, and start fresh at the beginning of the chart.

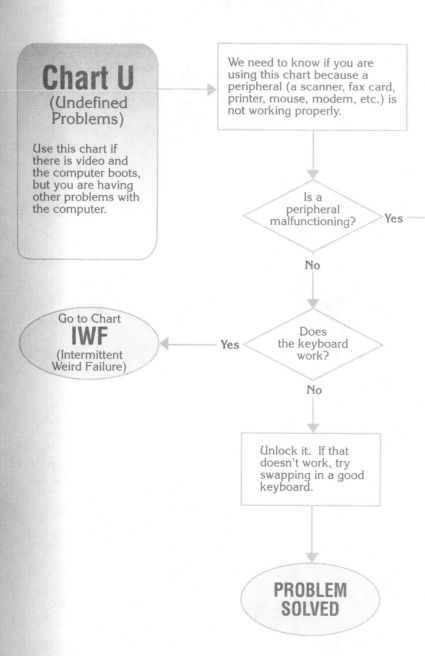

Chart U
(Undefined Problems)

Use this chart if there is video and the computer boots, but you are having other problems with the computer.

We need to know if you are using this chart because a peripheral (a scanner, fax card, printer, mouse, modem, etc.) is not working properly.

Is a peripheral malfunctioning?

Yes → Some peripherals (e.g., bus mouse, many scanners, fax cards) use a proprietary interface card rather than the computer's parallel or serial ports.

No

Go to Chart
IWF
(Intermittent Weird Failure)

← Yes — Does the keyboard work?

No

Unlock it. If that doesn't work, try swapping in a good keyboard.

PROBLEM SOLVED

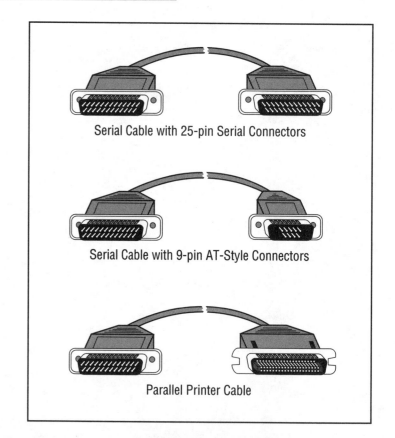

Serial Cable with 25-pin Serial Connectors

Serial Cable with 9-pin AT-Style Connectors

Parallel Printer Cable

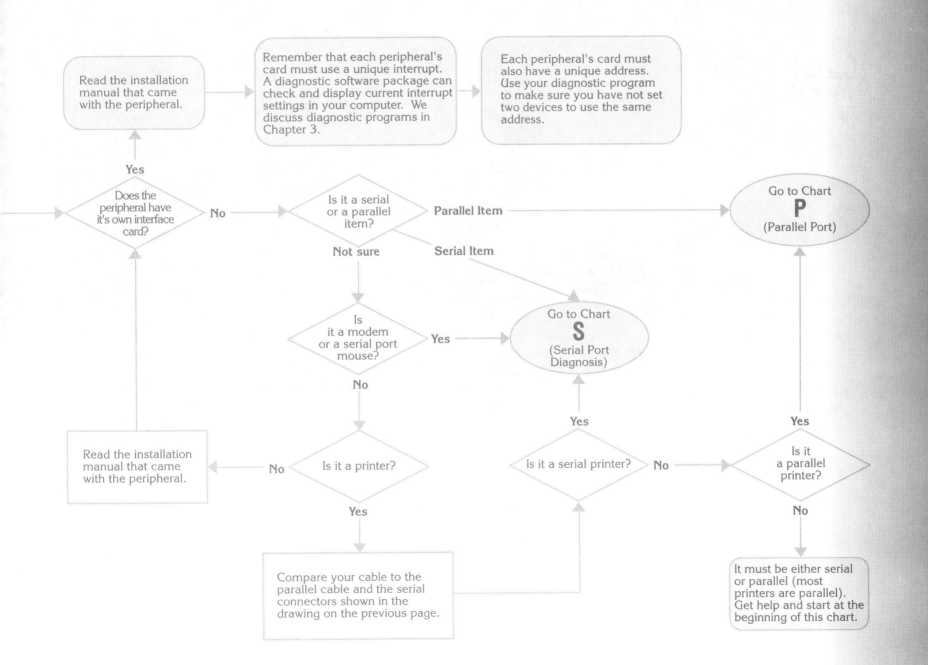

Read the installation manual that came with the peripheral.

Remember that each peripheral's card must use a unique interrupt. A diagnostic software package can check and display current interrupt settings in your computer. We discuss diagnostic programs in Chapter 3.

Each peripheral's card must also have a unique address. Use your diagnostic program to make sure you have not set two devices to use the same address.

Yes

Does the peripheral have it's own interface card?

No

Is it a serial or a parallel item?

Parallel Item

Go to Chart
P
(Parallel Port)

Not sure

Serial Item

Is it a modem or a serial port mouse?

Yes

Go to Chart
S
(Serial Port Diagnosis)

No

Read the installation manual that came with the peripheral.

No

Is it a printer?

Yes

Is it a serial printer?

No

Yes

Is it a parallel printer?

No

Yes

Compare your cable to the parallel cable and the serial connectors shown in the drawing on the previous page.

It must be either serial or parallel (most printers are parallel). Get help and start at the beginning of this chart.

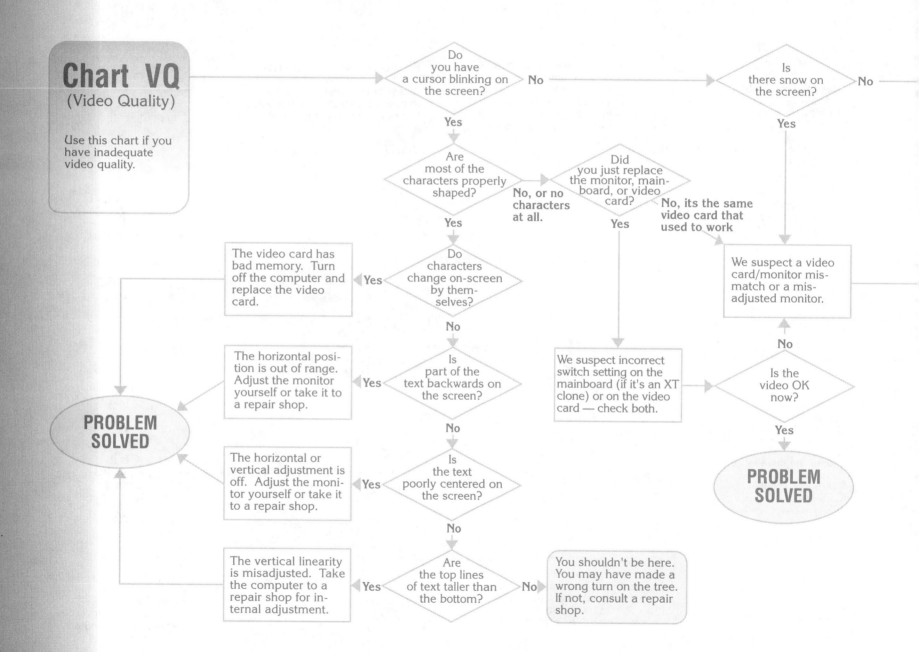

Chart VQ
(Video Quality)

Use this chart if you have inadequate video quality.

Do you have a cursor blinking on the screen?

No → Is there snow on the screen? → **No**

Yes ↓

Are most of the characters properly shaped?

No, or no characters at all. → Did you just replace the monitor, mainboard, or video card?

No, its the same video card that used to work → **Yes** ↓

Is there snow on the screen? → **Yes** ↓

We suspect a video card/monitor mismatch or a misadjusted monitor.

Yes ↓

Do characters change on-screen by themselves?

The video card has bad memory. Turn off the computer and replace the video card. ← **Yes**

No ↓

Is part of the text backwards on the screen?

The horizontal position is out of range. Adjust the monitor yourself or take it to a repair shop. ← **Yes**

No ↓

Is the text poorly centered on the screen?

The horizontal or vertical adjustment is off. Adjust the monitor yourself or take it to a repair shop. ← **Yes**

No ↓

Are the top lines of text taller than the bottom?

The vertical linearity is misadjusted. Take the computer to a repair shop for internal adjustment. ← **Yes**

No → You shouldn't be here. You may have made a wrong turn on the tree. If not, consult a repair shop.

Did you just replace the monitor, mainboard, or video card? **Yes** ↓

We suspect incorrect switch setting on the mainboard (if it's an XT clone) or on the video card — check both. →

Is the video OK now?

No ↑ We suspect a video card/monitor mismatch or a misadjusted monitor.

Yes ↓

PROBLEM SOLVED

PROBLEM SOLVED

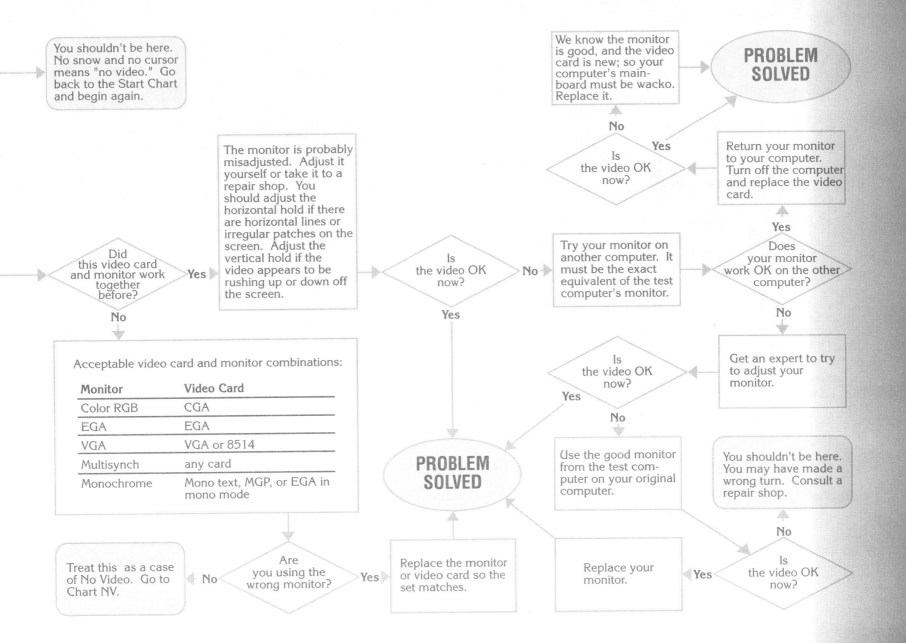

You shouldn't be here. No snow and no cursor means "no video." Go back to the Start Chart and begin again.

We know the monitor is good, and the video card is new; so your computer's mainboard must be wacko. Replace it.

PROBLEM SOLVED

The monitor is probably misadjusted. Adjust it yourself or take it to a repair shop. You should adjust the horizontal hold if there are horizontal lines or irregular patches on the screen. Adjust the vertical hold if the video appears to be rushing up or down off the screen.

Is the video OK now? — No — Return your monitor to your computer. Turn off the computer and replace the video card.

Did this video card and monitor work together before? — Yes

Is the video OK now? — No — Try your monitor on another computer. It must be the exact equivalent of the test computer's monitor. — Does your monitor work OK on the other computer? — Yes

No

Yes — Does your monitor work OK on the other computer? — No

Acceptable video card and monitor combinations:

Monitor	Video Card
Color RGB	CGA
EGA	EGA
VGA	VGA or 8514
Multisynch	any card
Monochrome	Mono text, MGP, or EGA in mono mode

Is the video OK now? — Yes

No — Get an expert to try to adjust your monitor.

PROBLEM SOLVED

Use the good monitor from the test computer on your original computer.

You shouldn't be here. You may have made a wrong turn. Consult a repair shop.

Treat this as a case of No Video. Go to Chart NV. — No — Are you using the wrong monitor? — Yes — Replace the monitor or video card so the set matches.

Replace your monitor. — Yes — Is the video OK now? — No

Section 4
The Appendices

Appendix A
Numeric Error Codes

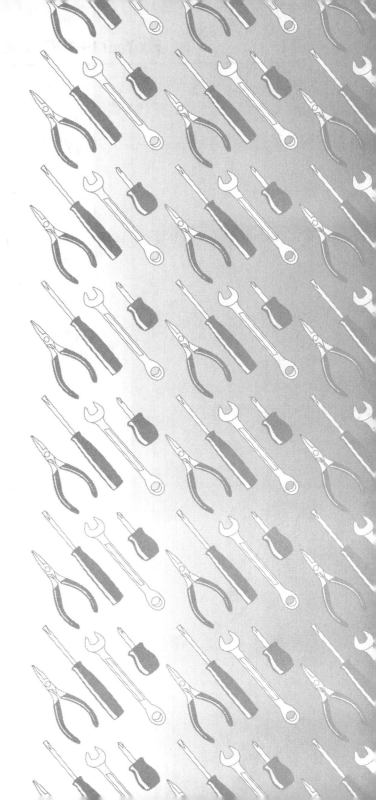

IBM and IBM look-alikes (Compaqs or clones using ERSO BIOS ROM, for example) use numeric error codes. This appendix lists these codes and tells you what to do when one of them appears on your monitor.

Each entry includes the error code number displayed on the screen, followed by the official name of the BIOS error. Note that some clone ROMs display the official name, but IBM ROMs display only the number. The paragraphs following the error number and name describe the possible causes of the error and give recommendations for correcting it.

If you see a text error message, refer to Appendix B, where we list these types of error messages. In Appendix B you'll find the official Phoenix ROM error messages plus a selection of AMIBIOS and DOS error messages.

101
"SYSTEM INTERRUPT FAILED"

If you have an XT/PC clone (8088 or 8086 CPU chips), this error code means that something is wrong with the mainboard. No further details are available from the computer's self-tests—you will have to replace the mainboard.

If you have an AT clone (80286 or 80386 CPU chips), this error code indicates that you have an unusual error. You have a bad mainboard or a board is interfering with the interrupt controller chip. We've only seen this particular problem once during years of troubleshooting at the clone store. If you have this problem, you will have to replace the mainboard.

102
"SYSTEM TIMER FAILED"

There is a bad timer chip on the mainboard—you will have to replace the mainboard.

103
"SYSTEM TIMER INTERRUPT FAILED"

The timer chip cannot get the interrupt controller chip to send interrupt zero (the timer interrupt). You have a bad mainboard and you will have to replace it.

104
"PROTECTED MODE OPERATION FAILED"

This error code applies to the AT only. The computer must switch into protected mode to count and check the extended memory in an AT, even if there is no extended memory (it must check and see there is zero kilobytes of extended memory). A bad mainboard can cause failure to switch into protected mode, as can a bad keyboard.

A bad keyboard in combination with particular 8042 (keyboard controller chip) firmware can cause the 8042 to keep sending signals on address line 20 to the processor. The processor needs to use address line 20 as a regular address line when it is in protected mode, but the 8042 chip will not get off the line. Eventually the BIOS ROM sends the message listed above. A Phoenix BIOS sends a similar error, "Gate A20 failure," to complain about a continuously busy address line 20.

Check the keyboard switches to see if they're set right, then try a new keyboard. If that doesn't work, put in a new mainboard.

105
"8042 COMMAND NOT ACCEPTED. KEYBOARD COMMUNICATION FAILURE"

You have a bad 8042 (keyboard controller chip) or a bad keyboard. Try another keyboard first. If this doesn't work, try replacing the 8042 (which is on the mainboard). Note that you can only do this if the 8042 is socketed. If it's soldered to the mainboard, you'll have to put in a whole new mainboard.

106
"POST LOGIC TEST PROBLEM"

This is the catch-all error code. It covers any problem found during the Power-On Self-Test (POST) that doesn't fit into any of the other baskets (errors 101-105 or 107-109), but is believed to be caused by a bad system mainboard. Other factors, like faulty cards, could also cause this error.

Turn off the computer, pull all the cards out of the machine except the video card, then turn on the computer again. If the error has gone away, try replacing one card at a time and retesting until the bad card is isolated. Don't worry about additional error messages that appear when your cards are removed. If the 106 error message doesn't go away when only the video card is installed, then unfortunately it's probably time to replace the mainboard. There is a slight chance, however, that the video card is the culprit. To check this, swap out the video card. If this doesn't work, you will have to replace the mainboard.

107
"NMI TEST FAILED"

The microprocessor on the mainboard has failed. 8088 and 8086 CPUs (microprocessors) are easy to replace, and are cheap. 80286 and 80386 microprocessors are not field serviceable by the average person. Replace the whole mainboard if you don't feel like working with the processor.

108
"FAILED SYSTEM TIMER TEST"

The timer chip on the mainboard is not working—you will have to replace the mainboard.

109
"PROBLEM WITH FIRST 64K RAM"

As the name of this error code suggests, there's a problem with the first 64K of RAM. You will have to replace these memory chips—or the whole mainboard. If you have a genuine IBM, with the first 64K soldered to the mainboard, you will have to replace the mainboard since the chips can't be individually replaced. Clones, however, generally have all the memory socketed. If this is the case with your computer, then you can just replace the chips.

The number of chips you'll have to locate and replace depends on what type of mainboard you have. If you have an 8088 mainboard, the 109 error code indicates that one or more chips in the first row of nine—marked Bank 0—is bad. Locate and replace these nine chips. If you have an 80286 or 8086 mainboard, the 109 code indicates that one or more of the chips in the first two rows of nine—marked Bank 0 and Bank 0 or Bank 0 and Bank 1, depending on the manufacturer—are bad. Locate and replace these 18 chips. If you have an 80386 or 80486 mainboard, the 109 code indicates that any of the first 36 memory chips could be bad. Use your manual to locate and replace these 36 chips. See Chapter 6 for more information.

161
"SYSTEM OPTION NOT SET," "POSSIBLE BAD BATTERY" or
162
"SYSTEM OPTION NOT SET," "INVALID CHECKSUM," "CONFIGURATION INCORRECT" or
163
"TIME AND DATE NOT SET"

The CMOS memory has forgotten the setup program. Replace the battery and rerun the program.

If you have already replaced the battery, replace the power supply and run your setup program again.

Another possibility is a failing RTC-CMOS chip. If you have replaced the power supply and the problem still persists, the only solution is to replace the RTC-CMOS chip (if it's socketed). If the chip is soldered to the mainboard, you must replace the mainboard.

164
"MEMORY SIZE ERROR"

The CMOS memory has probably forgotten the setup program. Run your setup program and retest. If the error is still there, replace the battery and run your setup program again.

If you still have the error, turn off the computer, open the case, and press down on all the memory chips. Make sure that they are firmly seated into their sockets. Then turn on the computer, and retest. If the error is still there, remove all the memory chips and take them to a repair shop equipped with a memory tester. The memory tester takes only a couple seconds per chip. Replace any chips that fail the test.

Most clones have all the memory chips socketed, but genuine IBMs, Coronas, Compaqs, and some other brand clones have at least the first 64K or 256K soldered in place. If you have such a machine, remove any socketed RAM and test it.

If no RAM chips fail in the memory tester, replace the power supply. If this doesn't work, replace the mainboard. This error is very seldom traced to a bad mainboard, though, so be sure to explore the other possibilities thoroughly first.

201
"MEMORY ERROR"

If you have an XT/PC clone (8088 or 8086 CPU chips), this error code means that something is wrong with the RAM memory located on the mainboard. No further details are available from the computer's self-tests. You'll have to manually test the RAM, replacing memory chips as necessary. If you're really unlucky, you may have bad addressing chips on the mainboard. As always, thoroughly check the cheap and easy solutions (a bad memory chip or two) before spending the big bucks on a new mainboard. Try reading the memory error codes for AT clone machines (201,

202, 203) for ideas. The newer machines have been designed with more discriminating power-on self-tests coded into the ROM. XT ROMs throw all the memory errors into code 201 and let you sort things out yourself.

If you have an AT clone, (80286, 80386, or 80486 CPU chips), this error code means there are one or more bad memory chips. Turn off the computer, open the case, and press down on all the memory chips. Make sure that they are firmly seated into their sockets, then close the case, turn on the computer, and retest. If the error is still there, remove all the memory chips and take them to a repair shop equipped with a memory tester. The memory tester takes only a couple of seconds per chip. Replace any chips that fail the test. Note that most clones have all the memory chips socketed, but genuine IBMs, Coronas, Compaqs and some other branded clones have at least the first 64K or 256K soldered in place. If you have such a machine, remove any socketed RAM and test it. In any case, if no RAM chips fail in the memory tester, replace the mainboard.

202
"MEMORY ADDRESS ERROR LINES 0-15" or
203
"MEMORY ADDRESS ERROR LINES 16-23"

There are one or more bad memory chips. Turn off the computer, open the case, and press down on all the memory chips. Make sure that they are firmly seated into their sockets, then close the case, turn on the computer, and retest. If the error is still there, remove all the memory chips and take them to a repair shop equipped with a memory tester. The memory tester takes only a of couple seconds per chip. Replace any chips that fail the test.

Note that most clones have all the memory chips socketed, but genuine IBMs, Coronas, Compaqs, and some other brand clones have at least the first 64K or 256K soldered in place. If you have such a machine, remove any socketed RAM and test it. In any case, if no RAM chips fail in the memory tester, replace the mainboard.

301
"KEYBOARD ERROR"

As the name of this error code suggests, there is a problem with the keyboard. Make sure that the keyboard is connected and no keys are stuck. Also check to make sure no books or other objects are resting on the keyboard.

302
"SYSTEM UNIT KEYLOCK IS LOCKED"

This code appears when you lock the keylock—the key on the front of the computer that grounds out the keyboard to mainboard circuit—or accidentally disconnect the jumper wires from the keyboard lock to the mainboard (while installing a new hard disk or card, for instance). This code may also appear if you have a faulty keylock switch or if a keyboard key is stuck down. Check all these possibilities.

303
"KEYBOARD OR SYSTEM UNIT ERROR" or
304
"KEYBOARD OR SYSTEM UNIT ERROR, KEYBOARD CLOCKLINE ERROR"

The keyboard controller chip tests the keyboard during POST. Error codes 303 and 304 indicate that the keyboard is not sending the right replies to the controller's POST signals. Either the keyboard cord or the keyboard itself is bad.

Check the AT/XT switch on the bottom of your keyboard. Is this keyboard intended for use on either an XT or AT only? Are you using it on an appropriate machine? Is a key stuck down?

401
"CRT ERROR #1"

This error code applies to the XT only. It indicates that the monochrome display adapter is malfunctioning. It probably has a bad chip, in which case you will have to replace the whole card.

501
"CRT ERROR #2"

This error code applies to the XT only. It indicates that the color graphics adapter (CGA) card is malfunctioning. It probably has a bad chip, in which case you will have to replace the whole card.

601
"DISK ERROR"

Most manuals say this error is caused by a bad disk, drive or controller, but we have most often seen it when the computer looks for a nonexistent floppy drive. If the CMOS chip contains setup information about a drive, but you have removed the drive from the machine (or unplugged a cable from the drive), the computer gives this error on bootup.

602
"DISK BOOT RECORD ERROR"

Many things can cause this problem, starting with a simple bad disk. Try several new boot disks. Be absolutely certain that these boot disks are good. Test them by booting another computer equipped with an equivalent 720K, 360K, 1.2 Mb, or 1.44 Mb drive.

Have you just been working inside the computer? If so, 99 percent of the time you just knocked a cable loose or installed the floppy drive cable incorrectly. See Chapter 14 for complete cable installation instructions.

If the problem persists, a bad floppy drive is the most likely cause. Try swapping a good equivalent floppy drive. If the machine still doesn't boot, replace the controller.

1701
"HARD DISK FAILURE"

The hard disk controller has not received the response from the hard disk that it expected. Possible causes are: (1) the power cord may not be connected to the hard disk, (2) the cables connecting the hard disk and its controller may be installed incorrectly, (3) the drive select jumper on the hard disk may be set wrong, (4) the hard disk may be dead, or (5) the hard disk controller may be dead.

Check all these possibilities.

Note that error code 1701 refers to the first hard disk (logical drive C) in most cases, but it could be either hard drive. 1701 is not an official IBM error. It's an error message programmed into the BIOS of the hard disk controller card. Therefore, each controller card manufacturer will display this error message slightly differently. OMTI controller cards, made by SMS, Inc., will report 1701a through 1701e, for example. All of these error messages are subsets of another manufacturer's 1701 error, with each letter pointing toward a different suspect portion of the hard drive/controller subsystem.

1780
"DISK 0 FAILURE"

The hard disk controller has not received the response from hard disk 0 that it expected. Possible causes are: (1) the power cord may not be connected to the hard disk, (2) the cables connecting the hard disk and its controller may be installed incorrectly, (3) the drive select jumper on the hard disk may be set wrong, (4) the hard disk may be dead, or (5) the hard disk controller may be dead. Check all these possibilities.

Note that hard disk 0, the first physical hard disk, is always named logical drive C. Sometimes this hard disk is split into more than one logical drive. Error code 1780 does not refer to any particular logical drive, though, just to the first physical hard disk assembly, whether mounted inside the computer case or attached externally via a cable to a hard disk controller card inside the computer.

1781
"DISK 1 FAILURE"

The hard disk controller has not received the appropriate response from hard disk 1. Possible causes are: (1) the power cord may not be connected to the hard disk, (2) the cables connecting the hard disk and its controller may be installed incorrectly, (3) the drive select jumper on the hard disk may be set wrong, (4) the hard disk may be dead, or (5) the hard disk controller may be dead. Check all these possibilities.

Note that hard disk 1, the second physical hard disk, is often named logical drive D. Sometimes the first physical hard disk may be split into two logical drives (in other words, treated by the computer as if there were two separate drives, each with its own directory tree and its own physical space). If so, the first two logical drives (drives C and D) are on the first hard disk and the second hard disk is logical drive E.

Error code 1781 does not refer to any particular logical drive, though, just to the second physical hard disk assembly, whether mounted inside the computer case or attached externally via a cable to a hard disk controller card inside the computer.

1782
"DISK CONTROLLER FAILURE"

The hard disk controller is almost certainly bad. A few controllers will give this error if the hard disk cables are installed upside down on the controller card, however, so check that first before replacing the controller card. Occasionally, another card will also have a BIOS ROM at the same address area as the hard disk controller card's ROM. If you have just put a new card into the computer and you get this message the first time you boot up, try pulling the new card out. Retest the computer to see if the card was interfering with the hard disk controller.

1790
"DISK 0 ERROR"

The hard disk controller has not received the response from hard disk 0 that it expected. Possible causes are: (1) the power cord may not be connected to the hard disk, (2) the cables connecting the hard disk and its controller may be installed incorrectly, (3) the drive select jumper on the hard disk may be set wrong, (4) the hard disk may be dead, or (5) the hard disk controller may be dead. Check all these possibilities.

Note that hard disk 0, the first physical hard disk, is always named logical drive C. Sometimes the first physical hard disk may be split into more than one logical drive. Error code 1790 does not refer to any particular logical drive, though, just to the first physical hard disk assembly, whether mounted inside the computer case or attached externally via a cable to a hard disk controller card inside the computer.

1791
"DISK 1 ERROR"

The hard disk controller has not received the appropriate response from hard disk 1. Possible causes are: (1) the power cord may not be connected to the hard disk, (2) the cables connecting the hard disk and its controller may be installed incorrectly, (3) the drive select jumper on the hard disk may be set wrong, (4) the hard disk may be dead, or (5) the hard disk controller may be dead. Check all these possibilities.

Note that hard disk 1, the second physical hard disk, is often named logical drive D. Sometimes the first physical hard disk may be split into two logical drives (in other words, treated by the computer as if there were two separate drives, each with its own directory tree and it's own physical space). If so, the first two logical drives, drives C and D, are on the first hard disk and the second hard disk is logical drive E.

Error code 1791 does not refer to any particular logical drive, though, just to the second physical hard disk assembly, whether mounted inside the computer case or attached externally via a cable to a hard disk controller card inside the computer.

Appendix B
Text Error Messages

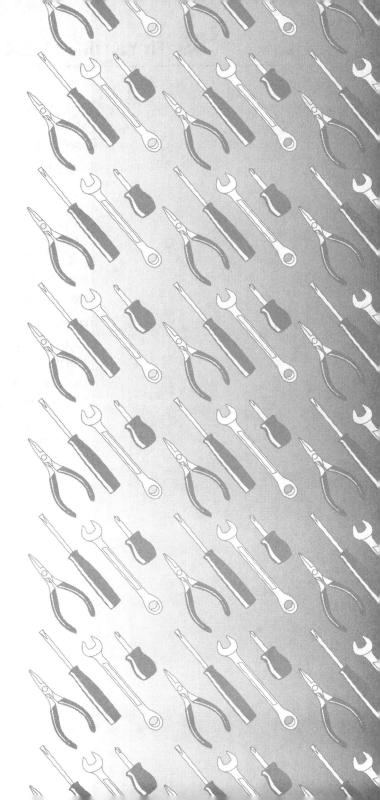

Text error messages are more common than the original IBM-style numeric error codes. This appendix lists Phoenix BIOS ROM error messages and the American Megatrends, Inc. AMIBIOS messages. Computers equipped with Phoenix and AMIBIOS look-alike BIOS ROMs use similar error messages, but the wording varies slightly from one ROM BIOS version to the next.

DOS also displays a number of error messages that imply hardware failure, so we have included a selection of DOS errors in this appendix as well. Each version of DOS has characteristic error message wording; don't be concerned if your error messages do not match our MS-DOS, AMIBIOS, or Phoenix BIOS examples word for word.

Each entry includes the error message displayed on the screen, followed by a description of the possible causes of the error and our recommendations for how to correct it. We list error messages that start with a variable number—for example, "*xx*=scancode, check keyboard"—under the first word in the message (in this case

"Scancode"). Messages that start with a fixed number—for example, "128 not OK, Parity Disabled"—appear at the beginning of the list, in numeric order.

If you have a numeric error message (numbers only, or numbers plus a short phrase), refer to Appendix A, where we have listed the IBM-style numeric ROM error messages. In Appendix C, we catalog computer beep error codes.

"128K NOT OK, PARITY DISABLED"

The first 128K of RAM has failed the POST. Turn off the computer, then turn it on and reboot. If the error message repeats, there is a problem with the RAM.

For some reason, the first 128K of RAM is not responding to the CPU. Perhaps the memory chips are bad. Remove the first 128K and take the chips to a computer repair shop to be tested. Alternatively, you can switch the high and low memory on your mainboard. In 8086 and 8088 machines the first bank of memory contains the first 64K (or the first 256K if the computer is using 256K chips), so switching the first and second banks (or the third and fourth banks) should solve the problem. Read your mainboard owner's manual to find out which is the first bank on your particular mainboard. If all this seems boring and/or intimidating, you can, of course, take the whole machine to the computer repair shop and let them fuss with the chips.

A bad mainboard can also cause this problem. If the memory chips all test good, you will have to replace the whole mainboard.

"8042 GATE—A20 ERROR"

This is usually a bad keyboard. See our discussion of the "GATE A20 FAILURE" error for more details.

"8087 NMI AT *xxxx:xxxx*. TYPE (S)HUT OFF NMI, (R)EBOOT, OTHER KEYS TO CONTINUE"

The 8087 math coprocessor chip has generated a nonmaskable interrupt (NMI) error. This means there is some problem with the 8087 chip. It must be tested thoroughly, and replaced if it is bad. Meanwhile, you probably don't want to lose the data you were working on when you got this error message. Type **S** to shut off the NMI message and you will be able to proceed with your task temporarily. Do an orderly shutdown of your task, then test the 8087 using one of the popular 8087 software test programs.

"ACCESS DENIED"

You tried to replace a write-protected, read-only, or locked file. Check to see if the disk is write-protected. Occasionally the part of the floppy drive responsible for detecting the write-enable notch (on a 5.25-inch disk) or the covered write-enable slide (on a 3.5-inch disk) is broken. If so, the drive will assume all disks are write-protected. You can also get this same message if you try to access a directory name as if it were a file.

If this error occurs because a particular file is write-protected or read-only, you can use a utility to change the file attributes if you really do want to change the file.

"ADDRESS LINE SHORT!"

Reseat the memory chips. If the problem persists, you'll have to decide whether to try replacing the memory chips or go straight to replacing the mainboard. The mainboard is probably the culprit, but it's so expensive that we would probably try replacing the memory with known-good memory from another machine and retesting first.

"ALLOCATION ERROR, SIZE ADJUSTED"

CHKDSK compared the apparent physical file size on this disk to the allocated size in the disk directory and the two didn't match. If the physical file seemed too long, CHKDSK truncated the file (cut off the tail end of the cluster chain) to match the size allocated in the directory. If the physical file seemed too short, CHKDSK changed the directory entry to reflect the real file size.

This error can happen to any user on rare occasions (like once a year). If you get this error more than once in a six-month period, look out. Your hard disk is starting to act up. Read the information about the "Hard Disk Read Failure" message and take steps to safeguard your data. Back everything up, run a hard disk diagnostic/repair utility, and keep alert to possible new symptoms. Chapters 5 and 10 should also be helpful.

Next time, use PC Tools DISKFIX or Norton's Disk Doctor rather than CHKDSK because they'll save more of your data rather than arbitrarily truncating the file.

"ATTEMPTED WRITE-PROTECT VIOLATION"

You tried to format a write-protected floppy disk. Occasionally the part of the floppy drive responsible for detecting the write-enable notch (on a 5.25-inch disk) or the covered write-enable slide (on a 3.5-inch disk) is broken. If so, the drive assumes all disks are write-protected. If this error occurs because a particular floppy is write-protected or read-only, you can use a utility to change the file attributes if you really want to format the disk.

"BAD DMA PORT = *xx*"

The DMA chip has failed the POST. Replace the mainboard; the DMA chip is soldered to the mainboard and is not individually replaceable.

"BAD OR MISSING COMMAND INTERPRETER"

Your computer can't find the DOS COMMAND.COM file. Trying to boot from a nonbootable disk? If you are using the network copy of COMMAND.COM on the file server, then log off the network, you'll get this error because the computer can't find COMMAND.COM anymore. Same problem if you neglect to tell your shell program (DOSSHELL in DOS 5.0, PC Tools PCShell, and so forth) where to find the COMMAND.COM file.

"BAD PARTITION TABLE"

You should only get this error message while you are attempting to format the hard disk. It means you ran FDISK improperly. Rerun FDISK, then and try to format again.

If you get the message again, you may have low-level formatted this drive improperly. Back up to the beginning of the format instructions for your machine (XT clone or AT clone) in Chapter 15. Read the instructions carefully, and try the entire format sequence again. If you find the formatting instructions baffling or just too much of a hassle, buy Disk Manager—it will do most of the work for you, since it is semiautomated, and is very quick.

If you are absolutely certain that you have low-level formatted and run FDISK and FORMAT correctly, yet you still get this error, it's a bad hard disk, so you will have to replace it. The disk is incapable of recording a readable partition table. Though it is theoretically possible to get this error from a bad hard disk controller, we've never seen that. In our experience it is almost always software, an operator error, or the occasional bad hard disk.

"*nnn*K BASE MEMORY" (FOR EXAMPLE, 640K BASE MEMORY)

This is not an error message. It is an informational message. Your computer has successfully tested *nnn* kilobytes of base (system) memory.

"BASE MEMORY SIZE = *nn*K" (FOR EXAMPLE, BASE MEMORY SIZE =640K)

This is not an error message. It is an informational message. Your computer is reporting base memory size.

"BUS TIMEOUT NMI AT SLOT X"

This is an EISA error. Run the EISA configuration utility, making certain you have correctly configured the EISA boards in your computer. If that doesn't fix things, better talk to the board vendor for the board in slot *x*. Though this problem can theoretically be caused by a bad mainboard, the board in slot *x* is more likely to be the problem.

"C: DRIVE ERROR"

The hard disk C:, the first hard disk in your machine, is not set up properly in CMOS. Run the CMOS SETUP. Also see "Hard Disk Configuration Error."

"C: DRIVE FAILURE"

See "Hard Disk Failure."

"CACHE MEMORY BAD, DO NOT ENABLE CACHE!"

The cache memory on this mainboard is malfunctioning. Reseat the cache memory chips and retest. This is an AMIBIOS error message; run AMIDiag if it's available. If not, try replacing the cache memory. Though the cache controller chip on the mainboard could also cause this problem, it's not likely—replace the mainboard only as a last resort.

"CANNOT CHDIR TO (*your pathname here*) TREE PAST THIS POINT NOT PROCESSED"

One of your directory files is trashed. You'll have to run SpinRite II or PC Tools DISKFIX. Either one should be able to correct this problem. Read the information about the "Hard Disk Read Failure" message, too. Directory files should not get trashed. Perhaps this is an early warning of hard disk troubles. Back up your data, run hard disk diagnostic/repair utilities, and keep alert for possible new symptoms.

"CANNOT CHDIR TO ROOT"

Your root directory file is trashed. Run SpinRite II or PC Tools DISKFIX. Either one should be able to correct the problem. Read the information about the "Hard Disk Read Failure" message, too. Directory files should not get trashed. Perhaps this is an early warning of hard disk troubles. Back up your data, run hard disk diagnostic/repair utilities, and keep alert for possible new symptoms.

"CANNOT RECOVER (.) ENTRY PROCESSING CONTINUED"

The entry (working directory) has been trashed. You'll have to run either SpinRite II or PC Tools DISKFIX. Either one should be able to correct the problem. Read the information about the "Hard Disk Read Failure" message, too. Directory files should not get trashed. Perhaps this is an early warning of hard disk troubles. Back up your data, run hard disk diagnostic/repair utilities, and keep alert for possible new symptoms.

"CANNOT RECOVER (..) ENTRY PROCESSING CONTINUED" or "CANNOT RECOVER (..)ENTRY, ENTRY HAS A BAD ATTRIBUTE (OR LINK SIZE)" or "CHDIR (..) FAILED, TRYING ALTERNATE METHOD"

The entry (parent directory) has been trashed. You'll have to run either SpinRite II or PC Tools DISKFIX. Either one should be able to correct the problem. Read the information about the "Hard Disk Read Failure" message, too. Directory files should not get trashed. Perhaps this is an early

warning of hard disk troubles. Back up your data, run hard disk diagnostic/repair utilities, and keep alert for possible new symptoms.

"CH-2 TIMER ERROR"

The timer chip 2 or interrupt controller logic on the mainboard is malfunctioning. Replace the mainboard.

"CMOS BATTERY STATE LOW"

Replace the clock/CMOS battery.

"CMOS CHECKSUM FAILURE"

The checksum used to check the CMOS setup chip's data integrity shows the CMOS data is corrupted. Replace your clock/CMOS battery and run SETUP. If you still get the error, the CMOS chip must be bad; replace the mainboard.

"CMOS DISPLAY TYPE MISMATCH"

The CMOS chip thinks you have a monochrome video card installed, but you actually have CGA or VGA, or vice versa. Run SETUP so the CMOS information matches the actual video card installed.

"CMOS MEMORY SIZE MISMATCH"

The CMOS chip thinks you have more or less memory installed than you actually have. Run SETUP.

Poorly seated memory chips or SIMM memory strips might not show up when the computer examines its physical memory during the boot process. If you know for sure how much memory is in the computer, and you know for sure that you told the CMOS chip the truth during SETUP, better turn off the computer and carefully examine each memory chip and SIMM strip. One is probably loose. See also the error message "Errors Found; Incorrect Configuration Information, Memory Size Miscompare."

"CMOS SYSTEM OPTIONS NOT SET"

The CMOS setup chip's data is corrupted. Run SETUP. You must use the correct SETUP program for your computer, not any old setup diskette lying around. Most new computers have SETUP in ROM BIOS (you'll see a message to "Hit <DEL> if you want to run SETUP" or "Press <DEL> if you want to run SETUP or DIAGS" whenever you boot the computer). Older computers used customized setup disks, which often malfunctioned if used in a different brand of computer.

"CMOS TIME & DATE NOT SET"

Run SETUP. You must use the SETUP program for your computer, not any old setup disk lying around. Most new computers have SETUP in ROM BIOS (you'll see a message to "Hit <DEL> if you want to run SETUP" or "Press <DEL> if you want to run SETUP or DIAGS" whenever you boot the computer). Older computers used customized setup disks, which often malfunctioned if used in a different brand of computer.

"COM PORT DOES NOT EXIST"

You are trying to use an invalid COM port. Check the COM ports in your machine, using diagnostic software like CheckIt, QA Plus, or Norton Utilities, to make sure your computer recognizes the COM port you are trying to use. For example, a machine with two physical serial ports with both set to COM1 will give this error if you try to send printer output through COM2. As far as the computer is concerned, COM2 doesn't even exist. For more information about serial port setup, see Chapter 8 and "Installing Serial Cards" in Chapter 16.

"CONFIGURATION ERROR FOR SLOT n"

You have just added an EISA card and haven't configured it, or you unplugged your CMOS backup battery, or the battery is low.

In all cases you must run the ECU (EISA configuration utility). If the battery is bad, replace it first, then run the ECU.

"CONVERT DIRECTORY TO FILE?"

Tell CHKDSK "No," or you'll lose this whole directory. Use PC Tools DISKFIX or Norton's Disk Doctor instead to save the directory and all its files.

"CONVERT LOST CHAINS TO FILES (Y/N)?"

You get this error if CHKDSK finds lost chains while inspecting a disk. A *lost chain* is a chain of clusters that are not connected to any known file. None of the files in the disk directory contains thechains of clusters. A chain clearly exists in the File Allocation Table (FAT), but there is no clue to its meaning.

These lost chains are not very significant. When you delete a number of files, the delete process may miss a link in the file chain. If you have a thunderstorm, you may get this error because a blip of electrical current wrote a tiny blip of trash information to the FAT. Neither of these random events are particularly important. They are not predictors of future hard disk problems. So go ahead and run CHKDSK/F to correct the errors and don't worry about it unless you start getting new lost chains every week or sooner.

If you think the lost chains might be useful data, use PC Tools DISKFIX or Norton's Disk Doctor— they're more precise and gentler than CHKDSK.

"D: DRIVE ERROR"

The second hard disk, drive D:, is not set up properly in CMOS. Run the CMOS SETUP. Also see "Hard Disk Configuration Error."

"D: DRIVE FAILURE"

See "Hard Disk Failure."

"DATA ERROR READING DRIVE x:"

Run PC Tools DISKFIX, SpinRite II, Norton's Disk Doctor, QA/WIN, or QA Plus on this disk. It is not necessarily a significant error, if only because all drives eventually start to go out of alignment and give this error. Luckily, DOS gives this error fairly early on in the aging process. The disk utilities we mentioned are capable of reading the data even when it starts to get tricky. So use the utilities. They will cause the drive to rewrite the data, often moving it to a better-quality spot on the disk. Once it's rewritten, the data are in alignment with the aging drive's alignment—so you should have no more trouble with this particular disk until the drive gets many more miles on it.

"DECREASING AVAILABLE MEMORY"

This is not an error message per se—the computer only displays it in conjunction with a memory error or a CMOS memory configuration error. Check out the other error message on the screen. It will tell you what the problem is.

"DISK BAD"

Some part of the hard disk system is bad. As usual, you should check the cheapest possibilities first. Check the hard drive cables inside the computer. If you have just been working inside the computer, you may have knocked one of the hard drive cables loose.

Next, check to see if the hard disk is spinning. You can feel a slight vibration or hear a low whine when the hard disk is on. Try unplugging the four-wire power connector at the hard disk, then plugging it back in—this makes it easy to distinguish the hard disk hum from other miscellaneous computer sounds. No spin? Try plugging in a second power supply cable (all the four-wire cables are identical). Still no spin? You have a bad hard disk. Replace both the hard disk and the controller. We always recommend replacing the hard disk and the hard disk controller together. If you want more details, see Chapter 15.

If the hard disk is spinning, then you may be able to get away with replacing only the hard disk controller. Still, we think it is smartest to replace both the controller and the hard disk together.

"DISK BOOT ERROR, REPLACE AND STRIKE KEY TO RETRY"

The computer is trying to boot, but cannot find a system disk. Check to make sure that there's a disk in drive A. It should be a system disk. Try using a known-good system disk.

If you have no disk in drive A and you are trying to boot from the hard disk, you might get this error too. If the hard disk has no DOS system files on it, you'll have to install them. Read Chapter 5 and

"Installing Hard Disks" in Chapter 15 for directions. On the other hand, the DOS system files may have been damaged. Read Chapter 10. This chapter includes information on hard disk data recovery.

"DISK CONFIGURATION ERROR"

The CMOS chip, which holds the hardware configuration information for 286, 386, and 486 computers, has an illegal code stored in it. The BIOS ROM on the system mainboard must read the information inside the CMOS chip each time the computer boots up. Suppose, for example, you have installed a 1.44 Mb 3.5-inch floppy drive in an ancient 286, a computer built before 1.44 Mb floppy drives existed. You use a new setup program disk to store information about this new drive in the CMOS chip. When the ancient ROM tries to read the CMOS chip, it runs into a code it doesn't recognize.

In general, configuration errors occur when you use a setup disk that is newer than your BIOS ROM. To fix these errors, use your original setup disk or, if you need a ROM with features not built into your old ROM, upgrade the ROM.

"DISK DRIVE 0 SEEK FAILURE"

Check the A drive cables first. Most manuals say this error is caused by a bad disk drive or controller, but we have most often seen it when the computer looks for a non-existent floppy drive.

If you have an XT clone, check for a bad or unformatted floppy disk. If you have an AT/286/386/486 clone or an EISA computer, note that the CMOS chip contains setup information about a drive. If you have removed the drive from the machine (or unplugged a cable from the drive), the computer will give this error on bootup.

"DISK DRIVE 1 SEEK FAILURE"

Check the B drive cables first. Most manuals say this error is caused by a bad disk drive or controller, but we have most often seen it when the computer looks for a nonexistent floppy drive. If the CMOS chip contains setup information about a drive, but you have removed the drive from the machine (or unplugged a cable from the drive), the computer will give this error on bootup.

"DISK DRIVE RESET FAILED"

The floppy disk controller card is unable to reset and you will have to replace it.

"DISK ERROR READING (OR WRITING) DRIVE *x*."

Run PC Tools DISKFIX, SpinRite II, Norton's Disk Doctor, QA/WIN, or QA Plus on this disk. It is not necessarily a significant error, if only because all drives eventually start to go out of alignment and give this error. Luckily, DOS gives us this error fairly early on in the aging process. The disk utilities we mentioned are capable of reading the data even when it starts to get tricky. So use the utilities. They will cause the drive to rewrite the data, often moving it to a better-quality spot on the disk. Once it's rewritten, the data are in alignment with the aging drive's alignment—so you should have no more trouble with this particular disk until the drive gets many more miles on it.

"DISK ERROR READING (OR WRITING) FAT"

There is a bad sector in the FAT. Luckily, DOS provides two copies of the FAT and simply starts using the second copy. This is a warning, though, that the fail-safe mechanism is already in use; you don't have any additional copies of the FAT if this second one goes bad.

Run PC Tools DISKFIX or SpinRite II on this drive, if it's a hard drive. If the failing disk is a floppy, just save the data you want to a new floppy and trash this one.

"DISK BOOT FAILURE"

The boot disk in drive A: is probably bad. Try another boot disk. If that doesn't sove the problem, see "Disk Read Failure—Strike F1 to Retry Boot."

"DISK DRIVE FAILURE" or
"DISKETTE DRIVE *x* FAILURE"

See "Disk Drive 0 Seek Failure," "Disk Drive 1 Seek Failure."

"DISKETTE READ FAILURE"

See "Disk Read Failure—Strike F1 to Retry Boot."

"DISK READ FAILURE—STRIKE F1 TO RETRY BOOT"

Many things can cause this problem, starting with a simple bad disk. Try a new boot disk, and another, and another. Be absolutely certain that the boot disks are good. Test them by booting another computer equipped with an equivalent 720K, 360K, 1.2 Mb, or 1.44 Mb drive.

Have you just been working inside the computer? If so, 99 percent of the time you just knocked a cable loose or installed the floppy drive cable. See "Floppy Drives" in Chapter 14 for full cable installation directions.

If the problem persists, a bad floppy drive is the most likely cause. Try swapping in a good equivalent floppy drive. If the machine still doesn't boot, replace the controller.

"DISPLAY ADAPTER FAILED; USING ALTERNATE"

The mono/color jumper on an AT/286/386/486 clone mainboard has been set wrong. Check your manual for the location and proper position of this jumper.

"DISPLAY SWITCH NOT SET PROPER"

The mono/color jumper on an AT/286/386/486 clone mainboard has been set wrong. Check your manual for the location and proper position of this jumper.

"DIVIDE OVERFLOW"

Reboot the computer. If you get the divide overflow message again while running this particular software program, contact the manufacturer.

"DMA BUS TIMEOUT"

American Megatrends, Inc. BIOS ROMs display this message when a device has driven the bus signal for more than 7.8 microseconds. Some fancy card in your computer is doing DMA transfers and it (or your DMA chip) has glitched out. Reboot the computer. This could simply be a random failure and not worth bothering about.

If you get the error message again, try to isolate the offending card. Turn off the computer and pull out the most high-tech card in the machine. Retest. If that card isn't causing the problem, try pulling out another card. One by one, pull out all the cards (you'll eventually have to substitute a known-good video card and hard disk with its controller, of course, or you won't be able to run the computer to test it). When you find the culprit, call the bad card's vendor. If you still get the error message when every card has been removed, it's got to be the mainboard.

"DMA ERROR" or
"DMA 1 ERROR" or
"DMA 2 ERROR"

The DMA chip has failed. Replace the mainboard; the DMA chip is soldered to the mainboard and is not individually replaceable.

"(.)(..) DOES NOT EXIST"

The (.) entry (current directory) or the (..) entry (parent directory) has been trashed. You'll have to run either SpinRite II or PC Tools DISKFIX. Either program should be able to correct this problem. Read the information about the "Hard Disk Read Failure" error message, too. Directory files should not get trashed. Perhaps this is an early warning of hard disk troubles. Back up your data, run hard disk diagnostic/repair utilities, and keep alert for possible new symptoms.

"DRIVE NOT READY ABORT, RETRY, IGNORE, FAIL?" or
"DRIVE x: NOT READY. MAKE SURE A DISK IS INSERTED INTO THE DRIVE AND THE DOOR IS CLOSED"

If drive *x* is a floppy, make sure a disk is installed right side up and the drive door is closed. If the disk works fine in other floppy drives, perhaps the floppy drive cable is damaged or the drive door-closed sensor is broken. Try replacing the cable first, then the drive. If the floppy disk doesn't work fine in another drive, use PC Tools DISKFIX or Norton's Disk Doctor to repair the disk.

Occasionally people get this error from a hard drive. In this case, a SCSI or an ESDI controller may be having trouble talking to your mainboard—it's usually timing incompatibilities. If you have this problem, there's not much to do except press **R**(etry). Generally the problem goes away on the second attempt to read. You'll just have to put up with the occasional error message.

If the hard disk will not respond on the first or second R(etry), use PC Tools DISKFIX (and your PC Tools Recovery Disk, if you made one).

"EISA CMOS CHECKSUM FAILURE" or "EISA CMOS INOPERATIONAL"

The checksum for the EISA CMOS data is bad (the data are corrupted) or there has been a read/write error in CMOS RAM. The EISA CMOS chip holds information under battery power when the computer is turned off. Therefore, a low battery is our prime suspect. Read the discussions of "Invalid Configuration Information. Please Run SETUP Program" and "Invalid EISA Configuraton Storage. Please Run the Configuration Utility."

"(.)(..) ENTRY HAS A BAD ATTRIBUTE (or LINK or SIZE)"

The (.) entry (current directory) or the (..) entry (parent directory) has been trashed. You'll have to run either SpinRite II or PC Tools DISKFIX. Either one should be able to correct this problem. Read the information about the "Hard Disk Read Failure" error message, too. Directory files should not get trashed. Perhaps this is an early warning of hard disk troubles. Back up your data, run hard disk diagnostic/repair utilities, and keep alert for possible new symptoms.

"ERROR READING/WRITING THE PARTITION TABLE"

You should only get this error while you are attempting to format the hard disk. It means you ran FDISK improperly. Rerun FDISK and try to format again. If you still get the same error, you may have low-level formatted this drive improperly. Reread the format instructions for your drive in Chapter 15. If you find the formatting instructions baffling or just too much of a hassle, buy Disk Manager—it will do most of the work for you, since it is semi-automated, and is very quick.

If you are absolutely certain that you have low-level formatted and run FDISK and FORMAT correctly, yet you still get this error, it's a bad hard disk, so you will have to replace it. The disk is incapable of recording a readable partition table. Though it is theoretically possible to get this error from a bad hard disk controller, we've never seen that. In our experience, it is always software, an operator error, or the occasional bad hard disk.

"ERRORS FOUND; DISK *x*: FAILED INITIALIZATION"

The hard disk does not report back on initialization. The possible causes range from a simple CMOS configuration error to a major hardware catastrophe. As always, start with the cheapest and simplest likely cause. Run your setup program and enter correct hard disk configuration information. If this doesn't resolve the problem, start checking the hardware.

Possible causes are: (1) the power cord may not be connected to the hard disk, (2) the cables connecting the hard disk to its controller may be misinstalled, (3) the drive select jumper on the hard disk may be set wrong, (4) the hard disk may be dead, or (5) the hard disk controller may be dead. Check these possibilities.

"ERRORS FOUND, F PARAMETER NOT SPECIFIED. CORRECTIONS WILL NOT BE WRITTEN TO DISK"

You get this error if CHKDSK finds lost chains or other errors while inspecting a disk. A lost chain is a chain of clusters that are not connected to any known file. None of the files in the disk directory contains this chain of clusters. There is clearly a chain in the FAT, but there is no clue to its meaning.

Lost chains are not very significant. When you delete a number of files, the delete process may miss a link in the file chain. If you have a thunderstorm, you may get this error because a blip of electrical current wrote a tiny blip of trash information to the FAT. For the most part, these random events are not particularly important. They are generally not predictors of future hard disk problems. On the other hand, problems reading the boot directory or a subdirectory can be much more threatening. It is wise to run a hard disk diagnostic/repair utility to correct possible directory errors. PCTools DISKFIX and Norton's Disk Doctor save more data than CHKDSK does.

"ERRORS FOUND; INCORRECT CONFIGURATION INFORMATION MEMORY SIZE MISCOMPARE"

The CMOS memory has probably forgotten the setup program. Run the setup program and retest. If the error is still there, replace the battery and run your setup program again.

If you still have the error, turn off the computer, open the case, and press down on all the memory chips. Make sure that they are firmly seated into their sockets. Then turn on the computer and retest. If the error is still there, remove all the socketed memory chips and take them to a repair shop equipped with a memory tester. The memory tester takes only a couple of seconds per chip. Replace any chips that fail the test. If all the chips in your computer are soldered, you'll have to replace the mainboard.

If no RAM chips fail in the memory tester, replace the power supply. If this doesn't work, replace the mainboard. This error is very seldom traced to a bad mainboard, though, so be sure to explore the other possibilities thoroughly first.

"ERRORS ON LIST DEVICE INDICATE THAT IT MAY BE OFF-LINE. PLEASE CHECK IT"

This message refers to the printer. Make sure it's not turned off or off-line. Also check the printer cable—it should be tightly plugged into the back of the printer and tightly connected to the printer port on the back of the computer. If you have a parallel printer, refer to Chapter 7 or to "Parallel Ports" in Chapter 16. If you have a serial printer, look at Chapter 8 and "Serial Ports" in Chapter 16.

"ERROR WRITING FAT"

See "Disk Error Reading (or Writing) FAT."

"*nnn*K EXPANDED MEMORY" (FOR EXAMPLE, 384K EXPANDED MEMORY)

This is not an error message, it is an informational message. Your computer has successfully tested *nnn* kilobytes of expanded (LIM) memory.

"EXPANSION BOARD DISABLED AT SLOT *X*"

This is not an error message, it is an informational message. The board in slot *X* has been disabled. Use the EISA configuration utility to disable or enable a board.

"EXPANSION BOARD NMI AT SLOT *X*"

The board in slot *X* generated a nonmaskable interrupt. This board is very unhappy. Call the board vendor's tech support line.

"EXPANSION BOARD NOT READY AT SLOT *X*"

The computer does not see a board in slot *X*, but you told it one would be there when you ran the EISA configuration utility. Make sure the board is firmly seated in the slot where you said it would be.

"*nnn*K EXTENDED MEMORY" (FOR EXAMPLE, 384K EXTENDED MEMORY)

This is not an error message, it is an informational message. Your computer has successfully tested *nnn* kilobytes of extended memory.

"EXTENDED MEMORY SIZE = *nnnnnn*K" (FOR EXAMPLE, EXTENDED MEMORY SIZE = 00000K)

This is not an error message, it is an informational message. Your computer is reporting extended memory size.

"*nnn*K EXTRA MEMORY" (FOR EXAMPLE, 384K EXTRA MEMORY)

This is not an error message. It is an informational message. Your computer has successfully tested *nnn* Kilobytes of extra memory.

"FAIL-SAFE TIMER NMI"

Some device has gone crazy and is hogging the bus in your EISA computer. It might be a random event (Mars in retrograde combined with the mirror you broke 6-1/2 years ago). Try rebooting and retesting.

If you get the error message again, try to isolate the offending card. Turn off the computer and pull out the most high-tech card in the machine. Retest. If that card isn't causing the problem, try pulling out another card. One by one, pull out all the cards (you'll eventually have to substitute a known-good video card and hard disk with its controller, of course, or you won't be able to run the computer to test it). When you find the culprit, call the bad card's vendor.

"FAIL-SAFE TIMER NMI INOPERATIONAL"

The fail-safe timer on your EISA board has failed. You'll have to replace your mainboard.

"FDD CONTROLLER FAILURE"

This error generally points to a bad floppy disk drive (FDD) and floppy disk drive controller subsystem. Make sure the controller card is seated firmly in the bus slot. Check for missing or misinstalled cables. You should replace the controller only after you explore these possibilities.

"FDD A IS NOT INSTALLED"

The computer cannot find the disk controller for floppy drive A. Make sure the controller card is seated firmly in the bus slot. Check for missing or misinstalled cables. You should replace the controller only after you explore these possibilities.

"FDD B IS NOT INSTALLED"

The computer cannot find the disk controller for floppy drive B. Make sure the controller card is seated firmly in the bus slot. Check for missing or misinstalled cables. You should replace the controller only after you explore these possibilities.

"FILE ALLOCATION TABLE BAD" or "FILE ALLOCATION TABLE BAD DRIVE *x*:"

There is a problem with the FAT. You may be able to save this disk by running Norton Disk Doctor or PC Tools DISKFIX. Chapter 10 covers data protection and recovery.

"FIRST CLUSTER NUMBER IS INVALID, ENTRY TRUNCATED"

CHKDSK has effectively deleted the file. It has zero clusters and now exists only as a name in the disk directory. Start running some hard disk diagnostic/repair utilities. Truncating is not something you want to have happen and it should be stopped right here.

Unfortunately, this particular file might be gone forever, though PC Tools DISKFIX will take care of some of these truncated entries. Next time, use PC Tools DISKFIX or Norton's Disk Doctor rather than CHKDSK.

"FIXED DISK CONFIGURATION ERROR"

See "Hard Disk Configuration Error."

"FIXED DISK CONTROLLER FAILURE"

See "Hard Disk Configuration Error."

"FIXED DISK FAILURE"

See "Hard Disk Failure."

"FIXED DISK READ FAILURE"

See "Hard Disk Read Failure—Strike F1 to Retry Boot."

"GATE A20 FAILURE"

This error message applies to the AT clone only. The computer must switch into protected mode to count and check the extended memory in an AT clone, even if there is no extended memory (it must check and confirm that there is indeed no extended memory). A bad mainboard can cause failure to switch into protected mode, as can a bad keyboard. A bad keyboard in combination with particular 8042 (keyboard controller chip) firmware can cause the 8042 to keep sending signals on address line 20 to the processor. The processor needs to use address line 20 as a regular address line when it is in protected mode, but the 8042 chip will not get off the line. Eventually the Phoenix BIOS sends the error message listed above to complain about a continuously busy address line 20.

Check the keyboard switches to make sure they're set right. Then try a new keyboard. If that doesn't work, put in a new mainboard.

"GENERAL FAILURE READING (OR WRITING) DRIVE X: (A)bort, (R)etry, (I)gnore?"

Press I (Ignore) first. If the drive reads now, run diagnostic tests on it. The diagnostics may not detect a problem, though, because the general failure may have been a transient problem that will never show up again. For example, a friend of ours has a SCSI hard drive and typically gets this "General

Failure" message once a day. The mainboard and the hard drive controller card do not like each other, so once a day there is some kind of timing error between them. He presses **I** (Ignore), the error goes away, and there has never been a problem with corrupted data. In his case, what looks like a major error is actually insignificant.

If **I** (Ignore) won't work, then press **A** (Abort) to get out of the prompt and start looking for a hardware problem. Anything could be wrong. Check the power cable and the ribbon cables to this drive. Make sure the disk controller is firmly seated in the mainboard card expansion slot (press it down hard, while the computer is turned off, of course).

If you have a floppy drive, a bad floppy disk can cause this error. Try another disk. And another. Run CheckIt, QA/WIN, or QA Plus. See "5.25-inch Floppy Disk Drives" in Chapter 14 for more testing suggestions.

If the problem drive is a hard disk, see Chapters 5 and 15 for testing and repair suggestions. No matter which drive is failing, you'll find useful data protection and resurrection ideas in Chapter 10.

"HARD DISK CONFIGURATION ERROR"

The CMOS chip, which holds the hardware configuration information for 286/386/486 computers, has an illegal code stored in it. The BIOS ROM on the system mainboard must read the information inside the CMOS chip each time the computer boots up.

Suppose, for example, you have installed a type 44 hard drive in an ancient AT/286 clone. The computer BIOS was written to comprehend type 1-15 hard drives, but knows nothing about type 44. If you use a new setup program disk to store information about this new drive (the type 44 drive) in the CMOS chip, the ancient ROM will run into a code it doesn't recognize when it tries to read the hard disk configuration information.

In general, configuration errors occur when you use a setup disk that is newer than your BIOS ROM. To fix these errors, you can either use your original setup disk or—if you need a ROM that includes features that are not built into your old ROM—you can upgrade the old ROM.

The wrong setup disk can also cause the same problem. For example, a Kaypro Phoenix BIOS uses slightly different CMOS codes than another manufacturer's Phoenix BIOS. If you record information designed to be read by a Kaypro, using a Kaypro setup disk, another computer's BIOS may think the CMOS information is gibberish.

"HARD DISK FAILURE"

This message indicates that the hard disk controller has not received the response from the hard disk that it expected. The controller tries to do a seek on the last head on the last cylinder of the hard disk. If this is successful (if the head can successfully move to that last cylinder) the system BIOS assumes that the hard disk type has been correctly set, the hard disk is working, and all is well.

Sometimes, however, the system BIOS sends out the command but doesn't get a response in the maximum time allotted. So the BIOS gives a "time-out error" and puts the "Hard Disk Failure" message on the screen. Possible causes are: (1) the power cord may not be connected to the hard disk, (2) the cables connecting the hard disk and its controller may be misinstalled, (3) the drive select jumper on the hard disk may be set wrong, (4) the hard disk may be dead, or (5) the hard disk controller may be dead. In most cases, this message refers to the first hard disk (logical drive C), but it could be either hard drive.

"HARD DISK READ FAILURE—STRIKE F1 TO RETRY BOOT"

Many things can cause this problem. If you've just been working inside the computer, you may have knocked a cable loose or misinstalled one of the hard drive cables. See the installation information in Chapter 15 for the particular hard disk and cables installed in your computer.

If you haven't just been working inside the computer, try pressing **F1** to see if the computer boots on the second try. If it does, great. Nevertheless, something was apparently wrong on the first boot attempt. It makes sense to run hard disk diagnostic/correction software—such as PC Tools DISKFIX, Norton Disk Doctor, or SpinRite II—that will read and rewrite the boot segment on the hard disk drive. If the drive is getting slightly out of alignment, this software will often head off more expensive data losses.

If the hard drive won't boot when you press **F1** a second time, you'll have to boot from a floppy disk with the system on it. Type **C:** to look at the hard disk. If you get an "Invalid Drive" message, the computer can't read the C drive. Run the setup program to make sure the configuration information for the hard disk is correctly stored in the CMOS. Try to boot again. If it still won't boot, the steps you follow depend on whether you've backed up.

If you are fully backed up, reformat the hard disk and reload the data. Retry booting. Everything should be fine, but if it isn't, the hard disk and controller should be replaced. Of course, the hard

disk is usually the first of these two parts to fail, but why run the risk of messing up a new hard disk because you guessed wrong and the defective controller is killing hard disks?

If you haven't backed up your data; you may still be able to rescue it if you send the hard drive to a data recovery service.

"HAS INVALID CLUSTER, FILE TRUNCATED"

CHKDSK has found an invalid cluster—a crazy reference to a nonexistent cluster, for example. It has deleted the tail end of the file (from the bad cluster to the end).

Start running PC Tools DISKFIX, Norton's Disk Doctor, or SpinRite II. Truncating is not something you want CHKDSK to do, and it should be stopped right here. Unfortunately, the tail end of this file is probably gone—but sometimes PC Tools DISKFIX will recover it.

"ID INFORMATION MISMATCH FOR SLOT *n*"

The computer thinks you've moved cards around and haven't told it what you've done. If that's true, use the EISA Configuration Utility (ECU) to tell the computer what cards are where. If you haven't moved the cards around, the computer's memory must have forgotten what used to be where. Replace the backup battery and retest.

"INFINITE RETRY ON PARALLEL PRINTER TIMEOUT"

Your printer is not turned on or it is not on-line.

"INSUFFICIENT MEMORY"

This is a software error, not a memory error. You are trying to use more memory than is installed in the machine.

"INTERNAL CACHE TEST FAILED—CACHE IS DISABLED"

Reboot your computer. If the message reoccurs, run QA Plus or QA/WIN to test your mainboard. It is likely that your 486 CPU chip is dead.

"INTERNAL ERROR"

This is a software error. Check your DOS manual for explanations.

"INTERNAL STACK OVERFLOW"

This is generally a software error. Check your DOS manual to correct the problem. If you still have this error, check the memory on your mainboard. It could be any kind of memory problem in the bottom 64K of memory.

"INTR1 ERROR"

The interrupt controller logic has failed. Replace the mainboard.

"INTR2 ERROR"

The interrupt controller logic has failed. Replace the mainboard.

"INVALID BOOT DISKETTE"

See "Not a Boot Disk—Strike F1 to Retry Boot."

"INVALID CONFIGURATION INFORMATION. PLEASE RUN SETUP PROGRAM"

If you have additional error messages displayed along with this one, try to eliminate them. You can then deal with the message listed above.

Begin by running your setup program. Are you absolutely certain that you are entering the correct answers to the setup questions? Saying you have a color monitor when you actually have a color EGA monitor would be a typical mistake. If the problem disappears when you run the setup program, then recurs when you turn the computer off and on again, replace the battery and run the setup program again. Another possible cause of this problem is a bad power supply. If new batteries don't fix the problem, you will have to replace the power supply, run the setup program again, then retest.

The final possibility—and this is very unlikely indeed—is a bad CMOS chip on the mainboard. Because the CMOS chip is soldered in place, you will have to replace the whole mainboard if this is indeed the cause of the problem.

"INVALID CONFIGURATION INFORMATION FOR SLOT *X*"

Rerun the ECU, making certain that you have entered the correct information for the board and the correct slot number for the board. Double-check your CMOS battery backup. If it's worn out your computer can lose setup information.

"INVALID EISA CONFIGURATION STORAGE. PLEASE RUN THE CONFIGU-RATION UTILITY."

Run the ECU. Double-check your CMOS battery backup. If it's worn out your computer can lose setup information.

"I/O CARD PARITY ERROR AT *xxxxx* (R)" or "I/O CARD PARITY INTERRUPT AT *xxxx:xxxx*. TYPE (S)HUT OFF NMI, (R)EBOOT, OTHER KEYS TO CONTINUE" or "I/O CARD NMI AT *xxxx:xxxx*. TYPE (S)HUT OFF NMI, (R)EBOOT, OTHER KEYS TO CONTINUE" or "I/O CARD PARITY INTERRUPT AT *xxxx:xxxx*. TYPE (S)HUT OFF NMI, (R)EBOOT, OTHER KEYS TO CONTINUE"

There is a bad peripheral card. First you must figure out which card is bad. If you absolutely must continue work, press **S** to shut off the NMI and save the file. The message goes away, but you haven't fixed the error.

When you're ready, turn off the computer, pull out all the cards except the video card, and reboot. If the error message doesn't reappear, reinstall the cards one at a time—turning the computer off as you install each card—and test until you find the bad card. If the error remains with only the video card installed, you will have to replace the video card, then retest. The last possibility to check is a bad mainboard. Before you do this, though, try installing a plain mono or CGA card from another computer to make sure the problem is in the mainboard, not the video card.

"KEYBOARD BAD"

The keyboard has failed the POST. Turn the computer off, then turn it back on and reboot. If the message persists, you have a bad keyboard and you will have to replace it.

"KEYBOARD CLOCK LINE FAILURE" or "KEYBOARD DATA LINE FAILURE" or "KEYBOARD CONTROLLER FAILURE" or "KEYBOARD STUCK KEY FAILURE"

The keyboard controller chip tests the keyboard during POST. These messages indicate that the keyboard is not sending the right replies to the controller's POST signals. Either the keyboard cable or the keyboard itself is bad. Check the AT/XT switch on the bottom of your keyboard. Is this keyboard intended only for use on an XT? Or only for use on an AT? Are you using it on an appropriate machine? Is a key stuck? Check all these possibilities.

"KEYBOARD ERROR"

If your computer has an American Magatrends, Inc. AMIBIOS, the keyboard may be incompatible with the BIOS ROM. American Megatrends suggests "The keyboard has a timing problem. Make sure a Keyboard Controller AMIBIOS is installed. Set *keyboard* in Standard CMOS Setup to *Not Installed* to skip the keyboard POST routines.

"LAST BOOT INCOMPLETE"

This message is tripped only by a malfunctioning chip in the Intel 82335 chip set. This chip set is used in some, but by no means all, AT clone mainboards. These chips have extended features that need to be set in the extended CMOS. Run your Intel 82335 setup program, paying strict attention to the memory interweaving and EMS configuration parameters.

"x LOST CLUSTER(S) FOUND IN y CHAINS CONVERT LOST CHAINS TO FILES (Y/N)?"

You get this error if CHKDSK finds lost chains or other errors while inspecting a disk. None of the files in the disk directory contains these chain(s) of clusters. There is clearly one or more chains in the FAT, but there is no clue to their proper place in the file.

Lost chains are not very significant. When you delete a number of files, the delete process may miss a link in the file chain. If you have a thunderstorm, you may get this error because a blip of electrical current wrote a tiny blip of trash information to the FAT. For the most part, these random events are not particularly important. They are not generally predictors of future hard disk problems. On the other hand, problems reading the boot directory or a subdirectory can be much more threatening. It is wise to run a hard disk diagnostic/repair utility to correct possible directory errors and save any useful data in the lost chains.

"MEMORY ADDRESS LINE FAILURE AT xxxx:xxxx, READ HEX VALUE xxxx, EXPECTING xxxx"

This error is deceptively explicit. You are given a particular memory address location where the failure occurs, but have no way to repair this problem in the field. Replace the mainboard.

"MEMORY ALLOCATION ERROR. CANNOT LOAD DOS, SYSTEM HALTED"

This is a software error. Check your DOS manual. You may have a trashed DOS boot disk.

If the hard disk is your boot disk, boot from a floppy disk containing the same DOS version. Run SYS to copy the DOS hidden files and copy COMMAND.COM to the hard disk.

"MEMORY DATA LINE FAILURE AT xxxx:xxxx, READ xxxx, EXPECTING xxxx"

This problem is caused by a bad or slow memory chip. The hexadecimal number in the first line of this error message tells you what row of memory chips contains the defective chip(s). The message provides enough information to locate the specific malfunctioning chip.

At a computer repair store, the technician may either do a number of hexadecimal calculations and replace the particular bad chip or he or she may pull the whole suspect bank of chips and send them through a memory tester. You have the same options. Although calculating the particular bad chip is more elegant, many of us do not have the necessary patience. You may choose to yank all the chips and take them to the repair shop. Let the computer repair shop run them through their memory tester (checking them at 20 nanoseconds faster than the minimum speed recommended for your mainboard). CheckIt diagnostic software is another alternative. CheckIt has the capacity to do the necessary calculations—if you run the memory test program and answer the memory location setup questions, it will locate the bad chip for you. Or you can take the whole machine into the repair shop and ask them to slog through the chip-pulling and testing routine. All these approaches work fine. Pick the one that appeals to you.

Here's how to convert the hexadecimal address into a particular memory address in K (kilobytes). In this example we will use hexadecimal number 1EAF:45FF.

1. Start with hex number 1EAF:45FF.

2. Shift the first half of the number (before the colon, called the segment) one place to the left.
   For example: 1EAF becomes 1EAF0 hexadecimal.

3. Add the second part of the number (after the colon, called the offset) to the shifted number.

   For example: 1EAF0 hexadecimal
                         +45FF hexadecimal
                         230EF hexadecimal (remember hexadecimal is a base 16 number)

   This is the address of the bad chip. The first numeral (number 2 in our example) tells you what bank of memory is the problem.

   Here is a list of hex addresses and the associated memory chips:

   - 0xxxx = error in the first 64K of memory.
   - 1xxxx = error in the second 64K of memory.
   - 2xxxx = error in the third 64K of memory.
   - 3xxxx = error in the fourth 64K of memory.
   - 4xxxx = error in the fifth 64K of memory.
   - 5xxxx = error in the sixth 64K of memory.
   - 6xxxx = error in the seventh 64K of memory.
   - 7xxxx = error in the eighth 64K of memory.

- 8*xxxx* = error in the ninth 64K of memory.
- 9*xxxx* = error in the tenth 64K of memory.

Thus, in our example, the problem is in the third 64K of memory.

4. Locate the correct row of chips. When computers were built with nothing but 64K chips, this step was easy. Each bank of nine 64K chips corresponded to one segment. Now that 256K, 1 Mb, and 4 Mb chips are popular you'll have to do a bit of figuring.

Each 256K chip contains four 64K segments (64 x 4 = 256K)

✔A simple XT clone (one equipped with 640K of system memory) may well have two rows of 256K chips (each with four segments of 64K) and two banks of 64K for the final two segments.

✔A 386 or 486 computer loaded with memory might have eight or more banks of 1 Mb or 4 Mb chips on the mainboard. The entire 640K (ten 64K segments)) is in a single bank of 1 Mb chips. Read your computer manufacturer's system manual to determine which bank—each mainboard manufacturer handles the memory mounting slightly differently.

5. Once you've located the correct row of chips, you can locate the specific bad chip using the hex data values in the second line of the error message. You do this by comparing the data the computer attempted to store with the hexadecimal number it read back from memory. The difference between the two numbers points to the bad chip.

For example: If you have the error message "Memory Data Line Failure at Hex Value 1EAF:45FF, Read C3B6, Expecting B3B6," subtract the smaller number from the larger number:

C3B6

-B3B6

1000 (a hex number that needs to be changed to binary)

1000H (1000 hexadecimal) = *xxxx xxxx xxxx xxxx* with each hexadecimal digit equal to a group of four binary digits. So 1000H is 0001 0000 0000 0000 in binary—the number that points to the bad chip.

The error message in our example occurs on a 16-bit computer (it might be a 286 clone, in which the data is stored in 16-bit numbers). Because a 386 or 486 computer boots up in the real mode (functioning as a 286) it will also give this 16-bit error message. At any rate, we have a computer that stores a 16-bit word of data in 16 separate chips.

Each digit of the binary number corresponds to a particular chip. In our example, the thirteenth chip (out of sixteen) is malfunctioning. It is permanently stuck on, giving a data value that is too high (remember the message "Read C3B6, Expecting B3B6").

6. Having identified the bad chip, you must now physically locate it on the mainboard or the memory expansion card.

   Sometimes you will be lucky—the board manufacturer has screened the bit numbers on the board. If so, you will see 0, 1, 2, 3, 4, 5, 6, 7, P. The next bank will be numbered 8, 9, 10, 11, 12, 13, 14, 15, and P. Other manufacturers use hex numbers. However, most manufacturers do not bother to print this information on the board. Look it up in your mainboard owner's manual. If you have no owner's manual, you'll have to use a series of guesses to locate the problem. For instance, look for an erroneous thirteenth bit of data in the fourth chip from the end of the bank. You may not know which end is the first chip and which is the sixteenth, but you can at least narrow it down to a couple of possibilities.

"MEMORY FAILURE AT *xxxx:xxxx*, READ *xxxx*, EXPECTING *xxxx*"

See "Memory Data Line Failure At *xxxx:xxxx*, Read *xxxx*, Expecting *xxxx*."

"MEMORY HIGH ADDRESS LINE FAILURE AT *xxxx:xxxx*, READ *xxxx*, EXPECTING *xxxx*"

You have a bad mainboard and you'll have to replace it.

"MEMORY DOUBLE WORD LOGIC FAILURE AT (HEX VALUE), READ (HEX VALUE), EXPECTING (HEX VALUE)"

You have a bad memory chip. Read the directions for the error "Memory Data Line Failure at *xxxx:xxxx*, Read *xxxx*, Expecting *xxxx*."

"MEMORY ODD/EVEN LOGIC FAILURE AT (*hex value*), READ (*hex value*), EXPECTING (*hex value*)"

You have a bad mainboard and you will have to replace it.

"MEMORY PARITY ERROR AT (*hex value*)"

You have a bad memory chip. It could be either a data-storing memory chip or one of the memory chips dedicated to parity checking. Read the directions for the error "Memory Data Line Failure at *xxxx:xxxx*, Read *xxxx*, Expecting *xxxx*" remembering that the problem could be either the data-storing chip or the parity chip in the suspect bank of memory chips.

"MEMORY PARITY FAILURE AT (*hex value*), READ (*hex value*), EXPECTING (*hex value*)"

You have a bad memory chip. It could be either a data-storing memory chip or one of the memory chips dedicated to parity checking. Read the directions for the error "Memory Data Line Failure at *xxxx:xxxx*, Read *xxxx*, Expecting *xxxx*" remembering that the problem could be either the data-storing chip or the parity chip in the suspect bank of memory chips.

"MEMORY PARITY NMI AT *xxxx:xxxx* TYPE (S)HUT OFF NMI, (R)EBOOT, OTHER KEYS TO CONTINUE" or "MEMORY PARITY INTERRUPT AT *xxxx:xxxx*. TYPE (S)HUT OFF NMI, (R)EBOOT, OTHER KEYS TO CONTINUE."

Most of the time this error is caused by a bad memory chip, but not always. Let's deal with the most likely cause first—the bad memory chip.

First, press **S** to shut off the NMI. Then save the file you have been working on. The error message goes away, but you haven't fixed the error.

The bad memory chip will almost certainly *not* be at the address mentioned in the error message. You may choose to take all the memory chips (from your mainboard and from any memory expansion cards) to the repair shop. Ask the shop to run them through their memory tester (checking them at 20 nanoseconds faster than the minimum speed recommended for your mainboard). On the other hand, you may prefer to take the whole machine into the repair shop and ask them to slog through the chip-pulling and testing routine. These are both good options; pick the one that appeals to you.

If no memory chip tests bad, you'll have to use some horse sense to point you to the next step. One of us has a computer which routinely gives this error when formatting a disk to 1.44 Mb. We believe the controller card driving the 1.44 Mb drive is drawing a little too much power. The manufacturer of that card says the power supply must be weak. Either explanation could be true. The drive/card draws a little too much power on the 5-volt line, the 5-volt line drops (perhaps to 4.0 or 4.5 volts, outside the minimum voltage tolerances specified for memory chips), there is not enough voltage on this 5-volt line to hold the information in the weakest memory chip, the memory chip blanks out, parity check fails, and the computer puts up the error message. So yes, a memory chip fails in this computer, but the real cause is the drain on the 5-volt line. If you have a similar problem, you can ignore it, as he is doing (after all, it causes no problem, the disk is properly formatted, and he has already stored his data before starting to format a floppy). Or you can track it down and fix it. Keep in mind, however, that it's going to require some fancy detective work to isolate the offending part.

"MEMORY TESTS TERMINATED BY KEYSTROKE"

You are allowed to stop the initial POST memory tests by pressing the space bar. When you do, the computer displays this message and proceeds with the rest of the POST routine.

"MEMORY WRITE/READ FAILURE AT (*hex value*), READ (*hex value*), EXPECTING (*hex value*)"

You have a bad memory chip. Read the directions for the error "Memory Data Line Failure at *xxxx:xxxx*, Read *xxxx*, Expecting *xxxx*."

"8087 NMI AT *xxxx:xxxx*. TYPE (S)HUT OFF NMI, (R)EBOOT, OTHER KEYS TO CONTINUE"

The 8087 math coprocessor chip has generated an NMI error. This means there is some problem with the 8087 chip. Test it thoroughly, and replace it if it's bad. Meanwhile, you probably don't want to lose the data you were working on when you got this error. Press **S** to shut off the NMI message and you will be able to proceed with your task temporarily. Do an orderly shutdown of your task, then test the 8087 using one of the popular 8087 software test programs.

"NO BOOT DEVICE AVAILABLE—STRIKE F1 TO RETRY BOOT"

The computer is unable to boot. Many things can cause this problem. Clones try drive A first, looking for a bootable system disk. If a disk is found, but the machine won't boot, the ROM BIOS displays this error on the screen. If no disk is found in the A drive, the clone tries to boot from the C drive (the hard disk). If there is no hard disk, or the hard disk won't boot, then the ROM BIOS displays this error.

If you've been working inside the computer, you may have knocked a cable loose or misinstalled one of the hard or floppy drive cables. See Chapter 14 (floppy disks) and Chapter 15 (hard disks) for full cable installation directions.

Make sure you don't have an unbootable disk in your drive A. If you're sure the disk in the floppy drive is bootable, try some other disks. If you still can't get the computer to boot, test the disks in another computer with an equivalent floppy drive (for example, if the suspect computer has a 360K drive, you must test your boot disks in another computer with a 360K drive—a 1.2 Mb drive won't work).

What happens if you don't have a disk in the floppy drive, and you still get this error? When the computer sees no disk in drive A, it tries to boot from the hard disk. You can watch the machine turn the red light on in the floppy drive, look for a floppy, then turn off that light and turn on the red light associated with the hard drive. Apparently the hard disk will not boot.

Try pressing **F1** to see if the computer boots on the second try. If it does, great. Nevertheless, something was apparently wrong on the first boot attempt. It makes sense to run hard disk diagnostic/correction software—such as SpinRite II, Norton's Disk Doctor, or PC Tools DISKFIX. Any of these programs will read and rewrite the boot segment on the hard disk drive. If the drive is getting slightly out of alignment, using this software will often head off more expensive data losses.

If the hard drive won't boot even when you press **F1** a couple times to get the computer to retry the hard disk, boot from a floppy disk with the DOS system files on it. If this works, you may be able to run the hard disk diagnostic/repair software mentioned above (SpinRite II, Norton's Disk

Doctor, or PC Tools DISKFIX). Type **C:** to look at the hard disk. If you get the message "Invalid Drive," skip down to the next paragraph. If you can read drive C at all, thank your lucky stars and get started with the hard disk repair software.

The "Invalid Drive" message indicates the computer can't read drive C. Run the setup program to make sure the configuration information for the hard disk is correctly stored in the CMOS. Try to boot again. If it still won't boot, the steps you take depend on whether or not you're fully backed up.

If you're fully backed up, reformat the hard disk and reload the data. Retry booting. Once formatted, the hard disk should be fine, but if it isn't, the hard disk and controller should be replaced. Of course, the hard disk is usually the first of these two parts to fail, but why run the risk of messing up a new hard disk because you guessed wrong and the defective controller is killing hard disks?

If you're not fully backed up, remove the hard disk and send it to a data recovery service. The back pages of *BYTE* magazine are full of ads from data recovery people.

See also our suggestions for the error "Hard Disk Read Failure—Strike F1 to Retry Boot."

"NO FAIL SAFE TIMER NMI"

The fail-safe timer on your EISA board has failed.

Run QA Plus or QA/WIN to check your system board. If it's really true, you'll have to replace your mainboard.

"NO SCAN CODE FROM THE KEYBOARD"

This message applies only to XT clones. Either there is no keyboard connected to the computer or the keyboard is locked out.

"NO SOFTWARE PORT NMI"

Run QA Plus or QA/WIN to check your system board. If it's really true, you'll have to replace your mainboard.

"NON-DOS DISK ERROR READING (OR WRITING) DRIVE *x*."

The boot track on this disk is dead, so DOS can't recognize the disk. This is not an easy mistake to repair. SpinRite II, PC Tools DISKFIX, and Norton's Disk Doctor sometimes fix these disks. If they don't, you'll have to back up your data and reformat the disk.

"NON-SYSTEM DISK OR DISK ERROR. REPLACE AND STRIKE ANY KEY WHEN READY"

Normally this error is caused by trying to boot from a nonsystem (nonbootable) floppy disk. If you get this error on your hard disk, recopy COMMAND.COM to your hard disk. The file is trashed.

"NON-SYSTEM DISK OR DISK ERROR. PRESS A KEY TO CONTINUE."

The computer is trying to boot, but can't find a system disk. Check to make sure there is a disk in drive A. Try using a known-good system disk. You might also get this error if you don't have a disk in drive A and you are trying to boot from the hard disk. If the hard disk has no DOS system files on it, you'll have to install them. Or perhaps the DOS system files have been damaged. If you suspect that may be the case, you should read Chapter 10, which includes information about hard disk data recovery.

"NO TIMER TICK INTERRUPT"

The timer chip can't get the interrupt controller chip to send interrupt 0 (the timer interrupt). This means you have a bad mainboard and you will have to replace it.

"NOT A BOOT DISK—STRIKE F1 TO RETRY BOOT"

The computer is unable to boot from the floppy drive. Make sure that there's a bootable disk in your A Drive. If you're sure the disk is bootable, try a couple of other disks. Test all these boot disks in another computer equipped with an equivalent floppy drive (e.g., if the suspect computer has a 360K drive, you must test your boot disks in another computer with a 360K drive—a 1.2 Mb drive won't work).

If the disks test good, the error may be caused by the floppy disk controller or by a bad floppy drive. Have you had problems in the past? For instance, have you occasionally received data error messages inside DOS—messages that pointed to read/write problems with this drive? If so, try replacing the drive first. The second step would be to replace the controller.

"NOT ENOUGH MEMORY"

This is a software error. Check your DOS manual.

"NOT READY READING DRIVE x:" or
"NOT READY ERROR READING (OR WRITING) DRIVE x:"

The drive door is probably not closed. If the error message persists after you close the door, try a couple of different disks. If that doesn't work, you might have a bad drive. Another possibility is that the drive's door-closed sensor is broken.

If the disk is the problem, not the drive, or if drive x: is a hard drive, try PC Tools DISKFIX.

According to the DOS manual, you can also get the "writing to" version of this error if the printer is off-line or turned off.

"(hex value) OPTIONAL ROM BAD CHECKSUM = (hex value)"

The ROM on an optional Input/Output expansion card is trashed. Look for a bad ROM on the hard disk controller, the EGA card, or the VGA card. We have listed the most popular addresses for these optional ROMs. Unfortunately, these are not standardized locations. The technician who built your computer could have installed the hard disk ROM at C800, CA00, or D800, for example. Most hard disk controller cards have jumpers allowing the ROM address to be moved to two or three additional addresses if that is necessary to prevent interference with other equipment installed in your machine. C800, CA00 and D800 are used for the hard disk controller; ROM C000 is an EGA or VGA card; CE00 is used for high-density floppy controllers; and DC00 is a network card

If the ROMs on your computer have other addresses, you will just have to use judgment coupled with trial and error. Turn off the computer, remove all the cards except the video card, then turn the computer back on. If you still have the error it must be caused by a damaged video card ROM. If you don't have the error, try turning off the computer, reinstalling one card, and rebooting the computer. Eventually the culprit will reveal itself.

"OUT OF ENVIRONMENT SPACE"

This is a software error. See your DOS manual.

"PARITY CHECK 1"

There is a parity error on an expansion card. Hard disk controller cards, for example, have memory on them, complete with parity checking. Memory expansion cards also have parity checking. Turn off the computer, pull out all of your expansion cards except the video card, turn the computer back on, and retest. The error should be gone. Reinstall these expansion cards, one at a time, and restart the computer after you install each one. The culprit should reveal itself.

"PARITY CHECK 2"

This error message applies to XT clones only. One or more of the memory chips located on the mainboard is probably the culprit. Turn off the computer, open the case, pull the memory chips out, and take the chips to a computer repair shop equipped with a memory chip testing machine. If you prefer, you can bring the whole computer in and let the shop hassle with removing and reinstalling the chips. Nine times out of ten, a bad memory chip causes this error. But, unfortunately, a bad mainboard can also provoke this error message. Make sure the memory chips have been thoroughly tested before you buy a new mainboard.

"POINTER DEVICE FAILURE"

Your mouse (or pen, trackball, etc.) attached to the PS/2-style mouse port on the mainboard has failed. Most likely cause: the mouse is not plugged in. If it's still bad, run the test program that came with your mouse.

"PRINTER ERROR"

Check the printer. Is it turned on? Is it on-line?

"PROBABLE NON-DOS DISK. CONTINUE (Y/N)?"

The boot track on the disk is dead, so DOS cannot recognize the disk. We have only seen this error on computers used during thunderstorms. Electrical voltage blips during storms can write some gibberish to a hard disk. This is not an easy mistake to repair. SpinRite II, PC Tools DISKFIX, and Norton's Disk Doctor sometimes fix these disks. If they don't, back up your data and reformat the disk, or send the disk to a data recovery service.

"PROCESSING CANNOT CONTINUE"

You get this error when you try to run CHKDSK without enough memory. The solution is to add more RAM to your computer.

"RAM BAD"

The RAM failed the POST. You will have to test the RAM and replace the bad chips. Most well-equipped computer repair shops have a RAM chip tester which will test the chips after you remove them from the mainboard. If you don't want to pull and reinstall the chips yourself, take the whole machine to the repair shop and let the technician figure it out.

Most of the time one or two bad memory chips cause this error message. Occasionally, though, the circuitry on the mainboard is bad, so even good RAM chips will not perform properly. If you are unlucky, and all your RAM chips test good, yet the error message still remains, replace the whole mainboard.

"READ FAULT ERROR READING DRIVE *x*."

Double check your disk. Is it installed in the drive correctly? It could be upside down, or not fully installed. Type **R** for retry.

If you still have the error, there is at least one bad spot on the floppy or hard disk. Run Norton's Disk Doctor, SpinRite II, or PC Tools DISKFIX on this disk. It is not necessarily a significant error, if only because all drives eventually start to go out of alignment and give this error. Luckily, DOS gives us this error fairly early in the aging process. The disk utilities we mentioned are capable of reading the data even when it starts to get tricky. So use the utilities. They will cause the drive to rewrite the data, often moving it to a better-quality spot on the disk. Once rewritten, the data is in alignment with the aging drive's alignment—so you should have no more trouble with this particular disk until the drive gets a whole lot more miles on it.

"REAL TIME CLOCK FAILURE"

The real time clock or battery has failed. See "Time-Of-Day Not Set Up—Please Run Setup Program."

"RESUME = "F1" KEY"

An error has occurred. Press the **F1** key to continue processing.

"ROM"

If you're using an XT, this message means that the system ROM BIOS located on the mainboard has been damaged and you will have to replace it.

"ROM BAD SUM = "

This message applies only to XT clones; the system BIOS ROM on the mainboard could not be read. Replace the ROM.

"ROM BAD CHECKSUM = "

This message applies only to XT clones; the system ROM located on the mainboard has been damaged and you will have to replace it.

"ROM ERROR"

This message means the BIOS ROM on the system mainboard has gone to BIOS heaven. Buy a new BIOS ROM and replace it yourself, or take the machine in to the repair shop for them to do it. On very rare occasions we have gotten this error, and the whole mainboard has turned out to be bad—it was so bad that it couldn't run the ROM test properly and so it looked as if the ROM was malfunctioning. If this is the case with your system, you will have to replace the whole mainboard.

"XX = SCANCODE, CHECK KEYBOARD"

An erroneous scancode was received from the keyboard. A stuck key or a bad keyboard connector can send a bad scancode from the keyboard to the CPU. Try swapping in another keyboard. If the keyboard has an XT/AT switch on the back, make sure to set this switch to XT.

"SECTOR NOT FOUND ERROR READING (OR WRITING) DRIVE x." or "SEEK ERROR READING (OR WRITING) DRIVE x."

The floppy may not be seated properly. Remove the floppy disk from the drive, then reinstall it. Try to read it or write again.

If you still have the error, there is at least one bad spot on the floppy or hard disk. Run Norton's Disk Doctor, SpinRite II, or PC Tools DISKFIX on this disk. It is not necessarily a significant error, if only because all drives eventually start to go out of alignment and give this error. Luckily, DOS gives us this error fairly early in the aging process. The disk utilities we mentioned are capable of reading the data even when it starts to get tricky. So use the utilities. They will cause the drive to rewrite the data, often moving it to a better-quality spot on the disk. Once rewritten, the data is in alignment with the aging drive's alignment—so you should have no more trouble with this particular disk until the drive gets a whole lot more miles on it.

"SHARING VIOLATION READING DRIVE x."

This is a software error. Check your DOS manual.

"SHUTDOWN FAILURE"

This error message applies to only AT clones. The computer must switch into protected mode to count and check the extended memory in an AT, even if there is no extended memory (it must check and confirm that there is indeed no extended memory). Then the computer shuts down and reboots itself in real mode.

The error is caused by either a keyboard controller chip on the mainboard, a bad mainboard, or a bad keyboard. As always, check the simplest, cheapest things first. The XT/AT keyboard switch and the keyboard itself must be eliminated as possible causes. If a new keyboard doesn't solve the problem, you will have to replace the whole mainboard.

"nnnK STANDARD MEMORY" (FOR EXAMPLE, 384K STANDARD MEMORY)

This is not an error message, it is an informational message. Your computer has successfully tested nnn kilobytes of standard memory.

"STRIKE THE F1 KEY TO CONTINUE"

This message indicates that an error was found during the POST. The computer will display an error message describing the problem. You can try to boot the system despite this error. Correct the problem (for example, a nonbooting disk in drive A), then press **F1** to try booting the system.

"STUCK KEY SCANCODE = *xx*"

A key is stuck on the keyboard. Locate and repair the stuck key. If the stuck key is not visually obvious, try pressing each of the keys in turn. The stuck key will feel different when you press it.

"TARGET DISK IS WRITE PROTECTED"

This error message should appear only if you are attempting to DISKCOPY to a write-protected floppy disk. Occasionally, the part of the floppy drive responsible for detecting the write-enable notch (on a 5.25-inch disk) or the covered write-enable slide (on a 3.5-inch disk) is broken. If so, the drive will assume all disks are write-protected.

"TIMER OR INTERRUPT CONTROLLER BAD" or "TIMER CHIP COUNTER 2 FAILED"

Either the timer chip or the interrupt controller chip has failed. Both are soldered to the mainboard, so you will have to replace the mainboard.

"TIME-OF-DAY CLOCK STOPPED" or "TIME-OF-DAY NOT SET UP—PLEASE RUN SETUP PROGRAM"

Run the setup program that came with your computer. If this error persists, try replacing the batteries (that power the CMOS chip whenever the computer is turned off), then run the setup program again.

If the error message still appears, the error is probably caused by the power supply. Replace the power supply and run the setup program again. On a couple of occasions we have had to replace a mainboard to fix this error, but these cases were exceptions.

"TIMER CHIP COUNTER 2 FAILED"

The timer chip has failed. Since it is permanently soldered to the mainboard, you will have to replace the mainboard.

"TIMER OR INTERRUPT CONTROLLER BAD"

The timer and/or interrupt controller chips are bad. Since both of these chips are soldered onto the mainboard, you will have to replace the mainboard.

"TRACK 0 BAD—DISK UNUSABLE"

You get this error when you try to format a 1.2 Mb floppy disk in a 360K drive. Most 1.2 Mb disks are not suitable for use in 360K drives, even if they are perfect. The error may also occur when you try to format a 360K disk in a 1.2 Mb drive.

Another possibility is that the floppy disk actually has a bad track 0. In this case, throw away the floppy disk and use another one.

If you get this error on a hard drive, it means exactly what it says. Track 0 is bad. This means that the hard drive is bad, and you will have to replace the hard drive.

"UNEXPECTED HW INTERRUPT *xx*H AT *xxxx:xxxx*. TYPE (R)EBOOT, OTHER KEYS TO CONTINUE" or "UNEXPECTED SW INTERRUPT *xx*H AT *xxxx:xxxx* TYPE (R)EBOOT, OTHER KEYS TO CONTINUE."

According to Phoenix, the company who wrote the system BIOS responsible for posting this error message on the screen, absolutely any hardware-related problem can cause this error.

For example, both a poorly designed card that is installed without its accompanying software driver and one with malfunctioning driver software can cause this error message. The message means this: an interrupt is being sent on an interrupt line which has not been properly initialized. The bad card, for example, a Systems Network Architecture (SNA) card, sends interrupt signals before it is initialized—certainly an ill-mannered quality in any card. Either no software has yet initialized it (told the CPU what to do if that interrupt is tripped), or bad driver software has improperly initialized the interrupt or initialized the wrong interrupt.

Most of the time, however, we've found that the error is caused by a software problem, not by bad hardware. So check your drivers, especially drivers for oddball cards like SNA boards, X.25 boards, and analog-to-digital boards. You should also consider the software running your serial card. If the error only occurs when you use the serial port software, the software is a likely suspect.

"UNEXPECTED INTERRUPT IN PROTECTED MODE"

Either a bad expansion card or a bad mainboard can cause this error. Bad VGA or network cards can produce this error, since both can use the NMI line to communicate with the CPU. In either case, though, the card is sending interrupts during bootup, a time when it should not be using the NMI circuit.

Turn off the computer, pull out all the cards except the video card, and reboot. If the error is gone, reinstall the cards one at a time (turning the computer off as you install each card) and test until you find the bad card. If the error remains with only the video card installed, you will have to replace the video card and then retest.

The last possibility is a bad mainboard. Before you check this, though, try installing a plain monochromatic or CGA card from another computer to make sure the problem is in the mainboard, not the video card.

"UNLOCK SYSTEM UNIT KEYLOCK"

This message appears when you lock the keylock—the key on the front of the computer that grounds out the keyboard to mainboard circuit. Unlock the keylock and reboot the computer.

"UNRECOVERABLE ERROR IN DIRECTORY. CONVERT DIRECTORY TO FILE (Y/N)?"

Press **N**(No). If you press **Y**(Yes), you will lose everything in this directory and in all the subdirectories inside it. Sometimes Norton's Disk Doctor or PC Tools DISKFIX will fix the error.

"UNRECOVERABLE READ (OR WRITE) ERROR ON DRIVE *x*:"

Your floppy disk may not be seated properly. Remove the disk from the drive, reinsert it, and try to read it or write again.

If you still have the error, there is at least one bad spot on the disk. Run Norton's Disk Doctor, SpinRite II, or PC Tools DISKFIX. This is not necessarily a significant error, if only because all drives eventually start to go out of alignment and give this error. Luckily, DOS gives us this error fairly early in the aging process. The disk utilities we mentioned are capable of reading the data even when it starts to get tricky. So use the utilities. They will cause the drive to rewrite the data, often moving it to a better-quality spot on the disk. Once rewritten, the data is in alignment with the aging drive's alignment—so you should have no more trouble with this particular disk until the drive gets many more miles on it.

"WRITE FAULT ERROR WRITING DRIVE *x*:"

The drive door is probably not closed. If the error persists after you close the door, try a couple of different disks. If this doesn't work, you might have a bad drive. Another possibility is that the door-closed sensor is broken.

According to the DOS manual, you can also get this error if the printer is off-line or turned off.

"WRITE PROTECT ERROR WRITING DRIVE *x*:"

This error message should appear only if you are attempting to record data on a write-protected floppy disk. Occasionally the part of the floppy drive responsible for detecting the write-enable notch (on a 5.25-inch disk) or the covered write-enable slide (on a 3.5-inch disk) is broken. If so, the drive assumes all disks are write-protected.

Appendix C
Beep Error Codes

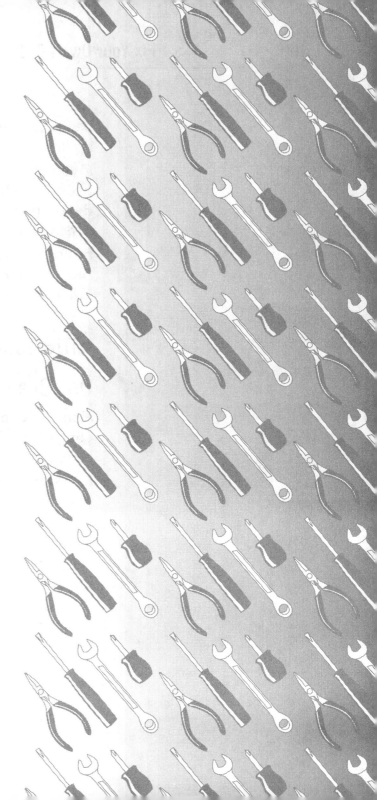

ndustry Standard Architecture (ISA) 286/386/486 bus computers and Extended Industry Standard Architecture (EISA) computers use beep codes for errors that are so severe that they prevent video display (the computer can't put a written error on the screen). Because these beep codes are built into the BIOS ROM chip on the mainboard, each BIOS ROM manufacturer is free to use whatever beep codes they wish. We list the beep codes for American Megatrends, Inc. BIOS ROMs and for Phoenix BIOS ROMs, the two dominant BIOS ROM makers. This appendix lists these beep codes and tells you what to do if you hear one. Each entry begins with the beep code itself and the manufacturer's official error name. We then discuss possible causes of the error and give our recommendations for correcting it.

Computers with an American Megatrends, Inc. BIOS ROM (an AMIBIOS) use an uninterrupted series of beeps to signal a fatal error (an error that halts the boot process before the video screen is useable). These AMIBIOS codes are listed in numeric order below. Count the number of beeps you hear—turn the machine off and on again to recount the beeps if necessary—then look up the error code in the list. We'll tell you what it means in plain English.

If you have a Phoenix BIOS, the beep error codes sound like three sets of beeps separated by pauses. We have listed these codes as a sequence of three numbers. For example, "Beep <pause> Beep <pause> BeepBeepBeep" is coded 1-1-3. Look for these three-part Phoenix BIOS error codes, directly following the AMIBIOS beep codes.

For more information on the American Megatrends, Inc. BIOS, see *Programming ISA and EISA BIOS,* from McGraw-Hill. *System BIOS for IBM PCs, Compatibles, and EISA Computers, second Edition,* from Addison-Wesley covers the Phoenix BIOS ROMs.

American Megatrends, Inc. BIOS ROM Beep Codes

One Beep "REFRESH FAILURE"

Many XT computers beep once or twice when booting up normally. So do a few AT 286/386/486 computers. If your computer has video (shows any message at all on the screen) you shouldn't be here, even if it beeped once. If there is anything wrong, the computer will display a screen error message.

If you don't remember whether you have an AMIBIOS, but have no video display, check the simple things first. Is the video monitor plugged in and turned on? Did the video cable from monitor to computer become disconnected? If you still have no video, take the cover off the computer and look at the mainboard. The BIOS ROM chip is roughly 3/4 inch by 2 inches, and has a bright decal with the manufacturer's name. 286/386/486 computers use a pair of ROMs, so don't be surprised if you find two chips, side by side, with the same decal. Don't let ROMs on the hard disk controller card, the video card, or your network card mislead you, we need to know the manufacturer of your mainboard ROM.

If your computer has no video and is equipped with an American Megatrends, Inc. BIOS ROM, this single beep tells you there is faulty memory refresh circuitry on your mainboard. The timer chip told the DMA chip to go into RAM and refresh the memory. The DMA chip did this, but the refresh process failed. The possible causes of this malfunction are: (1) bad memory chips, (2) a bad DMA chip, (3) bad memory addressing chips on the mainboard. Turn off the computer. Reseat the memory chips or the SIMMs, then retest the computer. Since the DMA chip is soldered to the mainboard—as are the memory address logic chips—any problems with these chips can only be solved by replacing the mainboard.

If your computer doesn't have an AMIBIOS, yet gives the single beep and displays no video, better get some help from a more experienced technician. It's probably something simple that you've overlooked (could be a bad 110-volt outlet for the video monitor, or a loose SIMM strip or video card, for instance).

Two Beeps "PARITY ERROR"

Many XT computers beep once or twice when booting up normally. So do a few AT 286/386/486 computers. If your computer has video (shows any message at all on the screen) you shouldn't be here, even if it beeped twice. If there is anything wrong, the computer will display a screen error message.

If you don't remember whether you have an AMIBIOS, but have no video display, check the simple things first. Is the video monitor plugged in and turned on? Did the video cable from monitor to computer become disconnected? If you still have no video, take the cover off the computer and look at the mainboard. The BIOS ROM chip is roughly 3/4 inch by 2 inches, and has a bright decal with the manufacturer's name. 286/386/486 computers use a pair of ROMs, so don't be surprised if you find two chips, side by side, with the same decal. Don't let ROMs on the hard disk controller card, the video card, or your network card mislead you, we need to know the manufacturer of your mainboard ROM.

If your computer has no video and is equipped with an American Megatrends, Inc. BIOS ROM, this double beep tells you there is a parity error in the first 64K of memory. This is the same as Phoenix BIOS error 1-4-2 "PARITY FAILURE FIRST 64K OF RAM." If you're lucky a memory chip has simply worked itself loose on the mainboard. Reseat the memory chips or the SIMM memory strips. If that doesn't work, follow the directions for error 1-3-3.

Three Beeps "BASE 64K MEMORY FAILURE"

This error, like the Phoenix ROM error 1-3-3, can be caused either by bad memory chips or by a bad mainboard. Try reseating the memory chips or the SIMM memory strips. If that doesn't work, follow the directions for error 1-3-3.

Four Beeps "TIMER NOT OPERATIONAL"

According to American Megatrends, Inc., a memory failure in the first 64K of RAM memory or a malfunctioning timer 1 will provoke this error. Theoretically, bad memory chips should cause a three-beep error, not this four-beep error, but you never know. Turn off the computer, reseat any loose memory chips, and retest. If the beep error persists, you might choose to test the mainboard with known-good memory from a comparable computer before you spring for a new mainboard. If so, replace the first 64K of memory (that would be a single row of chips in an XT clone, two rows of chips in a 286-based computer, and four rows of chips in a 386 or 486 computer). If you still get the four-beep error message, replace the mainboard.

Five Beeps "PROCESSOR ERROR"

The CPU chip is dead. Turn off the computer, reseat the memory chips, then retest. This probably won't help, but it costs nothing to try. If the error remains, replace the whole mainboard—the CPU chip is 90 percent of the cost of a new mainboard, and hard to install. If you're a techno-hobbiest, you might want to look around for a dead mainboard with a good CPU chip that you can transplant onto your otherwise-good mainboard. The transplant CPU chip should ideally be the same speed as your old CPU chip, though a slower CPU will work (more slowly, of course).

Six Beeps "8042—GATE A20 FAILURE"

This error, like the Phoenix ROM error 4-2-3, can be caused either by keyboard problems or a bad mainboard. American Megatrends, Inc. recommends reseating the keyboard controller chip. If it still beeps, replace the keyboard controller. If it still beeps, try a different keyboard, or replace the keyboard fuse, if the keyboard has one.

Seven Beeps "PROCESSOR EXCEPTION INTERRUPT ERROR"

The CPU chip is dead. Turn off the computer, reseat the memory chips, then retest. This probably won't help, but it costs nothing to try. If the error remains, replace the whole mainboard—the CPU chip is 90 percent of the cost of a new mainboard, and hard to install. If you're a techno-hobbiest, you might want to look around for a dead mainboard with a good CPU chip that you can transplant

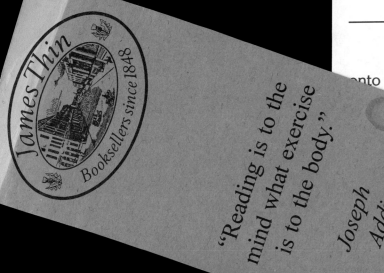

onto your otherwise-good mainboard. The transplant CPU chip should ideally be the same speed
old CPU chip, though a slower CPU will work (more slowly, of course).

LAY MEMORY READ/WRITE ERROR"

all a new one or replace the bad memory on the defective video

RROR"

is caused by a damaged BIOS ROM. Replace it.

REGISTER READ/WRITE ERROR"

up it transfers into protected mode, then transfers back to
real mode (to run DOS). The chip has to reboot to transfer to real mode.
Before it reboots,   ote to itself in CMOS RAM saying "I've just booted. I'm trying
to get into real mode to   work. Don't send me back into protected mode to initialize
everything—I've just done that." The CMOS shutdown register on this computer is busted, so the
CMOS won't hold that note. Replace the mainboard.

Eleven Beeps "CACHE MEMORY BAD—DO NOT ENABLE CACHE"

American Megatrends, Inc. says "The cache memory test failed. Cache memory is disabled. Do
not press <Ctl> <Alt> <Shift> <+> to enable cache memory." They recommend reseating the
cache memory on the mainboard and retesting. If the computer still beeps eleven times, replace
the cache memory.

Phoenix BIOS ROM Beep Codes

1-1-3 "CMOS WRITE/READ FAILURE"

The computer is unable to read the configuration that should be stored in CMOS. Replace the
mainboard.

1-1-4 "ROM BIOS CHECKSUM ERROR"

The BIOS ROM has been damaged, and you'll have to replace it.

1-2-1 "PROGRAMMABLE INTERVAL TIMER FAILURE"

There is a bad timer chip on the mainboard. You'll have to replace the mainboard.

1-2-2 "DMA INITIALIZATION FAILURE" or
1-2-3 "DMA PAGE REGISTER WRITE/READ FAILURE"

The DMA chip is probably bad. Since this chip is permanently soldered onto the mainboard, you will have to replace the whole mainboard. There's a remote possibility that a bad card is permanently grabbing control of one of the DMA lines, but this is extremely unlikely. If the computer gives you a beep error code with a new mainboard, perhaps you have this one-in-a-million situation. In this case, you'll have to remove all the expansion cards from the computer and see if the error message returns with only a video card installed. Keep in mind, however, that this scenario is extremely unlikely. In the vast majority of cases, this problem is caused by a simple bad chip.

1-3-1 "RAM REFRESH VERIFICATION FAILURE"

The timer chip told the DMA chip to go into RAM and refresh the memory. The DMA chip did this, but the refresh process failed. The possible causes of this malfunction are: (1) bad memory chips, (2) a bad DMA chip, or (3) bad memory addressing chips on the mainboard. Turn off the computer, remove all the memory chips, and test them. Replace any bad chips and retest the computer. Since the DMA chip is soldered to the mainboard—as are the memory address logic chips—any problems with these chips can only be solved by replacing the mainboard.

1-3-3 "FIRST 64K RAM CHIP OR DATA LINE FAILURE, MULTI-BIT"

For some reason, the first 64K of RAM is not responding to the CPU. Perhaps the memory chips are bad. Remove the memory chips for the first 64K and take them to a computer repair shop to be tested. Alternatively, you can switch the high and low memory on your mainboard. In 8086 and 8088 machines, the first bank of memory contains the first 64K, so switching the first and second banks should solve the problem. Read your mainboard owner's manual to find out which is the first bank on your particular mainboard. If you have an 80286 computer, remember that AT clones use 16-bit memory; therefore, the first 64K of memory on an 80286 will be stored in 16 data chips and two parity chips (a total of 18 chips in the first bank of memory). Be sure to switch all 18 chips with 18 different chips from high memory. If you have a 386 or 486 computer, the first bank of memory has 32 chips. If all this seems boring and/or intimidating you can, of course, take the whole machine to the computer repair shop and let them fuss with the chips.

A bad mainboard can also cause this problem. If the memory chips test good, you will have to replace the whole mainboard.

1-3-4 "FIRST 64K ODD/EVEN LOGIC FAILURE" or 1-4-1 "ADDRESS LINE FAILURE 64K OF RAM"

You have a bad mainboard, and you'll have to replace it.

1-4-2 "PARITY FAILURE FIRST 64K OF RAM"

You have a bad memory chip. It could be either a data-storing memory chip or one of the memory chips that is dedicated to parity checking. Read the directions for beep error code 1-3-3, keeping in mind that the problem could be either the data-storing chip or the parity chip in the suspect bank(s) (first 64K) of memory chips.

There are also chips on the mainboard that are responsible for calculating the memory parity. If these chips go bad, the whole mainboard needs to be replaced. Test the memory chips thoroughly first, though, before replacing your mainboard.

1-4-3 "FAIL SAFE TIMER FAILURE"

The fail safe timer on your EISA mainboard has failed. Replace your mainboard.

1-4-4 "SOFTWARE NMI PORT FAILURE"

The software port allows the EISA software to talk to EISA expansion boards. Replace your mainboard.

2-1-1 "BIT 0 FIRST 64K RAM FAILURE"
2-1-2 "BIT 1 FIRST 64K RAM FAILURE"
2-1-3 "BIT 2 FIRST 64K RAM FAILURE"
2-1-4 "BIT 3 FIRST 64K RAM FAILURE"
2-2-1 "BIT 4 FIRST 64K RAM FAILURE"
2-2-2 "BIT 5 FIRST 64K RAM FAILURE"
2-2-3 "BIT 6 FIRST 64K RAM FAILURE"
2-2-4 "BIT 7 FIRST 64K RAM FAILURE"
2-3-1 "BIT 8 FIRST 64K RAM FAILURE"
2-3-2 "BIT 9 FIRST 64K RAM FAILURE"
2-3-3 "BIT 10 FIRST 64K RAM FAILURE"
2-3-4 "BIT 11 FIRST 64K RAM FAILURE"
2-4-1 "BIT 12 FIRST 64K RAM FAILURE"
2-4-2 "BIT 13 FIRST 64K RAM FAILURE"
2-4-3 "BIT 14 FIRST 64K RAM FAILURE"
2-4-4 "BIT 15 FIRST 64K RAM FAILURE"

These beep codes all indicate that there is a bad memory chip in the first 64K of RAM. Each word of data has 16 bits (in an AT-style 80286 computer). Since each bit in a particular word is stored in a different memory chips, there are 16 chips for each word. The computer uses the different beep codes in the list above to identify, in a logical sense, which chip is bad. For example, beep code 2-4-2 indicates that bit 13 is defective.

Unfortunately, when you look at the mainboard, it is not intuitively obvious which particular memory chip holds bit 13. Your mainboard owner's manual may provide specific memory chip location diagrams, but many mainboard manuals do not. Other mainboards have the bit number silkscreened onto the mainboard next to the memory chip sockets. *P* stands for parity chip, *1* for bit 1, and so on. If you don't have any specific information, you'll have to guess which chip holds bit 13, pull all the chips in the first 64K out of the mainboard, and take them to the computer store for testing, or try the chip-switching maneuver described in beep code 1-3-3.

386 and 486 computers boot up as 16-bit computers, not as 32-bit computers. That's why these codes only cover 16 bits.

3-1-1 "SLAVE DMA REGISTER FAILURE" or
3-1-2 "MASTER DMA REGISTER FAILURE"

You have a bad DMA chip. Since the DMA chip is soldered onto the mainboard, you will have to replace the mainboard.

3-1-3 "MASTER INTERRUPT MASK REGISTER FAILURE" or
3-1-4 "SLAVE INTERRUPT MASK REGISTER FAILURE"

You have a bad interrupt controller chip. Since the interrupt controller is soldered onto the mainboard, you will have to replace the mainboard.

3-2-4 "KEYBOARD CONTROLLER TEST FAILURE"

The keyboard controller chip is not sending the right replies to the controller's post signals when it tests the keyboard during POST. This means that the keyboard cable or the keyboard itself is bad. Check the AT/XT switch on the bottom of your keyboard. Is this keyboard intended only for use on an XT? Or only for use on an AT? Are you using it on the appropriate machine? Is a key stuck down? Check all these possibilities.

3-3-4 "SCREEN INITIALIZATION FAILURE"

There is no video card installed in the computer. You will have to install one.

3-4-1 "SCREEN RETRACE TEST FAILURE"

The video chip on the video card is failing. You will have to replace the video card.

3-4-2 "SCREEN RETRACE TEST FAILURE"

There is a problem with your video card, it won't reset the retrace bit in the appropriate period of time. Replace your card.

4-2-1 "TIMER TICK FAILURE"

The timer chip cannot get the interrupt controller chip to send interrupt 0 (the timer interrupt). You have a bad mainboard and will have to replace it.

4-2-2 "SHUTDOWN TEST FAILURE"

This code applies only to the AT clones. The computer must switch into protected mode to count and check the extended memory in an AT, even if there is no extended memory (it must check and see there is zero kilobytes of extended memory). Once the computer performs this check, it shuts down and reboots itself in real mode.

This error is caused by either a keyboard controller chip on the mainboard, a bad mainboard, or a bad keyboard. As always, check the simplest, cheapest things first. The XT/AT keyboard switch and the keyboard itself must be eliminated as possible causes. If a new keyboard doesn't solve the problem, you will have to replace the whole mainboard.

4-2-3 "GATE A20 FAILURE"

This code applies only to the AT clones. The computer must switch into protected mode to count and check the extended memory in an AT, even if there is no extended memory (it must check and see there is zero kilobytes of extended memory). A bad mainboard can cause failure to switch into protected mode, as can a bad keyboard. A bad keyboard in combination with particular 8042 (keyboard controller chip) firmware can cause the 8042 to keep sending signals on address line 20 to the processor. The processor needs to use address line 20 as a regular address line when it is in protected mode, but the 8042 chip will not get off the line. Eventually the microprocessor sends an error, saying the protected mode operation has failed. Check the keyboard switches to make sure they're set right. If you don't find a problem there, try a new keyboard. If that doesn't work, put in a new mainboard.

4-2-4 "UNEXPECTED INTERRUPT IN PROTECTED MODE"

Either a bad expansion card or a bad mainboard can cause this error. Bad VGA or network cards, for example, can produce this error, since both can use the nonmaskable interrupt (NMI) line to communicate with the CPU. In either case, though, the card is sending interrupts during bootup, a time when it should not be using the NMI circuit.

Turn off the computer, pull out all the cards except the video card, and reboot. If the error is gone, reinstall the cards one at a time (turning the computer off as you install each card) and test each card in turn until you find the bad card. If the error remains with only the video card installed, you will have to replace the video card, then retest. The last possibility is a bad mainboard. Before you check this out, though, try installing a plain mono or CGA card from another computer to make sure the problem is in the mainboard, not the video card.

4-3-1 "RAM TEST ADDRESS FAILURE"

The chips that are responsible for memory address logic have failed. Since these chips are soldered to the mainboard, you will have to replace the mainboard.

4-3-2 "PROGRAMMABLE INTERVAL TIMER CHANNEL 2 TEST FAILURE"

The programmable interval timer is used to refresh memory. Replace the mainboard.

4-3-3 "INTERVAL TIMER CHANNEL 2 FAILURE"

The timer chip has failed. Since this chip is soldered to the mainboard, you will have to replace the whole mainboard.

4-3-4 "TIME OF DAY CLOCK FAILURE"

Run the setup program that came with your computer. If this error persists, try replacing the batteries (which power the CMOS chip whenever the computer is turned off), then run the setup program again.

If the error code still sounds, the error is probably caused by the power supply. Replace that and run the setup program again. On a couple of occasions we have had to replace a mainboard to fix this error, but these cases were definitely exceptions.

4-4-1 "SERIAL PORT TEST FAILURE"

The serial port has failed the POST tests.

4-4-2 "PARALLEL PORT TEST FAILURE"

The parallel port has failed the POST tests.

4-4-3 "MATH COPROCESSOR FAILURE"

Your math coprocessor may be bad. Use any of the popular math coprocessor testing software to double-check it.

Appendix D
Standard I/O Addresses

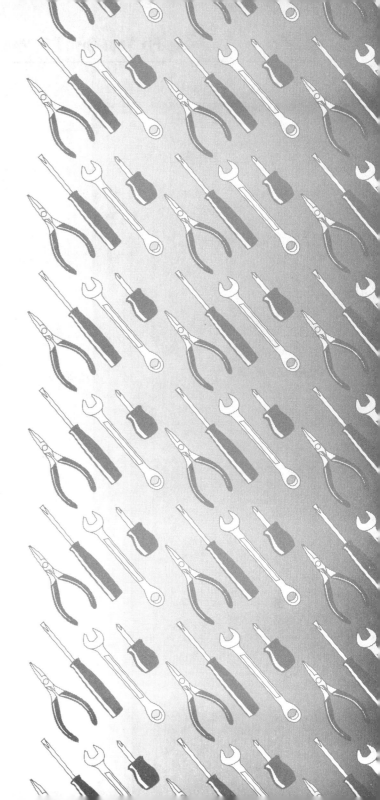

T he following is a list of the standard PC input/output (I/O) addresses. You can find a more complete list in *The Programmer's PC Sourcebook* by Thom Hogan (Microsoft Press, 1988).

Port	I/O Address	IRQ/DMA
Com1	3F8-3FF	4
Com2	2F8-2FF	3
Com3	3E8-3EF	4
Com4	2E8-2EF	3
Com5	2F0-2F7	4
Com6	2E8-2EF	3
Com7	2E0-2E7	4
Com8	260-267	3
LPT1	378-37F	7
LPT2	278-27F	5
System timer		0
Floppy	3F0-3F7	6
Hard disk-AT	1F0-1F8	14
Hard disk-XT	320-32F	5
Key press	060-06F	1
Real time clock	070-07F	8
Math coprocessor	0F0-0FF	13
Mono card	3B0-3BF	
CGA card	3D0-3DF	
EGA card	2B0-2DF and 3C0-3CF	
DMA controller 1	000-01F	
DMA controller 2	0C0-0DF	
Interrupt controller 1	020-03F	
Interrupt controller 2	0A0-0BF	
Game port	200-207	
Unused		10, 11, 12
Used to reroute of IRQs 8-15	NA	2
Used to reroute other interrupts	NA	9

Most boards have jumpers to select the memory locations the board will use. It's a good idea to note the addresses taken up by the boards in your machine.

Segment	Used by
A000-A800	MDA display memory
B000-BFFF	MDA display memory
B800-BFFF	CGA display memory
A000-BFFF	EGA display memory
A000-BFFF	VGA display memory
C000-C3FF	VGA, EGA BIOS
C800-CBFF	Hard disk BIOS
D000-D7FF	Cluster adapter BIOS
D800-DFFF	EMS bank switch area
E000-EFFF	Expansion area for system BIOS (hardly ever used)
F000-FFFF	System BIOS
FF000-FFFFF	Copy system BIOS

Appendix E
Reference List

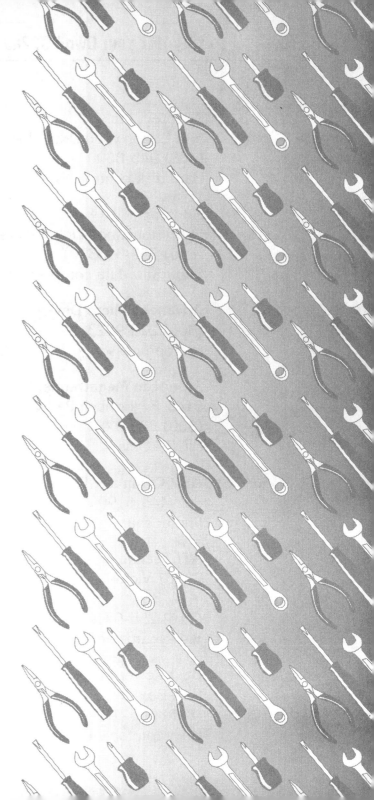

The following companies supply PCs, software, and other computer accessories.

Adaptec, Inc.
580 Cottonwood Dr., Milpitas CA 95035
(408) 945-8600
Hard disk controllers

Addstor
3905 Bohannon Dr., Menlo Park CA 94025
(800) 732-3133
SuperStor data compression software for hard disks

Advanced Micro Devices
(800) 222-9323
Microprocessors

American Megatrends, Inc.
6145-F Northbelt Parkway, Norcross, GA 30071
(800) 828-9264
BIOS ROMs

ASP Computer Products, Inc.
800-445-6190
Printer sharing devices

ATI Technologies
23761 Victoria Park, Scarborough, Ontario, CAN
M1W 3SC
(416) 756-0718
Video cards and modems

Best Power Technology
P.O. Box 280, Nececah WI 54646
(800) 365-5794
Uninteruptable Power Supplies

Black Box
(412) 746-5530
Cabling, connectors, and serial devices

Central Point Software
(503) 690-8090
Publisher of PC Tools Deluxe

Conner Peripherals
3081 Zankel Rd., San Jose, CA 95129
(408) 456-4500
Hard disks

Corporate Systems Center
730 North Pastoria Ave., Sunnyvale CA 94086
(408) 737-7312
Hard disks and the *Hard Drive Bible*

Creative Labs, Inc.
1901 McCarthy Blvd., Milpatas CA 95035
(408)428-6600
Sound Blaster cards

Cristina Foundation
(800) CRISTINA
Clearinghouse for charitable donations of computers

Dariana Technology Group
7439 La Palma Ave., Ste. 278, Buena Park, CA 90620
(714) 994-7400
WinSleuth Windows troubleshooting/configuration software

DiagSoft
(408) 438-8247
QA Plus and QA/WIN diagnostics, Power Meter bench-
mark software

Dynamic Electronics
(714) 855-0411
Memory chip supplier

Elek-Tek, Inc.
(800) 621-1269
Clone parts dealer

Everex
(800) 233-8555
Clone and clone board maker

GammaLink
(415) 856-7421
Fax cards

Gibson Research
(714) 830-2200
SpinRite II hard disk utilities

Hewlett-Packard
(800) 752-0900
HP Help Line

I-Bus Systems
(619) 569-0646
Large bus (many expansion slots) clones

Intel Corp.
(800) 538-3373
Microprocessors, PC enhancement parts

Iomega Corp.
1821 West 4000 South, Roy, Utah 84067
(800) 456-5522
Bernoulli drives and optical mass storage devices

JDR Microdevices
2233 Smaritan Dr., San Jose, CA 95124
(800) 538-5000
PC hardware and accessories

Jensen Tools, Inc.
(602) 968-6231
(800) 366-9662 FAX
Computer, LAN, and electronic tools

Logitech
(800) 231-7717
Mice (see mouse photos in this book)

Maxtor
(408) 942-1700
Hard disks

Novell
(800) 453-1267
(408) 729-6700
LAN operating system software and DR DOS 6.0
for PCs

Ontrack
(800) 752-1333
Disk Manager and Dr. Solomon's Anti-Virus Toolkit for DOS, plus Disk Manager-N, NetOptimizer, and NetUtils for Novell file server hard disks

Ontrack Data Recovery, Inc.
(800) 872-2599
They repair corrupted data and recover data from dead hard drives

PC Power and Cooling
31510 Mountain Way, Bonsall, CA 92003
FAX (619) 723-0075
(619) 723-9513
Clone power supplies and Compaq power supplies (see power supply photos in Section 2 of this book)

Phoenix Technologies
(617) 551-4000
ROM BIOS

Qualitas, Inc.
7101 Wisconsin Ave, Ste. 1386, Bethesda, MD 20814
(301) 907-6700
386MAX memory management software

Qume
(408) 942-4000
Hard disks and controllers

Specialized Products Co.
(800) 527-5018
PC, LAN, electronics, and telecommunications tools

Stac
5933 Avenida Encinas, Calsbad, CA 92008
(619) 431-7474
Stacker data compression software for hard disks

Storage Dimensions
(408) 879-0300
SpeedStor hard disk installation, management and diagnostic software

Swan Technologies
3075 Research Dr., State College, PA 16801
(800) 468-9044
286, 386, and 486 PCs, ISA and EISA computers (see 486 EISA photos in this book)

Symantec
10201 Torre Avenue, Cupertino, CA 95014
(408) 253-9600
(408) 253-4092 FAX
Norton Utilities, Norton Backup, Norton AntiVirus

Texas MicroSystems, Inc.
(713) 933-8050
Large bus (many expansion slots) clones

TouchStone Software Corp.
2130 Main St., Ste. 250, Hintington Beach, CA 92648
(213) 598-7746
CheckIt diagnostic software

Viteq Corp.
(800) 678-4877
Uninterruptible Power Supplies

Western Digital Corp.
(714) 863-0102
Video, LAN, and hard disk controller cards

Xebec
(702) 883-4000
Hard disk subsystems

Glossary

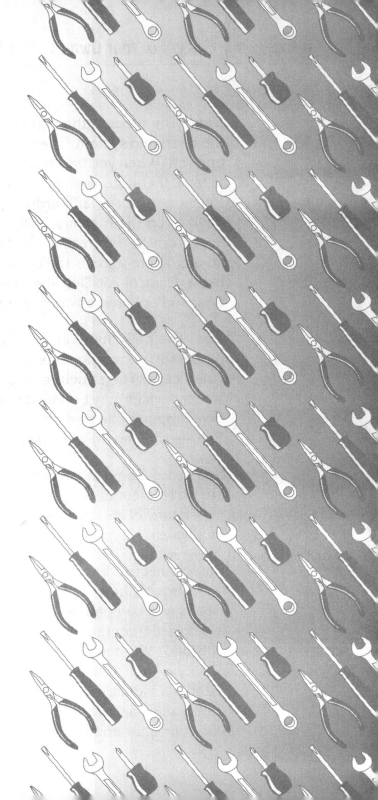

A

AIX IBM's name for their version of Unix.

Application software The program your computer uses to do work, such as word processing or a spreadsheet program.

B

BIOS Basic Input/Output System. An IBMism for firmware; that is, software written and "burned" into a piece of hardware called a Read Only Memory (ROM) chip. The BIOS ROM tells the computer how to boot, contains a Power-On Self-Test (POST) routine, and generally acts as the interface between the hardware and the software. Video cards, such as extended graphics adapter (EGA) cards, and hard disk controllers also contain ROMs with accompanying instructions (firmware) to tell them what to do.

Bit The smallest "thing" or number in a digital computer. A bit is either ON or OFF; we say it has the value 1 or 0, or TRUE or FALSE.

Boot The process the computer goes through to load the operating system. There are two kinds of boot, hard and soft. When you turn on the computer or hit the reset button, the system performs a hard boot. A *hard boot* forces a check of all hardware and creates a table of devices on the machine, such as number and type of floppy drives, the presence and size of the hard disk, and so on, before it loads the operating system. When you press **Control-Alt-Del**, the computer performs a *soft boot* and only reloads the operating system.

Bus The path that control information takes from the processor to components such as the hard disk and video card. The structure of the bus determines what sort of devices may be added to a computer and how fast the computer can perform certain types of operations. *See also* bus board and bus connector.

Bus board Some manufacturers have chosen to put the bus and bus connectors on one board, and the rest of the mainboard chips on a separate processor board. Examples are Kaypro and Wells American.

Bus connector Expansion cards are connected to the bus through bus connectors on the mainboard. XT clones and compatibles use 8-bit bus connectors, with a single 64-contact socket for each expansion card. 286/386/486-based machines built use either the IBM AT-style industry standard architecture (ISA) bus, the extended industry standard architecture (EISA) bus or the Micro Channel bus. ISA is a 16-bit bus with a double bus connector on the mainboard for 16-bit cards. Most 286/386/486/AT clones with the ISA bus also provide a couple of the short, XT-style, 8-bit connectors for older cards that won't physically fit into 16-bit slots. Some 386 and 486 computers also have a proprietary bus connector for the manufacturer's proprietary memory expansion card. EISA uses a 32-bit bus that is backward-compatible with ISA cards (the 8-bit XT-style and 16-bit AT-style cards used in ISA computers). EISA bus connectors fit either EISA cards or ISA cards. Micro Channel is IBM's proprietary 32-bit bus.

Bus master The guy who's in control of the bus. In ISA computers only the microprocessor (CPU) can be the bus master. EISA computers allow any EISA board to be the bus master (as well as the CPU, of course). Micro Channel Architecture (MCA) computers also allow multiple bus masters. The CPU arbitrates among contending bus master applicants.

Byte Eight bits, the smallest unit of data moved about in a computer.

C

Cache Memory used to store data that the computer can reasonably guess it will need next. It is a bridge between a slow device and a fast device—for example, a hard disk (slow) and main memory (fast). A hard disk controller with cache memory will store most-recently-used hard disk data in the cache. Main memory is slow by comparison to the CPU (microprocessor chip). The CPU cache stores most-likely-to-be-needed-next data from the main memory so the CPU can gobble it up quick when the CPU is ready for another bite. Cache performance (how much it speeds up your work) depends on two factors: the size of the cache (fairly important) and the intelligence of the cache controller (supremely important).

Chip The name for a integrated circuit. Chips are silicon wafers with circuits photo-etched into the silicon surface in layers.

CMOS Complementary Metal Oxide Semiconductor. CMOS chips require very little electricity. Therefore, they are used to store information with battery backup.

Conducted noise Erratic electrical fluctuations in the electric power running into your computer.

Coprocessor A chip that performs a function parallel with the processor. It has no responsibility for control of the machine. The usual example is the x87 (8087, 80287, etc.) math coprocessor that handles floating-point calculations for the microprocessor.

CPU Central Processing Unit. The part of the computer that processes. In microcomputers, the chip that actually executes instructions and manipulates information. Also called the processor or the microprocessor.

D

Data separation circuit The circuit in the path

betweenthe controller and the heads on the hard disk. It encodes the data so it may be consistently read back from the media surface. *See* encoding scheme.

Device driver An extension of the BIOS, a device driver allows DOS to access specific hardware in a hardware-blind fashion. DOS doesn't need to know about the hardware details in a mouse, for example. Instead, the mouse device driver is located at interrupt 33, and DOS just interrupts at hex 33 to access this mouse-control subroutine.

Dip switch Dual Inline Package Switch. A little module containing several tiny switches. It is designed as a dual inline package (two rows of little legs) so it can be mounted on a circuit board exactly like a chip.

DMA Direct Memory Access. Data is transferred inside a computer through the DMA chip, not through the microprocessor, thus increasing the transfer speed. The hard disk controller uses DMA to read data from the hard disk and store it directly into RAM.

DOS Disk Operating System. This operating system is a CP/M variant. It was originally written by Microsoft, at the request of IBM in 1979. Since that time, many features from Xenix have been added (like directories, for example). It is an extension of the BIOS ROM. It allows simple access to peripherals by a higher (hardware-blind) program—for example, COMMAND.COM. See *Inside The IBM PC* by Peter Norton (Brady Books, frequently updated) for all the gory details.

DRAM   Dynamic Random Access Memory. Memory chips that need to be refreshed regularly. *See also* memory, RAM, refresh, and SRAM.

E

EISA   Extended Industry Standard Architecture. Extensions to the standard 16-bit AT bus (the ISA bus) to allow 32-bit transfers. This bus is one of the alternatives to IBM's MCA bus (used in the PS/2 line).

EMS   Expanded Memory System. Also known as (Lotus/Intel/Microsoft [LIM], for the vendors that defined the standard) and as bank-switched memory. *See* expanded memory for a complete definition.

Encoding scheme   Used to process data before it is stored on floppy diskettes, hard disks, tape, or other media. The encoding scheme massages "raw" data and turns it into a stream of signals designed to make error detection easier. Encoding schemes are also used to compress data.

ESDI   Enhanced Small Device Interface. Interface for hard drives in which the data separation (encoding) circuit is in the hard drive. The cabling scheme is the same as the ST412/ST506 interface, but in ST412/ST506 the data separation circuits are on the hard drive controller. ESDI allows the manufacturer of the hard drive to use any encoding scheme they wish, so the manufacturer can pack more data onto the physical drive surface.

Expanded memory   The same as LIM, EMS, or bank-switched memory. This is a memory management scheme designed to get around the 1 meg memory barrier in 8088 CPU chips. EMS exploits a window of available address space above 640K but below the 1 Mb barrier. Banks of memory are switched into and out of the 16K window as needed, which provides effective access to as much as 8 Mb of additional memory. Many application programs have been written to utilize LIM to store data or to store programs until they are needed.

Extended memory   The memory in an 80286, 80386, or 80486 computer with an address above 1 Mb. It can be used under DOS by programs that throw the 286/386/486 CPU chip into protected mode, where it can take advantage of this memory. Examples: Windows 3.x and Lotus 3.1.

F

Format (high-level)   The process of preparing the media (disk or tape) for addressing by DOS. DOS checks the media for defects and creates certain tables. These tables allow DOS to find the stored data.

Format (low-level)   The process of placing marks on the media so data stored on the media can be found again.

I

IAPX86 Intel Advanced Processor X86; X being blank, 1, etc. The name Intel uses for the 80X86 family of microprocessors and support devices. Examples include 8086, 80286, 80386, and 80486.

IBM clone A computer that is functionally the same as an IBM PC, XT, or AT. *Clone* and *compatible* mean the same thing since the Phoenix and AMIBIOSs came on the market. Some earlier IBM-compatible machines, such as the Sanyo, were unable to run standard software without modification.

I/O, Input/Output The name for the process by which the computer communicates with the external world. Input comes from keyboards, mice, scanners, modems, and digital tablets. Output goes to printers, monitors, modems, and so forth. The term I/O is very context dependent. For example, data that is output from one program may become input for another program.

Interleave Data is loaded onto the hard disk one sector at a time, but not necessarily in contiguous sectors. An interleave of two uses every other sector. An interleave of three uses one sector, then skips two, then loads one, skips two, and so on. Slow CPUs require higher interleave numbers if they are to successfully read a hard disk. SpinRite II hard disk diagnostics will find your computer's ideal interleave number and set up the hard disk for maximum access speed.

Interrupt There are three levels of interrupt. *Hardware interrupts* break in on the CPU's internal meditations and ask for attention from the CPU. *Nonmaskable interrupts (NMIs)* demand attention right now. The CPU must suspend operations for an NMI. Most hardware interrupts are maskable, though; they are mediated by an interrupt controller chip. The interrupt controller chip queues up the interrupts and asks the CPU to service each one in its order of priority. *Software interrupts* are a jump to a subroutine. The subroutine locations and the interrupt numbers assigned to each subroutine are stored in the Interrupt Vector Table.

Interrupt Vector Table A table of 256 interrupts, located in the first kilobyte of memory, which contains the subroutine address assigned to each interrupt.

K

K Kilo, as in 1,000. In computers, K means 1024.

L

Laser printer Essentially, a Xerox machine which makes copies based on electronic signals from the computer, rather than reflected light patterns from a paper original. These boxes seem to be the greatest of mysteries in the electronic age—once set up, though, they are easy to use.

LIM Lotus-Intel-Microsoft (for the vendors who developed the standard): A technique to expand the amount of memory the computer can use for data. This method only works with special LIM or EMS cards and programs designed to use this memory. *See* expanded memory.

Logic Name for the internal parts of the computer that do functions defined by the rules of logic, as in philosophy.

M

Mainframe A computer that is able to handle hundreds of users at the same time. Prices start in the millions of dollars.

Mb *See* megabyte.

MCA Micro Channel. The name of the bus in the IBM PS/2 Model 50s and up. This bus is supposed to allow multi-processors. On any bus only one processor at a time can have control, but the MCA design allows any one of the processors in the machine to be in control. By comparison, ISA allows only the CPU to have control of the computer; all other processors are slaves to the CPU. EISA, like Micro Channel, is a 32-bit bus and allows other processors to take over the bus. *See also* EISA, ISA, and PS/2.

Media The name for the actual channel of communication. Floppy disks and hard disks are magnetic media. Compact disk/read only memory (CD-ROM) is optical media.

Mega Computer engineering term for multiple by 1,048,576 which is used casually to mean a million. Also abbreviated as Mb (megabyte).

Megabyte Approximately 1 million bytes. In computers, this is 1,048,576 bytes. Also abbreviated as Mb.

Memory That part of the computer that remembers things. Unlike human memory, it cannot remember any context or any emotion. It can only remember a past state. *See also* expanded memory, extended memory, nostalgia, RAM, refresh, ROM, and system memory.

Memory refresh *See* refresh.

MFM Modified Frequency Modulation. One of many possible encoding schemes. MFM uses clock bits interspersed with the data. The ST412/ST506 standard for MFM was the most common hard disk controller encoding scheme for years. *See also* ESDI, RLL, and SCSI, all competing hard disk controller designs.

Micro Channel Architecture *See* MCA.

Microcomputer So-called because it is smaller than a minicomputer or is a computer on a chip, (though some minicomputers now are not much more than a computer on a chip). It can support a handful of users, depending on the operating system. Prices start at $500 or so.

Microcontroller A microprocessor that is used in the control of a specific operation. The microprocessor in your microwave, keyboard, or car engine is a microcontroller. Intel also calls microcontrollers "imbedded controllers."

Microprocessor The part of the computer that processes. In microcomputers, the chip that actually executes instructions and manipulates information. Also called the CPU or the processor.

Minicomputer A computer smaller than a mainframe in both power and cost. These computers tend to support under a hundred users and cost several hundred thousand dollars.

Multi-tasking An operating system that is able to do multiple jobs simultaneously.

Multi-user An operating system that allows many users doing different tasks to run on the same computer. Not so long ago, this was what was meant by operating system, since computers cost so much that every instant of processor time had to be used to justify the expense. Example: Unix/Xenix.

N

Noise interference Noise from any source that interferes with your computer. Examples: erratic electrical, magnetic, or radio waves. Likely causes: the air conditioner compressor or a thunderstorm (electrical noise), the local radio station (magnetic/radio waves).

Numeric coprocessor A special chip (8087, 80287, and 80387) designed to do floating-point calculations, logarithms, and trigonometry.

O

Operating system The program that allows the computer to load programs and that controls the screen, the drives and other devices. The more the computer does, the more complex the operating system.

OS/2 Operating System 2, by IBM/Microsoft. (Operating System 1 is DOS.) IBM originally intended this operating system for the 80286, but released it for PS/2s.

P

Paged memory *See* expanded memory and LIM.

Parity A system used to check each byte of data for errors. The parity bit plus the 8 bits in the byte must add up right. For even parity, the number of 1s in the byte plus the parity bit must add up to an even number—if they don't, the computer knows there has been an error transmitting the signal. For odd parity they must add up to an odd number.

POST Power-On Self-Test. The BIOS ROM contains a series of hardware test instructions (POST), which runs each time the computer is turned on.

Processor The part of the computer that executes instructions and manipulates information. In microcomputers, this is a single chip. It is also called the CPU or the microprocessor. XT-compatible microcomputers are equipped with 8088 or 8086 microprocessors. AT-compatible computers use the 80286 microprocessor. 386 computers are built around the 80386 microprocessor. 486 computers are built around the 80486 microprocessor chip. *See also* IAPX86.

Protected mode The mode of an 80286, 80386, or 80486 in which the processor executes instructions that are extensions to the original set of 8086 instructions. 80286/80386/80486 chips are capable of operating either in real mode, where they are limited to the 8086 instruction set, or in protected mode. The 80386 and 80486 also have a virtual mode which allows them to impersonate multiple 8086 or 8088 computers running on the big 386 or 486 machine.

PS/2 Personal System 2. This 1987 IBM family of microcomputers incorporates a patented bus called MCA. We classic-bus partisans feel IBM designed this line to thwart cloning. *See also* MCA.

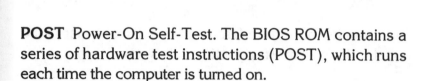

R

RAM Random Access Memory. Any part of this memory can be used by the microprocessor. Each storage location in RAM has a unique address, and each address can be either written to, or read, by the processor. System memory, maximum 640K, is the area DOS uses to manipulate programs. Expanded Memory or Extended Memory (see these two terms in the glossary) are also RAM. When people are using the term RAM casually, as in "How much RAM does your computer have?" they are usually talking about the system memory, plus expanded and extended memory. Windows, unlike DOS, uses both system memory and extended memory. *See also* DRAM, ROM, refresh, and SRAM.

Real mode 80286 microprocessors can operate in two modes, real mode and protected mode. 80386 and 80486 microprocessors also have a virtual mode, one where 386/486 computers can masquerade as multiple 8088 machines. In real mode these microprocessors pretend to be a very fast 8086 or 8088. These processors operate in real mode when running DOS; they operate in protected mode when running Windows.

Refresh DRAM forgets the information stored unless it is refreshed (read and rewritten). DMA channel 0 is dedicated to continuous memory refresh in a microcomputer.

RLL Run Length Limited. This is a method of encoding data on hard disk surfaces. It is similar to MFM, but does not require clock bits, so it can record more data in the same space. Instead of clock bits, it uses a rule about the number of consecutive zeroes that are written in any data stream. The method was developed by IBM some 15 years ago for mainframe use. It is as reliable as MFM for recording data but the recording surface must be very good. If the hard disk is not RLL-certified by the manufacturer of the drive, don't use an RLL controller on the drive. *See also* ESDI, MFM, and SCSI.

ROM Read Only Memory. Recorded once, at the factory, ROM is the ideal way to hold instructions that should never change, such as the instructions your computer requires to access the disk drive. *See also* BIOS and RAM.

ROM address The memory location for an expansion card's ROM chip, this is also called Base I/O Address. When the computer boots up it searches for any additional ROM chips in the system, reading the setup information from each ROM chip as it finds it. A typical ROM is 8, 16, or 32K long. Therefore, it uses up an 8, 16, or 32K block of memory addresses beginning at the "ROM address" (the starting address). No two ROMs can be at the same starting address, and their blocks of memory cannot overlap each other. You'll find ROMs on your video card (EGA and above), hard drive controller and/or SCSI host adapter, and many other expansion cards. There are no ROMs for parallel or serial ports, game ports, or ordinary floppy controllers because the computer already knows how to use these simple devices—the instructions are stored in the computer's ROM BIOS on the mainboard.

S

SCSI An industry standard 8-bit intelligent interface to exchange data. The standard covers hard drives and tape drives. A SCSI controller will support up to eight devices. The interface allows the drive manufacturer to use any encoding scheme they choose. However, SCSI is not supported in a standard way by the BIOS in ATs, posing interesting installation problems at times.

Seek time The length of time it takes for a hard disk head to find a track; expressed in milliseconds (ms). Average seek time is how long it will take to find a track, on average. Though fast seek times are often touted as an indication of a fast hard disk, seek time alone is rather useless as an expression of hard disk speed. Transfer rate is more meaningful. *See also* settle time.

Settle time How long it takes for the heads to settle down to the process of reading the hard disk once the specified track is found. *See also* seek time.

Setup A program used to store hardware information in the CMOS chip of a 286/AT, 386/AT, or 486 computer.

SIMM Single Inline Memory Module. Memory chips used to be individually installed in sockets, one chip at a time. A SIMM is an 8- or 9-chip unit which slips into a single socket.

Single user An operating system that allows only one user to use the computer at a time. *See also* Unix.

Single user, Single task A version of single user that allows only one user at a time to do one task at a time. DOS is an example.

Single user, Multitask A version of single user (see above) that allows only one user to do multiple tasks simultaneously. Examples: OS/2, Windows 3.1, and VM/386.

SRAM Static Random Access Memory chips that do not require refresh. Typically used as cache memory.

Stack A scratch pad for the microprocessor. When the microprocessor is interrupted in the middle of a task by a more urgent task, it saves notes to itself about the contents of registers, and so on. These notes are essential if the microprocessor is to resume the first task where it left off.

State Condition, as in ON-OFF, HIGH-LOW, or ZERO-ONE. In computers this means the particular way all the memory locations, registers and logic gates are set, for example, "wait state." State is also used casually to indicate the particular condition and status of the computer.

ST412/ST506 The names of the original hard drives in micros. The drives are no longer made, but the interface Seagate developed for them is still used. This interface is used on inexpensive XT and AT drives and controllers. *See also* MFM and RLL.

System memory The memory in the computer that DOS (or the chosen operating system) can use to store information and execute programs. On most DOS computers this is a maximum of 640K. DOS 5.0 and DR DOS 6.0 tuck data in high memory (the last 64K of memory in a 286/386/486 computer) that we used to put in the first 640K of memory, so these operating systems have an effective system memory of 704K.

T

Task The job (usually an application program) that the computer does. A task is not the same as a user—a task is what the computer is doing. One person can simultaneously perform multiple tasks on a single computer. *See* Multitasking.

Track-to-track access time How long it takes for the heads of a drive to move from one track to another. This number determines much of the speed with which data is read from the drive.

Transfer rate The amount of data, measured in bytes per second, the computer can read from the hard disk.

TSR Terminate and Stay Resident. A program that pops back into use when a hotkey sequence is pressed. Sidekick is an example. TSRs sometimes present problems when they clash with each other or programs loaded subsequent to them, and cause symptoms that you might think are hardware-related.

U

Unix An operating system developed by AT&T in the early 1970's to run their computerized phone switching system on PDP-11s. This operating system is known for low overhead with easy connecting of different tasks. Unlike DOS, Unix is a true multiuser, multitasking system.

V

Virtual mode The mode of the 80386 and 80486 where it pretends to be multiple 8086/8088s. This is the mode Windows 3.1 uses.

Voltage spike An electrical geyser.

Voltage surge A big electrical wave.

W

Word The smallest unit of data the processor can do anything in. For the 8088 a word is 1 byte. For the 8086, 80186, 80286, 386/SX, and 486/SX a word is 2 bytes (16 bits). For the 80386, 80486, and 80586 a word is 4 bytes (32 bits). When you upgrade memory, you must add a complete word at a time. So to add 256K to an 8088 requires eight chips. To add the same 256K to an 80286 or a 386/SX you need 16 chips. To add 256K to an 80386 or 80486 you need a whopping 32 chips. Memory chips come, of course, in 256K, 1 Mb, 4 Mb, and 16 Mb sizes—but you still have to add a full word of chips (that's 32 chips in a 386/486).

Write Precompensation As the head on a hard disk starts to write on the smallest inner tracks, data errors can occur if the data is recorded exactly as it was on the large, outer tracks. Write precompensation, subtle timing changes as the data is recorded, provides clean, clear data storage even on the innermost tracks.

X

Xenix A version of Unix developed for microcomputers. Slowly being replaced by Unix as the microcomputers of today develop the power of minicomputers of ten years ago.

Index